MEXICAN AMERICAN CHILDREN AND FAMILIES

D1712890

Offering new insight on Mexican American culture and families, this book provides an inter-disciplinary examination of this growing population. Contributors from psychology, education, health, and social science review recent quantitative and qualitative literature on Mexican Americans. Using current theories, the cultural, social, inter- and intra-personal experiences that contribute to the well-being and adjustment of Mexican Americans are examined. As such, the book serves as a seminal guide to those interested in moving away from the dominant deficit model that characterizes the majority of the literature. To ensure consistency and accessibility, each chapter features an introduction, literature review, summary, future directions and chal-lenges, policy implications, and references. Contributors review current education and health care policies and research that impact this population, with the hope of guiding the develop-ment of policies and interventions that support well-being and adjustment.

Highlights include:

- Normative and strength-based perspective on Mexican American families
- Generational perspective that is common among Mexican American families
- Multidisciplinary review of the values, beliefs, practices, identities, educational resilience, and physical and mental health issues for a deeper understanding of this growing population
- Specific focus on Latinos of Mexican origin, with a highlight on the cultural, social, inter- and intra-personal experiences that contribute to well-being and adjustment
- Empirically-grounded resource to guide the development of public policy and intervention approaches that support the well-being of families of Mexican origin.

Ideal for advanced students, researchers, policy makers, and practitioners in human develop-ment and family studies, psychology, sociology, social work, education, and community health interested in Mexican Americans. This book serves as an excellent resource in graduate or advanced undergraduate courses on Mexican American culture, (Latin) Mexican American/ Chicano or cross-cultural studies, cross-cultural development, diversity, or race and ethnicity. Knowledge of social science or developmental theory is not assumed.

Yvonne M. Caldera is Professor of Human Development and Family Studies at Texas Tech University.

Eric W. Lindsey is Professor of Applied Psychology at Penn State University—Berks Campus.

MEXICAN AMERICAN CHILDREN AND FAMILIES

MULTIDISCIPLINARY PERSPECTIVES

Edited by Yvonne M. Caldera and Eric W. Lindsey

NEW YORK AND LONDON

First published 2015
by Routledge
711 Third Avenue, New York, NY 10017

and by Routledge
27 Church Road, Hove, East Sussex BN3 2FA

Routledge is an imprint of the Taylor & Francis Group, an informa business

Library of Congress Cataloging in Publication Data
Mexican American children and families : multidisciplinary perspectives / [edited] by Yvonne M. Caldera & Eric W. Lindsey.
    pages cm
Includes bibliographical references.
1. Mexican Americans—Social conditions.   2. Mexican American children—Social conditions.
3. Mexican American families—Social conditions.   4. Mexican Americans—Statistics.   5. Mexican American children—Statistics.   6. Mexican American families—Statistics.   7. United States~Social conditions~1980–
8. United States—Ethnic relations.   I. Caldera, Yvonne M.   II. Lindsey, Eric W.
E184.M5M495 2015
973'.046872—dc23

                                                                                    2014026605

ISBN: 978-0-415-85453-5 (hbk)
ISBN: 978-0-415-85454-2 (pbk)
ISBN: 978-1-315-81461-2 (ebk)

Typeset in Bembo
by RefineCatch Limited, Bungay, Suffolk, UK

Printed and bound in the United States of America by Publishers Graphics,
LLC on sustainably sourced paper.

We would like to dedicate this book to the following individuals:

To my beautiful and loving daughter Carmen–Sophia Caldera, whose birth forever changed and enriched my life. May the pages of this book make it possible for you to reach your potential and achieve your dreams as well as those of other Mexican American children.

To all the Mexican American students I have had the privilege of knowing during my tenure at Texas Tech University, especially in memory of Laura Villa Quezada. You ignited my passion for your culture and I forever will remain humbled by your lives and spirit.

Yvonne M. Caldera

I would like to dedicate my work on this book to my mentor Dr. Jacquelyn Mize, to whom I owe all my professional accomplishments.

Eric W. Lindsey

CONTENTS

ABOUT THE EDITORS

Yvonne M. Caldera is currently a Professor of Human Development and Family Studies (HDFS) at Texas Tech University (TTU). Since arriving at TTU she has obtained over two million dollars in federal funds to serve and study ethnic minority children and families in Lubbock, Texas. She has conducted and published studies on normative socio-emotional and ethnic identity development of Mexican American children, and on the parent–infant relationship. She recently completed a three-year study, En Sus Manos, focusing on childcare use and socialization goals of Mexican American families with infants and toddlers. In addition to her research endeavors Dr. Caldera devotes her energies to mentoring ethnic minority and/or first generation graduate and undergraduate students. She is passionate about improving the conditions of Hispanics in the US in her work, her teaching, and service.

Eric W. Lindsey is a Professor of Applied Psychology at Penn State University—Berks Campus. He received his PhD in Human Development and Family Relationships at Auburn University, Auburn, Alabama in 1996. His research focuses on issues in applied family psychology with a particular emphasis on connections between marital relationships, parent–child relationships, and children's social competence with peers. His work has been published in journals within the fields of developmental and family psychology. In 2003 Dr. Lindsey, together with his colleague Dr. Yvonne Caldera, received funding from the Department of Health and Human Services for a three-year longitudinal study to examine the childcare practices of Mexican American families. The goal of this study was to provide much needed data concerning the childcare choices made by Hispanic families, how family characteristics and childcare quality combines to affect Hispanic children's adjustment.

CONTRIBUTORS

Daniela Aldoney is a doctoral student at the University of Maryland, College Park. She is interested in how the home environment/parenting practices influence development in disadvantaged populations during early childhood.

Elva M. Arredondo, PhD, is Associate Professor and Co-Director of the San Diego State University–University of California San Diego Joint Doctoral Program in Health Behavior, Graduate School of Public Health, San Diego State University; Senior Core Investigator of Institute for Behavioral and Community Health and Director of Communication and Dissemination, San Diego Prevention Research Center.

Angela E. Arzubiaga is Associate Professor in Justice Studies and Social Inquiry in the School of Social Transformation at Arizona State University. Her research focuses on the education of children of immigrants, socio-cultural perspectives on family life and home–institution connections, and immigrant families' adaptations.

Guadalupe X. Ayala, PhD, MPH, is Professor, Graduate School of Public Health (GSPH), San Diego State University (SDSU); Co-Director of the Institute for Behavioral and Community Health (IBACH) and the San Diego Prevention Research Center (SDPRC).

Alfredo H. Benavides, PhD, is Professor of Bilingual Education and Diversity Studies at Texas Tech University. He has been in this field for over forty years and served as Co-Editor of the *Bilingual Research Journal*.

Joaquin P. Borrego, Jr., PhD, is the Director of the Clinical Psychology Doctoral Program at Texas Tech University. His research centers on Parent–Child Interaction Therapy and culturally appropriate interventions for ethnic minority populations.

Jennifer A. Brinkerhoff, PhD, is a visiting Assistant Professor in the Department of Religion at Brigham Young University. Her research focuses on female identity and ritual contexts, particularly Ethiopian women.

Natasha J. Cabrera, PhD, is the Director of the Family Involvement Laboratory and an Associate Professor in the Department of Human Development in the Maryland Population Research Center. Dr. Cabrera's research focuses on father involvement and children's social development; ethnic and cultural variations in parenting; and the mechanisms that link early experiences to children's school readiness.

Margaret O'Brien Caughy, PhD, is Professor of Behavioral Sciences at the University of Texas School of Public Health. Her research is focused on how race/ethnic disparities in early childhood affects development and school readiness.

Thomas A. Chávez, PhD, is a Research Scientist at the University of New Mexico—Center on Alcoholism, Substance Abuse, and Addictions (CASAA). His research focuses on adolescent health-risk behaviors, with particular emphasis on improving intervention outcomes among underserved youth.

Luisa Franzini, PhD, is Professor of Health Economics at the University of Texas School of Public Health. Her research is focused on the socioeconomic determinants of health disparities.

James García, is a doctoral student in Clinical Health Psychology at the University of North Texas with an emerging expertise in Latino health.

Nancy A. Gonzales, PhD, is a Foundation Professor of Psychology at Arizona State University. Her research examines cultural and contextual influences on family processes and youth development in low income communities.

Heidi A. Hamann, PhD, is Assistant Professor in the Departments of Psychiatry and Clinical Sciences at University of Texas Southwestern Medical Center with expertise in psychosocial and behavioral aspects of cancer survivorship.

Nicole L. Harris is a Clinical Psychology doctoral student at Texas Tech University. Her research centers on the influence of socio-cultural factors on the health risk behaviors of ethnic minority adolescents.

Michaeline Jensen is a doctoral student in Clinical Psychology at Arizona State University. Her research focuses on the roles of individual and contextual factors in adolescent development.

Elizabeth Karberg is a doctoral student at the University of Maryland and is interested in how family functioning can attenuate the association between environment and children's development. She is specifically interested in the unique influence of fathers on child development.

Chelsea Klinkebiel is a Clinical Psychology doctoral student at Texas Tech University. Her research and clinical interests include risk for child maltreatment and parenting interventions, including Parent–Child Interaction Therapy.

George P. Knight, PhD, is a Developmental Psychologist in the Department of Psychology at Arizona State University. His research investigates cultural adaptation in Mexican American families and methodological issues associated with research on ethnic minority families.

Fatih Koca is a doctoral student in Educational Psychology at Texas Tech University with a Masters from Purdue. His interests include the social and cultural contexts in the development of children.

Simon J. Craddock Lee, PhD, is Assistant Professor of Clinical Sciences (Medical Anthropology) at the University of Texas Southwestern Medical Center, with expertise in socio-cultural difference, biological variation, and cancer health disparities.

Angélica López, PhD, received her doctorate in Developmental Psychology from University of California Santa Cruz. Her work focuses on children's helping and attention among children from Mexico and the US.

Rebecca A. Lopez, PhD, teaches in the areas of human behavior, policy and research at both the undergraduate and graduate levels. Administrative responsibilities as Associate Director include serving as Coordinator of Academic Programs, as well as Graduate Advisor for the Department's six hundred Masters level students. She entered academia after a decade of work as a Congressional Aide. She has extensive experience in macro practice in community organizing, civic involvement and local political empowerment. Publications have focused on cultural issues related to ethnic minority populations and their behaviors and belief systems. She is considered an expert lecturer on immigration policy and immigrant adjustment.

Jenessa L. Malin is a doctoral student at the University of Maryland, College Park. Her research focuses on the early educational outcomes of Latino immigrant children.

Eva Midobuche, PhD, is Professor of Bilingual Education and Diversity Studies at Texas Tech University. She has been in bilingual education for over thirty years and has held academic appointments at several universities.

Zorash Montano is a doctoral student in Clinical Psychology at Arizona State University. She is interested in how family processes and culture impact youth mental and physical health.

Stephen M. Quintana, PhD, is Professor of Counseling Psychology at the University of Wisconsin, Madison. He investigates children's and youth's understanding of race, ethnicity and other forms of social identity.

Alyssa M. Ramírez Stege received her *Licenciatura* (BA) in Psychology from the Universidad de las Américas Puebla and is a master's student in Counseling Psychology at the University of Wisconsin–Madison. She is interested in research related to Latino counselor's bicultural and bilingual skills development, and extending research ties internationally to other Latin American countries.

Lucila Ramos-Sánchez, PhD, is an Associate Professor and Chair in the Department of Counseling Psychology at Santa Clara University. She has published numerous articles that examine factors that impact the counseling process, such as counselor bilingual ability, counselor credibility, counselor ethnicity, and help-seeking intentions of Latinos clients. Her most recent work is a comparative analysis of the differences in mental health between documented and undocumented Latino immigrants.

James L. Rodriguez is a Professor in the Department of Child and Adolescent Studies at California State University, Fullerton. He received his undergraduate degree in psychology from Pomona College and a PhD in education with a specialization in child and adolescent development from Stanford University. His research examines the intersection of language, culture, and learning among Latino children and families with particular emphasis on educational access, opportunity, and achievement among immigrants and English learners.

Barbara Rogoff, PhD, is Professor of Psychology at University of California Santa Cruz. She recently received an Award for Distinguished Lifetime Contributions from Society of Research in Child Development. Her book *Developing Destinies* received the Maccoby Award from the American Psychological Association in August 2014.

Mark W. Roosa, PhD, is a Professor in the T. Denny Sanford School of Social and Family Dynamics, Arizona State University. He studies the roles of culture and context in Mexican American youth development.

John M. Ruiz, PhD, is an Assistant Professor of Clinical Health Psychology at the University of North Texas with expertise in Latino health as well as psychosocial determinants of cardiovascular disease.

Omar Ruvalcaba is currently working on his PhD in the Department of Psychology at University of California Santa Cruz. His research focuses on the relationships between culture and collaboration. Especially of interest are the relationships between Mexican-heritage children's practices and values while they learn computer science skills.

Bridget Granville Seeley, PhD, is a faculty lecturer at Arizona State University in the T. Denny Sanford School of Social and Family Dynamics.

Marie-Anne Suizzo, PhD, is an Associate Professor in the Department of Human Development, Culture, & Learning Sciences at the University of Texas. She earned a Doctorate in Human Development and Psychology at Harvard University. She studies children's development, socialization, and Parent–Child relationships in cultural contexts from a strengths-based, resiliency perspective.

Lauren Thompson is a PhD student in the Department of Human Development and Family Studies at Texas Tech University. She received her Bachelor's in forensic psychology and her Master's in forensic science. She completed training at the Department of Homeland Security's Federal Law Enforcement Training Center and is interested in a career in forensic interviewing.

Paulina Velez-Gomez is a Fulbright Fellow from Colombia, completing her doctoral degree in Human Development and Family Studies at Texas Tech University. Her research interests include social and emotional development in minority and international youth, and identity negotiations among international students.

Rebecca M. B. White, PhD, MPH, is an Assistant Professor in the T. Denny Sanford School of Social and Family Dynamics, Arizona State University. Her research examines Mexican American families, developmental, and cultural processes within neighborhood contexts.

Henry Wynne is a doctoral student in Clinical Psychology at Arizona State University. His research interests are in the development and implementation of culturally robust interventions for ethnic minority youth.

Marlene Zepeda, PhD, is Professor Emerita in the Department of Child and Family Studies at California State University, Los Angeles. A former preschool and elementary school teacher, Dr. Zepeda's current scholarship focuses on dual language learning in Spanish speaking preschool children. For the California State Department of Education, Dr. Zepeda led a group of national experts in the development of California's Early Learning Foundations for English Language Development for three- and four-year-olds—the first effort of its kind in the nation. More recently she has authored a report focused on early educator competencies for teachers who work with dual language learners. Dr. Zepeda received her BA in Child Development from California State University, Los Angeles and her MA and PhD degrees in Developmental Studies from the University of California, Los Angeles.

PREFACE

In recent years, research scholars have criticized existing knowledge on Latinos of Mexican Origin as being biased by a deficit perspective in which differences from mainstream American culture were framed as problematic and detrimental. In response to such criticism there has been an increase in empirical work on Mexican Origin populations guided by a normative and strength-based perspective. This work has focused on a diverse range of phenomena such as family values, beliefs and practices, ethnic identity development, educational resilience, as well as physical and mental health. In a short period of time, a wealth of information has been obtained on these topics by researchers following this new perspective. To date, however, there has yet to be a synthesis of this knowledge in a form that is easily accessible to a wide audience. The goal of this book is to present an organized, representative sampling of scholarly work on Mexican American children and families through models that emphasize normative developmental processes and strengths.

At the same time, the book goes beyond simply describing the state of existing knowledge on Latinos of Mexican Origin. Using current developmental and cultural theories, from an interdisciplinary perspective and a rich empirical base, the volume is intended to offer a thorough examination of the cultural, social, inter-personal, and intra-personal experiences that contribute to the well-being and adjustment of Latinos of Mexican origin. In this way, the book is meant to offer a seminal guide to theorists, researchers, advanced students, and educators who are interested in moving away from the dominant deficit model that characterizes the majority of existing literature.

Given its unique combination of theory, method, and topic, this compendium is also intended to serve as a text in any number of university courses. The chapters are written in a straightforward style which do not presume knowledge of social science or developmental theory, and in addition, it is written to be accessible and compelling, so as to appeal to the widest range of educated readers.

To ensure consistency and accessibility, each chapter features an introduction, literature review, summary, future directions and challenges, policy implications, and references. The introduction of each chapter serves to acquaint readers with the topic, and is followed by a review of extant empirical research. The "future directions and challenges" sections summarize author views of where research on the topic should be directed and what hurdles scientists are likely to face in continuing to study the area. The "policy implications" sections offer guidance to practitioners in how to translate existing knowledge on the subject to direct interventions in working with Mexican American populations.

Finally, we believe that this book provides practitioners and policy makers with a valuable resource for understanding and implementing practices that support the well-being and adjustment of families and children of Mexican origin. The dramatic increase and projected growth of the Latino population in the United States has sparked a public debate about the character of the nation in the next century. A significant reorientation in the realms of public policy, education, and health care appear to be underway in connection with the increase in the population of Latinos. This reorientation is accompanied by significant political decisions that affect all citizens of the United States. Much of the discussion about the changing demographics is flavored by essential views about what the character of the nation should be, and by personal experiences. In contrast, this book offers a theoretically-principled and empirically grounded source of information to guide decision-making regarding public policy and intervention approaches that impact the lives of Latinos of Mexican Origin.

In order to achieve these goals, this book consists of eighteen chapters divided into six parts. The order of the parts loosely follows an ecological perspective, beginning with the question of "who are Mexican Americans?" and a focus on the individual, followed by the different ecological systems that envelop Mexican American children and their families. "Part I: Introduction" provides the reader with a basic understanding of Mexican Americans. Caldera, Velez-Gomez, and Lindsey's Chapter 1, "Who Are Mexican Americans: An Overview of History, Immigration, and Cultural Values" provides a brief historical and demographic overview of Mexican Origin peoples in the US. The chapter begins with the signing of the Treaty of Guadalupe in 1848 when the Northern part of Mexico became the US. The chapter follows with a demographic profile and ends with cultural characteristics. Chapter 2, "What Does It Mean to Be Mexican American? Children's and Adolescents' Perspectives" by Quintana, Chávez, and Ramírez Stege focuses on the development of ethnic identity in Mexican American children and adolescents. The authors also highlight the protecting role that ethnic identity provides for ethnic minority youth. Part I concludes with White, Knight, and Roosa's Chapter 3, "Using Culturally Informed Theory to Study Mexican American Children and Families", proposing culturally informed theorizing in conducting research with Mexican-Origin populations.

The remaining parts of the book focus on the various ecological contexts that encompass Mexican American youth development and family life. Part II highlights the family context in which Mexican-origin children and adolescents develop. Aldoney, Karberg, Malin, and Cabrera's Chapter 4, "Mexican American Children and School Readiness: An Ecological Perspective" discusses the family characteristics that promote school readiness in Mexican American children. The authors suggest that parenting practices reflecting cultural values and encouraging bilingual development support school readiness. Chapter 5, "Coparenting in Mexican American Families" discusses the process of coparenting in Mexican American families. As Mexican heritage family are more likely to have two-parent families, Lindsey and Caldera focus on coparenting and the demographic and cultural values that promote successful coparenting in Mexican American families. In turn, Rogoff and colleagues in Chapter 6, "Attentive Helpfulness as a Cultural Practice of Mexican-Heritage Families" describe a unique process by which Mexican heritage children "Learn by Observing and Pitching-in"—a value commonly known as *acomedido la* in Mexico. Parents seem to emphasize the value of children's helpfulness in families, a characteristic not promoted in American schools. The helpfulness of Mexican heritage children should instead be supported and recognized for the important role in children's learning. The section concludes with a discussion of the concept of space and the role it has on socialization of Mexican American children in Arzubiaga, Brinkerhoff, and Granville Seeley's Chapter 7, "The Study of Mexican Immigrant Families' Space".

The school context is the focus of Part III. Chapter 8, "Issues in Educating Mexican American English Language Learners" by Midobuche, Benavides, and Koca, and Chapter 9, "Bilingual Development in Early Childhood: Research and Policy Implications for Mexican American Children" by Zepeda and Rodriguez, address the challenges that Mexican American children and bilingual children in particular face as they enter and move through the school system. The authors delineate the factors that contribute to these challenges and propose ways in which school systems and teachers can support the learning and development of these young people. These chapters highlight the role that bilingualism plays in children's success in school. The last chapter in this section, Chapter 10, "Mexican American Parents' Involvement in their Children's Schooling" by Suizzo, reviews the research on Mexican-origin parents' involvement in their children's schooling, challenging the stereotype that parents in this cultural group do not value education. Suizzo lists the specific cultural values of Latinos that promote academic performance.

The last two sections of the volume are concerned with the larger contexts of the mental and physical health systems. Part IV begins with Chapter 11, "Mexican American's Help-Seeking of Counseling Services: Removing Barriers to Access and Focusing on Strengths" by Ramos-Sánchez: like the other chapters in the book, this takes a strength-based perspective to suggest ways in which mental health care providers can draw from specific Mexican cultural values, to improve participation and the quality of services provided. Klinkebiel, Harris, and Borrego's Chapter 12, "Parenting and Children's Mental Health in Mexican American Families" emphasizes the social and contextual factors that influence Mexican American parenting and the role these play in their children's mental health. Gonzales and colleagues' Chapter 13, "The Cultural Adaptation and Mental Health of Mexican American Adolescents" follows, focusing on the impact of acculturation and enculturation in the mental health of Mexican American adolescents. Furthermore, this last chapter in the section highlights the potential risks youth encounter as they lose their culture of origin, contrasted with the protective role a bicultural orientation plays in the mental health of Mexican American youth.

The physical health in Mexican-heritage children and families is the focus of Part V. Three of the chapters in this section focus on the phenomenon called the Hispanic Paradox: the findings of better health outcomes in immigrants compared to their US born counterparts. The chapters discuss the discrepancy between risk and outcome and attempt to disentangle the role that culture plays in the Hispanic Paradox. Ayala and Arredondo in Chapter 14, "Nutritional Resilience in Mexican Immigrant/Mexican Americans: How might Food Intake Contribute to the Hispanic Paradox?" emphasize the benefits associated with some traditional Mexican dietary practices and suggest ways in which dietician and nutritionist can utilize these to promote the nutritional intake of Mexican Americans. Chapter 15, "Indigenous Health and Coping Resources in Mexican American Communities" by Lopez reviews the literature on informal and complementary health care practices that are traditional in the Mexican heritage and the factors that influence their usage and the perception of health and illness. Chapter 16, "The Psychology of Health: Physical Health and the Role of Culture and Behavior in Mexican Americans" by Ruiz and colleagues concentrates on studies with Mexican-origin individuals, while Caughy and Franzini in Chapter 17, "Promoting the Health of Mexican American Infants and Young Children" focus on maternal and infant health. The book concludes with Chapter 18, "Perspectives and Recommendation for Future Directions" by Lindsey and Caldera in Part VI.

Our goal in this compendium has been to present a representative multidisciplinary perspective of Mexican American children and families as well as to provide a deeper and more complex understanding of this growing population. We acknowledge that much is left to be said about Mexican descendants and the existing research in ours and other fields, but hope that our attempt will serve as the impetus for further collaboration amongst the various disciplines in order to increase the depth and scope of our understanding of Mexican Americans.

Yvonne M. Caldera
Eric W. Lindsey

ACKNOWLEDGMENTS

This book was made possible by a small grant from the Society of Research in Child Development (SRCD) Small Conference fund and a donation by the Texas Tech University Cross Cultural Academic Advancement Center awarded to Yvonne M. Caldera and Elizabeth Trejos Castillos in 2009. These funds were used to convene ten national scholars from diverse disciplines whose research focused on Mexican American children and families, to present original work reviewing the state of knowledge of this group in their respective fields. The scholars came together for the symposium titled "Mexican American Children and Families: Multidisciplinary Perspectives", which was held in April of 2010, in Lubbock, Texas. The original scholars were Drs. Enrique Aleman, Elva M. Arredondo, Angela E. Arzubiaga, Guadalupe X. Ayala, Alfredo H. Benavides, Natasha J. Cabrera, Margaret O'Brien Caughy, Eric W. Lindsey, Eva Midobuche, Stephen M. Quintana, and Lucila Ramos-Sánchez. All but Dr. Aleman and Dr. Trejos-Castillo agreed to publish their presented work in a compendium which eventually materialized as this book. We are extremely grateful to these scholars and to SRCD for the funds they awarded us; this book would not have been a reality without their support.

There are several individuals who have been instrumental in our professional lives and to whom we credit the completion of this book. First we are deeply indebted to our mentors, Drs. Aletha C. Huston and Jacquelyn Mize. You have inspired us to pursue our dreams, reach our goals, and find passion for our work.

We are grateful for the administrative assistance of Lauren Thompson. Your eagerness and support have been invaluable in putting together this volume.

We also would like to thank our editor Debra Riegert at Routledge publishers. We are grateful for your trust and belief in our volume and all your support during this exciting but arduous process.

We also wish to thank the following reviewers who provided feedback: Amado M. Padilla of Stanford University, Melanie Domenech Rodriguez of Utah State University, Yvette G. Flores of University of California, Davis, and one reviewer whose name remains anonymous.

Last, but not least, we would like to thank all the Mexican American families with infants and toddlers who participated in the longitudinal study, En Sus Manos. We will be forever indebted for letting us into your lives and sharing your stories.

Yvonne M. Caldera
Eric W. Lindsey

PART I

Introduction

1

WHO ARE MEXICAN AMERICANS?

An Overview of History, Immigration, and Cultural Values

Yvonne M. Caldera, Paulina Velez-Gomez, and Eric W. Lindsey

Introduction

The largest group of Latinos in the United States is from Mexican origin, accounting for almost two-thirds of Hispanics (US Census Bureau, 2010). Mexican-heritage people in the United States have evolved from a small, mostly regionally based group, into a large and nationally significant population. In the early 1900s, most of the Mexican-descent population lived in the southwest of the United States; today Mexican descendants live and work in every State of the country, including Alaska and Hawaii (Martínez, 2001).

Although Mexican descendants share common characteristics, such as language, culture, religion, and identification with Mexico, there is also much diversity among them. Immigrants have come from many States in Mexico, some of which are predominantly rural while others have large urban centers, each with its own cultural characteristics and traditions. Contrary to what is typically expected, most Mexican immigrants to the US have come from the center-west region of the country, from the States of Michoacán, Zacatecas, Guanajuato, and Jalisco. Surprisingly, this region is about 1,000 miles from Texas (Indexes of Migration Intensity Mexico–US, 2010).

Within the United States, the life experiences of Mexican descendants vary significantly from coast to coast depending, in part, on ethnic density and proximity to Mexico (Martínez, 2001). Among the States with the highest Hispanic populations are those that share a border with Mexico. Specifically, Texas ranks first in percentage of population from Mexican origin with 33%, followed by California with 32%, New Mexico with 30%, and Arizona with 27%. Following is Colorado with 16% of its population being of Mexican origin, then Illinois with 13% and Georgia with 6% (Pew Hispanic Center, 2013c). In addition, among the Mexican origin population there are differences by generation in US, level of acculturation and enculturation, as well as in English proficiency. Sixty-four percent of those aged five years and older speak proficient English, with the remaining 36% reportedly not speaking English very well (vs. 35% of all Hispanics). Finally, Mexican-origin people are a phenotypically diverse group, with a large proportion of racially mixed individuals. Their appearance shows traces of Indian and European ancestries, and they are thus considered *mestizos* (Alba, 2006).

Mexican-origin people in the US can be divided in two major sub-groups: Native-born and foreign-born. The majority of Mexican Americans, 66% or 22.3 million, are native born, with the remaining 34%, or 11.7 million, being foreign born. Among those born in the US, however, about half have at least one immigrant parent (Pew Hispanic Center, 2013b), strengthening the group's ties to Mexico and creating a Mexican identity. Indeed, 52% of Mexican descendants refer to themselves as Mexican, 26% as Hispanic or Latino, and 19% as American.

This volume primarily focuses on the native born population and thus utilizes the term Mexican Americans. Until recently, however, the research on Latinos did not differentiate between countries of origin, much less between nativities within a given country. As a result, it is often difficult to identify if the populations sampled in the empirical literature refer to native- or foreign born Mexicans. For this reason in this chapter the terms *Mexican-origin* people and *Mexican descendants* will be used interchangeably when referring to both native and foreign born, or when the distinction is not made clear in the original source. The term *Mexican* or *Mexican immigrant* will be used when referring specifically to the foreign born, and *Mexican American* or *native-born* will be used to denote US born Mexican descendants. This chapter begins with a brief history of Mexican descendants in the US, followed by a current demographic profile and concluding with an overview of cultural values and beliefs.

Literature Review

Brief History and Immigration

Mexican-origin people have a unique history that differentiates them from other ethnic groups in the United States and includes experiences of land loss, immigration, and discrimination.

Land Loss

With the signing of the Treaty of Guadalupe Hidalgo on February 2, 1848, the US acquired more than 500,000 square miles of valuable Mexican territory, and as many as 100,000 Mexican citizens living in that region became citizens of the US with the promise of civil and property rights (Taylor, 2002). Unfortunately, by the beginning of the 20th century most had lost their land either through force or fraud. Unlike any other ethnic group, Mexican descendants today inhabit an area that was once part of their native country (Marger, 2000). "By a single stroke of the pen, a large group of Mexican citizens right in their very own homes, found themselves smack in the middle of another country whose laws, political and social institutions, and fundamentally WASP traditions were alien to them" (Novas, 1998, pp. 78–9). The ceded territory is now the Southwestern United States, and includes the states of California, Texas, New Mexico, and Arizona.

Immigration

In a report from the Woodrow Wilson International Center for Scholars, Rosenblum and Brick (2011) surmise migration patterns from Mexico to the US have gone through three main phases since the beginning of the 20th century: An initial slow flow of immigration that continued until the beginning of World War II; a legal flow of mostly male Mexican workers during and shortly after the War; and a third more recent flow of mostly illegal immigrants since 1965.

The first phase of immigration consisted of temporary seasonal Mexican workers who were employed in railroad construction and agriculture. At the turn of the 20th century around 60,000 workers per year came to the US to work, with the majority returning to Mexico when the work was completed or after an agreed-upon specified period of time. When this phase of immigration began in 1900 there were about 100,000 Mexican-born individuals in the US. Between the 1910s and 1920s immigration rates increased more than twofold, and by 1930 the total number had grown to 640,000 (Rosenblum and Brick, 2011).

The 1930s, however, proved to be troubled times for Mexican immigrants in the United States. Initially, the strong anti-immigration sentiment that had been growing in the country began to be applied to Mexicans, and as a result stricter visa screenings reduced the inflow by 75 percent. In addition, high unemployment rates during the Great Depression resulted in a repatriation movement that required Mexicans and Mexican Americans to be sent back to Mexico (op. cit.). Local government agencies began rounding up anyone who looked Mexican and sent them "home" (Novas, 1998, p. 95). Hundreds of thousands of Mexicans—and US-born Mexican Americans—were deported to Mexico during this period.

Immigration restrictions and repatriation were eased when World War II created a serious labor shortage, and the second phase of Mexican immigration began. Needing to address the shortage of agricultural laborers created by the draft, Congress enacted the Emergency Labor Program, also known as the Braceros Program, in 1942. This program allowed immigrants from Mexico to work legally and temporarily in the United States, primarily as seasonal labor to replace the American men who had joined the armed forces (Marentes and Marentes, 1999). The program provided many benefits to Mexican workers, including guaranteed minimum wage (at a time when American farm workers did not earn minimum wage), and assistance with transportation, housing, and health. The program ceased at the end of the War, but was reinstated again during the Korean War in 1950. When this second war ended in 1953, however, around two million documented and undocumented Mexican workers were once again returned home in the "Operation Wetback" campaign. The Braceros Program, nonetheless, remained in effect until 1964 when it was officially terminated, and after about 4.8 million Bracero contracts had been signed. Unfortunately, by the time the program ended, a demand for low-wage foreign workers had been created throughout the US, and large numbers of Mexican workers had come to rely on emigration as the main source of employment (Rosenblum and Brick, 2011).

The third phase of Mexican immigration began in 1965 by the passage of the US Immigration and Nationality Act (INA) which still provides the basic outline of immigration policy today. The INA replaced the 1924 race-based national origin immigration system with a new variable-per-country allocation of up to 20,000 visas per country, per year. The INA also created a family-based immigration system that favored family unification visas versus employment ones, and a cap of 29,000 (including the worker's family members) employment-based visas per year was established. This new system, however, did not take into consideration the continued demand for foreign workers that the Braceros program had created, nor the previous legislation that had exempted businesses from being liable for hiring illegal immigrants. As a result, the decade of the 1970s began a sharp rise in undocumented immigrants from Mexico, leading to an "illegal alien problem" that has created much political tension in the US over the past several decades (Rosenblum and Brick, 2011).

By 1980 Mexico had become the top country of origin for immigrants to the US with a Mexican-born population of 2.2 million, about half of whom were unauthorized. Then the Immigration Reform and Control Act (IRCA) of 1986 allowed unauthorized immigrants who had entered the country before 1982 to acquire legal status as permanent residents. The IRCA also provided funding for stricter border patrol, and penalties for employers hiring unauthorized immigrants. By 1990 around 2 million Mexican immigrants had become legal residents of the US. Two more acts passed in the 1990s, the Immigration Act (IA) of 1990 and the Illegal Immigration Reform and Illegal Activity Act of 1996, introduced additional enforcement measures. The IA of 1990 increased the annual limit of permanent employment visas, issuing around 900,000 green cards per year since then (Rosenblum and Brick, 2011).

In early September of 2001 the US and Mexico appeared close to enacting major immigration reforms that were halted by the terrorist attacks of 9/11. After that, six additional laws focusing on tougher enforcement of immigration were passed by the US between 2002 and 2006. Nonetheless, immigration from Mexico continued growing until 2007. By then, the failing US economy, increased border patrol, violence in the border area, and changes from within Mexico, resulted in a halt to immigration. Nonetheless, in 2011 about 51 percent of immigrants from Mexico were unauthorized. The growth has continued, driven by economic opportunities, as well as social networks of friends and family already living in the US (op.cit.).

Discrimination

Discrimination refers to the unfair treatment of a person or groups, based on prejudice. It is a social stressor experienced by members of subordinate groups, and found to impact well-being and adjustment (Berkel *et al.*, 2010). The historical circumstances previously introduced continue to influence the discrimination Mexican Americans face, living in a mostly European American society. "If there is a common theme that runs through the unique histories and experiences of several Hispanic groups in the United States, it is their intermediate ethnic status—between Euro-American groups, on one hand, and African American, on the other. In several respects, Hispanics are an ethnic minority "in between"(Marger, 2000, p. 283).

Because of their "in between" minority status, Mexican descendants have not been subjected to the same prejudices as African Americans, but neither have they been treated as European immigrant groups have. This status also has made it more difficult for their discrimination to be acknowledged.

Much of the prejudice and discrimination to which Mexican descendants—to this day—are subjected has its origins in the method by which their people became a part of the US society. In the middle of the nineteenth century, Telles and Ortis (2008) argue that Manifest Destiny deemed Mexicans as belonging to an inferior race unable to "govern and develop their precious land" (p. 76). This belief gave White Americans, who perceived themselves as superior, the right to the land and unfair treatment of Mexicans. Subsequently, the Mexican–American War and the bloody Battle of the Alamo provided further fuel to the belief that Mexicans were lazy, inferior, and deserving of their subordinate status because they were a conquered people (Martínez, 2001).

Even though the 1896 *Plessy vs. Ferguson* ruling by the US Supreme Court legalizing segregation of Blacks under the "separate but equal" concept did not technically apply to Mexican descendants. By the early 1900s Mexican origin people had become victims of segregation and a divided employment market (Telles and Ortiz, 2008). Public facilities routinely banned Mexicans and Mexican Americans from their establishments, or directed them to sections deemed least desirable. Public pools reserved specific times for Mexicans so that after they swam, at the end of the day or week, the water in the pool could be changed (Martínez, 2001). School segregation was seen as necessary for various reasons including protecting Anglos from "the intellectual inferiority and dirtiness of Mexicans" (Telles and Ortiz, 2008), teaching Mexicans English, and the need to accommodate for seasonal employment. In addition to segregation, schools attended by Mexican origin children had poorer school facilities, less educated or trained teachers, extremely basic curriculum (which prohibited speaking Spanish), and less funding for their schools than White children (Martínez, 2001).

After the United States Congress passed Civil Rights legislation in the 1960s, discrimination began to decrease. Mexican American leaders were instrumental in the Mexican American Civil Rights movements which helped win their right to fair pay and humane treatment, and began the challenging journey toward equal treatment and opportunities for Mexican Americans. These historical conditions, however, continue to influence current dropout rates, poverty, and the low educational achievement for Mexican American children (Telles and Ortiz, 2008). Indeed, Pérez, Fortuna, and Alegría (2008) suggest that nationally, 30 percent of Mexican American adults experience discrimination as a result of their group membership. For young adults, however, Pérez and colleagues estimate that one half of 18- to 24-year-old Mexican Americans experience discrimination.

Current Statistical Profile

According to the 2010 US Census Bureau there were 32.9 million Mexican descendants comprising 64% of Latinos living in the US and 11% of the total US population. Two out of three immigrants from Mexico arrived in the US in 1990 or after. In the decade between 2000 and 2010 the Mexican-origin population increased by 54%, and Mexico became the country with the highest numeric rise in immigrants to the US (from 20.6 million in 2000 to 32.9 million in 2010). Today this growth is primarily the result of births rather than immigration: 7.2 million births versus 4.2 million immigrants.

The Mexican-origin population is young, with a median age of 25 years; 35% are under 18 years of age (vs. 25.7% in Non-Hispanic Whites). Native born Mexican Americans are younger than Mexican immigrants (median age 17 vs. 38 years respectively) (Pew Hispanic Center, 2013b). Children in immigrant and native-born families account for one of every seven children age 0 to 17 in the United States (Hernandez *et al.*, 2010). The majority of Mexican-origin people, 73%, are US citizens, while only 23% of Mexican immigrants are citizens (Pew Hispanic Center, 2013b).

Employment and Income

Today a large segment of the Mexican origin population in the United States lives in disadvantaged and marginalized conditions. In terms of employment, 42.4% of Mexican descendants have a full time job (vs. 43.5% of all Latinos and 47.2% of the US population). Of those who are employed 18.4% are in managerial positions; 24.3% are in service positions; 21.4% are in sales and office support; 14.4% are in construction; and 21.4% work in maintenance or production (Pew Hispanic Center, 2013a).

Similar to other Hispanic groups living in the US, Mexican-origin people earn low wages, with the median yearly salary for persons 16 and older being $20,000 (Pew Hispanic Center, 2013a). In contrast, at the family level, Mexican origin people fare worse than other Hispanic groups, with the median household income for Mexican Americans being $38,700, and only 20.6% earning more than $35,000, as compared to 29.6% of Puerto Ricans and 34.4% of Cubans (US Bureau of the Census, 2010). In addition, 27% of Mexican origin people live in poverty. Approximately one fifth of Mexican-origin children from native-born and immigrant families, in which at least one parent is English fluent, live below the official poverty threshold. This figure jumps to one third living below the poverty line when considering children from families in which parents are English learners (Hernandez *et al.*, 2010).

Education

According to the 2010 Census, 43% of Hispanics aged 25 and above had attained less than a high school education compared to 11.5% of non-Hispanic Whites. Within the Hispanic group, Mexican descendants were the least likely to have completed a high school education at 51% (vs. 64.3% for Puerto Ricans and 73% for Cubans), and only 9% of those older than 25 had earned a bachelor's degree (vs. 13% of all Hispanics). Furthermore, nearly 20% of children in native-born Mexican-origin families had fathers who had not graduated from high-school. For those in immigrant families, this number jumps to 32% for children with English-fluent parents, to 50% for those whose parents have mixed language skills, and to 69% for those whose parents are English learners (Hernandez *et al.*, 2010).

Considering the statistics presented above, most Mexican-origin families have fewer economic and educational resources to support their child-rearing efforts (Cauce and Domenech Rodríguez, 2002). According to Martínez (2001) only some of Mexican Americans are representatives of the middle-class in this country. This is, in part, due to the fact that starting from the 1960s, a social restructuring took place among Mexican Americans: More people of Mexican ancestry obtained well-paying jobs; an increased number of students graduated from college and universities, and many founded new businesses (Martínez, 2001).

Characteristics of Mexican-Origin Families

Family Structure

Mexican-origin families tend to be larger than families in general in the US. This difference is due to fertility rates and household composition. The mean household size is 3.7 people (vs. 3.5 for Latinos and 2.6 in the US), and the average number of children born to Mexican descent women is 2.5 children (vs. 1.8 in Non-Hispanic Whites). Mexican-origin families also tend to live with extended family members. Among both immigrants and native born families, 9–20 percent have at least one grandparent at home, and 17–33 percent have at least one additional adult relative, including older siblings (Hernandez *et al.*, 2010). Furthermore, Van Hook (2010) noted that Mexican immigrants with fewer than five years of experience in the United States are more likely to live in extended families than Mexicans living in Mexico.

In 2010, Mexican descendants older than 15 years were, overall, more likely to be married than Hispanics (45% vs. 43%), although this percentage was less than the US average of 48%. In the same year, 8% of Mexican-origin women aged 15–44 years gave birth, which was higher than the 6% rate for all US women. About 45% of these women were unmarried, which is similar to the percentage for all Hispanic women (47%), but higher than all US women (38%).

Values and Beliefs

Cultural values and beliefs represent central or desirable goals that shape family interaction patterns and parental socialization strategies (Gamble and Modry-Mandell, 2008). In representing broad cultural differences in values, the terms individualism and collectivism are often used (Greenfield and Cocking, 1994; Harwood *et al.*, 2002). Cultures that adhere to individualistic values focus on *independence*, which emphasizes separation, individuation, and self-creation (Greenfield, 1994). In contrast, cultures embracing collectivistic values focus on interdependence and group collaboration (Ruiz, 2005). The cultural emphasis on independence or interdependence, in turn, influences parenting beliefs and child-rearing practices that ultimately organize relationship patterns and interactions within families.

Independence and interdependence are intertwined phenomena, as all human beings are both individuals and members of the social group. However, every group selects a point along the independence and interdependence continuum as its developmental ideal. Interdependence or collectivism is a belief system that is held by about 70 percent of the world's population (Greenfield, 1994). American value orientation is generally characterized as individualistic, and Mexican Americans' value orientation is characterized as being collectivistic.

Rooted in their collectivistic orientation, Latino families have distinctive values and beliefs that guide parents' socialization practices. The social and cultural context of child-rearing in Mexican families is characterized by an emphasis on respect and obedience, less emphasis on independence and separation during childhood, and greater maintenance of kinship ties throughout the life course (Tapia-Uribe *et al.*, 1994). Mexican American families value face-to-face contact, physical touch, and sharing with nuclear- as well as extended family members (Cauce and Domenech Rodríguez, 2002). Values such as *familismo, personalismo, respeto* and *simpatía* have been identified in the empirical literature as being representative values among many Latino families, including Mexican-origin families. The following section will describe values and beliefs generally attributed to Mexican Americans.

Familismo—refers to the importance of family closeness, getting along with the family and contributing to the well-being of its members (Cauce and Domenech Rodríguez, 2002). Mexican-origin parents promote a sense of family unity by encouraging close relationships with siblings and relatives (Delgado and Ford, 1998). Family connection, interdependence, and closeness are integral parts of the Mexican American culture influencing individuals' beliefs and actions through their importance.

Familism is also evident in the structure of Mexican American families. The family unit includes extended family, and the ties remain closely intertwined within the nuclear family and beyond. In many Mexican American families grandparents live with their children and help with the care of grandchildren. In addition to grandparents, the family network includes aunts, uncles, cousins, and *padrinos/madrinas* (godparents).

Godparents are expected at celebrations, such as communions, baptisms, and weddings, and play an important role in the child's life. In addition, the relationship between a child's parents and godparents takes on a special meaning, represented by the term *compadres/comadres*, which is non-existent in the English language and refers to the relationship that parents have with each of their children's godparents.

Respeto—is another value that Mexican American families consider important. This value is related to the idea that cooperative behavior and deference to authority is expected (Garza and Watts, 2010). *Respeto* means that interactions "should be guided by a sense of caring that is communicated through politeness" (Delgado-Gaitan, 1994, p. 65). The importance of respect is also evident in the Spanish language. The more formal "usted" form of the word "you" is used in the Spanish language to address adults, elders, and those in authority, rather than the more informal "tu" that is used to address friends or young children. This quality is especially highly desired for children, as their parents raise them to have a strong sense of respect for elders.

Personalismo—is defined as the importance placed on personal goodness and getting along with others (Cauce and Domenech Rodríguez, 2002). More specifically, *personalismo* refers to behaviors and actions that demonstrate a direct interest in, and concern for others (Garza and Watts, 2010). *Personalismo* and *familismo* are values that are characteristic of the collectivistic orientation in Latino Culture, as they place emphasis on family solidarity, obligation and parental authority (Cauce, op. cit.).

Simpatía—is also a central value for Mexican American families. This value refers to the importance of respect and politeness toward others, which leads to harmonious, smooth, pleasant, and empathetic interpersonal relationships (Triandis *et al.* 1984, cited by Yu *et al.*, 2008). Similarly, *Simpatía* accounts for individuals' higher interpersonal helping and behaving in a socially desirable manner (Levine *et al.*, 2001). The value of *simpatía* is linked with learning and practicing social skills to maintain harmony in relationships (Gamble and Modry-Mandell, 2008).

Mexican American culture thus consists of group orientation, strong membership with family, and a dependence on others within a hierarchical structure founded on respect and obedience. These cultural values highlight the importance that is placed on close relationships with others. Therefore, by promoting family closeness, close bonds and getting along with others, parents can prepare their children to be socially competent individuals.

Summary

As this chapter has attempted to illustrate, Mexican Americans are a distinct Latino group in the United States who have become a part of this country through unique historical circumstances and experiences which differentiates them from other Latino groups. Mexican Americans include individuals whose ancestors have inhabited this land for centuries. Some of these individuals trace their origins to the Indigenous population in the region before Spanish colonization, others are descendants of *Mestizos*, while yet others' ancestors were predominantly Spanish. Some Mexican Americans are children born of Mexican immigrant parents or descendants of Mexican immigrants from the near or distant past. Some Mexican Americans speak mostly Spanish, some are monolingual English speakers, while others are bilingual. Mexican Americans are nonetheless united through collectivistic values and socio-demographic characteristics including similar levels of education and income, and commonality of space.

Future Directions and Challenges

Two major recommendations can be gleaned from this chapter. The first is that future research needs to focus on individual Latino groups, Mexican Americans in particular, rather than collapsing all Latino as if they are one. The unique socio-historical experiences of Mexican Americans vis-à-vis other Latinos make it imperative that country of origin be a discriminate factor in all future research. The behavioral sciences have begun to move in this direction, but we still have a way to go. Second, because of the socio-demographic diversity of Mexican Americans, future research must examine the way in which this—uniquely or in combination— impacts the well-being of Mexican American children and families.

Policy Implications

The brief socio-historical account in this chapter suggests that policies aimed at bettering the lives of children and families must pay particular attention to the needs of families from diverse backgrounds. Because of their unique placement within American society, policies that are beneficial to Mexican Americans will be those that consider their vulnerabilities and risk factors as well as their strengths. Mexican Americans have faced substantial adversity as members of this country and this must be at the forefront when developing social service programs and policies that will affect children and families. As is evident in the chapters in this volume, Mexican Americans also have much strength—previously considered shortcomings—that must be supported and promoted in order that future generations of Americans can reach their potential.

References

Alba, R. (2005). Mexican Americans and the American Dream. *Perspectives on Politics*, *4*, 289–296.

Berkel, C., Knight, G. P., Zeiders, K. H., Tein, J., Roosa, M. W., Gonzales, N. A., and Saenz, D. (2004). Discrimination and adjustment for Mexican American adolescents: A prospective examination of the benefits of culturally related values. *Journal of Research on Adolescence*, *20*(4), 893–915.

Cauce, A. M., and Domenech Rodríguez, M. (2002). Latino families: Myths and realities. In J. M. Contreras, K. A. Kerns, and A. M. Neal-Barnett (Eds.), *Latino children and families in the United States: Current research and future directions* (pp. 3–25). Westport, CT: Praeger.

Consejo Nacional de Población. (2012). *Indices de intensidad migratoria Mexico-Estados Unidos*. México, D.F.

Delgado, B. M., and Ford, L. (1998). Parental perceptions of child development among low-income Mexican American families. *Journal of Child and Family Studies*, *7*(4), 469–481.

Delgado-Gaitan, C. (1994). Socializing young children in Mexican-American families: An intergenerational perspective. In P. M. Greenfield and R. R. Cocking (Eds.), *Cross cultural roots of minority child development* (pp. 55–86). Hillside, NJ: Lawrence Erlbaum Associates Publishers.

Gamble, W. C., and Modry-Mandell, K. L. (2008). Family relations and the adjustment of young children of Mexican descent: Do cultural values moderate these associations? *Social Development*, *17*, 358–379.

Garza, Y., and Watts, R. E. (2010). Filial therapy and Hispanic values: Common ground for culturally sensitive helping. *Journal of Counseling and Development*, *88*(1), 108–113.

Greenfield, P. M. (1994). Independence and interdependence as developmental scripts: Implications for theory, research, and practice. In P. M. Greenfield and R. R. Cocking (Eds.), *Cross cultural roots of minority child development* (pp. 1–37). Hillsdale, NJ: Lawrence Erlbaum Associates Publishers.

Greenfield, P. M., and Cocking, R. R. (1994). *Cross cultural roots of minority child development*. Hillsdale, NJ: Lawrence Erlbaum Associates Publishers.

Hernandez, D. J., Macartney, S., Blanchard, V. L., and Denton, N. A. (2010). Mexican–origin children in the United States: Language, family circumstances, and public policy. In N. S. Landale, S. McHale, and A. Booth (Eds.), *Growing up Hispanic: Health and development of children of immigrants* (pp. 169–185). Washington, DC: The Urban Institute Press.

Levine, R. V., Norenzayan, A., and Philbrick, K. (2001). Cross-cultural differences in helping strangers. *Journal of Cross-Cultural Psychology*, *32*, 543–560.

Marentes, C., and Marentes, C. P. (1999). *The Bracero Program*. Retrieved from http://www.farmworkers.org/bracerop.html

Marger, M. N. (2000). *Race and ethnic relations: American and global perspectives*. Belmont, CA: Wadsworth.

Martínez, O. J. (2001). *Mexican-origin people in the United States: A topical history*. Tucson, AZ: The University of Arizona Press.

Novas, H. (1998). *Everything you need to know about Latino history*. Revised Ed. New York, NY: Plume.

Pérez, D. J., Fortuna, L., and Alegría, M. (2008). Prevalence and correlates of everyday discrimination among U.S. Latinos. *Journal of Community Psychology*, *36*, 421–433.

Pew Hispanic Center. (2013a). *A demographic portrait of Mexican-origin Hispanics in the United States*. Washington, DC: Ana Gonzalez-Barrera and Mark Hugo Lopez.

Pew Hispanic Center. (2013b). *Diverse origins: The Nation's 14 largest Hispanic-origin groups*. Washington, DC: Mark Hugo Lopez, Ana Gonzalez-Barrera, and Danielle Cuddington.

Pew Hispanic Center. (2013c). *Mapping the Latino population, by State, county and city*. Washington, DC: Anna Brown.

Rodriguez, B. L., and Olswang, L. B. (2003). Mexican-American and Anglo-American mothers' beliefs and values about child rearing, education, and language impairment. *American Journal of Speech-Language Pathology*, *12*(4), 452–462. doi:10.1044/1058-0360(2003/091)

Rosenblum, M. R., and Brick, K. (2011). *US immigration policy and Mexican/ Central American migration flows. Then and now*. Washington, DC: Migration Policy Institute.

Ruiz, E. (2005). Hispanic culture and relational cultural theory. *Journal of Creativity in Mental Health*, *1(1)*, 33–55.

Tapia-Uribe, F., LeVine, R. A., and LeVine, S. E. (1994). Maternal behavior in a Mexican community: The changing environments of children. In P. M. Greenfield and R. R. Cocking (Eds.), *Cross-cultural roots of minority child development* (pp. 41–54). Hillsdale, NJ: Lawrence Erlbaum Associates, Inc.

Taylor, R. L. (2002). *Minority families in the United States: A multicultural perspective.* Upper Saddle River, NJ: Prentice Hall.

Telles, E., and Ortiz, V. (2008). *Generations of exclusion: Mexican Americans, assimilation, and race.* New York: Russell Sage Foundation.

U.S. Census Bureau. (2010). *The Hispanic Population: 2010 Census Briefs.* Washington, DC: U.S. Department of Commerce.

Van Hook, J. (2010). Structure and acculturation: Explaining outcomes for children in Mexican American families. In N. S. Landale, S. McHale, and A. Booth (Eds.), *Growing up Hispanic: Health and development of children of immigrants* (pp. 145–153). Washington, DC: The Urban Institute Press.

Yu, J., Lucero-Liu, A. A., Gamble, W. C., Taylor, A. R., Christensen, D., and Modry-Mandell, K. L. (2008). Partner effects of Mexican cultural values: The couple and parenting relationships. *Journal of Psychology: Interdisciplinary and Applied*, *142*(2), 169–192. doi:10.3200/JRLP.142.2.169–192

2

WHAT DOES IT MEAN TO BE MEXICAN AMERICAN?

Children's and Adolescents' Perspectives

Stephen M. Quintana, Thomas A. Chávez, and Alyssa M. Ramírez Stege

Introduction

"What does it mean to be Mexican American?" is a foundational component of Mexican American children's and adolescents' ethnic identities. The meaning that Mexican American and other children and youth attribute to their ethnic status represents a dynamic confluence of developmental, anthropological, sociological, racial, cultural, familial, and psychological perspectives. Children's ethnic identifications are formed through the maturation of developmental capacities, especially their social cognition abilities (Aboud, 2008; Quintana, 2008), in the context of socialization and inter-ethnic and intra-ethnic interactions. Mexican American children's and youth's cognitive abilities enable them to understand the social and personal significance of their Mexican and US heritages (Quintana, 1994) and to anticipate how their ethnicity influences their prospects, status, and treatment in US society (Quintana, 1998). Children's conceptions of their ethnicity reflect the cultural socialization from their immediate and extended families (Umaña-Taylor et al., 2009a), as well as enculturation provided by the larger Mexican American community (Quintana et al., 2010). These ethnic self concepts are also influenced by pressures to acculturate to dominant US cultural orientations (see Berry et al., 2006). Early in development, children's ethnic self concepts reflect an ascribed status, based on the ethnic status others assign to them. Later, ethnic self concepts become achieved forms of identifications that reflect searching for meaning related to being Mexican American (e.g. see Phinney 1989). The psychological and social significance of their ethnic status equip Mexican Americans and other Latinos with important resources to protect against psychological risks (Kiang et al., 2006), but can also be the mechanism by which they are exposed to other threats through stereotyping and internalized discrimination (Quintana et al., 2010). Given the complexity and myriad processes involved, how children and adolescents develop meaning about their ethnic status is a fascinating and remarkable process.

Our discussion of what it means to be Mexican American to children and youth is organized with a developmental framework, describing the influences and forms of their identifications and identities as they emerge during development. We apply a model of ethnic perspective-taking ability (EPTA) (Quintana, 1994; 1998) to organize this review. Each level of EPTA describes the perspective that children and youth bring to construe their psychological experience of ethnicity. As social cognitive abilities develop, children gain new perspectives on their ethnic identity (Quintana *et al.*, 2000). Moreover, as children grow, they tend to matriculate through increasingly broad and complex social contexts: from family to daycare or preschool and elementary schools and, during adolescence, through secondary schools. They become, consequently, exposed to new social stimuli associated with this expansion of their social kin. In keeping with the EPTA model, this review describes (a) how Mexican American children and youth make sense of the ethnic features of themselves, their familial heritage, and their social worlds; (b) the implications that their construal of these ethnic features has for their ethnic identity, and (c) how their ethnic identity reflects their social environment.

Mexican American children's ethnic perspective-taking ability is based on research conducted with Mexican American children and adolescents using individual interviews to understand the logic and reasoning that children and youth apply to understand what it means to be Mexican American to them and their families as well as across their social world. Each level of EPTA is defined by children's reasoning that is grounded in specific perspectives on the ethnic aspects of themselves and their social world. Acquisition of a new perspective on their ethnicity defines movement to a higher level of perspective-taking ability, and the movement to a new perspective of ethnicity results from social cognitive abilities that are applied to increasing complex social contexts.

The current review summarizes the contemporary theory and research of the prominent influences of children's intra-ethnic and inter-ethnic experiences and the sense the children make of those experiences at each level in the development of EPTA. We draw, when available, from research conducted on Mexican Americans, but will reference research on other Latino or Hispanic groups in the absence of research on Mexican American children or families. We also draw on more general research with non-Latino children if research on these topics for Latino children is not available and if the findings appear to be generalizable across racial groups. We use the term *Mexican American* only to refer to research that is specifically conducted on this group, and the term "Latino" or "Hispanic" if the research was conducted on a different Latino/Hispanic group or if the research involved a heterogeneous group of Latinos.

We describe below, four levels of EPTA, beginning at Level 0, in which children's conceptualizations of their ethnic status are grounded in more egocentric and superficial perspectives. Continuing through Levels 1 (literal perspective), 2 (social perspective), and 3 (ethnic group consciousness perspective), children's conceptualizations represent increasingly complex and integrated perspectives of what their ethnic status means. We then describe the challenges and public policy implications of the EPTA model and research.

Literature Review

Level 0: Egocentric and Observable Perspectives

Children's nascent ethnic identity is influenced primarily by the amount of cultural exposure they have received and by their level of cognitive development: variations in these factors are associated with different levels of development in ethnic identifications. Quintana's (1994; 1998) EPTA model identifies the cognitive development that is associated with children's ethnic identifications.

Early Cognitive Development

The social cognition of Mexican American preschool children, like other children, tends to be egocentric, and they rely on rudimentary cognitive skills to construe their sense of ethnicity.

Young children are in the process of acquiring the use and meaning of adult labels applied to their own and others' ethnic groups. Naïve and erroneous logic may be used to understand racial and ethnic classifications prior to elementary school. Children have been known to coin idiosyncratic terms for their own and others' ethnic and racial groups, such as referring to African Americans as "Brown" instead of terms that are more commonly used by adults, such as "Black" or "African American"—it should be noted that from a physical standpoint the young children may be more accurate in their labels than adults, who are using terms with socially constructed connotations.

Young Mexican American children seem able, perhaps due to limited cognitive skills, to classify only along dichotomous lines of race and ethnicity, only differentiating, for example, between *Black* and *not Black* (Quintana, 1994). It is not uncommon, therefore, for young Mexican American children to classify themselves as *White* largely because they are *not Black*, and be unable to differentiate themselves from Anglo children in their racial schema. Bernal, Knight and colleagues (1990; 1993) suggested that young Mexican American children can differentiate between racial groups, putatively because they can classify the phenotypical characteristics of race, but have difficulty inferring ethnic status, due to the relatively more subtle physical manifestations of race versus ethnicity. Although Mexican American children's tendency to identify as White is considered erroneous from a developmental perspective (Bernal *et al.*, ops. cit.), the young children's identifications as being White and Mexican American is consistent with federal government's classifications of Latinos as racially Caucasian or White, but of Hispanic ethnicity. Nonetheless, the tendency to identify as White appears to decline through adolescence (Quintana, 1998).

Quintana (1994) found that young Mexican American children tended to equate their ethnic status with the physical manifestations of ethnicity. For example, children associated skin coloration and other phenotypic characteristics, as well as spoken language, with ethnic and racial group membership (Quintana, 1994; 1998). Young children lack ethnic permanence, as some Mexican American children thought that ethnic status changed when skin coloration changed, while others equated ethnic status with language spoken and suggested that children's ethnic status would change if they spoke a different language. Physical appearances signal to children these differences and provide markers as they explore the meaning of their ethnic status.

Consistent with the tendency for young children's social cognition to be egocentric, young Mexican American children's understanding of the culture and status of other ethnic groups is more limited than that of their own. Young children are aware of ethnic and racial groups, but their knowledge of their own group exceeds their knowledge of the culture and manifestations of other cultural groups. They tend to think of other groups based only in the differences with their own group (e.g. "They don't speak Spanish") rather than in their own terms (e.g. "African Americans are descended from slaves"), which appears later in child development (Quintana *et al.*, 2000).

Cultural Socialization

An important component of young Mexican American children's development of an ethnic identification is their enculturation into Mexican American cultures. Implicit cultural socialization—in which cultural values influence parental behaviors but when cultural values are not explicitly discussed with children—occurs for all children early in life. Latinos, and others who have collectivistic cultural orientations, parent their infants differently than those with individualistic orientations. These parenting behaviors include, for example, the degree to which parents stimulate or calm the child, and the amount of physical contact between parent and infant (Greenfield *et al.*, 2003; Halgunseth *et al.*, 2006; Ispa *et al.*, 2004; Livas-Dlott *et al.*, 2010). Interestingly, some parenting behaviors that are inconsistent with the cultural orientation of one group of parents (e.g. parental "intrusiveness" and corporal punishment) are associated with later maladjustment, but those same behaviors are not associated with lower levels of later adjustment when the behavior is not prohibited in parents' culture (Ispa, op. cit.; Lansford *et al.*, 2005). In short, infants appear to be responsive to the cultural context of their parents' behaviors and their enculturation begins very early in infancy.

The important point for this chapter is the pervasiveness and influence of the implicit cultural socialization that children receive. Although young infants may not be able to identify explicitly with an ethnic or cultural group, implicit forms of cultural socialization lay the foundation for later cultural identifications. In this regard, collectivistic cultural values have been found to influence Mexican American and other Latino parents' socialization of their children. Namely, Mexican American parents' level of acculturation influences their ethnic socialization of their children, with those parents least acculturated to US norms, instilling stronger cultural identification in their children (see Umaña-Taylor *et al.*, 2009a; Umaña-Taylor and Guimond, 2010). Those Mexican American parents identifying closely with Mexican culture expose their children to Mexican cultural traditions, encourage collectivistic social values, such as familism, *personalismo*, and *dignidad* (Halgunseth *et al.*, 2006). In turn, parental enculturation of their children into Mexican culture is associated with the development of some aspects of children's ethnic identity (Bernal *et al.* 1990; Knight *et al.*, 1993).

Ethnic Identification

Bernal and Knight and their colleagues' (Bernal *et al.* 1990; Knight *et al.*, 1993) model of ethnic identity described four dimensions of Mexican American children's early ethnic identifications: ethnic self-identification, ethnic preferences, ethnic behaviors, and ethnic knowledge. First, ethnic self-identification refers to Mexican American children's ability to accurately identify their own ethnicity by selecting the relevant ethnic labels (Bernal, op. cit.), and their research indicated that Mexican American children first learn to accurately identify or label their own and others' ethnic group and then develop ethnic permanence—or an understanding of the constancy of ethnic status across time.

Second, Bernal and colleagues (1990; 1993) described Mexican American children's social preferences for other Mexican Americans as part of their ethnic identification. They suggested that the stronger the preference for other Mexican Americans the stronger the child's ethnic identity. Ethnic behaviors, the third component of Bernal *et al.*'s model, are behaviors associated with Mexican American children's performance of cultural activities (e.g. speaking Spanish, use of piñata at birthday parties). Young children's accurate ethnic self-identifications and performance of ethnic behaviors were predicted by parents' enculturation of their children into Mexican American culture (see Quintana *et al.*, 2000). The final and fourth component of Bernal *et al.*'s model, ethnic knowledge, is children's acquisition of knowledge of which cultural and social patterns are associated with Mexican Americans and that are different from the cultural and social patterns of Anglos. Of these four components of ethnic identity, ethnic knowledge is the more developmentally complex and was demonstrated later in children's development. Ethnic self-identifications and knowledge were predicted by children's cognitive abilities as well as parental enculturation (Quintana, op. cit.), but the performance of ethnic behaviors was only associated with parental acculturation, given that children's performance of ethnic behaviors reflects parents' acculturation level, rather than the child's level of development: parents choose whether or not to have piñatas at their children's birthday parties and whether the child eats Mexican food (see Bernal *et al.*, 1990).

It is important to note that the scope of ethnic identifications as defined by Bernal *et al.* (1990) and Knight and colleagues (1993), even for young children, is multifaceted and represents dimensions that are associated with acculturation and enculturation processes, as well as cognitive development. This broad scope reinforces the notion that development of ethnic identifications represents the confluence of multiple processes including familial socializations, broader anthropological trends in Mexican American culture that are handed down across generations, children's cognitive development, as well as social processes. Most of these processes do not involve the child's volition or reflect choices they make with respect to their cultural orientation, with variation in strength or centrality of these dimensions of ethnic identification reflecting familial enculturation and level of acculturation more so than individual variation specific to the child. It is also important to note that although children are being socialized with these cultural values, behaviors, and traditions, they do not make a conscious or explicit connection between their performance of cultural behaviors and their ethnic status (Quintana, 1994).

Level 1: Literal Perspective of Ethnicity

As Mexican American children enter and pass through the early elementary school grades, their perspective of ethnicity expands (Quintana, 1994). They are no longer limited by the egocentric and physical-oriented perspectives of ethnicity that led them to some erroneous conclusions about the permanence or nature of ethnic group membership. Indeed, at this level, Mexican American children apply ethnic terms and labels with consistency and accuracy (see Bernal *et al.*, 1990; Knight *et al.*, 1993). They show awareness of the more literal or apparent aspects of ethnic group membership, which include knowing that Mexican Americans (a) have heritage in Mexico and more recent connections to the US, (b) are often associated with speaking Spanish, and (c) are generally associated with those features that are labeled as Mexican (e.g. Mexican food, Mexican heritage, celebrating Mexican holidays). Children at this level are better able, relative to preschool children, to infer characteristics that are not directly observable, such as inferring that a Mexican American child has Mexican heritage. By understanding that ethnic heritage, rather than physical appearance and behavior, defines ethnic status, children realize that changes in skin coloration or language ability would not alter ethnic status, consistent with Bernal *et al.*'s (1990) model of ethnic identification.

At this level of perspective-taking, Mexican American children understand the connection between ethnic status and Mexican heritage and cultural traditions. They tend to have a literal understanding of ethnicity (Quintana, 1994) in the sense that characteristics that are labeled as being ethnic, such as Mexican food, Mexican heritage, Spanish language, will be associated with ethnicity, but that other coincidental characteristics, such as ethnic differences in social class, will not be connected to ethnicity. Bernal, Knight and colleagues' (1990; 1993) empirical definition of ethnic knowledge focused on the association of more literal aspects of Mexican culture (e.g. use of piñatas at birthday parties) with ethnic status. Not surprisingly, therefore, research has confirmed that children who acquire a literal perspective of their ethnicity have advanced levels of ethnic knowledge (Quintana *et al.*, 2000).

These more advanced cognitive skills allow Mexican American children to draw conclusions about the cultural characteristics associated with ethnicity from their observations of Mexican, Mexican American, and Anglo cultures (Quintana, 1994; 1998). That is, children's awareness of the connection between Mexican culture and Mexican American ethnic status helps them to classify their social world more reliably and, in turn, the increased accuracy helps them expand the foundation of their ethnic knowledge by (a) observing others, (b) making ethnic classifications and then (c) drawing connections between patterns in the behavior observed for Mexican versus Anglo or other ethnic/racial groups. In a sense, children operate like lay anthropologists conducting participant observations, investigating the cultural characteristics that are associated with their ethnic group.

Despite the developmental advances in their ethnic identifications, Mexican American children experience their ethnic identification as a personal characteristic, which they happen to share with other Mexican Americans. That is, their ethnic status and their cultural values, skills, and orientation are viewed as characteristics, much like their eye color, that they share with other individuals who have those same personal characteristics. To explain, when children say, for example, that they like being Mexican American, their affiliation with the ethnic status is based on their feelings about themselves rather than feelings about their ethnic group. What has not yet emerged at this level of development is a communion and kinship with other Mexican Americans. Their identification, therefore, with other Mexican Americans is through sharing these behaviors, patterns, and heritage, but there isn't the merging of their personal sense of self with their ethnic group in ways that are more typical during adolescence (see Cross, 1995). Consequently, ethnic pride for Mexican Americans and other children of elementary school age is associated with pride in their ethnic self, which may involve pride in their personal characteristics, such as cultural skills and ability to speak Spanish. Some Mexican American children appreciate the exotic nature of their background, and think, for example, that it is "cool" to be descended from the Aztecs (Quintana, 1994). Others feel proud of their bilingual skills, or may be proud of their parents and grandparents who are also Mexican American. In short, they like themselves and have learned to appreciate the immutable aspects of their Mexican American ancestry.

Mexican American children's sense and valuing of their ethnic self is also influenced by the discrimination and bias to which they are exposed directly and vicariously (Quintana and McKown, 2008). They are confused by what is experienced as isolated incidents of mistreatment they receive from peers, through name calling ("chocolate milk") and teasing (called "Chinese" for having almond-shaped eyes) and for being different from Anglo children, which represent the socially-constructed norms for children. Experiencing denigration for their ethnic status, an immutable aspect of themselves, is particularly psychologically challenging for children because of limitations in their social cognition. That is, they may be unable to challenge the legitimacy of stigmatization given that an understanding of why they are stigmatized requires advanced social cognitive skills. Consequently, they tend to be unable to attribute others' prejudice toward them as false beliefs (Brown, 2008). To construe the illegitimacy of others' bias and discrimination toward them, children must first develop theory-of-mind abilities, which are the abilities to attribute mental states to others (Brown, 2008; Brown and Bigler, 2005).

There seem to be important sequelae from being stigmatized for children's development of ethnic identity. The stigmatization of Mexican American children may account for important differences in their inter-ethnic and intra-ethnic attitudes relative to Anglo children. Anglo children tend to show bias favoring their own group and bias disadvantaging other groups, while Latino children do not show these same biases, neither for nor against their own ethnic group. For example, Brown (2008) found that Anglo children tend to privilege members of their own group at the expense of other groups. Moreover, Anglo children's tendency to perceive discrimination was based on the ethnicity of the target of discrimination, with discrimination being perceived more often when the target was Anglo and less often when the target was Latino. Conversely, Latino children's perception of discrimination was similar for Latino and Anglo targets (Brown, 2008). Interestingly, Anglo children's ratings of Latino children were more influenced by school context, in that Anglo children from classrooms with large portions of Latinos rated Latino children more favorably than Anglo children in classrooms with few Latino children, whereas Latino children's ratings of Anglo children were uniformly high across racial density of their classroom (Tropp and Prenovost, 2008).

These patterns of findings for Latino and Anglo children have important implications from the perspective of social identity theories. Social identity and categorization theories (Tajfel and Turner, 1986) anticipate that when a person identifies with a social status or categorizes themself as a member of a social group, the person develops bias in favor of other members of the ingroup and bias against outgroup members. Consequently, the emergence of bias in Anglo children toward their ingroup and the failure for similar bias to emerge for Latino children seems to suggest that while Anglo children develop a social identity with their ethnic ingroup, Mexican American children do not. Given that a prime function of social identities is to enhance self-esteem, it is easy to understand why Anglo children more readily identify with their ethnicity than Latino children, given that identification with a stigmatized group could lead to diminished self-esteem in the absence of advanced social cognitive abilities to compensate.

Level 2: Social Perspective of Ethnicity

As they matriculate to the upper elementary grades and enter middle school, Mexican American children develop a social perspective on their ethnicity (Quintana, 1994; 1998). This perspective is based on advances in children's social cognitive ability, especially in their theory-of-mind abilities. Advances in social perspective-taking skills lead to Mexican American children's ability to "see" their ethnicity through the "eyes" of others, or reflected self-appraisals (Cooley, 1902). They understand the social consequences of their ethnic status in terms of how members of other groups perceive them as well as how ingroup members may perceive them. They also understand the social consequences of ethnic group membership in terms of social patterns. Mexican American children recognize that same-race friendships may be easier to form than different-race friendships (Quintana, 1998). The transition from a literal to a social perspective of ethnicity corresponds to the transition from conceiving of ethnic status as reflecting an artifact of the past to having a daily reality.

That is, at the literal perspective, children conceive of their ethnicity as reflecting one's past or one's heritage and the culture associated with that past. Conversely, at the social perspective ethnic group membership has implications for mundane social behavior and dynamics—it has a contemporary reality on social interactions and relationships (Quintana, 1994).

These social cognitive abilities support the development of a social perspective of ethnicity that allows children to infer the mental state of others, including their ethnic attitudes and the social consequences of these attitudes (Brown and Bigler, 2005; Quintana, 1998). Recognizing that others may hold biases in favor of or against members of ethnic groups helps children anticipate possible social consequences of ethnicity (e.g. "My friend's parents may not like me because I'm Mexican American" or "I like being Mexican American because . . . [a bully] teases kids but he doesn't tease me because I'm Mexican American"). At the literal perspective of ethnicity, children associate cultural traditions to ethnic status, but at the social perspective children show awareness of social norms (e.g. *respeto*) associated with ethnic status. With only a literal perspective of ethnicity, younger children would attribute the relative ease of forming intra-ethnic relationships to having the same traditions, but at the social perspective of ethnicity children attribute the ease of intra-ethnic relationships because ingroup members may share similar social experiences.

Mexican American children acquiring a social perspective on their ethnicity understand more subtle features associated with ethnicity that are not connected to the more literal aspects of their culture. With a social perspective of ethnicity, children function like young sociologists in making observations about the ethnic components of their social world. Children notice the confounding of social class and ethnic status and show awareness that Mexican Americans may be disproportionally represented among low-income groups. One of the most important insights into ethnic status that is not associated with literal parts of culture is the awareness and prevalence of ethnic prejudice. Having a social perspective of ethnicity, Mexican American children make explicit connections between being stigmatized and their ethnic status. For example, when asked what being Mexican American means, children at this level often describe the experience of being an "other", reflecting their experiences of stigmatization. Importantly, with theory-of-mind abilities children at the social perspective can challenge the legitimacy of ethnic prejudice against them and develop critical consciousness on their stigmatization (e.g. see Quintana and Segura-Herrera, 2003). The development of critical consciousness in late childhood may provide important protective functions for ethnic identity in adolescence. Research documents that Mexican American children show more awareness and experiences of ethnic prejudice in the transition from childhood into adolescence (Brown, 2008; Quintana, 1998). Importantly, in late childhood and early adolescence peers and peer groups are also developing social perspective on ethnicity, potentially making more direct and explicit their stigmatization of Mexican Americans.

With a social perspective and greater awareness of the prevalence of ethnic discrimination, Mexican American children become cognizant of the ways in which their ethnicity is racialized through discrimination and bias. Much of the research on Mexican American children's ethnic identity has focused on acquisition of cultural skills, bicultural orientation, and ethnic pride (Padilla, 2006), but has neglected the racialized aspect of Mexican American ethnicity. Padilla articulated the need for researchers to investigate the racialization of Latinos, including Mexican Americans. Similarly, Quintana *et al.* (2010) suggested that children's exposure to discrimination puts them at risk for internalizing the discrimination. Qualitative studies of Latino identity have emphasized the racialized context of the development of Latino youth's ethnic identity (e.g. Holleran, 2003).

Parental ethnic socialization also evolves as Mexican American children mature and are exposed to more complex social contexts. As children get older Latino parents are more likely to have frank discussions about how to prepare for ethnic discrimination. Across ethnic groups, parents are more likely to discuss the reality of racism and ethnic prejudice as children enter adolescence (Hughes *et al.*, 2008). Despite the potential for their children to experience discrimination, Latino parents' ethnic socialization is focused on egalitarian messages to insure that Latino children consider themselves equal to children of other ethnic groups.

Quintana *et al.*, (2010) describe how youth can protect themselves against ethnic stigmatization. Youth recalled how their parents protected them against internalizing ethnic discrimination: Parents instructed what the youth should respond when stigmatized by making encouraging self-statements. (e.g. "You have to tell yourself . . .") or citing facts that countered the underlying assumption of the discrimination (e.g. "Remember how . . .[a Mexican American] made it [was successful]"), or simply to disregard the discrimination (e.g. "If they tell you that, don't pay any attention to them"). Quintana (op. cit.) traced connections between parental socialization to prepare for discrimination, to youth's self-statements and thereby internalizing the parental ethnic socialization. Youth were found to draw from parental ethnic socialization when faced with ethnic discrimination and bias.

Level 3: Ethnic Group Consciousness Perspective

As Mexican American children enter adolescence there are two important developments in their ethnic cognition that influence identity formation: improvement in the ability to generalize across discrete experiences associated with ethnicity, and development of ethnic group consciousness (Quintana, 1998). Earlier in development children tended to construe ethnic experiences, such as discrimination, as isolated or discrete experiences and conceived of their ethnic heritage as an ascribed status. Conversely, Mexican American adolescents realize that they are not simply passive recipients of their ethnic heritage and of the random or discrete experiences that are associated with their ethnicity. Adolescents appreciate that there is an active role for them and their peers to play in the expression of their ethnic heritage and identity. Moreover, moving from an ascribed to an achieved status, adolescents realize that ethnic identity is not simply ascribed by a youth's ethnic heritage, but represents an achieved status reflecting active expressions of ethnic identity and ethnic pride. In adolescence, ethnic identity represents the integration of ethnic-related experiences, such as exposure to discrimination or enculturation into Mexican culture. In childhood, ethnic-related experiences are interpreted as discrete events, not necessarily as being inter-connected. However, advances in social cognition during adolescence allow Mexican American youth to integrate these experiences into themes, such that the discrimination that they or their peers experience reflect not just isolated acts by individuals, but the systematic discrimination perpetuated by, for example, Anglo society. Mexican American adolescents also integrate discrete members of their ethnic group into a group connected by shared ethnic experiences with a perceived *esprit de corps*. Inter-ethnic experiences between individuals reflect not just the two individuals, but also some representation of the history of inter-ethnic relations among their respective ethnic groups. In this way, Mexican American adolescents develop an ethnic group consciousness in which the youth merge their personal identities with their ethnic identity. Allegiance to their ethnic group becomes a matter of personal pride and an expression of their personal identity.

These advances in social and ethnic cognition provide the foundation for ethnic identity development (Quintana *et al.*, 1999). Phinney (1989) proposed a model of ethnic identity development and measurement thereof that has been applied to Mexican American and other Latino adolescents (e.g. Matsunaga *et al.*, 2010; Quintana *et al.*, 1999). Phinney (1992) described ethnic identity statuses including unexamined ethnic identity, identity search/moratorium and identity achievement, and Phinney (1989) found that ethnic identity development involves ethnic minority youth exploring and then committing to an ethnic identity, representing the meaning that their ethnicity and ethnic identity have for them. The number of different dimensions for Phinney's (1992) measure of ethnic identity has evolved over the years, but we focus on two dimensions: ethnic identity achievement and ethnic affirmation and belonging. Although ethnic achievement scores tend to increase with age (French *et al.*, 2000) and were associated with cognitive development (e.g. Quintana *et al.*, 1999), the affirmation and belonging scores predict well-being, and positive views toward education for Mexican American and other Latino youth. Ethnic achievement tends to increase during early adolescence, while affirmation scores tend to form before or early in adolescence (Pahl and Way, 2006; Umaña-Taylor *et al.*, 2009b).

Extending Phinney's (1989; 1992) work, Umaña-Taylor (2004) proposed a model specific to Latino ethnic identity that includes exploration and affirmation, as well as identity resolution. The Umaña-Taylor (2004) model differentiates identity process and content, with the identity exploration and resolution scales reflecting the process of ethnic identity formation and the affirmation scale representing the content or attitudinal dimension of ethnic identity. Umaña-Taylor and colleagues (2009a) found support for the development of all three ethnic identity dimensions among adolescent girls, whereas only the affirmation dimension increased longitudinally for boys.

Like Umaña-Taylor (2004), Quintana et al., (2010) differentiate the process from the content of ethnic identity. In Quintana et al.'s research, the process or functioning of ethnic identity corresponds to Erikson's notion of ego identity, through which adolescents filter and integrate their experiences of self into a coherent self concept. Quintana et al. (2010) suggest that the process of ethnic identity is analogous to Erikson's self-identities, which represent the various self-concepts and are the products of the ego identity functioning in a way that integrates experiences into a cogent sense of self. Others have examined the specific ethnic label that Mexican American and other Latino youth have chosen to represent their ethnic identity (Eschbach and Gomez, 1998). Although the ethnic label that Latinos choose is very important to the youth, it appears that the psychological investment in the label, not the label per se, was associated with adjustment (Fuligni et al., 2008). The ethnic labels and investment in the label appear to represent the content and process, respectively, of ethnic identity formation.

There are three main determinants of the content and process of ethnic identity formation: ethnic cognition, ethnic socialization, and inter-ethnic relations. As previously mentioned, Quintana et al. (1999) found that Mexican American's ethnic perspective-taking ability—youth's ethnic cognition—were predictive of ethnic identity formation. Otherwise, there has been little investigation into the ethnic cognition associated with ethnic identity formation, despite repeated references to forms of adolescent cognition in relation to ethnic identity (e.g. Umaña-Taylor et al., 2009a).

Conversely, there has been considerable research into the role that ethnic socialization plays in ethnic identity formation, particularly for Mexican American and other Latino youth. Family ethnic socialization begins very early in life (see above) and continues through adolescence in explicit and implicit ways (Quintana et al., 2010; Umaña-Taylor and Fine, 2004). Levels of parental acculturation are strongly connected to adolescents' ethnic socialization (Umaña-Taylor and Yazedjian, 2006) and to the adolescents' ethnic identity, particularly their sense of affirmation and belonging to Mexican American and Latino ethnic groups (e.g. Matsunaga et al., 2010). Parental ethnic socialization has been found to be strongly connected to ethnic identity formation and affirmation (Quintana et al., 1999; Umaña-Taylor et al., 2009a; Umaña-Taylor and Fine, 2004). Particularly noteworthy are the results of Umaña-Taylor and Guimond's (2010) longitudinal study that found strong concurrent connections between ethnic socialization and ethnic identity exploration, affiliation, and resolution for both boys and girls. For boys only, family ethnic socialization was connected prospectively to ethnic identity resolution.

Mexican American and other stigmatized groups of adolescents are also socialized through their inter-ethnic interactions and relationships (Quintana et al., 2010). Like other stigmatized youth, Mexican Americans are at risk for internalizing negative stereotypes about them and their group. Dovidio and colleagues (2010) indicate that discrimination toward Latinos, compared to other minority groups, may be influenced by any apparent non-native appearance, including non-native linguistic accents. Quintana (1994) indicated that Mexican American youth need not be the direct targets of stigma to be impacted—they can also be impacted by vicarious exposure to ethnic stereotyping targeting their American peers. Indeed, ethnic identity exploration seems to accelerate at the same time that youth are exposed to increasing discrimination (French et al., 2000).

Longitudinal studies demonstrate that ethnic identity formation, especially identity exploration, appears to be stimulated by experiences of discrimination for Latinos (Pahl and Way, 2006; Umaña-Taylor and Guimond, 2010)—Umaña-Taylor having found that while discrimination increased ethnic identity exploration, it seemed to decrease ethnic affiliation. Guyll and colleagues (2010) suggested several mechanisms by which Latinos may be vulnerable to deleterious effects of discrimination including self-fulfilling stereotypes, stereotype consciousness, and stereotype threat. Quintana (1994) found that Mexican American adolescents were well aware of the potential that they could fulfill negative ethnic stereotypes.

Summary

Quintana *et al.* (2010) suggested that youth's internalization of parental and extra-familial ethnic socialization would help buffer them against the deleterious effects of racism and internalized racism. Cross-sectional research has generally supported the notion that components of ethnic identity are associated with adjustment, predicting, for example, self-esteem and low levels of psychological symptoms of anxiety and depression (Phinney, 1992; Umaña-Taylor and Updegraff, 2007). Romero and Roberts (2003) found connections between ethnic identity and self-esteem, with ethnic affirmation showing a strong relationship with ethnic identity. Several longitudinal studies by Umaña-Taylor and colleagues (Umaña-Taylor & Updegraff, 2007; Umaña-Taylor *et al.*, 2008; Umaña-Taylor *et al.*, 2009b) replicated the cross-sectional findings connecting self-esteem to components of ethnic identity, but found limited support for longitudinal connections (e.g. six months later), and in 2008 found that only ethnic identity resolution predicted coping with discrimination.

Future Directions and Challenges

A range of factors challenge ethnic identity development. For young Mexican American children it might be difficult to infer their own and other's ethnic status due to subtle physical manifestations of ethnicity between Latino and White as opposed to other racial groups (Bernal *et al.*, 1990; 1993). Other factors might include differences within a group, such as skin coloration, level of acculturation and enculturation, or even the extent to which Spanish language skills have been passed down from one generation to the next. For Mexican Americans it is important to understand individual ethnic identity development in the context of the group, and how the development of ethnic identity is similar and dissimilar to other groups of Latino descent, particularly given Mexican American's unique history as a group in the US.

Policy Implications

Because ethnic group membership has implications for social behavior, it has an impact on social interactions and relationships. Therefore, ethnic group membership and its formation is likely to have lasting effects on how Mexican Americans interact within their ethnic group and with others. Level of acculturation, for instance, can influence how parents socialize Mexican American children and may have a direct impact on their cultural identification (Umaña-Taylor *et al.*, 2009a; Umaña-Taylor and Guimond, 2010). Additionally, those who identify more closely with Mexican culture are more likely to encourage other group-ascribed values, such as familism, personalismo and dignidad (Halgunseth *et al.*, 2006). Ascription to these social values is likely to inform how Mexican Americans perceive themselves in the group, as well as the expectations they might have for ethnic group membership.

Given the complexity of ethnic identity development in Mexican American youth, it is recommended that school programs develop appropriate interventions to facilitate children's ethnic identity development according to their maturation level. These interventions are likely to increase cultural identification between Mexican American and other racial and ethnic groups, predictably fostering understanding and acceptance between peers and a sense of cultural pride and ownership.

Ethnic identification is also significant in Mexican Americans' interactions with other racial and ethnic groups due to the risk of experiencing prejudice and discrimination. Research shows a heightened awareness of experiences of ethnic prejudice in adolescence (Brown, 2008; Quintana, 1998). Consequently, the transition from childhood to adolescence seems like a critical time to develop social and school programs to help Mexican American youth navigate this transition and assimilate experiences of oppression.

The ethnic socialization children receive both within and outside their ethnic group impact their views on cultural identification. Future research on Mexican American ethnic identity development could benefit from focusing on the different resources children possess, and the strategies they learn to equip themselves with to use against psychological risks due to their ethnic identity. For example, more research could be conducted to address the types of conversations Mexican American parents have with their children about their ethnic identity and how these impact their ethnic identity development. It is important to note how messages focused on egalitarian views toward ethnic groups may impact the Mexican American's ability to cope with discrimination.

Research supports the idea that different components of ethnic identity can be associated with positive adjustment that leads to increased self-esteem and lower levels of anxiety and depression (Phinney, 1992; Umaña-Taylor and Updegraff, 2007). Consequently, further research is recommended on the implications ethnic identity resolution has on positive outcomes, such as developing coping strategies against discrimination, stereotyping, acculturative stress, as well as other outcomes such as affirmation and belonging in Mexican American and Latino ethnic groups.

References

Aboud, F. E. (2008). A social cognitive developmental theory of prejudice. In S. M. Quintana and C. McKown (Eds.) *Handbook of race, racism, and the developing child* (pp. 55–71). Hoboken, NJ: John Wiley.

Bernal, M. E., and Knight, G. P. (1993). *Ethnic identity: Formation and transmission among Hispanics and other minorities.* Albany, NY: State University of New York Press.

Bernal, M. E., Knight, G. P., Garza, C. A., Ocampo, K. A., and Cota, M. K. (1990). The development of ethnic identity in Mexican-American children. *Hispanic Journal of Behavioral Sciences, 12,* 3–24.

Berry, J., Phinney, J., Sam, D., and Vedder, P. (2006). Immigrant youth: Acculturation, identity, and adaptation. *Applied Psychology: An International Review, 55*(3), 303–332.

Brown, C. (2008). Children's perceptions of racial and ethnic discrimination: Differences across children and contexts. In S. M. Quintana and C. McKown (Eds.) *Handbook of race, racism, and the developing child* (pp. 133–153). Hoboken, NJ: John Wiley.

Brown, C. S., and Bigler, R. S. (2005). Children's perceptions of discrimination: A developmental model. *Child Development, 76*(3), 533–553.

Cooley, C. (1902). *Human nature and the social order.* New York: Scribner's.

Cross, W. E., Jr. (1995). The psychological of nigrescence: Revising the Cross model. In J. G. Ponterotto, J. M. Casas, L. A. Suzuki, and C. M. Alexander (Eds.) *Handbook of multicultural counseling* (pp. 93–122). Thousand Oaks, CA: Sage.

Dovidio, J. F., Gluszek, A., John, M.-S., Ditlmann, R., and Lagunes, P. (2010). Understanding bias toward Latinos: Discrimination, dimensions of difference, and experience of exclusion. *Journal of Social Issues, 66,* 59–78.

Eschbach, K., and Gomez, K. (1998). Choosing Hispanic identity: Ethnic identity switching among respondents to high school and beyond. *Social Science Quarterly, 79,* 74–90.

French, S., Seidman, E., Allen, L., and Aber, J. (2000). Racial/ethnic identity, congruence with the social context, and the transition to high school. *Journal of Adolescent Research, 15*(5), 587–602.

Fuligni, A. J., Witkow, M., and Garcia, C. (2005). Ethnic identity and the academic adjustment of adolescents from Mexican, Chinese, and European backgrounds. *Developmental Psychology, 41,* 799–811.

Fuligni, A. J., Kiang, L., Witkow, M. R., and Baldelomar, O. (2008). Stability and change in ethnic labeling among adolescents from Asian and Latin American immigrant families. *Child Development, 79*(4), 944–956. doi:10.1111/j.1467-8624.2008.01169.x

Greenfield, P. M., Keller, H., Fuligni, A., and Maynard, A. (2003). Cultural pathways through universal development. *Annual Review of Psychology, 54,* 461–490.

Guyll, M., Madon, S., Prieto, L., and Acherr, K. C. (2010). The potential roles of self-fulfilling prophecies, stigma consciousness, and stereotype threat in linking Latino/a ethnicity and educational outcomes. *Journal of Social Issues, 66,* 113–130.

Halgunseth, L., Ispa, J. M., and Rudy, D. D. (2006). Parental control in Latino families: An integrated review of the literature. *Child Development, 77,* 1282–1297.

Holleran, L. (2003). Mexican American youth of the Southwest borderlands: Perceptions of ethnicity, acculturation, and race. *Hispanic Journal of Behavioral Sciences, 25,* 352–369.

Hughes, D., Rivas, D., Foust, M., Hagelskamp, C., Gersick, S., and Way, N. (2008). How to catch a moonbeam: A mixed-methods approach to understanding ethnic socialization processes in ethnically diverse families. In S. M. Quintana and C. McKown (Eds.) *Handbook of race, racism, and the developing child* (pp. 226–277). Hoboken, NJ: John Wiley and Sons Inc.

Ispa, J. M., Fine, M. A., Halgunseth, L. C., Harper, S., Robinson, J., Boyce, L., Brooks-Gunn, J., and Brady-Smith, C. (2004). Maternal intrusiveness, maternal warmth, and mother-toddler relationship outcomes: Variations across low-income ethnic and acculturation groups. *Child Development, 75,* 1613–1631.

Kiang, L., Yip, T., Gonzales-Backen, M., Witkow, M., and Fuligni, A. J. (2006). Ethnic identity and the daily psychological well-being of adolescents from Mexican and Chinese backgrounds. *Child Development, 77*(5), 1338–1350.

Knight, G. P., Bernal, M. E., Garza, C. A., Cota, M. K., and Ocampo, K. A. (1993). Family socialization and the ethnic identity of Mexican-American children. *Journal of Cross-Cultural Psychology, 24,* 99–114.

Lansford, J. E., Chang, L., Dodge, K. A., Malone, P. S., Oburu, P., Palmerus, K., Bacchini, D., Pastorelli, C., Bombi, A. S., Zelli, A., Tapanya, S., Chaudhary, N., Deater-Deckard, K., Manke, B., and Quinn, N. (2005). Physical discipline and children's adjustment: Cultural normativeness as a moderator. *Child Development, 76,* 1234–1246.

Livas-Dlott, A., Fuller, B., Stein, G., Bridges, M., Mangual Figueroa, A., and Mireles, L. (2010). Commands, competence, and cariño: Maternal socialization practices in Mexican American families. *Developmental Psychology, 46*(3), 566–578.

Matsunaga, M., Hecht, M. L., Elek, E., and Ndiaye, K. (2010). Ethnic identity development and acculturation: A longitudinal analysis of Mexican-heritage youth in the southwest United States. *Journal of Cross-Cultural Psychology, 41,* 410–427.

Padilla, A. (2006). Bicultural social development. *Hispanic Journal of Behavioral Sciences, 28,* 467–497.

Pahl, K., and Way, N. (2006). Longitudinal trajectories of ethnic identity among urban Black and Latino adolescents. *Child Development, 77*(5), 1403–1415.

Phinney, J. (1989). Stages of ethnic identity development in minority group adolescents. *Journal of Early Adolescence, 9*(1), 34–49.

Phinney, J. (1992). The multigroup ethnic identity measure: A new scale for use with diverse groups. *Journal of Adolescent Research, 7*(2), 156–176.

Quintana, S. (2008). Racial perspective taking ability: Developmental, theoretical, and empirical trends. In S. M. Quintana and C. McKown (Eds.) *Handbook of race, racism, and the developing child* (pp. 16–36). Hoboken, NJ: John Wiley and Sons Inc.

Quintana, S., and McKown, C. (2008). Introduction: Race, racism, and the developing child. In S. M. Quintana and C. McKown (Eds.) *Handbook of race, racism, and the developing child* (pp. 1–15). Hoboken, NJ: John Wiley and Sons Inc.

Quintana, S. M. (1994). A model of ethnic perspective taking ability applied to Mexican-American children and youth. *International Journal of Intercultural Relations, 18,* 419–448.

Quintana, S. M. (1998). Development of children's understanding of ethnicity and race. *Applied and Preventive Psychology: Current Scientific Perspectives, 7,* 27–45.

Quintana, S. M., and Segura-Herrera, T. A. (2003). Developmental transformations of self and identity in the context of oppression. *Self and Identity, 2*(4), 269–285.

Quintana, S. M., Castañeda-English, P., and Ybarra, V. C. (1999). Role of perspective-taking ability and ethnic socialization in the development of adolescent ethnic identity. *Journal of Research on Adolescence, 9*, 161–184.

Quintana, S. M., Segura-Herrera, T. A., and Nelson, M. L. (2010). Mexican American high school students' ethnic self-concepts and identity. *Journal of Social Issues, 66*, 11–28.

Quintana, S. M., Ybarra, V. C., Gonzalez-Doupe, P., and de Baessa, Y. (2000). Cross-cultural evaluation of ethnic perspective-taking ability in two samples: US Latino and Guatemalan Ladino children. *Cultural Diversity and Ethnic Minority Psychology, 6*, 334–351.

Romero, A. J., and Roberts, R. E. (2003). The impact of multiple dimensions of ethnic identity on discrimination and adolescents' self-esteem. *Journal of Applied Social Psychology, 33*, 2288–2305.

Tajfel, H., and Turner, J. (1986). The social identity theory of intergroup behavior. In S. Worchel and W. Austin (Eds.) *Psychology of intergroup relations* (pp. 7–24). Chicago: Nelson-Hall.

Tropp, L. R., and Prenovost, M. (2008). Role of intergroup contact in predicting children's interethnic attitudes: Evidence from meta-analytic and field studies. In S. R. Levy and M. Killen (Eds.) *Intergroup attitudes and relations in childhood through adulthood* (pp. 236–248). New York: Oxford University Press.

Umaña-Taylor, A. J. (2004). Ethnic identity and self-esteem: Examining the role of social context. *Journal of Adolescence, 27*, 139–146.

Umaña-Taylor, A. J., and Fine, M. A. (2004). Examining ethnic identity among Mexican-origin adolescents living in the United States. *Hispanic Journal of Behavioral Sciences, 26*(1), 36–59.

Umaña-Taylor, A. J., and Guimond, A. B. (2010). A longitudinal examination of parenting behaviors and perceived discrimination predicting Latino adolescents' ethnic identity. *Developmental Psychology, 46*, 636–650.

Umaña-Taylor, A. J., and Updegraff, K. A. (2007). Latino adolescents' mental health: Exploring the role of discrimination, ethnic identity, acculturation, and self-esteem. *Journal of Adolescence, 30*, 549–567.

Umaña-Taylor, A. J., and Yazedjian, A. (2006). Generational differences and similarities among Puerto Rican and Mexican mothers' experiences with familial ethnic socialization. *Journal of Social and Personal Relationships, 23*(3), 445–464.

Umaña-Taylor, A. J., Gonzales-Backen, M., and Guimond, A. B. (2009b). Latino adolescents' ethnic identity: Is there a development progression and does growth in ethnic identity predict growth in self-esteem? *Child Development, 80*, 391–405.

Umaña-Taylor, A. J., Alfaro, E. C., Bámaca, M. Y., and Guimond, A. B. (2009a). The central role of familial ethnic socialization in Latino adolescents' cultural orientation. *Journal of Marriage and Family, 71*, 46–60.

Umaña-Taylor, A. J., Vargas-Chanes, D., Garcia, C. D., and Gonzales-Backen, M. (2008). A longitudinal examination of Latino adolescents' ethnic identity, coping with discrimination, and self-esteem. *Journal of Early Adolescence, 28*, 16–50.

3

USING CULTURALLY INFORMED THEORY TO STUDY MEXICAN AMERICAN CHILDREN AND FAMILIES

Rebecca M. B. White, George P. Knight, and Mark W. Roosa

Introduction

Against a backdrop of continued growth of the Mexican American population (see Caldera, this volume), it is no wonder that interest in research with Mexican American children and families has increased substantially over the last decade. Increased interest offers a reasonable guarantee of increased scholarship, but not necessarily for the quality of that scholarship. Attention to quality is needed if scholars are to effectively inform scientific theory, supply the necessary scientific foundation for the development of effective social services and interventions, and guide public policy. Usually the quality of a given research study is dependent upon the degree to which scientific inferences can be made about the causality (i.e., internal validity of a research design) and generalizability of those inferences (i.e., the external validity of a research design). In this chapter we introduce the concept of *culturally informed theorizing* as a necessary component of research with Mexican Americans, one that can facilitate high quality studies and more accurate scientific inferences. We then go on to highlight the ways in which culturally informed theorizing can inform three important methodological issues in research with Mexican American children and families: design, sampling, and measurement.

Culturally Informed Theorizing and Ethnic Correlates

To guide high-quality research with Mexican American children and families, scholars must engage in culturally informed theorizing (CIT), which will require knowledge and understanding about a range of ethnic correlates. An ethnic correlate is defined as any concept that relates to ethnic group membership. Ethnic correlates can be used to describe differences between two ethnic groups. Due to considerable heterogeneity within an ethnic group, they can also be used to describe diversity among members of a group. CIT is defined as the process of developing ideas about the ways in which ethnic correlates might intersect with existing knowledge and/or theoretical models of human behavior. There are numerous degrees of potential intersection. At one end of the continuum, a scholar may conclude that an existing theoretical model should explain human behavior among the target ethnic group in a manner consistent with work on other (often majority or mainstream) groups. In such a case no adjustments need to be made to the existing model to accurately explain behavior in the target ethnic group. At the opposite end of this continuum, a scholar may conclude that an entirely new theoretical model must be developed to accurately explain behavior in a target ethnic group. Between these two extremes, and likely to be the more common case, a scholar may conclude that ethnic correlates have meaningful implications for an existing theory. In consequence, the theory may not explain behavior in the ethnic group as accurately as it has previously explained behavior in another group, and modifications to existing theory may be necessary. In sum, intersection involves the degree to which ethnic correlates enhance, impact, or influence current knowledge and theory.

We present three domains of ethnic correlates: culture, minority status, and demographic. Cultural variables reflect an ethnic minority group's shared language, belief systems, values, and customs. Minority status variables reflect experiences, challenges, and threats that members of an ethnic minority group experience in the context of a dominant majority group. Demographic variables reflect general population characteristics (e.g. socioeconomic distributions, age distributions, family structures) of the target population. We offer these categorizations as a heuristic to guide CIT; we do not claim that the three domains are orthogonal, or somehow not related. Indeed, many ethnic correlates have demographic markers which have been employed as proxies of culture or minority status in research. Further, several demographic variables may, at least in part, reflect culture (e.g. the prevalence of two-parent households may reflect strong family orientation), minority status (e.g. socioeconomic status may be a function of discrimination), or both. In this discussion we merely aim to provide a tool to assist scholars as they engage in CIT.

Cultural variables are ethnic correlates that must be treated as central components of CIT. Cultural variables include numerous operationalizations of three overarching concepts: cultural adaptation, acculturative stress, and cultural orientation. Mexican Americans experience a process of dual cultural adaptation (Gonzales *et al.*, 2009) involving two processes—acculturation (adaptation to the mainstream US culture), and enculturation (adaptation to the ethnic culture)—that take place *over time*. These distinct processes impact individuals from numerous angles, including their cultural beliefs, values, behaviors, language, and sense of belonging to both cultures. Acculturative stress refers to stressful experiences that occur as a part of adapting to the language, lifestyles, and rules of another culture (Gonzales *et al.*, 2002). Cultural orientation refers to an individual's standing *at any one point in time* on factors affected by cultural adaptation. For example, the enculturation *process* may be reflected in, and operationalized by, an individual's changes in cultural values over time whereas an individual's cultural *orientation* might be operationalized as his or her cultural values at one point in time.

Cultural variables represent significant sources of heterogeneity—both between Mexican Americans and other groups, and among Mexican Americans—which may intersect with existing theory to influence families and development. For example, parents' socialization strategies are a mechanism through which socialization goals are expressed in the family context (White *et al.*, 2013). A population with diverse cultural beliefs and values may have similarly diverse socialization goals, resulting in heterogeneity of socialization strategies. In light of those same beliefs and values, there is likely to be diversity in the ways that children interpret the meaning and intent of diverse approaches to parent socialization. Consequently, any theory that examines predictors and consequents of parent socialization would benefit from careful theorizing about how cultural variables may intersect with the theory, before it is uniformly applied to research questions focused on Mexican American children and families (for examples see Li-Grining, 2012; White *et al.*, 2012).

Minority status variables are distinct from cultural variables in that, even though they may represent an experience shared by many members of an ethnic group, they are not inherently a part of being a member of that group. Rather, minority status variables are more a product of how members of that group are received by members of the ethnic majority in the US. Minority status variables can include, among others, experiences of stereotyping, discrimination, prejudice, oppression, segregation, profiling, and fear of deportation. Many of these constructs are employed in theoretical models designed to describe experiences of ethnic minority groups in the US generally (e.g. Garcia Coll *et al.*, 1996). Most of these are not, however, incorporated into models that were based on research with European American samples. Consequently, scholars are responsible for considering how these experiences might intersect with such models. Continuing from the parenting example above, careful theorizing about the impact that exposure to ethnic discrimination may have on Mexican American families would likely force parenting scholars to consider that adequate preparation for such experiences may be a major component of parent socialization that is not represented in parenting research among European American samples (Hughes, 2003).

Demographic variables can include, among others, nativity, generational status, migration, regional differences, socioeconomic differences, differences in educational attainment, family structure, and residential neighborhoods. These demographic variables may have meaningful implications for existing theory and may undermine scholars' ability to make inferences about Mexican Americans from research based on demographically distinct groups. For example, major theories that describe neighborhood effects on children and families need to consider that certain subgroups of Mexican Americans (e.g. immigrants) may experience US neighborhoods very differently than others due to their ability to make evaluative comparisons between their US neighborhoods and those they inhabited in Mexico. Mexican Americans that have not lived in Mexico cannot make those same comparisons; likewise for European- or African Americans (the subjects of much of this research) who have only lived in US neighborhoods. Consequently, our theorizing about neighborhood effects among Mexican Americans will benefit from careful consideration of these sources of within- and between-group demographic diversity.

Drawing on knowledge of ethnic correlates to engage in CIT is a necessary component of research with Mexican Americans. The goal of CIT is to facilitate explanation and understanding of human behavior in a cultural or ethnic group by ensuring that variables somehow salient to that group, or ones that represent significant sources of heterogeneity within that group, are given appropriate consideration. The process is central to scholars' ability to make accurate scientific inferences about causality and generalizability because, in all but the most extreme cases (i.e., no intersection), a failure to consider ethnic correlates will undermine both internal and external validity. In the sections that follow, we highlight the ways in which CIT will influence three important methodological issues and, consequently, study validity.

First, CIT should be the basis for selecting a study's *design*, via its impact on the development of research questions and hypotheses. Second, CIT can be used to delineate *sampling* strategies most capable of achieving accurate representation of the target population. Third, CIT is necessary to ensure accurate *measurement* of concepts of interest to the researcher.

Literature Review

Using Culturally Informed Theorizing to Inform Study Design

Researchers must conceptually embed the design of a study within a relevant and informed set of research questions and hypotheses based on CIT. This process benefits from both inductive reasoning (theorizing that relies on empirical findings) and deductive reasoning (theorizing that relies on culturally informed concepts). Using induction and deduction to theorize about the ways that ethnic correlates might intersect with existing knowledge will help scholars (a) ensure

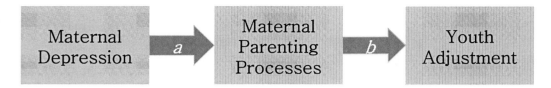

FIGURE 3.1 Conceptual Model of Maternal Depression, Parenting Processes, and Youth Adjustment

that the processes being examined are theoretically relevant and salient to Mexican American children and families (Knight *et al.*, 2009b), (b) develop research questions and hypotheses that are culturally informed (e.g. Garcia Coll *et al.*, 1996), and (c) choose a research design that can best test study hypotheses. To facilitate a discussion about the ways in which CIT should inform study design, we present a conceptual model of the relation between maternal depression, parenting, and youth adjustment (Figure 3.1).

Theoretical Relevance

One of the tasks of scientific inquiry is to identify a theory or model that proves useful for explaining the psychological processes impacting behavior in a given context and population. For scholars focused on Mexican Americans this involves specifying, via CIT, that a model is relevant and salient to Mexican Americans (Knight *et al.*, 2009b). Regarding the example in Figure 3.1, scholars have used both inductive and deductive approaches to engage in CIT and establish relevancy. Inductively, Corona *et al.* (2005) noted depressed Latinos are more likely to present with somatic complaints than interpersonal complaints, when compared to European Americans. Deductively, Corona (op. cit.) noted that it may be especially important to examine relations between maternal depression, parenting processes, and youth adjustment in collectivist societies, where family is central to identity and culture. Both inductive and deductive arguments suggest that ethnic correlates highlighting differences between Latinos and European Americans (i.e., somatic symptom presentation, cultural orientation) undermine scholars' ability to make scientific inferences about the relations between these variables among Mexican Americans from research based on European Americans. The arguments also offer a compelling rationale that such research questions are relevant to the population of Mexican American children and families.

Culturally Informed Research Questions and Hypotheses

CIT can also help scholars to develop a culturally relevant and informed set of research questions and hypotheses that will maximize research quality and, in turn, the degree to which sound scientific inferences can be made about causality and generalizability. Continuing with the example in Figure 3.1 and the previous CIT, because maternal depression results in more frequent somatic symptoms relative to interpersonal problems among Latinos compared to European Americans, we may expect that maternal depression will lead to comparatively less interpersonal difficulty and, thus, less negative influence on parenting and/or the parent–child relationship (Corona *et al.*, 2005) in Mexican American families. The corresponding hypothesis is that maternal depression will have a less substantial impact on the adjustment of Mexican American youths than has been found among their European American counterparts. In contrast, the emphasis on respect and familial support in the Mexican American family context might suggest that the impact maternal depression has on youth will be stronger because Mexican American youth rely more on their families for support than do their European American counterparts (Corona *et al.*, 2005). The corresponding hypothesis is that maternal depression will have a more substantial impact on Mexican American youth adjustment than it has on the adjustment of European American youth.

A common shortcoming in the literature is premature suspension of CIT. In the current example, the ethnic correlates employed in the inductive and deductive arguments (i.e., symptom presentation and cultural orientation, respectively) are discussed as having *opposite* effects (symptom presentation might decrease the impact maternal depression has on Mexican American youth, whilst Mexican cultural orientation might increase it). Advanced, high-quality CIT should be used to move beyond study justification and cross-cultural comparisons to the actual development of culturally informed research questions and hypotheses that reflect integration of inductive and deductive arguments. In the current case, integrating the two perspectives suggests that Mexican American mothers' *symptom presentation* might attenuate the relation between maternal depression and parenting (path *a*), whereas Mexican American children's *cultural orientation* might amplify the impact those processes have on youth (path *b*). The corresponding hypotheses are no longer contradictory; rather they are complimentary and could do much to advance our understanding of these processes in Mexican American families.

Study Design

The use of inductive and deductive reasoning to support CIT and the development of a culturally relevant and informed set of research questions and hypotheses has direct implications for study design. Notably, researchers must employ a study design that permits an examination of the hypotheses generated. A major choice facing scholars interested in Mexican American families is whether to conduct an ethnic comparative design (in which results are compared and contrasted between Mexican Americans and one or more other groups) or an ethnic homogenous design. The best choice depends largely on the research questions and hypotheses developed from CIT. In the examples that follow, we draw first from more preliminary research questions and hypotheses (i.e., those resulting from unintegrated inductive and deductive arguments) and second from more advanced research questions and hypotheses (i.e., those generated from integration of the inductive and deductive arguments). Each has different implications for study design.

The research questions generated from more preliminary stages of CIT suggest that differences between Mexican Americans and European Americans on ethnic correlates would result in maternal depression having a *more*, or a *less*, substantial impact on child adjustment among Mexican Americans. The ethnic-group comparative research question can only be addressed with an ethnic comparative research design. Scholars would examine the proposed model in a sample composed of both European Americans and Mexican Americans, hypothesizing that ethnicity would moderate the *a* and *b* paths (Figure 3.2, upper label). To the degree that ethnicity *did* moderate those paths, authors could discuss results in the context of *unmeasured differences* in the presentation of depression, and/or cultural orientation between the two groups. This approach would answer the comparative research questions. It would not, however, directly contribute to our understanding of the processes that contributed to these differences because the major concepts hypothesized to produce these differences are not measured.

The more advanced CIT results in different research questions. First, to what degree does variability in symptom presentation among Mexican American mothers moderate the relation

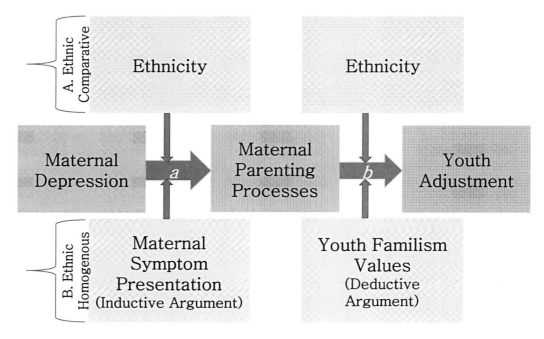

FIGURE 3.2 A. Proposed Ethnic Comparative Design; B. Proposed Ethnic Homogenous Design

between maternal depression and parenting? Second, to what degree does Mexican American youth cultural orientation moderate the relation between parenting and adjustment? This set of research questions is best addressed by an ethnic homogenous design, in which the ethnic correlates hypothesized to produce within-group diversity in the association between maternal depression, parenting, and adjustment are measured directly. An example of this model is presented in Figure 3.2 (lower label). This approach would allow scholars to directly test hypotheses generated from CIT and is best suited for making contributions to understanding family and developmental processes among Mexican Americans.

Using Culturally Informed Theorizing to Develop Sampling Strategies

Once theory and design have been considered, important decisions remain regarding other methodological issues, including three that affect sample quality:

- *Sampling*—involves selection of some number of members from a target population defined by the researcher;
- *Recruitment*—is the process of persuading sampled population members to participate in research;
- *Retention*—which is only relevant for longitudinal research designs, is the process of retaining as much of the original sample as possible over repeated assessments.

The aim of sampling, recruitment, and retention in research based on positivist ontologies and epistemologies is that the original sample (those members both selected *and* successfully recruited) and the subsequent samples (those members selected *and* successfully recruited *and* successfully retained) are representative of the target population. It is well understood that these procedures influence the initial (sampling and recruitment) and subsequent (retention) quality of a sample and, consequently, the extent to which scholars can infer that findings from a sample generalize to the population (i.e., external validity). However, in research questions aimed at comparing subgroups of a population on some variable (e.g. comparing 1st through 4th generation Mexican Americans on levels of adherence to familism values), sampling procedures represent the operationalization of the independent variable (e.g. generational status). To the degree that the sampling, recruitment, and/or retention strategies employed are not equally effective across groups, bias is introduced and internal validity is compromised. Consequently, all three processes should be informed by high-quality CIT.

Sampling

Sampling can involve probability-based strategies, non-probability strategies, or a combination of both. In probability sampling (e.g. simple random sampling, stratified random sampling) every member of the sampling frame has a known chance of selection into the sample. Probability sampling is less often used in research on Mexican Americans. Even when it has been employed, CIT suggests that many of the common approaches to probability sampling may present challenges to representation when employed among Mexican Americans. For example, random digit dialing of phone numbers is a way to ensure that every member of the sampling frame has an equal chance of selection into the sample, but the sampling frame itself may be a poor representation of the target population. Scholars can induce from demographic variables that low-income Mexican Americans may not have telephones or may rely on pay-as-you-go cell phone services not adequately captured by the sampling frame (Leonardi, 2003; Vertovec, 2004). Scholars might deduce from minority status variables that undocumented Mexican Americans may be reluctant to answer calls from strangers due to fears of immigration enforcement efforts. Alternatively, consideration of cultural variables suggests that the requirement to speak English, sometimes employed in large national studies, would lead to non- or under-representation of Mexican Americans who are monolingual Spanish speakers, and would challenge the external validity as well as the internal validity of the resulting scientific inferences (see Knight *et al.*, 2009b for details).

Non-probability sampling is relatively quick, easy, and inexpensive, so it is a common sampling technique in research with Mexican Americans. In non-probability (e.g. convenience, haphazard) sampling, members of the sampling frame and different subgroups within it have an unknown chance of selection into the sample. By virtue of the technique, some members will experience a very high probability of being sampled, and others will experience a zero probability of being sampled. Both situations are problematic and, for reasons already discussed, can undermine internal and external validity. A common approach to convenience sampling may involve identifying schools that serve large proportions of Mexican Americans and using their rosters to construct a sampling frame. Such schools, however, are likely to serve communities with high concentrations of Mexican Americans. Careful consideration of ethnic correlates will reveal some challenges to representation associated with such an approach. Specifically, within these communities there is often underrepresentation of higher-income, and later-generation Mexican Americans. Among those higher-income and/or later-generation Mexican Americans that do reside in such ethnic enclaves, it is likely that their choice to stay in those neighborhoods reflects differences in cultural orientation between them and their counterparts that chose to move to more integrated neighborhoods. Consequently, certain members of the population (e.g. higher-income, more acculturated Mexican Americans) may be excluded (or severely underrepresented) under these sampling circumstances and threats to both internal and external validity are a concern.

When conducting research with Mexican Americans, choices related to sampling—what technique to use, how to identify an adequate sampling frame—should be made in concert with CIT. Because it is a common approach, we use the example of sampling from schools to highlight the ways in which CIT might influence sampling decisions. For example, scholars wishing to obtain a sample of Mexican origin families with children under five years of age might commonly consider daycare center-, childcare program- and/or preschool rosters to construct a sampling frame. Deductively, we expect that families with a strong orientation toward traditional beliefs (e.g. *familism*) might be less likely to have their children in childcare centers because they are more likely to rely on extended family members for childcare. Similarly, families with fewer financial resources may not be able to afford center-based care. Inductively, empirical research with Latinos has found that they were significantly less likely to use non-parental childcare for children five and under (Chyu *et al.*, 2005). Both arguments converge on the culturally informed notion that childcare rosters may not offer a sampling frame with adequate coverage to capture a representative sample of Mexican American families with infants, toddlers, and young children.

When scholars are interested in sampling school-aged children, the theorizing should be adapted to consider the relative strengths or challenges associated with using school rosters as sampling frames. As a result of *Plyer v. Doe*, all children, regardless of immigration status, have access to both primary and secondary education in the US (Plyer v. Doe, 1982). An examination of both demographic and ethnic correlates across the K–12 spectrum, however, should be used to inform choices about sampling designs. For example, there is a much higher likelihood of Latinos being Catholic (Taylor *et al.*, 2012). Consequently, a sampling frame that excluded parochial schools may not achieve adequate coverage of the full-range of Mexican American families, particularly those that are later-generation and higher socioeconomic status. At earlier developmental stages (e.g. elementary and middle school), a sampling frame that includes public, charter, and parochial schools is likely to represent a wide spectrum of Mexican American families with young children. At later developmental stages (e.g. High School) however, additional ethnic correlates need to be considered. Dropout rates for Latino youth are still three times the rate of European Americans. Further, there are notable distinctions in dropout rates for foreign- vs. native-born youth (Fry, 2009). Sampling plans and/or scientific inferences will need to be adjusted according to CIT.

As the application of *Plyer v. Doe* has been limited to K–12 schooling, further challenges arise when scholars wish to sample Mexican American emerging adults. CIT will reveal that Mexican Americans do not experience a homogenous degree of access to institutions of higher education (Gonzales and Chavez, 2012). Undocumented Mexican Americans, depending on their state of residence, may be denied eligibility for in-state tuition, scholarships, or even enrollment at public institutions. Further, the shift for undocumented youth from a status that is legally protected (i.e., student in the primary and secondary US educational system), to one in which legal status serves as the basis for participation (i.e., in higher education or in work) is daunting (Gonzales, 2011). Those who, for example, successfully transition to higher education despite these challenges are likely to be very different than those that do not. Those differences will complicate scholars' abilities to make scientific inferences. Consideration of these ethnic correlates should be used to inform the design of alternative sampling plans and/or to qualify scientific inferences.

Recruitment and Retention

Once CIT has been used to design a sampling plan capable of achieving some degree of representation of the target population, scholars will need to develop recruitment strategies that ensure that diverse members of the sampling frame will be equally willing to participate in the research. Similarly, for longitudinal research efforts, scholars will need to develop a parallel set of strategies to retain as many people as possible who enrolled in the study. Even when CIT leads to the identification of an optimal sampling frame, obtaining and maintaining a representative sample of Mexican Americans is not possible if large numbers of those selected refuse to participate or drop out. Alternatively, if the recruitment/retention strategies favor certain subgroups of Mexican Americans over others, scholars' ability to make scientific inferences will be equally diminished. Consequently, the value of high quality CIT remains a central aspect of the methodological process through recruitment and retention. Knight and colleagues (2009a) presented recommendations for successfully recruiting and retaining Latino and low-income populations. We address most of them within a discussion of how CIT might inform the process, and examples of many of their recommendations are itemised here in advance, for reference:

Recommendations for recruitment:

1. Make recruitment materials available in Spanish.
2. Researchers follow culturally appropriate modes of interacting.
3. Researchers should emphasize the confidentiality of research data.
4. Use culturally attractive symbols.
5. Take a collectivist perspective when explaining benefits of research.
6. Respect traditional practices and beliefs.
7. Educate potential participants about research process and potential benefits.
8. Develop collaborations with trusted institutions or community leaders.
9. Keep communication as personal as possible.
10. Offer a concrete incentive whenever possible.

Recommendations for retention:

1. Obtain tracing information at first contact.
2. Systematically make contact between data collection intervals.
3. Follow up on mailings that do not generate a response.
4. Use the internet to search public records for participant contact information.
5. Prepare participants for timing of assessments with mailings and direct contact.

Note: adapted from Knight *et al.,* 2009a

Theorizing about the ways in which demographic variables might *intersect* with recruitment and retention strategies will help scholars to anticipate challenges, capitalize on opportunity, and facilitate acquisition and retention of a sample worthy of scientific inference. Socioeconomic correlates, such as income and education levels, will require scholars to consider how best to inform potential participants about research, because low-income Mexican Americans (like many other lower-income individuals; Knight *et al.,* 2009b) may have had very limited exposure to research or research institutions. Previously, scholars have addressed this challenge, in part, by developing collaborations with trusted institutions and community leaders (Cauce *et al.*, 1998; Roosa *et al.*, 2008). In light of financial correlates, it may be important to offer a reasonable incentive, to gain attention and commitment from low-income participants and differentiate researchers from other perceived authority figures the same participants might have reasons to avoid (e.g. police, landlords). Issues of mobility should also be considered when developing plans for retention. Ways to address this might include the use of tracers and location services (Knight, op. cit.).

Theorizing about cultural variables will also inform the development of various recruitment and retention strategies. Most scholars will probably readily recognize the need to address language preference as a source of between- and within-group variability when conducting research with Mexican Americans. Scholars can readily induce from demographic profiles (e.g. Motel and Patten, 2012) that about a third of Mexican Americans over the age of five years speak English less than very well. Deductively, however, there are additional considerations to be made. For example, collectivism (emphasizing interdependence of all humans, family integrity, and cooperation and support) is thought to be higher among Mexican Americans than non-Hispanics (Vazquez Garcia *et al.*, 2000). Consequently, research may benefit from recruitment and retention materials that emphasize the benefit to the community and family. Similarly, scholars must deduce what impact cultural values, like *respeto* (i.e., emphases on obedience to authority, deference and decorum; Calzada *et al.*, 2010) and *familism* (emphases on support, interdependence, and obligations among family and extended family members; Sabogal *et al.*, 1987) will have on the willingness of diverse Mexican Americans to participate and remain in a research study. Respect might suggest that those recruitment materials and scripts employing more formal modes of addressing adults would be most successful. Similarly, the combination of respeto, familism, and traditional gender roles can sometimes result in more hierarchical power structures within families. Processes that reflect an awareness of these structures are likely to be more successful (Roosa *et al.*, 2008).

Finally, theorizing about minority status variables will further inform the selection of recruitment and retention strategies. For example, among undocumented immigrants both deductive and inductive arguments would suggest that there may be substantial hesitation to participate in research for fear that information obtained during the research process might lead to deportation (Levkoff and Sanchez, 2003). Emphasizing confidentiality and obtaining a Certificate of Confidentiality may improve both recruitment and retention rates among undocumented Mexican Americans. Ultimately, scholars will need to develop recruitment and retention strategies that balance emphases on those demographic, cultural, and minority status variables that highlight differences between Mexican American and traditionally studied groups with those aspects that make them similar. Even when working with a sample of diverse Mexican Americans, there is a need to balance demographic/cultural/minority-based adjustments with a recognition that many Mexican Americans will not share those same exact demographic, cultural, or minority contexts. For this reason, some have argued for employing multiple recruitment/retention strategies simultaneously to be successful in highly diverse populations (Knight *et al.*, 2009a).

Using Culturally Informed Theorizing to Select and Develop Measures

Once CIT has been used to support the development of research questions, hypotheses, study design and sampling, scholars must continue to rely on it when important measurement decisions are being made. *Measurement* involves the process of operationalizing a concept of interest to researchers. *Measurement equivalence* involves the degree to which a measure is similarly reliable and valid across subgroups within the sample; the degree to which the measure, as applied to the diverse members of the sample, assesses the same psychological construct in the same way and to the same degree of accuracy. One noteworthy ethnic correlate affecting measurement in research with Mexican Americans is language. *Language availability* involves either the simultaneous development of a measure in multiple languages, or the translation of an existing measure into another language. Many measures used by social scientists have been developed with predominately European American and middle-class samples. Too often, the adoption of measures for use with Mexican Americans has occurred without the benefit of CIT.

Measurement

CIT should be used to identify a concept needing to be measured, theoretically define it, identify items that represent it, and specify expected relations between the measured concept and other concepts. A concept's theoretical definition specifies indicators of a measured construct by defining the basic nature of a concept (among Mexican Americans). It provides the basis for identifying the items or observations that reflect the concept (among Mexican Americans) as well as the relations the measured construct has to other concepts (among Mexican Americans). Consequently, the theoretical definition of a concept can be used to both identify items that can be used as indicators of the measured construct (for Mexican Americans) and to examine the degree to which those items, together, adequately represent the concept (as it manifests among Mexican Americans). We do not suggest that all concepts have culturally distinct theoretical definitions. Parallel to our suggestion that CIT is necessary to establish the degree of *intersection* between ethnic correlates and existing knowledge or theory, we suggest here that CIT is necessary to determine the degree that ethnic correlates *intersect* with a concept's theoretical definition, indicators, or relation to other concepts.

By way of example, consider a case where a scholar is interested in the *socioeconomic status* concept among Mexican American families. One of many common operationalizations of socioeconomic status is parent educational attainment. Before using this operationalization the scholar must employ CIT to consider whether educational attainment is likely to be an equally reliable and valid measure of socioeconomic status among all Mexican Americans in the sample. For example, does "high school completion" refer to comparable *amounts* of education, or have equal market value, between Mexican Americans who completed high school in Mexico vs. the US? Is the market value of a medical degree obtained in Mexico the same as the market value of a medical degree obtained in a US institution? If the answer to these questions is *no*, then the country in which the education was obtained may be an ethnic correlate that produces bias in the measure. Consequently, parental educational attainment may not be an equally reliable and valid measure of the socioeconomic status concept across diverse subsamples of Mexican Americans.

Measurement Equivalence

Measurement equivalence is a question of the similarity of reliability and construct validity coefficients of a measure across two or more groups. Unless a construct is measured similarly across two subsamples, findings from (a) data pooled across subsamples, or (b) subsample comparisons, may be misleading. Hui and Triandis (1985) defined several types of equivalence—conceptual, item, functional, and scalar:

- Conceptual equivalence—involves assessment of whether the concept is relevant to all the subsamples involved.
- Item equivalence—involves assessments of whether individual scale items relate to the theoretical concept similarly across subsamples.
- Functional equivalence (of a measure)—involves assessments of whether the degree to which the goals of the behaviors being measured are similar in all subsamples.
- Scalar equivalence—involves assessments of whether scale scores refer to the same degree, intensity, and magnitude of the construct in the subsamples being studied.

Conceptual Equivalence

Conceptual equivalence is determined by CIT. Consider, for example, the Children's Report of Parental Behavior Inventory (CRPBI). The CRPBI was developed by Schaefer (1965) to assess children's perception of their parents' behavior. Concepts measured by the CRPBI include parental acceptance ("spoke to you in warm and friendly voice"), rejection ("wished s/he didn't have children"), inconsistent discipline ("punished you for doing something wrong one time, but ignored it another time"), control ("insists you do exactly as you are told"), and hostile control ("screamed at you when you did something wrong"). Inductively, scholars can look for evidence of CRPBI constructs in the empirical literature. Specifically, researchers might note that CRPBI constructs have been replicated in data from diverse samples and ethnic groups (see Finkelstein *et al.*, 2001 for an example). Indeed, several works provide substantial evidence of the replicability of the CRPBI factor structure across diverse samples, and collectively suggest that children raised in different cultural contexts perceive their parents' behavior along similar dimensions (Knight *et al.*, 1994; Schludermann and Schludermann, 1970). Samples have included (a) French-speaking, urban, academic and vocational public school students in Liége, Belgium; (b) two independent samples of college students in Canada; (c) children from 20 Hutterite communities in rural Manitoba, and (d) English-speaking Latinos, mostly of Mexican origin. Within these samples a range of socioeconomic, individualist, collectivist, linguistic, rural, and urban groups are represented. The results suggest that constructs assessed by the CRPBI are theoretically relevant to high and low socioeconomic status, individualistic and collectivist, and urban and rural groups. Inductively, the CRPBI's constructs should be theoretically relevant to a broad range of Mexican Americans.

Deductively, culturally informed concepts can be used to inform researchers of each subscales' theoretical relevance to Mexican Americans. For example, the parental rejection and hostile control constructs, with their emphasis on negative interactions between parents and children, appear theoretically inconsistent with an emphasis on *familism* (i.e., loyalty, attachment, and solidarity)—likely present among more traditional Mexican American families (Triandis, 2001). That same emphasis, however, suggests that parental acceptance, emphasizing parental support of the child, has the potential to be theoretically relevant for Mexican Americans (Vazquez Garcia *et al.*, 1999). More traditional families may also place a strong emphasis on strict generational hierarchies (*respeto*), strict gender roles, and discouragement of independence (Vazquez Garcia, op. cit.). In this context, the emphasis on deference to authority theoretically supports the relevance of the control construct (e.g. parents insisting children do exactly as told) and undermines the theoretical relevance of the inconsistent discipline construct. That is, in a cultural context in which the position of elders is not contested by minors, it may be that children do not question the consistency of parenting behaviors. Deduction provides a slightly more nuanced picture of the potential theoretical relevance of the concepts assessed by the CRPBI, especially for more traditional Mexican Americans. Integration of the inductive and deductive elements suggests that acceptance and control are conceptually equivalent across diverse subsamples of Mexican Americans. Rejection, hostile control, and inconsistent discipline, however, may not be conceptually equivalent across diverse subsamples of Mexican Americans.

Item, Functional, and Scalar Equivalence

The processes used to establish item, functional, and scalar equivalence rely on a combination of analytical techniques and CIT. The analytical techniques establish the degree of similarity of the internal structure of a measure across groups (measurement invariance or factorial invariance) and the degree of similarity in the construct validity associations of that measure across groups (construct validity equivalence). These are described in great detail elsewhere (e.g. Knight *et al.*, 2009a). CIT is used to define what pattern of reliability and validity associations is to be considered consistent with *equivalence*. That is, it establishes what pattern of internal structural relations and construct validity associations is consistent with factorial invariance and construct validity equivalence, respectively. When CIT converges on a conclusion that ethnic correlates do not intersect appreciably with the measurement of a concept, a scholar would expect that both the internal structure and construct validity associations should be identical across subgroups. If, however, CIT suggests that ethnic correlates do intersect notably with a concepts' theoretical definition, indicators, or relation to other concepts, then the scholar should define a set of patterns regarding internal structure and/or construct validity relations that would be consistent with measurement equivalence under that intersection. For example, if theorizing indicates that the concept is differentially related to some other concept across two groups of Mexican Americans, or that some subtle differences in the item functioning and factor structures across these groups exists, then measurement equivalence would be indicated by somewhat different but theoretically consistent interrelationships with other concepts or among items.

CIT offers further implications for the interpretation of item, functional, and scalar equivalence analyses. Many of the variables across which scholars might be interested in establishing invariance and equivalence might be highly correlated. For example, a research question focused on differences in language versions of a measure that uses naturally occurring groups of Spanish- and English-speaking Mexican Americans will likely find that English- and Spanish-speakers differ on other important ethnic correlates that may impact measurement equivalence. Because young Mexican American adolescents who are Spanish-dominant may be less acculturated (Marin, 1992) and experience lower socioeconomic status than their English-dominant peers (Tienda and Neidert, 1984), the identification of non-equivalence between an English and Spanish version of a measure may be a symptom of cultural or demographic differences between the two groups. Evidence of measurement equivalence across these language versions, however, would provide indirect support for use of the measures across socioeconomic and cultural-orientation groups, as well as language groups.

Language Availability and Translation

Addressing the need to have multiple language versions can involve two unique processes: the translation of existing measures from English to Spanish, or the simultaneous construction of measures in both languages. Both processes should rely on CIT. Here, we focus on how CIT should influence translation processes, including translation approaches and procedures. The "literal translation approach" involves substitution of English words or phrases with Spanish words and phrases. The "conceptual translation approach" involves the substitution of concepts and ideas expressed in Spanish for comparable concepts and ideas expressed in English. Each of these approaches may be produced via one-way translation, back translation, or committee translation procedures. *One-way translation* involves one bilingual individual translating an instrument from one language (e.g. English) into a target language (e.g. Spanish). *Back translation* first involves a bilingual individual to translate the instrument from the source language (e.g. English) to a target language (e.g. Spanish). Then, another, independent, bilingual person translates the target-language version (e.g. Spanish) back into the source language (e.g. English). If the two source-language versions are reasonably comparable the procedure is complete. Otherwise, the procedure is repeated until comparable source-language versions are obtained. This process can also involve a decentering of the source-language version, adjusting *the source-language version* to resolve detected discrepancies. *Committee translation* involves a group of bilingual people who translate a measure and meet to review the translations.

CIT can, to some degree, inform the selection of a translation approach. On one end of the continuum there may be little-to-no intersection between ethnic correlates and the target concept. This scenario is most likely to occur for very simple psychological concepts that are expressed with ideas and words that have exact counterparts and grammatical structures in both languages (Knight *et al.*, 2009a). At this end of the continuum, literal approaches may meet the researcher's needs. Moving beyond simple psychological concepts, however, there is likely to be considerable intersection between ethnic correlates and target concepts. Consequently, conceptual approaches are more likely to achieve a valid and reliable Spanish-language version of the target measure or measures. The substitutions made in the process of conceptual translation will inherently involve CIT concerning the cultural (including sociolinguistic), ethnic minority, and demographic context of the Spanish-speaking Mexican American population (Martinez *et al.*, 2006).

CIT should also inform the translation procedure. Ultimately, a mix of back-translation, decentering, and committee procedures is likely to be most effective in producing valid and reliable measures in the target language (Bracken and Barona, 1991). Still, these procedures rely on bilingual individuals. An examination of ethnic correlates will reveal that a substantial proportion of Mexican Americans are not bilingual. Furthermore, there are numerous potential differences in the distribution of ethnic correlates between bilingual and monolingual Mexican Americans. Bilingual individuals may be, on average, more educated, more bicultural, more cognitively flexible, and less familiar with local sociolinguistic nuances than the target population. Consequently, to the extent that the make-up of the committee does not accurately reflect the cultural, ethnic minority, and demographic make-up of the target population, traditional committee procedures may pose significant threats to the validity and reliability of the target-language version, and—to the extent decentering was used—of the source-language version as well. Careful theorizing about the different distribution of ethnic correlates across these two groups results in uncertainty about whether translations conducted by a team of bilingual individuals will effectively generalize to the full range of Spanish- and English-speaking Mexican Americans. To combat some of this uncertainty, and produce translations that are a better match to the target population, Erkut and colleagues (1999) recommend the inclusion of Mexican American monolingual English and monolingual Spanish speakers on translation committees.

Summary

High-quality CIT can and should be used during all stages of research; in this chapter, we highlighted its utility for making key methodological decisions related to study design, sampling, and measurement. The best research questions and hypotheses are those that result from high-quality CIT. Likewise, the same process should influence the study's design so that the study might best be poised to address the most important research questions. We contend that CIT has important implications for identifying a sampling frame, sampling procedures, recruitment, and retention strategies and, via those implications, on the internal and external validity of the study. Finally, we believe that CIT should inform the selection or development of measures (and associated translation procedures, if necessary) to facilitate the best scientific inference-making. We hope that the discussion of how CIT can influence important methodological issues in research with Mexican Americans will assist your decision-making.

Future Directions and Challenges

We believe that major advances in our understanding of family and developmental processes among Mexican Americans can best be facilitated by active engagement in CIT at all stages of the research process. Investment in high-quality CIT that is informed by both inductive and deductive approaches, can make substantial contributions to both empiricism and theory development. We believe that the best research questions and hypotheses are those that result from high-quality CIT. Likewise, the same process should influence the study's design so that the study might best be poised to address the most important research questions. We contend that CIT has important implications for identifying a sampling frame, sampling procedures, recruitment, and retention strategies and, via those implications, on the internal and external validity of the study. Finally, we believe that CIT should inform the selection or development of measures (and associated translation procedures, if necessary) to facilitate the best scientific inference-making. The biggest challenge for scholars learning to use CIT will be integrating their theorizing across the range of ethnic correlates considered. As was shown in our discussion above, diverse ethnic correlates might have different implications for the model or theory being tested. To this end, we suggest team-based approaches and careful consideration of individual pathways (as opposed to entire theoretical models). We hope that you share our belief in the efficacy of CIT in influencing important methodological issues relating to research with Mexican Americans.

Policy Implications

CIT should be an integral part of any research involving Mexican American children and families. We have highlighted the ways in which CIT can benefit the development of research questions and hypotheses, study design, sampling, and measurement. Research designed with the benefit of CIT can better serve practitioners and policy makers needing to meet the needs of this large and growing population. Increases in scholarship quality, aided by CIT, can more effectively inform scientific theory, supply the necessary scientific foundation for the development of effective social services and interventions, and guide public policy.

References

Bracken, B. A., and Barona, A. (1991). State of the art procedures for translating, validating and using psychoeducational tests in cross-cultural assessment. *School Psychology International, 12*, 119–132.
Calzada, E. J., Fernandez, Y., and Cortes, D. E. (2010). Incorporating the cultural value of *respeto* into a framework of Latino parenting. *Cultural Diversity and Ethnic Minority Psychology, 16*, 77–86.

Cauce, A. M., Coronado, N., and Watson, J. (1998). Conceptual, methodological, and statistical issues in culturally competent research. In M. Hernandez and M. Isaacs (Eds.), *Promoting cultural competence in children's mental health services* (pp. 305–329). Baltimore, MD: Paul H. Brookes.

Chyu, L., Pebley, A., and Lara-Cinisomo, S. (2005). *Patterns of child care use for preschoolers in Los Angeles County*. Santa Monica, CA: RAND Corporation.

Corona, R., Lefkowitz, E., Sigman, M., and Romo, L. F. (2005). Latino adolescents' adjustment, maternal depressive symptoms, and the mother–adolescent relationship. *Family Relations*, *54*, 386–399.

Erkut, S., Alarcón, O., Coll, C. G., Tropp, L. and García, H. V. (1999). The dual-focus approach to creating bilingual measures. *Journal of Cross-Cultural Psychology*, *30*, 206–218.

Finkelstein, J. A. S., Donenberg, G. R., and Martinovich, Z. (2001). Maternal control and adolescent depression: Ethnic differences among clinically referred girls. *Journal of Youth and Adolescence*, *30*, 155–171.

Fry, R. (2009). *The changing pathways of Hispanic youths into adulthood*. Washington, DC: Pew Hispanic Center.

Garcia Coll, G., Crnic, K., Lamberty, G., Wasik, B. H., Jenkins, R., Garcia, H. V., and McAdoo, H. P. (1996). An integrative model for the study of developmental competencies in minority children. *Child Development*, *67*, 1891–1914.

Gonzales, N. A., Fabrett, F., and Knight, G. P. (2009). Acculturation, enculturation, and the psychosocial adaptation of latino youth. In F. A. Villarruel, G. Carlo, J. M. Grau, M. Azmitia, N. J. Cabrera and T. J. Chahin (Eds.), *Handbook of US Latino psychology* (pp. 115–134). Thousand Oaks, CA: Sage.

Gonzales, N. A., Knight, G. P., Morgan-Lopez, A., Saenz, D., and Sirolli, A. (2002). Acculturation and the mental health of Latino youths: An integration and critique of the literature. In J. M. Contreras, K. A. Kerns and A. M. Neal-Barnett (Eds.), *Latino children and families in the U. S.* (pp. 45–74), Westport, CT: Greenwood.

Gonzales, R. G. (2011). Learning to be illegal: Undocumented youth and shifting legal contexts in the transition to adulthood. *American Sociological Review*, *76*, 602–619.

Gonzales, R. G., and Chavez, L. R. (2012). Awakening to a nightmare. *Current Anthropology*, *53*, 255–281.

Hughes, D. (2003). Correlates of African American and Latino parents' messages to children about ethnicity and race: A comparative study of racial socialization. *American Journal of Community Psychology*, *31*, 15–33.

Hui, C. H., and Triandis, H. C. (1985). Measurement in cross-cultural psychology: A review and comparison of strategies. *Journal of Cross-cultural Psychology*, *16*, 131–152.

Knight, G. P., Roosa, M. W., and Umaña-Taylor, A. J. (2009b). *Studying ethnic minority and economically disadvantaged populations: Methodological challenges and best practices*. Washington, DC: American Psychological Association.

Knight, G. P., Virdin, L. M., and Roosa, M. W. (1994). Socialization and family correlates of mental health outcomes among Hispanic and Anglo American children: Consideration of cross–ethnic scalar equivalence. *Child Development*, *65*, 212–224.

Knight, G. P., Roosa, M. W., Calderón-Tena, C. O., and Gonzales, N. A. (2009a). Methodological issues in research on Latino populations. In F. A. Villarruel, G. Carlo, J. M. Grau, M. Azmitia, N. J. Cabrera and T. J. Chahin (Eds.), *Handbook of US Latino psychology: Developmental and community-based perspectives* (pp. 45–62). Thousand Oaks, CA: Sage.

Leonardi, P. M. (2003). Problematizing "new media": Culturally based perceptions of cell phones, computers, and the internet among U. S. Latinos. *Critical Studies in Media Communication*, *20*, 160–179.

Levkoff, S., and Sanchez, H. (2003). Lessons learned about minority recruitment and retention from the centers on minority aging and health promotion. *The Gerontologist*, *43*, 18–26.

Li-Grining, C. P. (2012). The role of cultural factors in the development of Latino preschoolers' self-regulation. *Child Development Perspectives*, *6*(3), 210–217.

Marin, G. (1992). Issues in the measurement of acculturation among Hispanics. In K. F. Geisinger (Ed.), "Psychological testing of Hispanics," *APA Science Volumes* (pp. 235–251). Washington, DC: American Psychological Association.

Martinez, G., Marín, B. V., and Schoua-Glusberg, A. (2006). Translating from English to Spanish. *Hispanic Journal of Behavioral Sciences*, *28*, 531–545.

Motel, S., and Patten, E. (2012). *Hispanics of Mexican origin in the U. S., 2010*. Washington, DC: Pew Hispanic Center.

Plyler v. Doe, 457 U.S. 202, 230 (1982).

Roosa, M. W., Liu, F. F., Torres, M., Gonzales, N. A., Knight, G. P., and Saenz, D. (2008). Sampling and recruitment in studies of cultural influences on adjustment: A case study with Mexican Americans. *Journal of Family Psychology, 22*, 293–302.

Sabogal, F., Marín, G., Otero-Sabogal, R., Marín, B., and Perez-Stable, E. (1987). Hispanic familism and acculturation: What changes and what doesn't? *Hispanic Journal of Behavioral Sciences, 9*, 397–412.

Schaefer, E. S. (1965). A configurational analysis of children's reports of parent behavior. *Journal of consulting psychology, 29*, 552.

Schludermann, E., and Schludermann, S. (1970). Replicability of factors in children's report of parent behavior (CRPBI). *The Journal of Psychology, 76*, 239–49.

Taylor, P., Lopez, M. H., Martinez, J. H., and Velasco, G. (2012). *When labels don't fit: Hispanics and their views of identity*. Washington, DC: Pew Hispanic Center.

Tienda, M., and Neidert, L. J. (1984). Language, education, and the socioeconomic achievement of Hispanic origin men. *Social Science Quarterly, 65*, 519–36.

Triandis, H. C. (2001). Individualism–collectivism and personality. *Journal of Personality, 69*, 907–924.

Vazquez Garcia, H., Garcia Coll, C. T., Erkut, S., Alarcon, O., and Tropp, L. (1999). Family values of Latino adolescents. In F. A. Villarruel (Ed.), *Latino Adolescents: Building on Latino diversity*. New York: Garland Press.

Vazquez Garcia, H. A., Garcia Coll, C., Erkut, S., Alarcón, O., and Tropp, L. R. (2000). Family values of Latino adolescents. *Making invisible Latino adolescents visible: A critical approach to Latino diversity* (pp. 239–64) NY: Falmer Press.

Vertovec, S. (2004). Cheap calls: The social glue of migrant transnationalism. *Global Networks, 4*, 219–24.

White, R. M. B., Roosa, M. W., and Zeiders, K. H. (2012). Neighborhood and family intersections: Prospective implications for Mexican American adolescents' mental health. *Journal of Family Psychology, 26*, 793–804.

White, R. M. B., Zeiders, K. H., Gonzales, N. A., Tein, J.-Y., and Roosa, M. W. (2013). Cultural values, neighborhood danger, and Mexican American parents' parenting. *Journal of Family Psychology, 27*, 265–275.

PART II

Family Contexts

4

MEXICAN AMERICAN CHILDREN'S SCHOOL READINESS

An Ecological Perspective

Daniela Aldoney, Elizabeth Karberg, Jenessa L. Malin, and Natasha J. Cabrera

Introduction

The empirical literature supports the view that children who have sufficient cognitive, language, and socio-emotional skills are "ready" to succeed in school, and are consequently more likely to achieve later academic success, attain higher levels of education, and secure future employment than children who are less prepared (Duncan *et al.*, 2007). There is also consensus that children growing up poor are at risk for school failure and exhibit considerable difficulties at school entry compared to their more affluent counterparts (Crosnoe, 2007). Because minority children disproportionately live in poor households, there is a tendency to equate minority ethnicity status with disadvantage and maladjustment. Consequently, we have tended to neglect variability not only within groups, but also across developmental domains. Recent studies show that while, on average, ethnic minority children lag behind their peers in early mathematics and readings skills, they match and even surpass their European American peers in terms of social skills (Guerrero *et al.*, 2013). These findings attest to the within-group variability of ethnic minority children, even among those living in disadvantaged homes.

Focusing on the variability within ethnic minority groups is important for several reasons. First, as the United States (US) population becomes increasingly heterogeneous, and as schools prepare to educate a culturally and ethnically diverse cohort of children, information about how minority children develop and how ready they are for school is needed, to inform research and practice (McLoyd *et al.*, 2000). Second, not all minority children grow up in poor households. Consequently, it is important to understand what aspects of development are constant across children who fall into the same economic status group, and what are the cultural/context factors that might promote school readiness among children within particular economic status groups. Third, focusing on the variability among minority children can help us send the message that being minority is not a risk for school failure and other difficulties. This recognition can help practitioners and policymakers to allocate resources accordingly, including paying more attention to how low-income European American children fare in school.

In this chapter, we highlight the variability in school readiness among Mexican American children because they are the largest and fastest growing ethnic group in the US (U.S. Bureau of the Census, 2002). Because most of the research on Latino children, in general, is conducted with Mexican American samples, we draw on research that focuses on Latinos, and identify studies that focus on Mexican American samples specifically whenever possible.

Using an ecological framework, we organize the chapter into three major sections designed to answer specific questions: (1) What are the pre-academic and social skills of Mexican American children? (2) How do proximal processes (parenting) support children's school readiness? and (3) What are the distal factors (parents education, income, and immigration experience) that indirectly influence children's school readiness? We conclude the chapter with recommended directions for future research.

Literature Review

What are The Pre-Academic and Social Skills of Mexican American Children?

According to the National Education Goals Panel (NEGP, 1995), being "ready" for school means having multiple skills in the following five dimensions: (1) physical well-being and motor development; (2) social and emotional development; (3) approaches to learning; (4) language development (including early literacy); and (5) cognition and general knowledge. Although all of these skills are important, recent findings show that pre-academic knowledge (i.e., mathematics, language, and literacy) and social competence are the strongest predictors of children's early school achievement (Duncan *et al.*, 2007). Thus, in this chapter we focus on children's pre-academic and social skills.

There is an implicit assumption that all Mexican American children are at risk for school failure (Fuller and García Coll, 2010). This perception is supported by findings showing that Latino children, on average, enter school with smaller vocabularies (when assessed in English or Spanish), weaker understanding of print materials, and lower comprehension of mathematical concepts when compared to European American children (Guerrero *et al.*, 2013; Han *et al.*, 2012). However, this general picture of disadvantage is not entirely accurate (see Midobuche, Benavides, and Koca, Chapter 8). More recent and detailed analyses show that most of these disadvantages originate from the disproportionately low socioeconomic status (SES) of Latino families. In fact, when controlling for SES and language background, the aforementioned differences between Latino and White children diminish or disappear altogether (Cabrera *et al.*, 2006; Crosnoe, 2007).

Although SES appears to predict group differences in school performance, other research has shown that low-income minority children also demonstrate strengths in some domains of school readiness. Research conducted with local and national samples show that Latino children exhibit social skills that rival their European American peers. For example, Guerrero and her colleagues (2013), using a nationally representative sample, found that four-year-old Mexican American and European American children show similar ratings of positive (i.e., child shares, pays attention, is eager) and negative (i.e., child has a bad temper, is unhappy, becomes angry) behaviors when rated by their parents. Other scholars have found that Latino children surpass their European American counterparts on measures of socio-emotional development. De Feyter and Winsler (2009) report that four-year-old Latino immigrants in Miami had higher teacher ratings on socio-emotional skills (initiative, self-control, attachment/closeness with adults, and behavioral concerns) relative to their non-immigrant peers. A comparable trend was found by Crosnoe (2007), in that Latino kindergarten children were reported by teachers to display fewer externalizing problems (aggressive behavior such as fighting or disturbing others' activities) than their European American counterparts.

High levels of socio-emotional skills exhibited by young Latino children may seem surprising when analyzed from a developmental-risk framework, which suggests that poor and low educated parents may be less able to foster strong social competence to their children (Galindo and Fuller, 2010). Mexican immigrant families, on average, have the lowest level of SES and the highest level of poverty compared to other immigrant groups and to the general US population (Crosnoe, 2007). What explains, then, Mexican American children's robust social skills? One possible answer is that many low-income Latino families rear their children in a cultural context that enables them to provide support and nurturance that prepare them to socially interact with peers at school (see Quintana *et al.*, Chapter 2).

These new findings focused on positive aspects of development resonate with recent attention to how protective factors, such as culturally bounded parenting practices, may help economically disadvantaged Latino parents raise socially competent preschoolers (Guerrero *et al.*, 2013). Core elements of Latino socialization goals, such as good comportment and respectful communication (being *bien educado* and displaying *respeto)* may explain the strong social–emotional growth of Latino preschoolers (Galindo and Fuller, 2010). However, these culturally bounded practices seem to be domain-specific buffers of low SES or other environmental risk factors disproportionately faced by Mexican American families. Thus, in the next two sections we discuss some of the literature that has related proximal and distal factors to children's school readiness skills.

Proximal Factors Affecting Children's School Readiness: Parenting

Parents are the first and primary influence on children's development, and are usually responsible for structuring their children's early experiences (e.g. Bornstein, 2002). Researchers often divide parenting into two categories: behaviors and beliefs (op.cit.). Behaviors, the more direct expressions of parenting, include diverse aspects of the parent–child interaction, such as the affective, verbal, and physical behaviors parents use during interpersonal exchanges with their child, the strategies parents use to engage children with their environment, and the ways in which parents organize their children's physical world (op.cit.). Parenting beliefs on the other hand, refers to parents' values, goals, and attitudes (Goodnow, 2002) and how they may generate and shape parental behaviors or help to organize parenting. Parents in different cultures may hold different parenting beliefs, which influence their behavior as they act on culturally defined values and goals (e.g. Bornstein, 2002). In this section we focus on specific parenting behaviors (the parent–child interaction, discipline, and home literacy experiences) because they are strongly linked to children's school readiness (Bradley *et al.*, 2001).

Parenting Behaviors

Quality of Parent–Child Relationship

Developmental theory posits that children develop best (e.g. socially, linguistically, and cognitively) with a supportive family environment that includes parents who are loving and responsive to children's needs. The quality of parent–child interaction, specifically mothers' warmth and responsiveness while interacting with their children, is positively associated with children's early social, linguistic, and cognitive outcomes, which subsequently contribute to children's school readiness and academic achievement. One study with Salvadorian, Puerto Rican, and Mexican mothers from an Early Head Start program showed that maternal responsiveness to child inputs was significantly associated with children's cognitive outcomes during kindergarten (Figueroa-Moseley *et al.*, 2006). In particular, higher maternal scores on responsiveness were related to children having higher scores on letter word identification and applied problem assessments. However, researchers have not systematically explored the mechanisms underlying maternal warmth and its benefits for children's development. This is an interesting finding that calls for future research especially in the context of cultural diversity.

A limitation of the extant research on the quality of parent–child relationships in Mexican families is that it has focused primarily on mothers. Thus, we know less about the parenting behaviors of fathers and their role in their children's school readiness. Given that many Latino children in the US live in two-parent households with their biological fathers, the lack of data on fathers may result in an inaccurate portrayal of how Latino parents help their children to succeed. Scholars have begun to address this limitation. Cabrera *et al.* (2007) found that greater levels of paternal supportiveness were positively associated with toddlers' cognitive, and language development. Other studies have also positively linked father involvement (measured by the frequency that fathers engaged in different activities with their offspring, such as reading and outings) with children's cognitive outcomes (Flouri and Buchanan, 2004; NICHD ECCRN, 2004; 2005; Tamis-LeMonda *et al.*, 2004).

Therefore, it is important to consider studies that address mothers' *and* fathers' involvement with their children. These studies are rare. The few that exist suggest that fathers have unique and independent effects on children's outcomes, over and above mothers' contribution (Cabrera *et al.*, 2006). A study based on an ethnically diverse sample (including European American, African American, and Latino families) showed that fathers' and mothers' supportive parenting independently predicted children's language and cognitive outcomes even after accounting for co-varying demographic factors (e.g. education and income) (Tamis-LeMonda *et al.*, 2004). Another study, using data from the NICHD Study of Early Child Care and Youth Development, showed that fathers' sensitivity was most beneficial to children when mothers' sensitivity was low, suggesting that maybe children, especially those living in disadvantage, need one "good" parent to succeed (Martin *et al.*, 2010). These findings are important and need to be replicated with other domains of development.

Researchers have also begun to examine how specific activities that mothers and fathers engage in with their children contribute to their children's positive development. Quality play interactions, for instance, are directly linked to children's well-being (Tamis-LeMonda *et al.*, 2004), and studies show that in contrast to mothers, fathers engage in proportionately more play than care-giving routines (Craig, 2006). Furthermore, fathers' play with children seems to be qualitatively different than mother's play. For example, father's play tends to be more physically stimulating than mothers' play (Bretherton *et al.*, 2005) and fathers tend to engage in more rough-and-tumble play (RTP; rough housing; vigorous physical interactions that would be aggressive outside of a playful context) than mothers (John *et al.*, 2012; MacDonald and Parke, 1984). RTP is important for self-regulation (i.e. inhibiting aggression) because it helps children practice navigating arousing situations and managing their aggressive impulses (Peterson and Flanders, 2005). Play is also associated with children's ability to manage emotions and develop fine motor skills, although this is not specific to RTP (Peterson and Flanders, 2005). There are few studies on father play in general, and none that specifically examine play within Latino families. Although there is no reason to believe that RTP among Mexican American fathers would not influence children's regulatory behaviors, the cultural context of play, in terms of frequency, type, or meaning, has not been extensively explored.

Discipline

Another important dimension of parenting behaviors that influences school readiness (especially social competence) is discipline. Discipline practices are used by parents to control their children's behaviors to the norms and values of their cultural group (Barber *et al.*, 2005). Although there are many approaches that parents use to discipline their children, much of the research in this area has focused on the use of physical discipline (e.g. spanking) and verbal abuse. Studies have consistently linked these types of discipline with negative emotional outcomes in children, specifically higher levels of child externalizing disorders (e.g. aggressive, hyperactive, deviant behaviors; Gershoff, 2013; McKee *et al.*, 2007). A study using a nationally representative sample replicated these findings with diverse ethnic groups (European American, African American, and Latino) (Berlin *et al.*, 2009), suggesting that the effects of discipline on children may not differ by culture or ethnicity.

The literature on how Mexican American mothers and fathers discipline their children is not very extensive. What exists is mostly based on mothers, and does not always disentangle SES and parenting practices. One study using nationally representative data explored spanking behaviors (1 = never spank, 0 = otherwise) in mothers and fathers. Findings showed that children of Mexican mothers (and other Latinos) were less likely to be spanked by their mother or father at age two than children from other ethnic groups, including European Americans, as reported by both parents (Han *et al.*, 2012). Using the same data set, Guerrero *et al.* (2013) found that Mexican American mothers of 24-month-old children reported less harsh discipline (a composite variable composed from the parent's willingness to spank, hit, or yell at the child to exert control) than European American mothers on average. In contrast, using a convenience sample of 76 Latino and European American mothers with 3–5 year old children, Cardona *et al.*, (2000) found that Latino mothers reported more use of verbal or physical punishment in response to their child's behavior than did the Anglo American mothers in the study. Cardona (op.cit.) also found that higher SES parents were more likely to report using corporal punishment than lower SES parents, though SES and ethnicity together were not examined. Therefore, these mixed results are likely the result of the difference in samples (different Latino subgroups and age of the children) and entanglements of SES and ethnicity.

Home Literacy Experiences

Parents also influence their children by providing learning experiences in the home and by teaching either directly (e.g. teaching letter-sounds) or indirectly (e.g. reading to children) (Brooks-Gunn and Markman, 2005). Research has shown that children who engage in a variety of literacy experiences, such as sharing a book with their parents, singing, or hearing stories and playing games (board games, others) are more likely to develop the necessary language and social skills they need to be ready for formal schooling (e.g. Forget-Dubois *et al.*, 2009). Specifically, shared book reading and exposure to print are associated, concurrently and longitudinally, with children's math skills, vocabulary size, phonemic awareness, print concept knowledge, and positive attitudes towards literacy, even in low-income families with low levels of literacy (Raikes *et al.*, 2006).

These findings have been replicated with Latino families. For instance, a study with low SES Latino mothers and their preschoolers showed that parents' direct involvement in and encouragement of literacy-related activities was associated with children's oral language skills (Farver *et al.*, 2006). Research has shown that children in low-income immigrant households (not restricted to Latinos) experience lower levels of language, literacy, and cognitive stimulation in the home than low-income non-immigrant children and that this link is best explained by low levels of language stimulation in the home (Mistry *et al.*, 2008). More recently, a study found that, on average, low-income Mexican American families read less to their children than their (middle-class) European American counterparts (Guerrero *et al.*, 2013). However, this study did not disentangle the effects of SES and ethnicity and did not capture other types of literacy activities, such as storytelling, that minority and low-income children might experience.

Cultural researchers have pointed out that reading is not the only way to teach children language and literacy skills; that there may be other cultural-specific literacy practices just as effective. Some studies have found that the narrative skills of African American children are superior to those of their peers, largely because these children are exposed to more storytelling from their parents (Gardner-Neblett *et al.*, 2012). This line of research is promising and begs the question whether there are some literacy-specific practices in Latino families that may stimulate language growth.

In addition to literacy practices, the quality and quantity of parental language used during parent–child interactions is an important predictor of children's later language skills (Rodriguez and Tamis-LeMonda, 2011). Fathers are especially important in fostering children's language skills, as they are more likely to use language that challenges a child's linguistic ability than mothers (Rowe *et al.*, 2004; Malin, Cabrera, and Rowe, 2014). However, paternal quality and quantity of language is influenced by paternal characteristics, such as education and depressive symptoms (Malin *et al.*, 2012). It is possible that Latino children hear less quality language from their fathers because fathers are more likely to have lower levels of education than mothers (Cabrera *et al.*, 2006).

Distal Factors Affecting Mexican American School Readiness

Children's school readiness is not only influenced by proximal processes, but also by distal factors (Bronfenbrenner, 1992) that reflect the contextual variables that are associated with a child's development. In this section, we focus on parents' education and income, because parenting research in general has identified these as important distal factors that influence how parents interact with their children (e.g. McLoyd, 1998). In addition we consider a third factor, immigration experience, which includes acculturation and nativity status, English proficiency, bilingualism, and documentation status, because diverse studies (e.g. García Coll and Marks, 2009; Hammer *et al.*, 2011) have shown that these characteristics affect the development of Mexican American children.

Parents' Education and Income

A parental investment model argues that families with greater economic resources (income and education) are better able to "invest" in their children by providing them with an enriched home learning environment (e.g. buying books, didactic toys, visits to museums, enrolling children in extracurricular activities), which in turn promotes children's educational outcomes (Conger *et al.*, 2010; Duncan and Magnuson, 2012). Lower SES parents, on the other hand, have more difficulties accessing these resources, which may compromise children's optimal development. Maternal education, in particular has been implicated in children's cognitive development (Bornstein and Bradley, 2003). Parents with higher levels of education promote their children's cognitive development (e.g. Davis-Kean, 2005) by providing a rich learning environment for their children that includes more stimulating learning materials and activities (e.g. Raviv *et al.*, 2004) and more varied and complex language in their interactions (Hoff, 2003). Because many Mexican immigrants in the US tend to be poorer and less educated than the average US citizen, many of the negative outcomes exhibited by Mexican American children may be driven by SES (Gonzalez-Barrera and Lopez, 2013).

Lack of education and income can also influence children through their effect on family functioning. The family stress model posits that the effects of low SES on children's development are mediated through its impact on parents' mental health and stress. Facing economic hardship may contribute to parents' mental health problems, inter-parental conflict, and disrupted parenting which, in turn, disrupts children's development (e.g, Conger *et al.*, 2010; Mistry and Wadsworth, 2011).

Immigration Context

Mexican Americans represent the largest foreign-born population in the US. Specifically, 29 percent of all foreign-born Americans are from Mexico. Thus, in discussing Mexican American children it is imperative to consider the immigration context. A number of factors associated with the immigration experience, including but not limited to acculturation, nativity status, English proficiency, bilingualism, and documentation status, may have important implications for children's early educational achievement because they shape the environments in which these children grow. In this section, we explore how such factors contribute specifically to Mexican American children's school readiness.

Acculturation and Nativity Status

An emerging line of research suggests that acculturation may pose a developmental risk factor for children and families (e.g. García Coll and Marks, 2012). The notion of an immigrant paradox has been bolstered by numerous studies that suggest that second-generation, or acculturated first-generation immigrants, on average, perform worse on measures of mental health (e.g. anxiety, substance use) and academic achievement (e.g. high school completion, grade point average, and standardized test scores) than children with US born parents (Glick and Hohmann-Marriott, 2007). However, these studies have primarily focused on adolescent samples and the few studies that have tested this notion with young children have produced mixed findings, suggesting a more nuanced view of how Latino immigrant children are faring. For example, in a study of low-income Latinos in Miami (de Feyter and Winsler, 2009), first- and second-generation immigrants were found to lag behind children from non-immigrant families (i.e. where the child and parents were born in the US) in cognitive and language skills, but excelled by comparison in socio-emotional skills. Specifically, teachers rated first-generation immigrant children as the strongest of the three groups (first-, second-, and non- immigrants) in initiative, self-control, and attachment with adults. Similarly, a nationally representative study of Mexican American children found that children of foreign-born parents, on average, exhibited fewer externalizing behavior problems than children of native-born parents, even after family background factors were taken into account (Crosnoe, 2007). Children of immigrant parents also show more emotional maturity and competence in peer relations and in-class behavior. Using the same data set, but comparing Latinos in general to their European American peers, Galindo and Fuller (2010) found that first-generation (immigrant) Latino children displayed slightly weaker social competencies than did later generation Latino children. However, these disparities in social competence were much smaller than the gaps in math achievement at entry to kindergarten.

Taken together, these results suggest that the immigrant paradox may in fact be domain specific. Acculturated children may fare better in cognitive domains, but worse in socio-emotional domains. However, few studies have probed these findings and examined why acculturation or generational status may in fact be a risk factor. One line of research has suggested that strong social skills among less acculturated Mexican American children might be related to a cultural emphasis on socializing children to be *bien educado* and socially competent. Another study found that parents' acculturation (i.e. English proficiency) differentially predicted their engagement with their children (Cabrera *et al.*, 2006). Yet, more research is needed to fully explore why acculturation or generational status is associated with Mexican American children's school readiness skills and the mechanisms, perhaps through the home environment and parenting practices, by which it functions (Glick *et al.*, 2009).

English Proficiency

Research with immigrants has consistently shown that English proficiency is strongly associated with better academic outcomes through adolescence (Glick *et al.*, 2009; Suárez-Orozco *et al.*, 2008). English proficiency may be a strong indicator of academic success because schools in the US assess children in English. Conversely, research has shown that it takes between three and ten years to become academically proficient in English (Garcia *et al.*, 2009), which leaves English language learning children struggling to understand lessons and concepts in the early years of school if they are not enrolled in a bilingual program. However, whether Mexican American children need to be proficient in English for conceptual learning, or if they need English proficiency to be able to communicate their knowledge, is unclear. Parents' English proficiency is also an important predictor of children's English proficiency and school success. However, recent data show that 24 percent of children with immigrant parents live in a linguistically isolated household where no one in the home over age 13 speaks English fluently (Hernandez and Napierala, 2012). Parents with proficient English may be more likely to be familiar with American school systems and social institutions, and thus may be better equipped to help children get ready for school. They are also more likely to expose their children to an English-speaking environment, and thus higher test scores would be predicted, given that most academic tests are administered in English (Han *et al.*, 2012).

In another study using representative data, children with immigrant parents who spoke a non-English language at home were found to perform significantly worse in English and math when entering school than children of immigrant parents who both spoke only English at home. However, the number of children's books in the home, the frequency of the child reading books, attending center-based care prior to kindergarten, attending a private school, and having a parent who had met with the teacher at least once, eliminated the gap in math scores between these groups (Lahaie, 2008).

Bilingualism

Researchers have found that being bilingual (i.e., proficient in immigrant children's native language in addition to English proficiency) confers an advantage in a variety of cognitive tasks (specifically those related to selective attention and cognitive flexibility such as inhibitory control) that are associated with school readiness (for review see Bialystok, 2001). A study using a nationally representative sample found that compared with children raised in homes where English or Spanish was the only language spoken, Latino children raised in homes where English was mixed with some Spanish displayed stronger growth in mathematical concepts understanding (Reardon and Galindo, 2009). Additionally, learning English and Spanish may help all bilingual children—including Mexican American children—develop better executive function skills (Bialystok, 2001). Executive functioning in turn, has been positively correlated with school readiness, academic ability (e.g. Blair and Razza, 2007; Riggs *et al.*, 2003), and social competence (e.g. Razza and Blair, 2009). Unfortunately, few studies of executive functioning have included Latino samples (for an exception see Carlson and Meltzoff, 2008; Caughy, Mills, Tresch, and Hurst, 2013), and even fewer have explored the effect of bilingualism and second language acquisition on executive functioning longitudinally. In addition, there is no consensus on what *degree* of bilingualism a person (or child) needs in order to show cognitive benefits, or on how different trajectories of second language acquisition influence school readiness. Thus, the positive influence of bilingualism on Mexican American children's school readiness is not well understood.

Documentation Status

More than half of the 11.1 million undocumented immigrants in the US are from Mexico, encompassing approximately half of all Mexican American immigrants (Passel and Cohn, 2011). Research suggests that a parent's documentation status is associated with children's cognitive development and educational progress (Yoshikawa, 2011). However, data on documentation status are extremely difficult for researchers to obtain and the few studies probing this domain have used proxies (e.g. lack of a driver's license) for documentation status, which have been linked to lower cognitive skills, but not to socio-emotional development (Yoshikawa, 2011).

Various mechanisms have been proposed to explain how parents' documentation status might influence children's learning and subsequent schooling outcomes (Yoshikawa and Kalil, 2011). Evidence suggests that unauthorized documentation status may function as a barrier to resources or serve as a source of stress (Gonzales, 2011; Yoshikawa, 2011). In particular, parent–child separation, lower access to means-tested programs that benefit children's development, poor work conditions, psychological distress, and economic hardship have been proposed as important stressors/factors that limit children's exposure to developmentally optimal environments (Yoshikawa and Kholoptseva, 2013). Yet, it is difficult to disentangle socioeconomic disadvantage and unauthorized status because both are highly correlated, and thus existing results may not truly reflect the influence of documentation status.

Summary, Future Directions and Challenges

Mexican American children, on average, arrive at school with some strengths and some weaknesses. It is important to note that many Mexican American children enter school with the skills they need to succeed; however, on average, Mexican Americans as a group lag behind their European American peers in pre-academic readiness, and rival or exceed them in social skills. While English language and literacy skills are important for classroom learning and specifically for assessment success in the US school system, the importance of social skills should not be underrated.

We focused on pre-academic and social competence skills as important predictors of school success, but there are other domains that are equally important that were not covered because the research base is still emerging. For instance, an important aspect of the socio-emotional domain that has been linked to better academic skills is self-regulation (Raver *et al.*, 2011). There is evidence that bilingual children may exhibit greater self-regulation than their monolingual peers (Carlson and Meltzoff, 2008), but empirical studies of Mexican American's self-regulation is scant. We still do not know what role cultural factors play in the socialization of Latino preschoolers' self-regulation (Li-Grining, 2012).

Another aspect that merits further exploration is Mexican American children's language development. Mexican American children's language proficiency, not only in English, but also in their native language, is important for future school success. Yet, few studies assess bilingual children in both English and their native language. Bilingualism can be considered a form of social and economic capital and can reflect aspects of biculturalism (i.e. embracing one's cultural values and ethnic identity as well as those of the host society), which can be protective because it provides children with adaptive skills with which to navigate the mainstream culture (Berry et al., 2006).

Policy Implications

Positive parenting is a predictor of school readiness that is universal to children across groups and ethnicities. However, there are culturally specific aspects of parenting that are important to underline, yet research has not addressed how mothers' *and* fathers' goals are reflected in their parenting practices. We need therefore, further research, to understand how Latino mothers and fathers employ culturally specific and novel practices to advance child development, and how their activities and practices differentially shape cognitive and social–emotional vitality. Additionally, the field would benefit from more longitudinal studies of Mexican American children from diverse socio-economic backgrounds, and including diverse types of families to help the debate about the idea that being minority is synonymous with being disadvantaged (Cabrera, 2013). Understanding what contributes to the diversity of Mexican American children's school readiness will help develop interventions and inform policy and practice, thereby building on their strengths rather than underlining their weaknesses.

References

Barber, B. K., Stolz, H. E., Olsen, J. A., Collins, W. A., and Burchinal, M. (2005). Parental support, psychological control, and behavioral control: Assessing relevance across time, culture, and method. *Monographs of the society for research in child development*, i–147.

Berlin, L. J., Ispa, J. M., Fine, M. A., Malone, P. S., Brooks-Gunn, J., Brady-Smith, C., Ayoub, C., Bai, Y. (2009). Correlates and consequences of spanking and verbal punishment for low-income White, African American, and Mexican American toddlers. *Child Development*, 80(5), 1403–1420.

Berry, J. W., Phinney, J. S., Sam, D. L., and Vedder, P. (2006). Immigrant youth: Acculturation, identity, and adaptation. *Applied Psychology*, 55(3), 303–332.

Bialystok, E. (2001). *Bilingualism in development: Language, literacy, and cognition*. Cambridge, UK: Cambridge University Press.

Blair, C., and Razza, R. P. (2007). Relating effortful control, executive function, and false belief understanding to emerging math and literacy ability in kindergarten. *Child Development*, 78(2), 647–663.

Bornstein, M. H. (2002). Parenting Infants. In M. H. Bornstein (Ed.), *Handbook of parenting: Vol.1. children and parenting*. (2nd edn, pp. 3–43). Mahwah, NJ: Lawerence Erlbaum.

Bornstein, M. H., and Bradley, R. H. (2003). *Socioeconomic status, parenting, and child development*. Mahwah, NJ: Lawrence Erlbaum Associates.

Bradley, R. H., Corwyn, R. F., Burchinal, M., McAdoo, H. P., and García Coll, C. (2001). The home environments of children in the United States Part II: Relations with behavioral development through age thirteen. *Child Development*, 72(6), 1868–1886.

Bretherton, I., Lambert, J. D., and Golby, B. (2005). Involved fathers of preschool children as seen by themselves and their wives: Accounts of attachment, socialization, and companionship. *Attachment and Human Development*, 7(3), 229–251.

Bronfenbrenner, U. (1992). Child care in the Anglo-Saxon mode. In M. E. Lamb, K. J. Sternberg, C. Hwang, and A. G. Broberg (Eds.), *Child care in context: Cross-cultural perspectives*. Hillsdale, NJ: Erlbaum.

Brooks-Gunn, J., and Markman, L. B. (2005). The contribution of parenting to ethnic and racial gaps in school readiness. *The Future of our Children, 15*(1), 139–168.

Cabrera, N. J. (2013). Positive development of minority children. *Social Policy Report, 27*(2), 1–22.

Cabrera, N. J., Fitzgerald, H. E., Bradley, R. H., and Roggman, L. (2007). Modeling the dynamics of paternal influences on children over the life course. *Applied Developmental Science, 11*(4), 185–190.

Cabrera, N. J., Shannon, J., West, J., and Brooks-Gunn, J. (2006). Parental interactions with Latino infants: Variation by country of origin and English proficiency. *Child Development, 77*(5), 1190–207.

Cardona, P., Nicholson, B., and Fox, R. (2000). Parenting among Hispanic and Anglo American mothers with young children. *The Journal of Social Psychology, 140*(3), 357–365.

Carlson, S. M., and Meltzoff, A. N. (2008). Bilingual experience and executive functioning in young children, *Developmental Science, 11*(2), 282–298.

Caughy, M. O., Mills, B., Tresch, M., and Hurst, J. R. (2013). Emergent self-regulation skills among very young ethnic minority children: A confirmatory factor model. *Journal of Experimental Child Psychology, 116*(4), 839–855.

Conger, R. D., Conger, K. J., and Martin, M. J. (2010). Socioeconomic status, family processes, and individual development. *Journal of Marriage and Family, 72*(3), 685–704.

Craig, L. (2006). Does father care mean fathers share? A comparison of how mothers and fathers in intact families spend time with children. *Gender and Society, 20*(2), 259–281.

Crosnoe, R. (2007). Early child care and the school readiness of children from Mexican immigrant families. *International Migration Review, 41*(1), 152–181.

Davis-Kean, P. E. (2005). The influence of parent education and family income on child achievement: The indirect role of parental expectations and the home environment. *Journal of Family Psychology, 19*(2), 294.

de Feyter, J. J., and Winsler, A. (2009). The early developmental competencies and school readiness of low-income, immigrant children: Influences of generation, race/ethnicity, and national origins. *Early Childhood Research Quarterly, 24*(4), 411–431.

Duncan, G. J., and Magnuson, K. (2012). Socioeconomic status and cognitive functioning: Moving from correlation to causation. *Wiley Interdisciplinary Reviews: Cognitive Science, 3*(3), 377–386.

Duncan, G. J., Dowsett, C. J., Claessens, A., Magnuson, K., Houston, A. C., Klebanov, P., Pagani, L. S., Feinstein, L., Engel, M., Brooks-Gunn, J., Sexton, H., Duckworth, K., and Japel, C. (2007). School readiness and later achievement. *Developmental Psychology, 43*(5), 1428–1446.

Farver, J. M., Xu, Y., Eppe, S., and Lonigan, C. J. (2006). Home environments and young Latino children's school readiness. *Early Childhood Research Quarterly, 21*(2), 196–212.

Figueroa-Moseley, C., Ramey, C. T., Keltner, B., and Lanzi, R. G. (2006). Variations in Latino parenting practices and their effects on child cognitive developmental outcomes. *Hispanic Journal of Behavioral Sciences, 28*(1), 102–114.

Flouri, E., and Buchanan, A. (2004). Early father's and mother's involvement and child's later educational outcomes. *British Journal of Educational Psychology, 74*(2), 141–153.

Forget-Dubois, N., Dionne, G., Lemelin, J.-P., Pérusse, D., Tremblay, R. E., and Boivin, M. (2009). Early child language mediates the relation between home environment and school readiness. *Child Development, 80*(3), 736–749.

Fuller, B., and García Coll, C. (2010). Learning from Latinos: Contexts, families, and child development in motion. *Developmental Psychology, 46*(3), 559–565.

Galindo, C., and Fuller, B. (2010). The social competence of Latino kindergartners and growth in mathematical understanding. *Developmental Psychology, 46*(3), 579–592.

García Coll, C., and Marks, A. K. (2009). *Immigrant stories: Ethnicity and academics in middle childhood*. Oxford: Oxford University Press.

García Coll, C., and Marks, A. K. E. (2012). *The immigrant paradox in children and adolescents: Is becoming American a developmental risk?* Washington, DC: American Psychological Association.

Garcia, E., Jensen, B., and Scribner, K. (2009). The demographic imperative: Supporting English language learners. *Educational Leadership, 66*(7), 8–13.

Gardner-Neblett, N., Pungello, E. P., and Iruka, I. U. (2012). Oral narrative skills: Implications for the reading development of African American children. *Child Development Perspectives*, 6(3), 218–224.

Gershoff, E. T. (2013). Spanking and child development: We know enough now to stop hitting our children. *Child Development Perspectives*, 7(3), 133–137.

Glick, J. E., and Hohmann-Marriott, B. (2007). Academic performance of young children in immigrant families: The significance of race, ethnicity, and national origins. *International Migration Review*, 41, 371–402.

Glick, J. E., Bates, L., and Yabiku, S. T. (2009). Mother's age at arrival in the United States and early cognitive development. *Early Childhood Research Quarterly*, 24(4), 367–380.

Gonzales, R. G. (2011). Learning to be illegal: Undocumented youth and shifting legal contexts in the transition to adulthood. *American Sociological Review*, 76(4), 602–619.

Gonzalez-Barrera, A., and Lopez, M. H. (2013). *A demographic portrait of Mexican-origin Hispanics in the United States* (Statistical profile). Retrieved from Pew Research Center website: http://www.pewhispanic.org/2013/05/01/a-demographic-portrait-of-mexican-origin-hispanics-in-the-united-states/

Goodnow, J. J. (2002). Parents' knowledge and expectations: Using what we know. In M. H. Bornstein (Ed.), *Handbook of parenting: Vol. 3. Status and social conditions of parenting* (2nd edn., pp. 439–460). Mahwah, NJ: Lawrence Erlbaum.

Guerrero, A. D., Fuller, B., Chu, L., Kim, A., Franke, T., Bridges, M., and Kuo, A. (2013). Early growth of Mexican–American children: Lagging in preliteracy skills, but not social development. *Maternal and Child Health Journal*, 17(9), 1701–1711.

Hammer, C. S., Jia, G., and Uchikoshi, Y. (2011). Language and literacy development of dual language learners growing up in the United States: A call for research. *Child Development Perspectives*, 5, 4–9.

Han, W. J., Lee, R. H., and Waldfogel, J. (2012). School readiness among children of immigrants in the US: Evidence from a large national birth cohort study. *Children and Youth Services Review*, 34(4), 771–782.

Hernandez, D. J., and Napierala, J. S. (2012). Children in immigrant families: Essential to America's future (Policy Brief). Retrieved from Foundation for Child Development website: http://fcd-us.org/sites/default/files/FINAL%20Children%20in%20Immigrant%20Families%20(2)_0.pdf

Hoff, E. (2003). The specificity of environmental influence: Socioeconomic status affects early vocabulary development via maternal speech. *Child Development*, 74(5), 1368–1378.

John, A., Halliburton, A., and Humphrey, J. (2012). Child-mother and child-father play interaction patterns with preschoolers. *Early Child Development and Care*, 183(3–4), 483–497.

Lahaie, C. (2008). School readiness of children of immigrants: Does parental involvement play a role? *Social Science Quarterly*, 89(3), 684–705.

Li-Grining, C. P. (2012). The role of cultural factors in the development of Latino preschoolers' self-regulation. *Child Development Perspectives*, 6(3), 210–217.

MacDonald, K., and Parke, R. D. (1984). Bridging the gap: Parent–child play interaction and peer interactive competence. *Child Development*, 55(4), 1265–1277.

Malin, J. L., Cabrera, N. J., and Rowe, M. L. (2014). Low-income minority mothers' and fathers' reading and children's interest: Longitudinal contributions to children's receptive vocabulary skills. *Early Childhood Research Quarterly*, 29(4), 425–432.

Malin, J. L., Karberg, E., Cabrera, N. J., Rowe, M., Cristaforo, T., and Tamis-LeMonda, C. S. (2012). Father–toddler communication in low-income families: The role of paternal education and depressive symptoms. *Family Science*, 3(3–4), 155–163.

Martin, A., Ryan, R. M., and Brooks-Gunn, J. (2010). When fathers' supportiveness matters most: Maternal and parental parenting and children's school readiness. *Journal of Family Psychology*, 24(2), 145–155.

McKee, L., Roland, E., Coffelt, N., Olson, A. L., Forehand, R., Massari, C., Jones, D., Gaffney, C. A., Zens, M. S. (2007). Harsh discipline and child problem behaviors: The role of positive parenting and gender. *Journal of Family Violence*, 22(4), 187–196.

McLoyd, V. C. (1998). Socioeconomic disadvantage and child development. *American Psychology*, 53(2), 185–204.

McLoyd, V. C., Cauce, A. M., Takeuchi, D., and Wilson, L. (2000). Marital process and parental socialization in families of color: A decade review of research. *Journal of Marriage and the Family*, 62(4), 1070–1093.

Mistry, R., Biesanz, J., Chien, N., Howes, C., and Benner, A. (2008). Socioeconomic status, parental investments, and the cognitive and behavioral outcomes of low-income children from immigrant and native households. *Early Childhood Research Quarterly, 23*(2), 193–212.

Mistry, R. S., and Wadsworth, M. (2011). Family functioning and child development in the context of poverty. *The Prevention Researcher, 18*(4), 11–15.

National Education Goals Panel. (1995). *Building a nation of learners.* Washington, DC: Government Printing Office.

NICHD Early Child Care Research Network. (2004). Fathers' and mothers' parenting behavior and beliefs as predictors of children's social adjustment in the transition to school. *Journal of Family Psychology, 18*(4), 628–638.

NICHD Early Child Care Research Network. (2005). *Child care and child development: Results from the NICHD study of early child care and youth development.* New York: Guilford Press.

Passel, J. S., and Cohn, D. (2011). *Unauthorized immigrant population: National and state trends, 2010.* Retrieved from Pew Research Center website: http://www.pewhispanic.org/files/reports/133.pdf

Peterson, J. B., and Flanders, J. L. (2005). Play the regulation of aggression. In R. E. Tremblay, W. H. Hartup, and J. Archer. (Eds.), *Developmental origin of aggression.* New York, NY: Guilford Press.

Raikes, H., Pan, B. A., Luze, G., Tamis-LeMonda, C. S., Brooks-Gunn, J., Constatine, J., Tarullo, L. B., Raikes, H. A., and Rodrigues, E. T. (2006). Mother–child bookreading in low-income families: Correlates and outcomes during the first three years of life. *Child Development, 77*(4), 924–953.

Raver, C. C., Li-Grining, C., Bub, K., Jones, S. M., Zhai, F., and Pressler, E. (2011). CSRP's impact on low-income preschoolers' preacademic skills: Self-regulation as a mediating mechanism. *Child Development, 82*(1), 362–378.

Raviv, T., Kessenich, M., and Morrison, F. J. (2004). A meditational model of the association between socioeconomic status and three-year-old language abilities: The role of parenting factors. *Early Childhood Research Quarterly, 19*(4), 528–547.

Razza, R. A., and Blair, C. (2009). Associations among false-belief understanding, executive function, and social competence: A longitudinal analysis. *Journal of Applied Developmental Psychology, 30*(3), 332–343.

Reardon, S. F., and Galindo, C. (2009). The Hispanic-white achievement gap in math and reading in the elementary grades. *American Educational Research Journal, 46*(3), 853–891.

Riggs, N. R., Blair, C. B., and Greenberg, M. T. (2003). Concurrent and 2-year longitudinal relations between executive function and the behavior of 1st and 2nd grade children. *Child Neuropsychology, 9*(4), 267–276.

Rodriguez, E. T., and Tamis-LeMonda, C. S. (2011). Trajectories of the home learning environment across the first 5 years: Associations with children's vocabulary and literacy skills at pre-kindergarten. *Child Development, 82*(4), 1058–1075.

Rowe, M. L., Cocker, D., and Pan, B. A. (2004). A comparison of fathers' and mothers' talk to toddlers in low-income families. *Social Development, 13*(2), 278–291.

Suárez-Orozco, C., Suárez-Orozco, M. M., and Todorova, I. (2008). *Learning a new land: Immigrant students in American society.* Cambridge, MA: Belknap Press of Harvard University Press.

Tamis-LeMonda, C. S., Shannon, J. D., Cabrera, N. J., and Lamb, M. E. (2004). Fathers and mothers at play with their 2- and 3-year olds: Contributions to language and cognitive development. *Child Development, 75*(6), 1806–1820.

U.S. Bureau of the Census. (2002). *Statistical abstract of the U.S.* (119th edn.). Washington, DC: Government Printing Office.

Yoshikawa, H. (2011). *Immigrants raising citizens.* New York, NY: Russell Sage Foundation.

Yoshikawa, H., and Kalil, A. (2011). The effects of parental undocumented status on the developmental contexts of young children in immigrant families. *Child Development Perspectives, 5*(4), 291–297.

Yoshikawa, H., and Kholoptseva, J. (2013). Unauthorized immigrant parents and their children's development. *Migration Policy Institute.* Retrieved from http://observatoriocolef.org/_admin/documentos/childrenspdf.pdf

5

COPARENTING PROCESSES IN MEXICAN AMERICAN FAMILIES

Eric W. Lindsey and Yvonne M. Caldera

Introduction

Family relationship research has witnessed a growing interest in coparenting over the past two decades. The way that mothers and fathers coordinate their parental roles, support one another in the performance of childrearing duties, reach agreements and work together harmoniously to raise a child, and evaluate each other's contribution to parenting have been identified as key characteristics of the coparenting relationship (Caldera and Lindsey, 2006; Solmeyer *et al.*, 2011). From this body of work it has become clear that coparenting is a process that is distinct from sharing perspectives or responsibilities in the marital or parent–child relationships (Margolin *et al.*, 2001; McHale *et al.*, 2004), distinctions that are central to the emergence of the coparenting construct as representing a unique family subsystem. In two-parent families, coparenting that is characterized by partner's efforts to endorse or compliment each other's childrearing efforts has been linked to a more positive family climate (Carlson *et al.*, 2008; Schoppe-Sullivan *et al.*, 2004) and more optimal adjustment outcomes for children (Schoppe *et al.*, 2001). Poor coparenting, on the other hand, is characterized by competitive, hostile, and adversarial behaviors, and has been linked to family conflict (McHale and Rasmussen, 1998) and child behavioral problems outside the home (McConnell and Kerig, 2002; Schoppe, op.cit.).

On the whole, however, most of the empirical database concerning coparenting within the United States focuses on non-Hispanic, White families (McHale *et al.*, 2000; Van Egeren and Hawkins, 2004). Consequently, there has been a notable lack of attention to the important impact of ethnicity, culture, and context when addressing questions about coparenting. Exceptions to this general lacuna in the research, as well as demographic data concerning changes in the US population, suggest that there is good reason to focus on coparenting processes within Mexican American families. In this chapter we review what is known in the empirical literature about coparenting in Mexican American families, to offer guidance for future research, as well as policy and practice, involving this unique population.

Literature Review

Definitions of Coparenting

"Coparenting" has been defined as how mother and father support or undermine one another in their mutual parenting roles (Gable *et al.*, 1995; McHale *et al.*, 2003). Significant components of the coparenting process identified by Feinberg (2003) include: (a) joint family management, (b) support-undermining for the coparental role, (c) childrearing agreement, and (d) division of labor. Each of these components is considered to represent separate, but overlapping areas of functioning, that together comprise the coparenting relationship. Because the database from which this model of coparenting was developed predominately included studies of Anglo American families, it is reasonable to question to what extent the construct of coparenting may be applied to Mexican American families. Although common, the practice of transferring concepts developed in reference to majority cultures and applying them to different cultural groups often leads to a misunderstanding of minority families (McHale *et al.*, 2004). Examining the meaning of a particular family pattern from within the perspective of the culture to which it is being applied allows for a more sensitive and deeper understanding of the cultural context that provides meaning to that practice.

Validity as a Construct

About the same time that Feinberg (2003) outlined his model of coparenting, Caldera, Fitzpatrick, and Wampler (2002) carried out a qualitative study examining the validity of coparenting as a construct applicable to Mexican American families. These authors conducted focus group interviews with 14 Mexican American couples who had at least one child under the age of 11. The majority of participating parents (70%) were born in the United States. The interviews included questions pertaining to how the parents worked together to raise their child, what parent's experiences were when interacting together with their child, and how parents handled disagreements about parenting. Interviews were transcribed and coded using a mapping procedure that first identified statements that fell into a global coparenting category, then these statements were subcoded into particular coparenting themes.

Caldera *et al.*'s (2002) analyses of the interviews revealed that across couples both parents consistently reported being highly involved in parenting activities. Furthermore, among the themes that emerged from parent's comments about their coparenting experiences was the importance of supporting one another while parenting, coordinating parenting tasks, and sharing tasks or parenting responsibilities. Both the mothers and fathers in these Mexican American families appeared to be keenly aware of the importance of aiding their partners and engaging in joint rather than unilateral decision-making. Parents also expressed the need to present a united front for their children, especially in dealing with decisions in response to a child's request. Supporting one another in times when a particular parent takes a lead in childrearing, by providing assistance, reinforcing what the lead parent says or does, and avoiding interfering, was also identified by parents as being critical to successful coparenting. In addition, the idea of one partner providing relief to the other for the stress that comes with childrearing, or on the occasion of role strain, was evident as a component of coparenting in parents' comments. At the same time, parents acknowledged that it was common for their coparenting to manifest itself in the form of compensating for gaps in each other's performance, when one parent had mastered a life skill that the other had not, or when one parent would take charge of a situation in which the other parent was not successful.

The data from Caldera *et al.*'s (2002) study clearly indicate that coparenting is a family process recognized by Mexican American parents. Not only did parents identify the manifestation of coparenting in their relationship, they also emphasized the importance of constructing a supportive and unified coparenting relationship for the well-being of their child. The results obtained by Caldera and her colleagues (2002) offer verification for extending conceptualizations of coparenting processes to Mexican American families. Furthermore, the content of statements made by the participating families support the four components outlined in Feinberg's (2003) definitional model of coparenting, suggesting that it may be a useful heuristic for understanding coparenting in Mexican American families, despite being developed primarily from information on European American families.

Concomitantly, however, the qualitative nature of the Caldera *et al.* (2002) study prevented the use of controls for confounding variables, such as generational and acculturation status, in parent's ideas about their coparenting relationship. That is, the authors were unable to explore the possibility that subtle distinctions exist in the ways that coparenting is understood across parents with different generational status, or different levels of acculturation. Moreover, the limited sample size of the study raises concerns about the generalizability of the findings to the broader population of Mexican American families. Additional qualitative research focusing on Mexican American parent's conceptualizations of coparenting would be worthwhile to further verify definitions of coparenting that have been developed from studies of other ethnic groups.

Theoretical Models of the Correlates of Coparenting

Beyond defining the structure of coparenting, theoretical and empirical work has explored the correlates of coparenting from the perspective of ecological models (Feinberg, 2003; Gable *et al.*, 1995; Lindsey *et al.*, 2005). The proposed linkages of constructs in various ecological models are similar to associations posited in the family systems perspective (Bronfenbrenner, 1986; Minuchin, 1985). From both theoretical viewpoints coparenting is considered to be a microsystem within the family, composed of the mother–father–child relationship, in which the quality of the marital relationship interfaces with how mothers and fathers coordinate their efforts to deal with issues related to childrearing. In this way, coparenting is considered to be an extension of the marital relationship that involves transactions with a third individual, namely the child (Minuchin, 1985). Located at a point of intersection between two family subsystems —the marital, and parent–child relationships—coparenting shares characteristics in common, but also unique from, other subsystems comprising the family. Thus, there is a conceptual distinction between parents' individual behavior with their children, the quality of the marital relationship, and parents' mutual support and involvement with the child.

Empirical evidence supports the theoretical distinction between coparenting and other relationship subsystems within the family (Floyd and Zmich, 1991; McHale and Rasmussen, 1998). For example, Floyd and his colleagues (Floyd *et al.*, 1998; Floyd and Zmich, 1991) found that the coparenting relationship is related to the quality of the marital relationship, but that both relationship subsystems contribute to the quality of parent–child relationships in different ways. Likewise, McHale *et al.* (2000) found that mothers' and fathers' levels of involvement and use of limit-setting with their child differed across dyadic parent–child interactions and triadic mother–father–child coparenting contexts. Together this evidence suggests that the coparenting relationship offers a window into family functioning that cannot be obtained from assessments of other family relationships.

The family itself is considered to be a subsystem located within a broader social and cultural context made up of multiple subsystems that reciprocally interact (Bronfenbrenner, 1986; von

Bertalanffy, 1968). Any given family member may interact or be a part of other systems outside of the family, and through the interface members of the family have with other ecological contexts outside, these systems also influence the family. In this way, an ecological systems perspective assumes that there are transactional influences across various subsystems, both from within and outside the family (Feinberg, 2003; Minuchin, 1985).

When applied to the phenomenon of coparenting, ecological models stipulate that patterns of coparenting may vary by race and ethnic group membership (Feinberg, 2003; Van Egeren and Hawkins, 2004). One way that ethnicity is viewed to influence coparenting—and other family subsystems—is through social position and social stratification factors, such as social class, prejudice, discrimination, and segregation—aspects of the larger societal system in which families are embedded, and that are acknowledged to play a potential role in coparenting. In the following section we review information pertaining to social position and social stratification characteristics that may influence coparenting in Mexican American families.

Social Position Trends in Mexican American Families

From 2000 to 2005, Latinos accounted for 75 percent of the growth in the number of families with children under 18 years old, and accounted for 143 percent of the growth in the number of two-parent families (Passel and D'Vera, 2008). Mexican Americans represent the largest Latino group in the US, making up almost three-quarters of the 15.2 million increase in the Latino population in America from 2000 to 2010 (U.S. Census Bureau, 2010). Given these demographic trends, there is a clear need to assess the proximal family context, or characteristics, of the growing number of what are predominately two-parent Mexican American families with young children. Such information will critically advance our knowledge of the developmental environment inhabited by a significant and increasing number of America's children, with which to inform policy and program development.

In studying Mexican American families it is important to recognize that there is variability in the generational status of parents and children that may contribute to sociocultural variations in family processes, including coparenting. Individuals of Mexican descent living in the United States are typically characterized as belonging to one of three generational groups: (a) those born in Mexico, (b) those born in the US of Mexican-born parents, and (c) those born in the US of US-born parents (Esteinou, 2007). Data suggests that there are important social and cultural differences between these three groups that may play a role in coparenting processes. For example, Mexican-born parents have less education and lower family income than their US born counterparts, factors that have been linked to variations in parenting practices (Buriel, 1993; Buriel *et al.*, 1991). This evidence suggests that across successive generations, Mexican American families undergo social and cultural changes that may influence coparenting. What is less obvious is how family processes within Mexican American families, such as coparenting, change across generations.

Acculturation

It also is important to recognize that within Mexican American families, independent of generational status, there is a wide range of variability in the extent to which individual family members have assimilated the sociocultural and psychological characteristics of the Anglo society (Esteinou, 2007; Ramirez *et al.*, 1974). These individual differences in "acculturation" appear to be critical to a variety of family processes (Baca Zinn, 1994; Rueschenberg and Buriel, 1989). Mexican Americans who are more "traditional" (least acculturated) show strong identification with the nuclear and/or extended family, their own ethnic group, and Mexican cultural ideology (Rodriguez *et al.*, 2007). On the other hand, Mexican Americans who are more "atraditional" (most acculturated) show little identification with the Mexican culture, or family ties (Phinney and Flores, 2002; Sarkisian *et al.*, 2006). Previous literature has also shown that by and large, the time Mexican American parents have spent in the USA is associated with the adoption of parenting practices that resemble the mainstream culture (Buriel, 1993; Livas-Dlott *et al.*, 2010). Thus, it seems reasonable to speculate that individual differences in level of acculturation may be linked to variations in coparenting across Mexican American families. To better understand coparenting in Mexican American families empirical work needs to consider how acculturation affects heterogeneity among Mexican American parents.

Generational Status

To date, to the best of our knowledge, there has been only one study to consider generational status in relation to coparenting in Mexican American families. Pinto and Coltrane (2009) examined patterns of household division of labor among 194 Mexican-origin and 199 Anglo families as part of a larger longitudinal study. Participating families included a child in the 7th grade with both parents of the same ethnic background living in the home. Interviews and questionnaires were used to obtain data from both parents. Parents' generational status was determined based on their own place of birth, their parents' place of birth, and age of arrival to the US. A total of 126 mothers and 122 fathers were identified as first-generation Mexican immigrants. Although not framed as an assessment of coparenting, a measure of maternal gate-keeping was obtained based on the average of mother's and father's scores on questions about the mother's regulation and assessment of the father's participation in household work and child care, with high scores indicating greater control on the part of the mother, which could be interpreted as a form of interfering and unsupportive coparenting. In addition, mothers reported on the number of hours both she and the father participated in housework.

Analyses revealed that mothers of Mexican origin performed more housework than Anglo mothers, with Mexican immigrant mothers performing the most housework of the three groups. Concomitantly, fathers of Mexican origin performed less housework than Anglo fathers, with Mexican immigrant fathers performing the least amount of housework. Mexican origin mothers and fathers reported more maternal gatekeeping than Anglo mothers and fathers, and Mexican immigrant mothers reported more gatekeeping and stronger gender segregation than Mexican American mothers. Interestingly, there were no associations between reports of maternal gatekeeping and participation in housework for Mexican American fathers and mothers. The findings of Pinto and Coltrane (2009) suggest that coparenting in Mexican American families may differ from that of Anglo families, and may vary among Mexican Americans based on generational status.

There are two studies that provide data concerning the role of acculturation status in coparenting processes of Mexican Americans. The first study was conducted by Formoso *et al.* (2007) who examined how the interparental relationship, and mother's and father's work hours influenced the quality of fathering among low-income Mexican American families. The sample included 115 two-parent Mexican American families with a school-age child (11- to 14-years-old). The majority of participating mothers (69%) and fathers (67%) were born in Mexico, as were almost half of the children (49%). There were approximately equal numbers of boys and girls. Acculturation status was determined by the amount of Spanish spoken by fathers in the home. Mothers and fathers also reported on the number of hours they worked per week. Dimensions of coparenting assessed in the study included interparental conflict, as well as shared parenting beliefs, the extent to which parents valued and respected their coparent's judgments, and supportive coparenting. In addition, fathers and children provided separate assessments of the quality of fathers' parenting.

Analyses revealed that fathers who spoke predominately Spanish reported a stronger coparenting alliance, and that when mothers and fathers reported a strong coparenting alliance, fathers reported higher-quality fathering. Thus fathers who were less acculturated appeared to have a stronger coparenting alliance. Mother's report of a strong coparenting alliance, regardless of father's acculturation level, was associated with children's report of higher-quality fathering. Although parental employment status was not associated with coparenting quality, in single-earner families where the father spoke predominately Spanish, fathers who reported more interparental conflict also reported lower-quality fathering, and mothers who reported more interparental conflict had children who reported lower-quality fathering. Also, in single earner families, irrespective of father's language use, interparental conflict reported by fathers and mothers was associated with children's report of lower-quality fathering. From this data it appears that parental acculturation status and employment outside the home are important social position factors accounting for variations in coparenting in Mexican American families.

Language

Further evidence for the influence of acculturation as a social position variable on coparenting in Mexican American families is provided by Cabrera *et al.*, (2009) who examined the connections between Mexican American parents' level of acculturation (based on English proficiency) and coparenting conflict, in relation to mother–child and father–child interaction and infant's social development. Using data from the nine month assessment of participants in the Early Childhood Longitudinal Study-Birth Cohort (ECLS-B), a nationally representative sample of families with children born in 2001, the authors identified 735 Mexican American infants living in two-parent homes. Mother's and father's response to a single question about the level of conflict they experienced regarding issues concerning their child served as a measure of coparenting conflict. Mothers and fathers also reported on their marital happiness and marital conflict, and fathers reported on their engagement with the target child. Observational measures of mother's positivity and responsiveness to her child, and children's emotionally regulated and responsive interaction with the mother, were obtained during a teaching task.

The authors found that after controlling for family SES and other demographic characteristics, father's English proficiency was associated with lower levels of mother-reported coparenting conflict. Thus, when fathers were more acculturated, mothers indicated there was less coparenting conflict. Analyses of the moderating role of parent English proficiency revealed that, among fathers who were more proficient in English, higher levels of coparenting conflict, as reported by mothers, was associated with fathers' report of being more involved in child caregiving. Likewise, among fathers who reported more coparenting conflict, greater English proficiency was associated with more involvement in child caregiving, whereas low English proficiency was associated with less child caregiving. These findings indicate that acculturation status accounts for individual differences in coparenting quality in Mexican American families, and interacts with coparenting quality to account for variations in individual parenting behavior.

Social Position

Together, the findings of Pinto and Coltrane (2009), Formoso *et al.* (2007) and Cabrera *et al.* (2009) point to a connection between social position characteristics and the quality of coparenting in Mexican American families, and suggest that multiple social position characteristics can interact to influence coparenting quality across families. Based on these data it appears that not only generational status, acculturation, and parental employment make unique contributions to the quality of coparenting, but that they also are intertwined in complex ways to account for variations in the coparenting experience and how coparenting influences other relationships within Mexican American families. Therefore, it seems clear that an adequate study of coparenting within Mexican American families must take into account social influences. Given the limited scope of the only three studies that have examined social position characteristics in relation to coparenting in Mexican American families to date, future research should consider additional ecological variables such as degree of societal discrimination, educational and employment opportunities, and opportunities to participate in the native culture, to name just a few, as social factors contributing to patterns of coparenting among Mexican Americans. It also will be worthwhile for future research to consider how changes in environmental systems (e.g. children's school, parental place of employment, religious institutions) outside the family can affect the sociocultural characteristics and coparenting practices of Mexican American families (McHale *et al.*, 2003).

It also is important to note that acculturation is a complex process (Keefe and Padilla, 1987; Padilla and Perez, 2003) that may not be adequately represented by a simple assessment of parents' English proficiency, as was done by Formoso *et al.* (2007) and Cabrera *et al.* (2009). Other domains of acculturation and cultural orientation among Mexican Americans, such as cultural awareness—the implicit knowledge that individuals have of their cultures of origin and of their host cultures—and ethnic loyalty—a person's preference for one cultural orientation or ethnic group (Chun and Akutsu, 2003; Rodriguez *et al.*, 2007)—are likely to be important determinations of coparenting. Distinctions between the process of acculturation—in which the main focus is on how individuals relate to the dominant society—and the process of ethnic identity, in which the focus is on how individuals relate to themselves and their own group (Padilla and Perez, 2003; Phinney and Flores, 2002), may provide important insight into coparenting processes. For example, Keefe and Padilla (1987) report that despite declines in cultural awareness across generations among Mexican Americans, ethnic loyalty remained consistently high from the first to the fourth generation. The implications of such findings are that more multidimensional measures of acculturation are needed in research on coparenting in Mexican American families.

Cultural Values of Mexican Americans

A second manner in which ethnicity may influence coparenting is through the distinctive values, beliefs, and attitudes that are held in common among individuals who share ethnic group membership. Not only may Mexican American families display unique patterns of coparenting relative to other ethnic groups, but also differences in coparenting among families of Mexican origin may be linked to variations in individual parent's adherence to particular cultural values. Cultural values and expectations that relate to how fathers and mothers participate in childrearing activities, or to the allocation of household chores and other obligations between parents are likely to be particularly relevant to coparenting processes. Empirical data suggest that there are at least four values inherent to the cultural background of Mexican Americans that may fall into this category: (a) the value of family closeness (*Familismo*; Becerra, 1998), (b) importance placed on traditional gender roles (*Machismo*; Goldwert, 1985), (c) emphasis on showing respect for others (*Respeto*; Garcia, 1996), and (d) the value of interpersonal harmony (*Simpatía*; Triandis *et al.*, 1984). In the following paragraphs we give specific attention to conceptual and empirical data indicating how each of these values may be linked to coparenting processes in Mexican American families.

Familismo

The cultural value that has arguably received the most empirical attention in studies of Mexican Americans is that of *Familism* or *Familismo*, which refers to an emphasis on duty to one's family, as well as cooperation, cohesion, and non-conflictual family interactions (Baca Zinn, 1994; Rodriguez *et al.*, 2007). The term *Familismo* includes the desire to maintain strong family ties, the expectation that the family will be the primary source of instrumental and emotional support, and commitment to the family over individual needs and desires (Lugo Steidel and Contreras, 2003; Sabogal *et al.*, 1987).

Empirical research indicates that *Familismo* is a multidimensional construct that includes both values and behaviors (Baca Zinn, 1994; Sabogal *et al.*, 1987). Familistic values emphasize family support, solidarity, and obligations, and familistic behaviors focus on involvement with nuclear and extended family. Thus, connections between familism and coparenting in Mexican American families may be complex, and vary depending on the specific component of familism, as well as other sociocultural characteristics of the family. In relation to coparenting, mothers and fathers who strongly endorse principles of *Familismo* may be more likely to coordinate their parenting to preserve family unity (Caldera *et al.*, 2002). To the extent that norms of familism are adopted within Mexican American families, one might expect to see coparenting subsystems characterized by high levels of agreement and cooperativeness.

Machismo

The Mexican American family has also been characterized as adhering to values that include traditional male/female gender roles (Becerra, 1998; Phinney and Flores, 2002), and more specifically the cultural value of *Machismo*, typified by male supremacy, and maternal submissiveness (Goldwert, 1985). A manifestation of this value is the strict division of childrearing responsibilities along gender lines, with the mother assuming primary responsibility for parenting and the father taking a peripheral role in children's lives (Mirandé, 1985). Based on this formulation of the value of *Machismo*, coparenting in Mexican American families might be expected to take on patterns of inequality and disjointed participation by mothers and fathers.

Recent evidence suggests, however, that the stereotypical meaning of *Machismo* does not accurately capture the behavior of Mexican American fathers (Cabrera and Garcia Coll, 2004; Felix-Ortiz *et al.*, 2001). Specifically, Mexican American fathers have been found to actively play with their children, to be highly affectionate, and emotionally supportive toward children (Davis and Chavez, 1995; Mirandé, 1991). Toth and Xu (1999) reported that a combined sample of 135 Mexican American, Cuban American, and Puerto Rican fathers spent more time in direct interactions with their children than a comparison group of 999 non-Hispanic White fathers. Furthermore, there was no difference between the three groups of Hispanic fathers in time spent with children. Together, this evidence suggests that among Mexican American families the link between the cultural value of *Machismo* and coparenting may be more complex than suggested by existing stereotypical perspectives of the meaning of *Machismo*.

Respeto

A third cultural value common among Mexican American families is that of *Respeto*, a belief in maintaining harmonious interpersonal relationships through respect for self and others (Arcia and Johnson, 1998; Valdes, 1996). Within the family, the value of *Respeto* extends beyond its English translation "to respect" in that it encompasses an appreciation of each family member's unique role (Valdes, 1996). Consequently, *Respeto* is likely to have a formative influence on the coparenting subsystem, which is composed of the mother, father, and child, and their intersecting roles. To the extent that individual family members adhere to their particular roles, one could expect an overall atmosphere of mutual respect that is likely to promote coordinated coparenting relationships. In addition, high levels of *Respeto* in Mexican American families may be conducive to more coordination in the behaviors of mothers and fathers, and parents and children, in that there is a hierarchical structure in patterns of deferring to the opinions and suggestions of other family members.

Indirect support for the possible role of *Respeto* in coparenting quality among Mexican American families comes from an ethnographic study conducted by Valdes (1996) who found that by the age of four, children in Mexican American families demonstrated an understanding and adherence to behavioral rules of respect toward parents and other family members, such as the use of polite salutations, not contradicting adults' opinions, and not interrupting adults' speech. At the same time, both adults and children manifested beliefs that children should be accorded respect when they followed behaviors appropriate to their role in the family. The pattern of child and adult adherence to *Respeto* observed in Valdes' study suggests that this cultural value may be significantly linked to coparenting quality in Mexican American families.

Simpatía

Another cultural value typical of Mexican American families is *Simpatía*, defined as "a permanent personal quality where an individual is perceived as likable, attractive, fun to be with, and easy going" (Triandis *et al.*, 1984, p. 1363). At a behavioral level the term *Simpatía*, which has no equivalent in English, refers to the demonstration of a willingness to conform, an ability to share in others' feelings, and striving for harmony in interpersonal relations by avoiding interpersonal conflict. Consequently, individuals who embody the value of *Simpatía* maximize agreeableness in their relationships, place others' needs before their own and avoid conflict even when disagreeing (Yu *et al.*, 2008). Within the family, a belief system or cultural script grounded in the value of *Simpatía* would likely translate into a coparenting relationship characterized by high agreement, sharing responsibilities, and cooperative decision-making. Likewise, parents who conjointly strive to adhere to the value of *Simpatía* would likely manifest low levels of conflict in their coparenting relationship.

Links Between Cultural Values and Coparenting in Mexican American Families

One of the first studies to provide direct evidence of links between Mexican American parent's cultural values and their coparenting relationship was conducted by Yu *et al.* (2008) who collected data from 45 mother–father dyads with a preschool-age child. Data were obtained from both mothers and fathers at time 1 and only from mothers at time 2, approximately 6 months apart. Spanish was the predominate language spoken in the home by 82 percent of mothers and 71 percent of fathers. The majority of parents were first-generation Mexican Americans (84 and 82 percent of mothers and fathers, respectively). Data were collected using in-home interviews, conducted separately with mothers, fathers, and children. Both mothers and fathers completed surveys assessing their cultural beliefs of simpatía and respeto, specifically in regard to expectations for the parent–child relationship. Coparenting quality was assessed based on parent's responses to questions concerning the degree to which they shared responsibilities over a broad domain of their child's life (e.g. "making day-to-day decisions," "discussing what rules to set," and "discussing finances"). Higher scores reflected greater levels of coparenting for mothers and fathers. In addition, mothers and fathers reported on their level of agreement regarding family life, level of happiness in their relationship, and level of conflict over childrearing issues, whereas only mothers reported on their satisfaction with the father's child rearing skills.

Analyses revealed that mother's and father's cultural values were related to coparenting quality in unique ways. Specifically, in families with fathers who placed a high value in simpatía, mothers reported greater parental agreement on childrearing at T1 and greater satisfaction with father's parenting at T2. In contrast, mothers' valuing of simpatía was not related to their own or to fathers' reports of parental agreement or coparenting. Similarly, in families where fathers placed a high value in respeto, mothers reported less parental agreement at T1 and less satisfaction with father's parenting at T2. In turn, in families where mothers placed a high value in respeto, fathers reported greater coparenting interaction. Thus, Yu *et al.*'s (2008) findings suggest that certain cultural values may be more, or less, conducive to the quality of coparenting in Mexican American families. Moreover, the nature of the connection between coparenting and cultural values appears to vary depending on the parent who adheres to the value, and the parent whose perception of the coparenting relationship is assessed.

Gender Roles

Another study that provides information concerning connections between coparenting and cultural values is that of Pinto and Coltrane (2009), described previously, who examined the role of beliefs regarding familism and gender roles in maternal gatekeeping among Mexican origin and Anglo families. In addition to assessing parents' generational status, mothers and fathers completed a 14-item survey measuring their endorsement of segregated gender roles in the family, as well as a 10-item familism beliefs questionnaire.

The authors found that Mexican origin mothers and fathers reported stronger beliefs in segregated gender roles and familism, than Anglo mothers and fathers, and that Mexican immigrant mothers reported stronger gender segregation and familism beliefs, than Mexican American mothers. Interestingly, however, among Mexican American families there was no connection between cultural beliefs and participation in housework, with the exception that fathers who held more segregated gender role attitudes performed less housework. Thus, overall, the cultural beliefs of machismo and familism did not appear to be a major influence on the coparenting processes of Mexican American families examined by these authors.

A more recent study by Solmeyer *et al.* (2011) examined the phenomenon of parental differential treatment of siblings in relation to coparenting quality and cultural values among Mexican origin families. Data were collected from a sample of 246 families in which the mother was of Mexican origin, two parents lived in the home, and 7th grader and older siblings were living in the home. Mothers and fathers had lived in the United States for an average of 12.44 and 15.10 years, respectively. Younger children were on average thirteen years of age, and older siblings were on average sixteen, with approximately half being males. The majority of parents (67%) chose to complete home interviews in Spanish. Mothers and fathers reported on their coparenting relationship based on questions concerning satisfaction with joint childrearing, and also completed measures of their acculturation level (strength of orientation to the Mexican culture relative to the Anglo culture), cultural beliefs regarding familism (importance of family to individual well-being), and traditional gender roles (division of male and female roles in the family along stereotypical gender norms). Parental differential treatment of siblings was assessed based on mother's and father's report of differences in their expression of affection and use of discipline toward one child compared to the other. Families were categorized into three groups based on parent's report of differential treatment of siblings:

- The equal treatment group—was composed of families in which the mother and fathers treated both offspring equally.
- The incongruent treatment group—was composed of families that had one parent who treated siblings differently and the one parent who treated siblings equally.
- The congruent treatment group—was composed of families that had parents who treated children differently, but favored the same child over the other child.

Solmeyer et al.'s (2011) analysis revealed that higher levels of coparenting satisfaction were found among parents who reported treating siblings equally in terms of affection, and discipline. In addition, higher levels of coparenting were observed among parents who were congruent in treating one child differently than the other in their use of discipline, than among parents who were incongruent in their use of discipline across children. The authors also found that parents who were more oriented toward the Mexican culture, and who adhered to traditional gender role beliefs were more likely to report treating both offspring equally with regard to affection. Likewise, parents who were more oriented toward the Mexican culture were more likely to report treating both offspring equally with regard to discipline. Parents who believed in more egalitarian gender roles were more likely to report treating both offspring equally with regard to discipline, whereas parents who believed in more traditional gender roles were more likely to treat one child consistently different from the other in the domain of discipline.

Cultural Beliefs

The findings of Solmeyer et al. (2011) suggest that Mexican American parents' adherence to the Mexican culture and to traditional gender role beliefs plays a role in coparenting processes within the family. Although the authors did not report analyses of direct associations between coparenting satisfaction and cultural beliefs, the finding that the group of parents who exhibited a pattern of equal treatment of their children with regards to affection reported not only higher levels of coparenting satisfaction, but also a stronger orientation to the Mexican culture and to traditional gender role beliefs, indirectly suggests that there may be a connection. That is, the fact that adherence to these cultural beliefs was common among parents who coordinated their parenting in a way so as to treat both children equally, and who were highly satisfied with their coparenting relationship, relative to parents who did not treat both children equally, lends support to the supposition that these family characteristics are linked.

Summary

Together these three studies suggest that the cultural values of (a) *Familismo*, (b) *Machismo*, (c) *Respeto*, and (d) *Simpatía* are related to coparenting processes in Mexican American families. Although frequently discussed as separate and unique cultural values in Mexican American families (Rodriguez et al., 2007; Triandis et al., 1984), it is important to recognize that within any given individual or family there is likely to be a complex interplay among different values (Gutierrez and Sameroff, 1990). It may be that values take on a hierarchical structure, so that particular beliefs supersede others in determining family processes (Arcia and Johnson, 1998). For example, a given family may place more emphasis on the importance of *Simpatía* than on *Machismo*, so that family harmony takes precedence over adherence to gender roles. Likewise, certain values may be more salient in particular family subsystems than others, or in particular contexts of family interaction. For example, although Mexican American mothers advocate an approach to childrearing that instills beliefs in *Respeto* when it comes to parent–child relationships (Arcia and Johnson, 1998), evidence suggests that Mexican American women's ideals toward marital relationships have shifted from *Respeto* to a belief in joint decision-making, companionship, and indistinct gender boundaries (Hirsch, 1999). To fully understand the role that cultural values play in coparenting within Mexican American families it will be necessary for researchers to assess multiple cultural values in a single study and examine interactions between values in connection to coparenting processes.

Parents' similarity in cultural values is likely to represent an important process in explaining coparental functioning within Mexican American families. Researchers have established that parental agreement in childrearing is associated with functional parental alliances (Margolin *et al.*, 2001) and the quality of parent–child interaction (Lindsey and Mize, 2001). Parental agreement in childrearing requires consensus on basic ideals of care and culturally preferred socialization strategies (McHale *et al.*, 2003). Such consensus or shared views between parents may be understood as the building block through which parents produce a stable and predictable environment for their children (Lindsey and Mize, 2001). Consequently, in studying coparenting among Mexican American families researchers need to assess the values of both parents, and evaluate the degree of similarity between mother's and father's beliefs.

Future Directions and Challenges

Despite an increased recognition of the important role of coparenting in family processes and a corresponding increase in the number of studies focusing on coparenting in Mexican American families, gaps and unanswered questions still remain. In particular, although there are notable exceptions identified in this review, much of the work on coparenting in Mexican American families has lacked a strong theoretical framework. Theoretically driven research is more likely to avoid the pitfalls of a deficit perspective, wherein coparenting processes of Mexican American families are compared to those of other ethnic groups and any differences are framed as a shortcoming on the part of Mexican Americans. Theoretical models and conceptual frameworks that take into account the unique context in which Mexican American families are embedded are more likely to reveal the adaptive significance of differences seen in the coparenting practices of Mexican Americans. Furthermore, empirical research on coparenting that is grounded on theory will help to integrate findings on different domains of Mexican American family functioning. Theorists and researchers can compare findings related to theoretically guided hypotheses that are specific to coparenting among Mexican Americans, with findings pertaining to other areas of family life, in order to judge the efficacy of broader theoretical explanations. Therefore an increase in theoretically grounded research will significantly contribute to building our knowledge base on Mexican American family life.

The study of coparenting is also lagging behind methodologically in that much of the research relies on measures developed for other populations and not validated in Mexican American samples. As a result, it remains unclear to what extent the concept of coparenting developed from the study of European American or African American families applies to Mexican American families. To address this limitation more qualitative studies are needed, such as the study by Caldera *et al.* (2002), in order to account for variations within Mexican American families based on acculturation, SES, or perhaps neighborhood characteristics. As the study of coparenting in Mexican American families moves forward, it will be important to increase the conceptual and methodological sophistication of approaches used to study them.

Another notable gap is a limited understanding of the broader context in which coparenting is affected in Mexican American families. In this regard, increased focus on the acculturation process and how it influences coparenting will be important. In addition, the available literature has begun to highlight coparenting processes and cultural values that appear specific to Mexican American families. Cultural values such as Familismo, Machismo, Respeto, and Simpatía, represent more proximal cultural constructs that give insight into how culture may influence family processes, and may offer a useful starting place given their relevance to current definitions of coparenting. Further development and refinement of measures to assess such cultural values is critically needed and will help to extend existing theorizing and model development regarding coparenting.

In reference to the more immediate family context, it also is important for research to explore the distinction between coparenting and other relationships within the Mexican American family. Given the demographic characteristics of Mexican American families, it will be helpful to study the role of siblings and members of the extended family as socializing agents, as well as family-level interactions involving both parents with multiple children, as well as parent and grandparents with children.

Policy Implications

Although limited, existing evidence does offer some guidance for policy makers. Most notably, the emerging database suggests that policies should move from an individual parenting perspective to one that considers the joint role of parents in the socialization of children. Policies that target the coparenting relationship, by helping to strengthen the way parents work together to raise children, may prove uniquely beneficial to Mexican American family dynamics and child outcomes, relative to policies that target only individual parents or parenting behavior. At a broad level this entails ensuring that policies acknowledge both parents as important contributors to childrearing—such as a more widespread adoption of offering both paternity and maternity leave. In more specific terms, policy interventions should be implemented that focus explicitly on strengthening parents' ability to work together in rearing their child.

Similar guidelines can be applied to settings where more direct interventions are employed in working with Mexican American families. For example, family interventions must carefully consider how the specific parenting and child behaviors that are targeted may affect the coparenting relationship and how parents work together. This should be done at the development stage as well as in adaptations made during the course of intervention. In educational settings, programs may need to provide additional supports to include both parents, and educational staff's effort to engage parents should be extended to include a coparenting perspective. Correspondingly, in clinical settings families presenting for treatment should be assessed for difficulties in coparenting relations and coordination, as clinical approaches to bolstering coparenting quality may be called for. Moreover, clinicians should be aware of interfamilial and intrafamilial factors that contribute to, or exacerbate, coparenting difficulty and conflict.

As we gain a richer understanding of coparenting processes in Mexican American families, it will be important for researchers to move beyond descriptive studies and test, prospectively, how coparenting relates to adjustment outcomes at both the individual and family level. In testing longitudinal associations, it will be critical to follow comprehensive conceptual frameworks that take into account the cultural and socio-demographic ecologies of Mexican American families and the developmental nature of parenting and other family processes, that pay attention to the great variability observed among Mexican American families, and that assess outcomes in terms of both mainstream as well as culture-specific constructs.

References

Arcia, E., and Johnson, A. (1998). When respect means to obey: Immigrant Mexican mothers' values for their children. *Journal of Child and Family Studies*, 7, 79–95.

Baca Zinn, M. (1994). Adaptation and continuity in Mexican-origin families. In R. L. Taylor (Ed.), *Minority families in the United States: A multicultural perspective* (pp. 64–94). Englewood Cliffs, NJ: Prentice Hall.

Becerra, R. M. (1998). The Mexican-American family. In C. H. Mindel, R. W. Habenstein, and R. Wright, Jr. (Eds.), *Ethnic families in America: Patterns and variations* (4th edn.). New Jersey: Prentice Hall.

Bronfenbrenner, U. (1986). Ecology of the family as a context for human development: Research perspectives. *Developmental Psychology*, 22, 723–742.

Buriel, R. (1993). Childrearing orientations in Mexican American families: The influence of generation and sociocultural factors. *Journal of Marriage and the Family*, 55, 987–1000.

Buriel, R., Mercado, R., Rodriguez, J., and Chavez, J. M. (1991). Mexican-American disciplinary practices and attitudes toward child maltreatment: A comparison of foreign- and native-born mothers. *Hispanic Journal of Behavioral Sciences*, 13, 78–94.

Cabrera, N. J., and Garcia Coll, C. (2004). Latino fathers: Uncharted territory in need of much exploration. In M. E. Lamb (Ed.), *The role of the father in child development* (pp. 98–120). Hoboken, NJ: Wiley.

Cabrera, N. J., Shannon, J. D., and La Taillade, J. J. (2009). Predictors of co-parenting in Mexican American families and direct effects on parenting and child social emotional development. *Infant Mental Health Journal*, 30, 523–548.

Caldera, Y., Fitzpatrick, J., and Wampler, K. (2002). Coparenting in intact Mexican American families: Mothers' and fathers' perceptions. In J. M. Contreras, K. A., Kerns, and A. M. Neal-Barnett (Eds.), *Latino children and families in the United States* (pp. 107–133). Westport, CT: Praeger.

Caldera, Y. M., and Lindsey, E. W. (2006). Coparenting, mother-infant interaction, and infant-parent attachment relationships in two-parent families. *Journal of Family Psychology*, 20, 275–83.

Carlson, M. J., McLanahan, S. S., and Brooks-Gunn, J. (2008). Coparenting and nonresident fathers' involvement with young children after a nonmarital birth. *Demography*, 45, 461–488. doi: 10.1353/dem.0.0007

Chun, K. M., and Akutsu, P. D. (2003). Acculturation among ethnic minority families. In K. M. Chun, P. B. Organista, and G. Marin (Eds.), *Acculturation: Advances in theory, measurement and applied research* (pp. 95–119). Washington, DC: American Psychological Association.

Davis, S. K., and Chavez, V. (1995). Hispanic househusbands. In A. M. Padilla (Ed.), *Hispanic psychology: Critical issues in theory and research* (pp. 257–287). Thousand Oaks, CA: Sage.

Esteinou, R. (2007). Strengths and challenges of Mexican families in the 21st century. *Marriage and Family Review*, 40, 309–334.

Feinberg, M. E. (2003). The internal structure and ecological context of parenting: A framework for research and intervention. *Parenting: Science and Practice*, 3, 95–131.

Felix-Ortiz, M., Abreu, J. M., Briano, M., and Bowen, D. (2001). A critique of machismo measures in psychological research. In F. Columbus (Ed.), *Advances in psychology research* (Vol. III, pp. 63–90). New York: NOVA Science Publishers.

Floyd, F., Costigan, L., and Gilliom, K. (1998). Marriage and the parenting alliance: Longitudinal prediction of change in parenting perceptions and behaviors. *Child Development*, 69, 1461–1479.

Floyd, F. J., and Zmich, D. E. (1991). Marriage and parenting partnership: Perceptions and interactions of parents with mentally retarded and typically developing children. *Child Development*, 62, 1434–1448.

Formoso, D., Gonzalez, N. A., Barrera, M., and Dumka, L. E. (2007). Interparental relations, maternal employment, and fathering in Mexican American families. *Journal of Marriage and Family*, 69, 26–39.

Gable, S., Belsky, J., and Crnic, K. (1995). Coparenting during the child's 2nd year: A descriptive account. *Journal of Marriage and the Family*, 57, 609–616.

Garcia, W. R. (1996). Respeto: A Mexican base for interpersonal relationships. In W. Gudykunst, S. Ting-Toomey, and T. Nishida (Eds.), *Communication in personal relationships across cultures*. Thousand Oaks, CA: Sage.

Goldwert, M. (1985). Mexican machismo: Flight from femininity. *Psychoanalytic Review*, 72, 161–169.

Gutierrez, J., and Sameroff, A. (1990). Determinants of complexity in Mexican-American and Anglo American mothers conceptions of child development. *Child Development*, 61, 384–394.

Hirsch, J. S. (1999). En el norte la mujer manda gender, generation, and geography in a Mexican transnational community. *American Behavioral Scientist, 42*, 1332–1349.

Keefe, S. E., and Padilla, A. M. (1987). *Chicano ethnicity*. Albuquerque, NM: University of New Mexico Press.

Lindsey, E. W., and Mize, J. (2001). Interparental agreement, parent–child responsiveness, and children's peer competence. *Family Relations, 50*, 348–354.

Lindsey, E. W., Caldera, Y., and Colwell, M. (2005). Correlates of coparenting during infancy. *Family Relations, 54*, 346–359. doi: 10.1111/j.1741–3729.2005.00322.x

Livas-Dlott, A., Fuller, B., Stein, G. L., Bridges, M., Mangual-Figueroa, A., and Mireles, L. (2010). Commands, competence, and cariño: Maternal socialization practices in Mexican-American families. *Developmental Psychology, 46*, 566–578.

Lugo Steidel, A. G., and Contreras, J. M. (2003). A new familism scale for use with Latino populations. *Hispanic Journal of Behavioral Sciences, 25*, 312–330.

Margolin, G., Gordis, E. B., and John, R. S. (2001). Coparenting: A link between marital conflict and parenting in two-parent families. *Journal of Family Psychology, 15*, 3–21.

McConnell, M. C., and Kerig, P. K. (2002). Assessing coparenting in families of school-age children: Validation of the coparenting and family rating system. *Canadian Journal of Behavioural Science/Revue Canadienne des Sciences du Comportement, 34*, 44.

McHale, J. P., and Rasmussen, J. R. (1998). Coparental and family group-level dynamics during infancy: Early family precursors of child and family functioning during preschool. *Development and Psychopathology, 10*, 39–58.

McHale, J. P., Kuersten-Hogan, R., and Rao, N. (2004). Growing points for coparenting theory and research. *Journal of Adult Development, 11*, 221–234.

McHale, J. P., Kuersten-Hogan, R., Lauretti, A., and Rasmussen, J. (2000). Parents' reports of coparenting behavior are linked to observed coparental process. *Journal of Family Psychology, 14*, 220–237.

McHale, J. P., Khazan, I., Erera, I., Rotman, T., DeCourcay, W., and McConnell, M. (2003). Coparenting in diverse family systems. In M. Borenstein (Ed.), *Handbook of parenting: Vol. 3. Being and becoming a parent* (pp. 75–108). Mahwah, NJ: Lawerence Erlbaum Associates.

Minuchin, P. (1985). Families and individual development: Provocations from the field of family therapy. *Child Development, 56*, 289–302.

Mirandé, A. (1985). *The Chicano experience: An alternative perspective*. Notre Dame, IN: University of Notre Dame Press.

Mirandé, A. (1991). Ethnicity and fatherhood. In F. W. Bozett and S. M. H. Hanson (Eds.), *Fatherhood and families in cultural context* (pp. 53–82). New York: Springer.

Padilla, A. M., and Perez, W. (2003). Acculturation, social identity, and social cognition: A new perspective. *Hispanic Journal of Behavioral Sciences, 25*, 35–55.

Passel, J. S. and D'Vera, C. (2008). *U.S. population projections: 2005–2050*. Washington, DC: Pew Hispanic Center.

Phinney, J. S., and Flores, J. (2002). "Unpackaging" acculturation: Aspects of acculturation as predictors of traditional sex role attitudes. *Journal of Cross-Cultural Psychology, 33*, 320–331.

Pinto, K. M., and Coltrane, S. (2009). Divisions of labor in Mexican origin and Anglo families structure and culture. *Sex Roles, 60*, 482–495.

Ramirez, M., Castaneda, A., and Herold, P. L. (1974). The relationship of acculturation to cognitive style among Mexican Americans. *Journal of Cross-Cultural Psychology, 5*, 424–433.

Rodriguez, N., Mira, C. B., Paez, N. D., and Myers, H. F. (2007). Exploring the complexities of familism and acculturation: Central constructs for people of Mexican origin. *American Journal of Community Psychology, 39*, 61–77.

Rueschenberg, E., and Buriel, R. (1989). Mexican American family functioning and acculturation: A family systems perspective. *Hispanic Journal of Behavioral Sciences, 11*, 232–244.

Sabogal, F., Marin, G., Otero-Sabogal, R., VanOss-Marin, B., and Perez, E. J. (1987). Hispanic familism and acculturation: What changes and what doesn't. *Hispanic Journal of Behavioral Sciences, 9*, 397–412.

Sarkisian, N., Gerena, M., and Gerstel, N. (2006). Extended family ties among Mexicans, Puerto Ricans, and Whites: Superintegration or disintegration? *Family Relations, 55*, 331–344. doi:10.1111/j.1741–3729.2006.00408.x

Schoppe, S. J., Mangelsdorf, S. C., and Frosch, C. A. (2001). Coparenting, family process, and family structure: Implications for preschoolers' externalizing behavior problems. *Journal of Family Psychology, 15*, 526–545. doi:10.1037//0893-3200.15.3.526

Schoppe-Sullivan, S. J., Mangelsdorf, S. C., Frosch, C. A., and McHale, J. L. (2004). Associations between coparenting and marital behavior from infancy to the preschool years. *Journal of Family Psychology, 18*, 194–207. doi: 10.1037/0893-3200.18.1.194

Solmeyer, A. R., Killoren, S. E., McHale, S. M., and Updegraff, K. A. (2011). Coparenting around sibling differential treatment in Mexican-origin families. *Journal of Family Psychology, 25*, 251–260.

Triandis, H. C., Marin, G., Lisansky, J., and Betancourt, H. (1984). Simpatía as a cultural script of Hispanics. *Journal of Personality and Social Psychology, 47*, 1363–1375.

Toth, J. F., and Xu, X. (1999). Ethnic and cultural diversity in fathers' involvement: A racial/ethnic comparison of African American, Hispanic, and White fathers. *Youth and Society, 31*, 76–99.

U.S. Census Bureau. (2010). *The Hispanic population: 2010 census briefs.* Washington, DC: U.S. Department of Commerce.

Valdes, G. (1996). *Con respeto: Bridging the distances between culturally diverse families and schools.* New York: Columbia University, Teachers College Press.

Van Egeren, L. A., and Hawkins, D. P. (2004). Coming to terms with coparenting: Implications of definition and measurement. *Journal of Adult Development, 11*, 165–178.

von Bertalanffy, L. (1968). *General system theory: Foundations, development, applications.* New York: Braziller.

Yu, J. J., Lucero-Liu, A. A., Gamble, W. C., Taylor, A. R., Christensen, D. H., and Modry-Mandell, K. L. (2008). Partner effects of Mexican cultural values: The couple and parenting relationships. *Journal of Psychology, 142*, 169–192. doi: 10.3200/JRLP.142.2

6

ATTENTIVE HELPING AS A CULTURAL PRACTICE OF MEXICAN-HERITAGE FAMILIES

Angélica López, Omar Ruvalcaba, and Barbara Rogoff

Introduction

The extensive collaboration and helping often observed among children from Índigenous American and Mexican communities, in both their homes and in research settings, may be based on a value system referred to in Mexico as being *acomedida/o*, which involves attentive helping without being asked. This cultural value system may encourage children's voluntary, spontaneous assistance to others in family and community work in such communities (de Haan, 2001; Delgado-Gaitán, 1987; Orellana, 2001; Paradise, 1996; Tharp *et al.*, 2000; Valenzuela, 1999; Weisner *et al.*, 1988).

Most scholarly discussions cast children's helping as developing with maturation, as an individual characteristic. Research findings indicate that helping is common among very young children and it develops further as children become able to detect subtle cues that someone needs help (Eisenberg and Fabes, 1998; Warneken *et al.*, 2007; Warneken and Tomasello, 2006). This work has primarily involved European American middle-class children. The research seldom considers children's helping in terms of its cultural context, which in some communities involves helping with shared or communal benefit or with reciprocity.

Young children in communities that encourage and expect children to help in everyday mature activities as a matter of contributing to the community may be more prepared to volunteer help and to recognize social cues that someone needs help. Children seem to show more prosocial behavior in communities where such behavior is encouraged and required or expected (Kartner *et al.*, 2010). Our chapter examines community-based aspects of helpfulness as a sociocultural process (Vygotsky, 1978), going beyond individually focused stage models that have characterized most of the research on prosocial development to date (see also López *et al.*, 2012).

In the sections to come, we examine background research on Mexican- and Índigenous-heritage children's helpfulness; we discuss the idea that helping without being asked is a key feature of learning through pitching in to ongoing family and community activities; and we suggest that being attentive is crucial to being able to pitch in appropriately. Then we present findings from interviews exploring the cultural value of helping without being asked—being *acomedida/o*—and its generality across rural and urban communities, migration to the US, and generational changes. We regard attentive helpfulness as part of a larger constellation of cultural practices that may characterize many Índigenous-heritage communities of the Americas. We conclude by putting the value system of being *acomedida/o* in a broader cultural and historical context and by considering implications of cultural differences in children's attentive helpfulness.

Children's Helpfulness in Mexican- and Índigenous-Heritage American Communities Helpfulness at Home

In a number of Mexican rural, Mexican-heritage, Índigenous and Índigenous-heritage communities of the Americas, children often provide help as a way to contribute to the larger community or group (Eriks-Brophy and Crago, 2003; Gaskins, 2000; Goodnow, 2000; Ramírez Sánchez, 2007; Rogoff *et al.*, 2007). Children from a very young age take on helpful responsible roles in family work and sibling care (Alcalá *et al.*, 2014; Coppens *et al.*, 2014; Delgado-Gaitán, 1987; Tharp *et al.*, 2000; Weisner and Gallimore, 1977).

For example, Mexican mothers of Índigenous background reported that their six- to eight-year-old children take initiative and contribute to the family by cooking, helping with younger siblings, and running errands; they provide dependable and capable help in their household. In contrast, Mexican mothers from a nearby professional middle-class community reported that their children take less initiative and make less extensive contributions to household work. These children reportedly focused more exclusively on self-care chores that were not for the benefit of the whole family and they often required inducements to be involved (Alcalá *et al.*, 2014).

Children's helpfulness may relate to community ideologies that treat responsibilities as being shared by the group. In both an Índigenous-heritage and a highly schooled Mexican community, nine- to ten-year-old children viewed household work as a shared family responsibility that children want to take part in. However, it was the children from the Índigenous-heritage community whom mothers reported taking initiative to pitch in to household work. These children also emphasized their shared responsibility with other family members, whereas children from the Mexican highly schooled community contributed less, with less initiative, and more often highlighted their personal, individual contributions (Coppens *et al.*, 2014).

Helpful contributing to shared family responsibilities appears to be more common in Índigenous-heritage communities than in European American middle-class communities (Farver, 1993; Whiting and Edwards, 1988; Whiting and Whiting, 1975). In contrast, European American middle-class children tend to provide help with tasks that are primarily for self-benefit, rather than for the benefit of the whole family (Bowes and Goodnow, 1996; Goodnow and Delaney, 1989; Ochs and Izquierdo, 2009). In middle-class communities, it is often considered unfair for an individual to be responsible for work that others create (Goodnow, 1998; Ochs and Kremer-Sadlik, 2013; Warton and Goodnow, 1991, 1995). Chores are usually assigned and children are sometimes paid, in an effort to teach responsibility and work life (Alcalá *et al.*, 2014; Furnham and Kirkcaldy, 2000). These family and community arrangements may discourage initiative in helping out.

Helpfulness at School

Índigenous-heritage and Mexican-heritage children often try to be helpful in classroom settings (Gaskins, 2000; López *et al.*, 2012), although such behavior may be penalized. In school settings in the US and Mexico, teachers often require children to work alone, or if they use cooperative learning, they often take charge of how children collaborate by dividing tasks among cooperative groups (Au and Mason, 1981; de Haan, 1999, 2001; Mehan, 1985; Philips, 1983). Children are discouraged from collaborating and provided few opportunities to help adults.

Nonetheless, helping may be a primary form of classroom interaction for many Índigenous-heritage and Mexican-heritage students (Mercado, 2001; Trueba and Delgado-Gaitán, 1985). For example, Inuit children often share information in order to help their peers (Eriks-Brophy and Crago, 2003). In Los Angeles, Mexican- and Central American-heritage children who often pitch in to ongoing activities in their household often offered and sometimes pleaded to help in the classroom, although this contrasted with many teachers' expectations and ideology (Orellana, 2001; Orellana et al., 2003).

Helpfulness in Research Situations

In a number of research situations, Índigenous American, Mexican, and Mexican-heritage children have been found to engage more collaboratively than other children. A more cooperative orientation while playing games has been noted among Mexican-heritage than European-heritage children (Knight and Kagan, 1977; Knight et al., 1982; Widaman and Kagan, 1987). US Mexican-heritage children who are likely to be familiar with Índigenous cultural practices collaborated and spontaneously helped each other more while folding origami figures or constructing a puzzle, compared with European American and US Mexican-heritage children whose mothers had extensive experience with Western schooling (Correa-Chávez, 2011; López et al., 2012; Mejía-Arauz et al., 2007). Mexican-heritage children from regions with Índigenous history more often attempted to become collaboratively involved in their sibling's toy-building activity than did Mexican-heritage children whose parents had extensive experience with Western schooling (Silva et al., 2010).

Similarly, pairs of Navajo children who were teaching a younger child how to play a researcher-designed game, remained actively engaged more often than European American children, even when their partner took the leading role in instructing the younger child. In contrast, the European American children more often became sidetracked to the point of going off task if they were not in charge (Ellis and Gauvain, 1992). The Navajo children were also more likely to extend or support information given by their peer to instruct the younger child, evidencing attentive collaboration, whereas European American children more often repeated their partner's statements or made comments unrelated to their peer's previous statements.

Thus, children from Mexican- and Índigenous-heritage American backgrounds seem to be especially helpful at home, in school, and in research settings. We speculate that children's helpfulness across these settings is encouraged by parental and community support and expectations for children to be present, observe closely, and contribute to productive activities.

Helpfulness is a Key Feature of Learning by Observing and Pitching in

Attentive helpfulness is a central feature of a theoretical model of organizing learning: *Learning by Observing and Pitching In* (Rogoff, 2014; Rogoff et al., 2007; Rogoff et al., 2003). Learning by Observing and Pitching In was formerly referred to as learning through intent community participation, and is a form of guided participation (Rogoff, 2003), influenced by sociocultural theory (Vygotsky, 1978). In Learning by Observing and Pitching In, children are included in the wide range of activities of the community and contribute to ongoing collaborative endeavors. This approach to organizing learning appears to be particularly prevalent in Índigenous communities of the Americas and Mexican-heritage communities, especially where Western schooling has not been prevalent.

Learning how to pitch in with initiative, with the demeanor and skills necessary to contribute and be part of the community, is an important aspect of this way of organizing children's learning and development (Rogoff *et al.*, 2014a). Children are expected to pay attention in order to contribute, and to learn through their contributions (Chavajay, 1993; Paradise and Rogoff, 2009). In turn, such inclusion seems to encourage children's active interest and attentiveness in knowing how to contribute to family and community work.

The Importance of Attentiveness in Being Able to Pitch in Appropriately

In some Índigenous communities, the organization of family and community endeavors involves multi-way collaborations in which participants attentively pitch in when they see something that needs to be done (Lamphere, 1977; Sindell, 1997). For example, Pelletier (1970) described a form of horizontal collaboration in an Índigenous community in Canada where everyone contributes as they are needed, learning through "observing and feeling" (p. 21), in the process of participating in ongoing community life. We argue that such attentiveness to what is going on is a crucial feature of helping without being asked. To know when and how to contribute to ongoing endeavors, it is essential to be alert to surrounding events.

Observation has long been regarded as an important aspect of learning (Bandura, 1977; Rotter, 1954). In particular, observing and listening to events in which one is not directly involved (third party attention) provides children with useful information, such as new vocabulary, how to make things, and how to interpret an ambiguous situation (Akhtar, 2005; Akhtar *et al.*, 2001; Barton and Tomasello, 1991; Correa-Chávez and Rogoff, 2009; Feiring *et al.*, 1983; Ochs, 1988; Oshima-Takane *et al.*, 1996). Observing and listening-in on surrounding events takes place worldwide.

Although it occurs worldwide, learning by attending to nearby events seems to be more prevalent in communities where children are included in a broad range of community events. Guatemalan Mayan children and Mexican-heritage children whose families are likely to have familiarity with Índigenous practices more often attended keenly to an interaction not directed toward them, than did children from families with extensive Western schooling (Correa-Chávez and Rogoff, 2009; López *et al.*, 2010; Silva *et al.*, 2010).

Children from families with extensive schooling may often narrow their attention to conform to the attention pattern common in schools, where the teacher often manages children's attention to focus them on the teacher, and discourages attention to surrounding events such as the actions of other children. Mothers who have extensive experience with schooling, including those with roots in Índigenous American communities, also tend to use such management practices associated with schooling (Chavajay, 2006; Chavajay and Rogoff, 2002; Laosa, 1980; Rogoff *et al.*, 1993; see also Paradise *et al.*, 2014).

Traditionally, in Índigenous communities of the Americas, observation and listening have been a prevalent method of learning and participation in family and community work and social activities (Chamoux, 1992; Corona and Pérez, 2005; de Haan, 1999; de León, 2000; Rogoff, 2003; Tsethlikai and Rogoff, 2013). Some Mazahua (Índigenous Mexican) adults reported that observation is a form of learning that is more crucial and direct than giving explanations, especially when dealing with complex skills and knowledge (de Haan, 1999).

In many communities of Mexico and other parts of Latin America, a cultural value of being *acomedida/o* may encourage children to be attentive and helpful. In the next section, we examine how Mexican and Mexican-heritage adults define this concept, and their observations of the settings where it is most likely to be used.

Interviews Regarding Being Acomedida/o

Many Mexicans whose interviews we report below defined being *acomedida/o* as spontaneously and attentively contributing to others' work, pitching in without being asked, by acting on an opportunity to contribute (also see López *et al.*, 2012). The cultural value of being *acomedida/o* may help explain the extent of collaboration and helping among many Mexican-heritage children.

The notion of being *acomedida/o* has rarely been the topic of academic discourse. The sole exception that we have been able to find is the work of González (2001; 2006), who described being *acomedida/o* as being able to accommodate to one's surroundings and make oneself useful to be able to fit in anywhere. She indicated that Mexican parents commonly teach children to be *acomedida/o(s)* wherever they may find themselves and to be aware of their surroundings and interpret sometimes hidden meanings of what is said. González suggested that an aspect of being *acomedida/o* is being able to empathize with others' needs in order to work collectively.

We conducted informal interviews with 34 adults in Guadalajara México and in several cities in California to examine how people conceptualize being *acomedida/o*, how they describe changes in practice with migration to the US, and how they believe this practice has changed across generations. Interviews were conducted by the first author. Participants were recruited through convenience and snowball sampling.

Guadalajara participants included 9 females and 8 males (ages 21–72) whose schooling ranged from a high school degree to a doctorate. Occupations included: taxi driver, nurse, radiologist, research assistant, university administrator, professor, and a retired watch maker. Participants residing in California were all of Mexican or Mexican-heritage backgrounds and included 9 females and 8 males (ages 26–76) with schooling that ranged from second grade to PhD. Occupations included: gardener, babysitter, janitor, professor, student, manager, truck driver, and retired blue collar workers (cannery and janitorial service). The responses to the questions were similar in the two nations.

How is Being Acomedida/o Conceptualized and Encouraged?

Respondents consistently reported that in being *acomedida/o*, one helps spontaneously without thinking of getting anything in return. It differs from simply helping, in that helping can be in response to a request or even feeling obliged to help; in being *acomedida/o* the desire to help comes from within. Almost all (33 of the 34) participants provided definitions along the following lines:

> *[Acomedirse] es ayudar, es estar dispuesto a ayudar a cualquier persona en cualquier momento, entregarte así de fácil, este sin tener nada a cambio, o desinteresadamente.*

> [Acomedirse] is helping, it's to be willing to help any person at any moment, to devote oneself, without getting anything in return, or without self-interest.
>
> *(42-year-old male radiologist, Guadalajara)*

> *[Acomedirse es] ayudar cuando hay necesidad sin que te lo pidan.*

> [Acomedirse is] to help when it's needed without being asked.
>
> *(38-year-old male professor, California)*

> (When asked about how *acomedirse* differs from helping) *Si está uno obligado a ayudar, no lo va hacer uno así de muy buena gana. Pero [ser acomedido] tiene que ser más voluntario de uno, que*

le salga. A veces al [ser acomedido] es engrandecer uno mismo. Dice, 'voy a ayudar a aquella persona, no importa si reconoce o no reconoce.'

If one is obliged to help, help will not be given in a generous spirit. But [being *acomedido*] has to be more voluntary, it needs to emerge from oneself. Sometimes [being *acomedido*] results in strengthening oneself. One says, 'I'm going to help that person, it doesn't matter if they acknowledge it or not.'

(72-year-old, male, retired watch maker, Guadalajara)

All 34 interviewees stressed that being *acomedida/o* has to do with values inculcated early in childhood. One participant explained,

Mi madre me enseñó a saber ayudar. Eso fue el primer conocimiento que yo tuve. Me dio responsabilidad desde temprana edad.

My mother taught me to know when to pitch in. That was one of the first things I learned. She gave me responsibilities at a young age.

(54-year-old male taxi driver, Guadalajara)

What is Involved in Being Acomedida/o?

All respondents indicated that being *acomedida/o* is an important value in their lives, and two respondents expressed that being *acomedida/o* connects qualities that makes one human, or "having human quality" (34-year-old male taxi driver in Guadalajara). Twelve out of 35 participants (35%) linked being *acomedida/o* to the idea of humility, *respeto* (mutual responsibility and consideration, as described by Garcia, 1996; Lorente Fernández, 2010; Ruvalcaba *et al.*, in preparation; Valdés, 1996), being *educada/o* (showing integrity, responsibility, and sociality, as described by Burciaga, 2007; Valenzuela, 1999), and being *buena gente* which is a "sense of interdependence and the desire to put the needs of 'others' before oneself" (Pimentel, 2009, p. 175). For example, participants stated:

Ser acomedida es, para mí es una forma de respeto*; como llegar a la casa de alguien y ofrecerse a ayudar.*

Being *acomedida*, for me is a form of *respeto* (respectful consideration); like to arrive at someone's house and offer to help.

(26-year-old female social worker, California)

Para mí es muy importante. Es un pilar para mí porque como yo tuve esa educación de ser agradecido y ayudar a los demás . . . para mí sí es muy importante por eso a mí sí me molesta mucho que la gente no sea acomedida.

For me it's very important. It's a pillar for me because I had that *educación* to be grateful and to help others. It's important to me and yes, it bothers me very much when others are not *acomedidas/os*.

(42-year-old male radiologist, Guadalajara)

Most respondents (27 out of 34, 79%) also emphasized that being *acomedida/o* involves initiative.

Yo creo que ser acomedido es tener, como sobre todo, la iniciativa, o sea, como no esperar a que te lo pidan, sino tu tener esa iniciativa para hacerlo.

> I think that being *acomedido* is to have, above all, initiative, that is to say, not waiting to be asked, but having the initiative to do it.
>
> *(29-year-old female research assistant, Guadalajara)*

In order to be *acomedida/o*, it is also necessary to be aware of one's surroundings and know when and how to pitch in. Many respondents (19 out of 34, 56 %) included attentiveness to one's surroundings as essential to being *acomedida/o*.

> *Se me hace un proceso muy complejo que como casi adivinarles el pensamiento a los demás. Estar atento, siempre estar listo de lo que necesitan.*
>
> It's a very complex process, you almost have to guess what others are thinking. Being alert; always being ready to do what is needed.
>
> *(27-year-old female research assistant, Guadalajara)*

> *. . . pero también tener la visión y la sensibilidad de saber cuándo es el momento para hacer las cosas y además, sí, tienes que a veces tener como conocimiento de la situación porque si yo quiero ser acomedida en algo pero no sé ni de que se trata pues a veces estorbas más de lo que ayudas.*
>
> . . . but also to have the vision and sensitivity to know when is the time to do things and also, yes, you do need sometimes to have knowledge of the situation, because if I want to be *acomedido* in something but I don't even know what it's about, well sometimes you get in the way more than you help.
>
> *(29-year-old female research assistant, Guadalajara)*

Does Being Acomedida/o Differ Across Generations, in Rural Versus Cosmopolitan Regions of Mexico, or with Migration to the US?

Most participants described the value of being *acomedida/o* changing across generations or being less prevalent with youth. Out of the 31 respondents who reported on changes across time, 25 (81%) expressed that the practice is less common among the youth but that it would also depend on the parents. (The other six respondents (19%) felt that there was no difference or that it depends on the person and the upbringing.)

When asked if they felt there was a difference in the prevalence of being *acomedida/o* in different regions of Mexico, such as in a small town or in a metropolitan city, 81% of the 32 respondents to the question said that people in small towns were more *acomedidas/os* (Three respondents (9%) reported there not being a difference and three (9%) mentioned that it depends, or did not know whether or not there was a difference.) Here are some examples:

> *Definitivamente sí, hay diferencias increíbles porque en el rancho se nota la diferencia y gente es como, y no quiero decir que es gente pobre porque también hay gente con lana, pero sí, gente más sencilla, entonces hay gente con más de esa actitud.*
>
> Definitely, there are incredible differences because in the countryside, you can see the difference and people are like, and I don't want to say poor people because there's also people with money, but yes, the people are less complicated, so there's people with more of that attitude.
>
> *(29-year-old female research assistant, Guadalajara)*

Pienso que en la cuidad se da menos, como la gente anda tan a la carrera y tiene miles de actividades y como que ya no se da tan espontáneamente eso. A diferencia de las poblaciones más pequeñas, yo creo que sí se da más.

I think there's less of it in the city, because people run around in such a hurry and have thousands of activities and it's like it doesn't occur as spontaneously. In contrast, with smaller towns, I think that yes, it occurs more.

(52-year-old female professor, Guadalajara)

Some respondents (13 of them, 38%) speculated spontaneously on several reasons that being *acomedida/o* is more common in rural areas. For example, both of the respondents quoted above reported that the pace of life in the countryside allows one to notice when people are in need. The fact that people in small towns know each other more was also something commonly mentioned as to why people in such settings are perhaps more *acomedidas/os*.

Respondents also mentioned individual variation depending on the family, emphasizing the importance of socialization of this value:

Puede ser una ciudad grande y puede ser alguien que sí le gusta ser acomedido. O puede ser también un rancho chiquito que también no son acomedidos. A lo mejor es la educación de la familia.

It could be a big city and it could be someone that does like to be *acomedido*. Or it could be some from a small village but they could also be not *acomedidos*. Maybe it's the *educación* of the family.

(60-year-old female janitor, California)

Most of the respondents with experience in the US (15 of 17, 88%) reported that the value is diminished among Mexican-heritage people in the US (The other two said that it depends.) One respondent reported,

Aquí no creo que tanto, porque aquí, como cuando yo llegue tenía 14 años y otros, como mis amigas, otros adolescentes, ellos no tenían que hacer quehaceres, no tenían que hacer muchas cosas, entonces pienso que no se les daba el valor de ser acomedida o a lo mejor ni siquiera conocían de la palabra, del concepto. Pero allá en el pueblo, allá sí, este era muy normal que mucha gente te dijera, "Mira, que acomedida es," o "Si sabe acomedirse." Así era algo que esperaban que fueras pero aquí pos obviamente no igual.

Here, I don't think so much, because when I arrived here I was 14 years old and others, like my friends, other teenagers, they didn't have to do chores, they didn't have to do much, so I don't think that they had that value of being *acomedida/o* or maybe they didn't even know of the word or concept. But back in el pueblo, yes, it was very normal for people to tell you, 'Look how *acomedida* she is,' or 'That one does know how to be *acomedida*.' So that was something that was expected but here it's obviously not the same.

(30-year-old female graduate student, California)

Most of the respondents reporting differences in values also mentioned that although there might be conflicting values in the US, transmission of the value would also depend on how it is inculcated by parents.

Depende en cómo se han criado también porque si no se han criado así . . .

It depends on how they were raised because if they weren't raised like that . . .

(69-year-old female retired janitor, California)

In sum, the participants in our interviews reported that being *acomedida/o*—being attentively helpful without being asked—is an important feature of being human, engaging in the family and community with consideration and initiative. It is commonly an important aspect of raising children in rural villages of Mexico, and also in urban settings in Mexico and among immigrants from Mexico to the US, although it seems to diminish in the urban settings and upon immigration.

The Historical Context of Helpfulness

The cultural value as well as cultural change of being *acomedida/o* described by the interviewees fits into a larger cultural historical context. We speculate that the importance of being *acomedida/o* in Mexican villages and small towns may fit with the collaborative Índigenous histories of the rural regions of Mexico around Guadalajara and many other parts of Mexico.

Indigenous Practices and Community Responsibility in Rural Mexico in the Face of "Modernization"

Although many rural Mexicans and Mexican immigrants to the US do not consider themselves Índigenous, many of their communities were Índigenous communities in past centuries, and a number of Índigenous practices persist (Frye, 1996; López, 2007; López *et al.*, 2010; Rogoff *et al.*, 2014b; Urrieta, 2003; Vigil, 1998).

In the early 20th century, Mexico's nationalistic agenda emphasized "modernizing" the nation by means of Western schooling and other institutions that involved cutting ties with Índigenous languages and traditions (Bonfil Batalla, 1988; Stavenhagen, 1988). During 1916–1935, beginning with the *Congresos Panamericanos del Niño* (Panamerican Congress on The Child), discussions on childhood revolved around "improving the race" (Corona Caraveo, 2003). This effort was directly related to efforts to "modernize" the population, by focusing on changing children both through Western schooling and home values (Iglesias *et al.*, 1995).

With the efforts to "modernize" the population, children's education emphasized individuality, without collective values (Corona Caraveo, 2003). Childrearing practices in the middle class emphasized child-focused activities and age segregation. Childhood began to be treated as a time of dependency on parents, with children incapable of contributing to their own care or to production activities, as portrayed in official documents issued by UNICEF that have inspired public policies, practices, and ideas (Hecht, 1998; Ramírez Sánchez, 2007; Strathern, 1988).

These ideas and practices differed radically from the education of children in rural and farm communities in which members defined themselves in terms of collective work and solidarity. According to authors of this time (1916–1935), there was no clear differentiation between adult and child work, in contrast with the upper and middle class who had instituted specialized activities (Corona Caraveo, 2003). Recent social welfare programs in Mexico continue to try to "correct" childrearing approaches in many communities that value community and family helpfulness (Escobar Latapí, 2009).

Over the past century, the identity of many rural towns changed from Índigenous to *campesino* or peasant (Urrieta, 2003; Vigil, 1998). However, families that remained in rural towns have been more likely to maintain Índigenous practices than families that migrated to cities and had more access to schooling and other Western practices. This continuity may include the value system related to being *acomedida/o*.

Voluntary Collaboration and Helping as a Value

Being *acomedida/o* seems to fit the organization of Índigenous communities, which appear to emphasize collaboration, collective action, and horizontal social relations, where the value system is for everybody to help out (Corona Caraveo, 2003; Pelletier, 1970). Although the Náhuatl concept of *tequio* has also been used to describe non-voluntary labor or tribute, this concept that is prevalent in Índigenous communities of Mexico has been described as a way that work is organized to benefit the collective. In this sense, it involves service or work for a community project such as constructing roads, other public service projects, or the introduction of schooling, potable water, or clinics. *Tequio* has been essential for marginal communities because of its public investment and because it has been one of the most vigorous institutions for perseverance and solidity of the community (Chamoux *et al.*, 2011; Flores *et al.*, in preparation; Warman, 2003).

This collective action is often accompanied by individual initiative (Alcalá *et al.*, 2014; Paradise and Rogoff, 2009; Rogoff, 2003). For example, Louise Lamphere, in her 1977 book on her work with the Navajo, indicated that Navajo community-mindedness is based on people's voluntary efforts—the success of collective community life is based on individual autonomy. People pitch in and expect others to pitch in, with a non-interference approach that respects and depends on individual decisions. In attentive helpfulness, children act with initiative and also have a sense of interdependence to help others (Coppens *et al.*, 2014; Kartner *et al.*, 2010; Mosier and Rogoff, 2003; Rogoff, 2003).

The importance of collective action was underlined in a study of family lives in a *Nahua* community of Tlaxcala, Mexico, where children and youth claim not to be working even when heavily involved in family work (Ramírez Sánchez, 2007). The youth refer to such "helping" as a matter of being part of the family; "working" is paid work outside the family. Childhood is part of a system of reciprocity and exchange where everyone helps members of their family, especially those in the same household. The definition of a good child in this community includes "being a child that helps out."

In our interviews, one respondent explained a similar idea: "*Es como una parte que te inculcan, como parte de tu comportamiento para que tu imagen sea agradable ante los demás* (It is like a part that they inculcate, like a part of your behavior so that your image is pleasant to others)." She further explained that people do not want to be labeled or want their children to be labeled as *desacomedida/o* (un*acomedida/o*).

In several Índigenous communities of Mexico, attentive helpfulness is associated more broadly with an idea of working and helping as an important aspect of human dignity and respect. For example, work and *icnoliz* (the Nahuatl word for respect) go hand in hand, as the reward of work is to give respect as well (Lorente Fernández, 2010; Ramírez Sánchez, 2007). Historically the concept of communal labor among the Nahua emphasized contribution to the community as humans' essential role in the universe (Chamoux *et al.*, 2011). Similarly, in a Mixe community, the dignity of work is regarded as what makes people human (Cardoso Jiménez, 2008).

Summary

This chapter puts children's helpfulness in a sociocultural context. Widespread research has focused on developmental changes in helping, but has hardly addressed cultural aspects of helping. We report findings that suggest that helpfulness varies among distinct cultural communities. We argue that cultural differences in helpfulness may be especially important when attentive helping *without being asked* is considered.

A large literature indicates that children from Índigenous backgrounds of the Americas are particularly helpful at home and also in research settings and in school. We suggest that their helpfulness is often characterized by initiative, helping without being asked, alert to what is going on around them. This form of spontaneous helping is an important feature of a hypothesized cultural tradition of Learning by Observing and Pitching in, and may connect with a cultural value system that promotes a collaborative approach. We argue that helping without being asked is part of a larger constellation of cultural practices that may characterize Índigenous-heritage communities of the Americas. Helping and working are regarded as contributing to human dignity in several Índigenous Mexican communities.

To examine the role of cultural values regarding helping without being asked, we discuss responses of Mexican and Mexican-heritage US adults to an interview regarding the Mexican cultural value of being *acomedida/o*. The respondents reported that being *acomedida/o* is characterized by helping without being asked, alert to what is needed and pitching in with initiative, based on a desire to contribute. They noted that children are commonly encouraged to be *acomedida/o*, although this value system is less commonly seen in Mexican cities and in the US than in rural Mexico, and it is decreasing among the younger generation.

Such historical changes make sense in the context of cultural changes across the past century in Mexico, where rural and, especially, Índigenous practices have been discouraged. It also relates to cultural contact, as rural populations of Mexico migrate to cities in Mexico and the US. With such changes, children's helping without being asked may decrease with widespread changes in the circumstances of families' and communities' lives. Their helping without being asked nonetheless still appears to be more common than among European-heritage children, who have been the main participants in research on helping.

Future Directions and Challenges

Being seen as *acomedida/o* can thus be considered a measure of success in many Índigenous American communities and in many Mexican immigrant communities. However, it may go unrecognized within mainstream European American institutions.

This "pedagogy of the home" is part of culture-specific ways of organizing learning that are ways of knowing; ways that have also been noted in Latino students in postsecondary education (Delgado Bernal *et al.*, 2006). Contributing to a community or being useful to one's people are intrinsic rewards that may be stronger incentives for learning than extrinsic rewards, in some communities (Pimentel, 2009). Further research on children's helping without being asked will help to understand better the circumstances that support this cultural value.

Policy Implications

There are several implications for practice and policy: In particular, teachers of young children may be more able to support children from Mexican-heritage and some other backgrounds if they understand the cultural importance of helping out. If they see it as a sign of maturity rather than misinterpreting it as cheating or depending on others, this would help them interpret and support their students' development.

Further, we speculate that making use of such students' interest in helping each other may be an important tool to motivate their academic achievement. In line with this speculation, Latino university students' motivation to succeed in college was supported by opportunities to help others and to contribute to their community, in a collaborative student society focused on academic success (organised by two of us, AL and OR).

We speculate that encouraging children's and youth's interest in helping other people would be of benefit to people of all backgrounds and to their communities. In discussing our team's work on cultural differences in collaboration and helpfulness, we have been asked by a vice president in a prominent New York firm, complaining, "So how do I get my staff to work together, to collaborate and help each other?" Despite pressures not to collaborate, many community endeavors (including workplaces) would benefit from people becoming skilled in collaboration and attentive helpfulness—learning to engage in a way of interacting that we believe develops through values and practices supportive of attentive helpfulness in childhood.

References

Akhtar, N. (2005). The robustness of learning through overhearing. *Developmental Science, 8,* 199–209.

Akhtar, N., Jipson, A., and Callanan, M.A. (2001). Learning words through overhearing. *Child Development, 72,* 416–430.

Alcalá, L., Rogoff, B., Mejía-Arauz, R., Coppens, A. D., Roberts, A. D. (2014). Children's initiative in contributions to family work in Índigenous-heritage and cosmopolitan communities in México. *Human Development, 57,* 150–161.

Au, K., and Mason, J. (1981). Social organizational factors in learning to read: The balance of rights hypothesis. *Reading Research Quarterly, 17,* 115–152.

Bandura, A. (1977). Self-efficacy: Toward a unifying theory of behavioral change. *Psychology Review, 84,* 191–215.

Barton, M. E., and Tomasello, M. (1991). Joint attention and conversation in mother-infant-sibling triads. *Child Development, 62,* 517–29.

Bonfil Batalla, G. (1988). Panorama étnico y cultural de México [Ethnic and cultural panorama of Mexico]. In R. Stavenhagen (Ed.), *Política cultural para un país multiétnico [Cultural policy for a multiethnic country]* (pp. 61–68). Mexico City: Secretaría de Educación Pública.

Bowes, J. M., and Goodnow, J. J. (1996). Work for home, school, or labor force. *Psychological Bulletin, 119,* 300–321.

Burciaga, M.R. (2007). Chicana Ph.D. students living *nepantla: Educación* and aspirations beyond the doctorate. Unpublished dissertation manuscript.

Cardoso Jiménez, R. (2008). *Wejën-Kajën (brotar, despertar): Noción de educación en el pueblo Mixe, estado de Oaxaca.* Unpublished master's thesis.

Chamoux, M. N. (1992). Aprendiendo de otro modo [Learning in other ways]. In M. N. Chamoux, *Trabajo, técnicas y aprendizaje en el México indígena* [Work, skills and learning in Índigenous Mexico] (pp. 73–93). México City: Centro de Investigaciones y Estudios Superiores en Antropología Social, Ediciones de la Casa Chata.

Chamoux, M.N., Flores, R., López, A., Lorente y Fernandez, D., Perez Martinez, E., and Urrieta, L. (2011). *Collaborative collaboration, el Trueque, Acomedido as Respect, the Cargo, Respeto entre los Nahuas, and Supervivencias de prácticas mesoaméricas* and the role of history in intent comunity participation. Result of a workshop help in Austin, Texas, February 11–13, 2001. N.P.

Chavajay, P. (1993). Afterword: Independent analysis of cultural variations and similarities in San Pedro and Salt Lake. *Monographs of the Society for Research in Child Development, 58*(8, serial no. 236), 162–165.

Chavajay, P. (2006). How Mayan mothers with different amounts of schooling organize a problem-solving discussion with children. *International Journal of Behavioral Development, 30,* 371–382.

Chavajay, P., and Rogoff, B. (2002). Schooling and traditional collaborative social organization of problem schooling by Mayan mothers and children. *Developmental Psychology, 38,* 55–66.

Coppens, A.D., Alcalá, L., Mejía-Arauz, R., Rogoff, B. (2014). Children's initiative in family household work in Mexico. *Human Development, 57,* 116–130.

Corona, Y., and Pérez, C. (2005, June). *The enrichment of community relations through children's participation in ceremonial life*. Paper presented at "Childhoods 2005: Children and youth in emerging and transforming societies." Oslo, Norway.

Corona Caraveo, Y. (2003). Diversidad de infancias: Retos y compromisos [Diversity of childhoods: Challenges and commitments]. *Tramas, 20*, 13–31.

Correa-Chávez, M. (2011, October). The organization of participation and communication in US Mexican heritage siblings' joint interaction. Presented at the Society for Advancement of Chicanos and Native Americans in Science Meeting. San Jose, CA.

Correa-Chávez, M., and Rogoff, B. (2009). Children's attention to interactions directed to others: Guatemalan Mayan and European American patterns. *Developmental Psychology, 45*, 630–641.

de Haan, M. (1999). *Learning as cultural practice: How children learn in a Mexican Mazahua community*. Amsterdam: Thela Thesis.

de Haan, M. (2001). Intersubjectivity in models of learning and teaching: Reflections from a study of teaching and learning in a Mexican Mazahua community. In S. Chaiklin (Ed.), *The theory and practice of cultural–historical psychology* (pp. 174–199). Aarhus, Denmark: Aarhus University Press.

de León, L. (2000). The emergent participant: Interactive patterns in the socialization of Tzotzil (Mayan) infants. *Journal of Linguistic Anthropology, 8*, 131–161.

Delgado Bernal, D. (2006). Learning and living pedagogies of the home: The mestiza consciousness of Chicana students. In D. Delgado Bernal, A. C. Elenes, F. Godinez, and S. Villenas (Eds.), *Chicana/Latina education in everyday life: Feminista perspectives on pedagogy and epistemology* (pp. 132–133). Albany: State University of New York Press.

Delgado-Gaitán, C. (1987). Traditions and transition the learning process of Mexican children: An ethnographic view. In G. and L. Spindler (Eds.), *Interpretive ethnography of education: At home and abroad* (pp. 333–362). New Jersey: Erlbaum.

Eisenberg, N., and Fabes, R. A. (1998). Prosocial development. In N. Eisenberg and W. Damon (Eds.), *Handbook of child psychology: Social, emotional, and personality development* (pp. 701–78). New York: Wiley and Sons.

Ellis, S., and Gauvain, M. (1992). Social and cultural influences on children's collaborative interactions. In L.T. Wineger and J. Valsiner (Eds.), *Children's development within social context (vol 2)* (pp. 155–180). Hillsdale, NJ: Erlbaum.

Eriks-Brophy, A., and Crago, M. (2003). Cultural or linguistic? Evidence from Inuit and non-Inuit teachers of Nunavik. *Anthropology and Education Quarterly, 34*, 396–419.

Escobar Latapí, A. (2009). Mexico's Progresa-Oportunidades programs: Where do we go from here? In M. J. Bane and R. Zentero (Eds.), *Poverty and poverty alleviation strategies in North America* (pp.203–232). Cambridge, MA: Harvard University Press.

Farver, J. A. (1993). Cultural differences in scaffolding pretend play: A comparison of American and Mexican mother-child and sibling-child pairs. In K. MacDonald (Ed.), *Parent-child play: Descriptions and implications*. SUNY series, children's play in society (pp. 349–366). Albany, NY: State University of New York Press.

Feiring, C., Lewis, M., and Starr, M. D. (1983, April). *Indirect effects and infants' reaction to strangers*. Presented at meetings of the Society for Research in Child Development, Detroit.

Flores, R., Urrieta, L., Chamoux, M.N., Lorente y Fernandez, D., and López, A. (in prep). *History and cultural practices in the analysis of intent community participation*. Unpublished Manuscript.

Frye, D. (1996). *Indians into Mexicans: History and identity in a Mexican town*. Austin, TX: University of Texas Press.

Furnham, A., and Kirkcaldy, B. (2000). Economic socialization: German parents' perceptions and implementation of allowances to educate children. *European Psychologist, 5*, 202–215.

Garcia, W. (1996). *Respeto*: A Mexican base for interpersonal relationships. In W. Gudykunst, T. Ting-Toomey, and T. Nishida (Eds.), *Communication in personal relationships across cultures* (pp. 137–155). Thousand Oaks, CA: Sage.

Gaskins, S. (2000). Children's daily activities in a Mayan village. *Cross-Cultural Research, 34*, 375–389.

González, N. (2001). *I am my language: Discourses of women and children in the borderlands*. Tucson: The University of Arizona Press.

González, N. (2006). Testimonios of border identities: Una mujer acomedida cabe donde quiera [An *acomedida* woman fits in anywhere]. In D. Delgado Bernal, A.C. Elenes, F. Godinez, and S. Villenas (Eds) *Chicana/Latina education in everyday life* (pp. 197–213). Albany, NY: SUNY Press.

Goodnow, J. J. (1998). Beyond the overall balance: The significance of particular tasks and procedures for perceptions of fairness in distributions of household work. *Social Justice Research, 11,* 359–376.

Goodnow, J. J. (2000). On being responsible for more than you have directly caused. In W. van Haaften, T. Wren, and A. Telling (Eds.), *Moral sensibilities and education, vol. 2—The schoolchild* (pp. 35–59). London: Concorde.

Goodnow, J. J., and Delaney, S. (1989). Children's household work. *Journal of Applied Developmental Psychology, 10,* 209–226.

Hecht, T. (1998). *At home in the street: Street children of Northeast Brazil.* Cambridge: Cambridge University Press.

Iglesias, S., Villagra, H., and Barrientos, L. (1995). *Un viaje a través de los espejos de los congresos panamericanos del niño* [A trip through the mirrors of the Pan American child congresses.] In *Derecho a tener derecho: Infancia, derechos y política social en América Latina y el Caribe*[The right to have rights: Childhood, rights, and social policy in Latin America and the Caribbean]. Unicef/Instituto Interamerico del Niño/Instituto Ayrton Senna.

Kartner, J., Keller, K., and Chaudhary, N. (2010). Cognitive and social influences on early prosocial behavior in two sociocultural contexts. *Developmental Psychology, 46,* 904–914.

Knight, G. P., and Kagan, S. (1977). Development of prosocial and competitive behaviors in Anglo-American and Mexican-American children. *Child Development, 48,* 1385–1394.

Knight, G. P., Nelson, W., Kagan, S., and Gumbiner, J. (1982). Cooperative-competitive social orientation and school achievement among Anglo-American and Mexican-American children. *Contemporary Educational Psychology, 7,* 97–106.

Lamphere, L. (1977). *To run after them: Cultural and social bases of cooperation in a Navajo community.* Tucson: University of Arizona Press.

Laosa, L. M. (1980). Maternal teaching strategies and cognitive styles in Chicano families. *Journal of Educational Psychology, 72,* 45–54.

López, A., Correa-Chávez, M., Rogoff, B., Gutiérrez, K. (2010). Attention to instruction directed to another by U.S. Mexican-heritage children of varying cultural backgrounds. *Developmental Psychology, 46,* 593–601.

López, A., Rogoff, B., Najafi, B., and Mejía-Arauz, R. (2012). Collaboration and helpfulness as cultural practices. In J. Valsiner (Ed.), *Handbook of cultural psychology* (pp. 869–884). NY: Oxford University Press.

López, A. A. (2007). *The farmworkers' journey.* Berkeley: University of California Press.

Lorente Fernández, D. (2010). *Ser respetuoso es ser "persona": el niño y la pedagogía moral de los nahuas del centro de Mexico.* [Being respectful is being a "person": the child and moral pedagogy of the Nahuas of Central Mexico.] Unpublished manuscript.

Mehan, H. (1985). The structure of classroom discourse. In T. A. van Dijk (Ed.), *Handbook of discourse analysis* (pp. 120–131). London: Academic.

Mejía-Arauz, R., Rogoff, B., Dexter, A., and Najafi, B. (2007). Cultural variation in children's social organization. *Child Development, 78,* 1001–1014.

Mosier, C. E., and Rogoff, B. (2003). Privileged treatment of toddlers: Cultural aspects of individual choice and responsibility. *Developmental Psychology, 39,* 1047–1060.

Ochs, E. (1988). *Culture and language development: Language acquisition and language socialization in a Samoan village.* Cambridge, MA: Cambridge University Press.

Ochs, E., and Izquierdo, C. (2009). Responsibility in childhood. *Ethos, 37,* 391–413.

Ochs, E., and Kremer-Sadlik, T. (Eds.). (2013). *Fast-forward family: Home, work, and relationships in middle-class America.* Los Angeles: University of California Press.

Orellana, M. F. (2001). The work kids do: Mexican and Central American immigrant children's contributions to households and schools in California. *Harvard Educational Review, 71,* 366–389.

Orellana, M. F., Dorner, L., and Pulido, L. (2003). Accessing assets: Immigrant youth's work as family translators or "para-phrasers". *Social Problems, 50,* 505–524.

Oshima-Takane, Y., Goodz, E., and Deverensky, J. L. (1996). Birth-order effects on early language development. *Child Development, 67,* 621–634.

Paradise, R. (1996). Passivity or tacit collaboration: Mazahua interaction in cultural context. *Learning and Instruction*, *6*, 379–389.

Paradise, R., and Rogoff, B. (2009). Side by side: Learning through observing and pitching in. *Ethos*, *37*, 102–138.

Paradise, R., Mejía-Arauz, R., Silva, K.G., Roberts, A.L.D., and Rogoff, B. (2014). One, two, three, eyes on me! Adults attempting control versus guiding in support of initiative. *Human Development*, *57*, 131–149.

Pelletier, W. (1970). Childhood in an Indian village. In S. Repo (Ed.), *This book is about schools* (pp. 18–31). New York: Pantheon Books.

Pimentel, O. (2009). Disrupting discourse: Introducing Mexicano immigrant success stories. *Reflections: A Journal of Writing, Community Literacy, and Service Learning*, *8*, 171–196.

Ramírez Sánchez, M. A. (2007). "Helping at home": The concept of childhood and work among the *Nahuas* of Tlaxcala, Mexico. In B. Hungerland, M. Liebel, B. Milne, and Wihstutz (Eds.), *Working to be someone: Child focused research and practice with working children* (pp. 87–95). London and Philadelphia: Jessica Kingsley.

Rogoff, B. (2003). *The cultural nature of human development*. NY: Oxford University Press.

Rogoff, B. (2014). Learning by observing and pitching in to family and community endeavors: An orientation. *Human Development*, *57*, 69–81.

Rogoff, B., Najafi, B., and Mejía-Arauz, R. (2014b). Constellations of cultural practices across generations: Indigenous American heritage and learning by observing and pitching in. *Human Development*, *57*, 2–3.

Rogoff, B., Mistry, J., Göncü, A., and Mosier, C. (1993). Guided participation in cultural activity by toddlers and caregivers. *Monographs for the Society for Research in Child Development*, *58*, (Serial No. 236).

Rogoff, B., Paradise, R., Mejía-Arauz, R., Correa-Chávez, M., and Angelillo, C. (2003). Firsthand learning through intent participation. *Annual Review of Psychology*, *54*, 175–203.

Rogoff, B., Alcalá, L., Coppens, A., López, A., Ruvalcaba, O., and Silva, K. (2014a). Children learning by observing and pitching in in their families and communities. Special Issue of *Human Development*, *57*(2–3), 65–171.

Rogoff, B., Moore, L., Najafi, B., Dexter, A., Correa-Chavez, M., and Solis, J. (2007). Cultural routines and practices. In J. Grusec and P. Hastings (Eds.), *Handbook of socialization* (pp. 225–263). New York, NY: Guilford Press.

Rotter, J. B. (1954). *Social learning and clinical psychology*. Englewood Cliffs, NJ: Prentice-Hall.

Ruvalcaba, O., Rogoff, B., López, A., Correa-Chávez, M., and Gutierrez, K. (in prep). *Children's consideration of others: Nonverbal respeto in requests for help by Mexican-heritage and European-heritage children*. Unpublished manuscript.

Silva, K., Correa-Chávez, M. and Rogoff, B. (2010). Mexican-heritage children's attention and learning from interactions directed to others. *Child Development*, *81*, 898–912.

Sindell, P. S. (1997). Some discontinuities in the enculturation of Mistassini Cree children. In G. D. Spindler (Ed.), *Education and cultural process: Anthropological approaches* (pp. 383–392). Prospect Heights, IL: Waveland Press.

Stavenhagen, R. (1988). Introducción [Introduction]. In R. R. Stavenhagen (Ed.), *Política cultural para un país multiétnico* [*Cultural policy for a multiethnic country*] (pp. 7–21). Mexico City, Mexico: Secretaría de Educación Pública.

Strathern, M. (1988). *The gender of the gift*. Berkeley: University of California Press.

Tharp, R. G., Estrada, P., Dalton, S. S., and Yamauchi, L. A. (2000). *Teaching transformed. Achieving excellence, fairness, inclusion, and harmony*. Boulder, CO: Westview Press.

Trueba, H. T., and Delgado-Gaitán, C. (1985). Socialization of Mexican children for cooperation and competition: Sharing and copying. *Journal of Educational Equity and Leadership*, *5*, 189–204.

Tsethlikai, M., and Rogoff, B. (2013). Involvement in traditional cultural practices and American Indian children's incidental recall of a folktale. *Developmental Psychology*, *49*, 568–578.

Urrieta, L., Jr. (2003). Las identidades también lloran: Identities also cry: Exploring the human side of indigenous Latina/o identities: *Educational Studies*, *34*, 147–168.

Valdés, G. (1996). *Con respeto*. New York: Teachers College Press.

Valenzuela, A. (1999). *Subtractive schooling: U.S.–Mexican youth and the politics of caring*. Albany, NY: State University of New York Press.

Vigil, J. D. (1998). *From Indians to Chicanos: The dynamics of Mexican-American culture*. Prospect Heights, IL: Waveland Press.

Vygotsky, L. (1978). *Mind in society: The development of higher psychological process*. Cambridge: Harvard University Press.

Warman, A. (2003). *Los indios mexicanos en el umbral del milenio* [The Mexican Indians in the threshold of the millennium]. México, FCE.

Warneken, F., and Tomasello, M. (2006). Altruistic helping in human infants and young chimpanzees. *Science, 31*, 1301–1303.

Warneken, F., Hare, B., Melis, A. P., Hanus, D., and Tomasello, M. (2007). Spontaneous altruism by chimpanzees and young children. *PLoS Biology, 5*(7), e184.

Warton, P. M., and Goodnow, J. J. (1991). The nature of responsibility: Children's understanding of "your job". *Child Development, 62*, 156–165.

Warton, P. M., and Goodnow, J. J. (1995). Money and children's household jobs. *International Journal of Behavioral Development, 18*, 335–350.

Weisner, T. S., and Gallimore, R. (1977). My brother's keeper: Child and sibling care-taking. *Current Anthropology, 18*, 169–190.

Weisner, T. S., Gallimore, R., and Jordan, C. (1988). Unpackaging cultural effects on classroom learning: Native Hawaiian peer assistance and child-generated activity. *Anthropology and Education Quarterly, 19*, 327–353.

Widaman, K. F., and Kagan, S. (1987). Cooperativeness and achievement: Interaction of student cooperativeness with cooperative versus competitive classroom organization. *Journal of School Psychology, 25*, 355–365.

Whiting, B. and Whiting, J. (1975). *Children of six cultures: A psycho-cultural analysis*. Cambridge: Harvard University Press.

Whiting, B. B., and Edwards, C. P. (1988). *Children of different worlds: The formation of social behavior*. Cambridge, MA: Harvard University Press.

7

THE STUDY OF MEXICAN IMMIGRANT FAMILIES' SPACE

Angela E. Arzubiaga, Jennifer A. Brinkerhoff, and Bridget Granville Seeley

Introduction

This chapter reviews literature on Mexican heritage families' practices, including parenting—broadly conceived, using a spatial lens or the notion of socially produced space. First we discuss how the construct of space has been used in the past and its relative recent resurgence as an analytical tool. Next we provide an overview on how a spatial lens contributes to an understanding of Mexican heritage families' socialization practices. We examine critically the state of the field. Further, through examples drawn from a study in Tennessee, we illustrate how spatializations, or the conceptualization of space, can add to our understandings of the practices of families of Mexican heritage.

Low and Lawrence-Zúñiga (2003) note the 1990s brought a renewed interest in issues of space and place across the social sciences. Studies from an urban and human geography perspective such as Soja's (1989), and educational theorists including Artiles (2008) and Gutiérrez (2008), have provided us with understandings about the important role space plays. In *The Anthropology of Space and Place: Locating Culture*, Low and Lawrence-Zúñiga (2003) provide an overview of the major changes in theory and method within the *subfield* of anthropological studies on space and place. They argued that anthropologists were rethinking and reconceptualizing their understandings of culture in spatialized ways.

An important premise in the theorization of space is that there are differences between space as an objective form of matter (physical space, e.g. a playground's equipment)—or space as a contextual given—and *socially produced space* (Soja, 1989; Tejeda, 2000). Socially produced space takes into account both where people act, and the relational dimensions associated with how spaces are understood and perceived (Van Loon, 2002). The relational dimensions refer to reciprocal and dynamic processes amongst people and their contexts. In this chapter our concern is the notion of space as socially produced. At the same time, we make the assumption that the social production of space takes place in ideologically and politically bound landscapes. From this standpoint, the organization and meaning of space is lived in, experienced, and changing (Soja, 1989).

One of the dimensions studied in regard to space is how people form meaningful relationships with the sites, locales, or localities they occupy; it is contended that in this way they transform space into *place*. Basso (1996) argues that the most basic human experience is a *sense of place*.

He contends the sense of place is relational and mutually constituted; place is built through both reciprocal and dynamic processes between and amongst people and their contexts. According to Basso "*sensing* of place is a cultural activity . . . an imaginative experience, a species involvement with the natural and social environment, a way of appropriating portions of the earth" (p. 83). In Basso's *Wisdom sits in places: Notes on a western Apache landscape*, the cultural activity of sensing of place is explained. After living and participating in daily routines, within a western Apache community, Basso came to associate places with stories bound to beliefs the community valued, and which taught community members how to live a balanced life. He found that the name of specific places conjured ancestral stories tied to the actual landscape; in one story, two sisters tease a lecherous old man and lead him to a cottonwood tree where he is deceived and defeated by the girls. The naming of the tree and its location help to remind community members of the story and the lessons it represented. That is, the story, and others like it, provide explicit mnemonics for ideologies about ways of living, illustrating from a space-as-socially-produced perspective how locations are tied to ways of thinking and ideologies (Basso, 1996). However, not all the spaces we inhabit are as explicitly tied to a specific ideology as in this example. In fact, at times, several conflicting ideologies may be connected to the same locality, and it is in this sense that these ideologies are politically contested.[1]

The concept of "third space" is directly related to the notion of space as a contested place.[2] For Soja (1996), thirdspace, is conceptualized as a limitless composition of lifeworlds[3] that are radically open and openly radicalizable. Lifeworlds include shared understandings about people and their identities. At times, these identities are associated with negative meanings or identities, considered inferior to other identities. For example, an immigrant identity on the border between the state of Arizona and Mexico may carry damaging connotations. From a border patrol perspective, for instance, the term *immigrant* may imply illicit action and be equated to a *criminal* identity. From this standpoint, those identified as immigrants elicit actions associated with being persecuted. However, a thirdspace perspective intends to push the boundaries of the meanings attached to people—the relational dimensions of how spaces are understood—and the concomitant implications for ways of both being identified and identifying self. A thirdspace perspective, with its limitless understandings about persons, has the potential to challenge identity hierarchies. In this sense, the notions of actors' or participants' differential power in the construction of identities are also at issue, as in Bhabha's (1995) call for a third-space, which is similar to Anzaldúa (1999) and Hooks' (1995) claim for position within interstices—peripheries or borders, real and imagined. All three authors call on us to transgress the impositions of our shared meanings about others and self, or in other words to see, feel, and hear, beyond our limiting classifications and hierarchies by moving to the edges where discourses collide. From a thirdspace perspective the example of a criminalized immigrant identity from a border patrol perspective is questioned. The imposed hierarchy, which places the immigrant beneath citizens, no longer stands if the perspective or identity constructions of the border crossers, their families, and support institutions, are taken into account. From such lifeworlds, for example, the border has other meanings including that of cemetery for victims of social and economic inequalities (see Harding, 2011).

There are different dimensions studied in regard to space, as discussed in this brief overview of some of the ways space is conceptualized. Underlying the conceptualizations, as noted, however, are the relational and situational dimensions of space. There is agreement, amongst current space theoreticians, that the role of space is essential in order to avoid decontextualization or disembodiment (Low and Lawrence-Zúñiga, 2000; Soja, 1989; Van Loon, 2002). Low and Lawrence-Zúñiga (2003) argue "the most significant change for anthropology is found not in the attention researchers increasingly pay to the material aspects of culture, but in the acknowledgement that *space* is an essential component of *sociocultural theory*" (p. 1, italics added). In other words, the focus is no longer on descriptions of the material landscape, or the components or parts of a physical area, but rather on what people are doing together, or the performativity of everyday life (Van Loon, 2002) and the need to account for this. The concern is about representing embodied, contextualized, placed in space and time, persons, in order to avoid disembodied, decontextualized, anchoristic accounts (Soja, 1989).[4] In other words, the argument is that what is general about human experience is its grounding in particular realities.

Literature Review

Perspectives on Methodology: Sociocultural Research and The Study of Families of Mexican Heritage

Over the past two decades there has been an increased concern with making strides in the understanding of the particular realities of Mexican heritage families from a sociocultural perspective. However, space is not always explicitly referenced in such sociocultural studies. This happens despite the fact that space is an essential component of *sociocultural theory*. Nonetheless, a close examination of the approaches and methods used in socioculturally driven studies reveals that spatialization has been a central concern of the research. Psychological and educational research grounded in sociocultural theory has shifted the focus from studying the individual and the influences of external context as the unit of analysis, to studying how person(s) and context(s) mutually constitute each other. In other words, what people do together—how, when, and where—or *repertoires of practices*, have become the focal points of analysis. Rather than making causal inferences based on external variables, the focus has shifted to explaining and representing the processes of engagement. The shift has provided much needed approaches to study the practices of non-dominant groups (Rogoff and Chavajay, 1995).[5] Approaches used prior to this shift fell short in that they assumed a universal subject, or the belief that individuals should be treated essentially the same in research. Such approaches placed individuals in categories, which failed to account for the particular or situated realities of the individual.

In the following paragraphs, we discuss studies that illustrate the need for a consideration of space in understanding the particular realities of Mexican heritage families and that suggest directions for future research. The studies presented do not represent an exhaustive review of the literature on Mexican heritage families, but rather a selection of studies intended to illustrate some of the issues involving the use of space and place by these families; however, as noted earlier, there is a relative scarcity of studies that reference spatial terms in relation to the parenting of families of Mexican heritage. Our search of the literature from 2000 to the present included the terms Mexican/Mexican American/Chicano/Latino heritage "parenting," "parents and parenting," "children and youth," "family and family life," and yielded few results. In addition to articles on space and place, we have included some articles on the parenting of Mexican heritage families even when they did not use a spatial lens or the terms used in the space and place literature.

Socially Produced Space

We begin with a study that illustrates how space is socially produced. Specifically, Mangual Figueroa (2011) conducted a study with mixed legal status families composed of members who were (a) undocumented in the United States, (b) legal residents, and (c) United States born citizens. Using discourse analysis, Mangual Figueroa examined differences amongst particular or situated realities while taking into account both the way people spoke to each other and the relational aspects associated with how the inhabited space was perceived by participants. Marked differences emerged between the documented and the undocumented members of families. Families socially produced space where legal status was referenced, to enforce compliance with school demands. A mother, for example, attempted to control her child's behavior by emphasizing the advantages of his legal status in contrast to her undocumented status. In this manner, what emerged was a socially produced space where children with documented status needed to live up to the expectations associated with their legal status.

Arzubiaga *et al.*, (2000) noted there are also examples of studies in which the parenting styles of Mexican heritage families were misunderstood and misrepresented. A lack of consideration of space and a failure to take into account how families adjust to their different contexts contributed to erroneous conclusions being drawn. Specifically, the authors argued that when families' sociocultural context was not taken into account their parenting appeared to be predominantly controlling, and their acts of responsiveness or nurturance went unrecognized. In this manner, Mexican heritage parents were classified as authoritarian parents. However, a closer examination of the ecological context in which the families lived would have revealed that parents were in fact being responsive in asserting strong control in dangerous neighborhoods—where misbehavior had greater consequences than it did in safer neighborhoods. Through the use of an ecocultural approach—which uses a mixed-methods approach, including structured and semi-structured interviews, clinical and anthropological stances, and the quantification of assessments—findings pointed to ways that parents engaged in numerous acts of responsiveness that had gone unrecognized because expectations about what these acts should look like were constrained (Arzubiaga *et al.*, 2000). The study of families' daily routines, as the unit of analysis, exposed how families afforded their children socio-emotional support or nurturance, which was conducive to school success (Arzubiaga *et al.*, 2002). Understandings of the sociocultural context—including the role of space—have afforded us with more accurate representations of families. The shift towards a sociocultural lens has placed the focus on particular and situated realities. As a result, theoretical and empirical representations of Mexican heritage families have moved from a categorical approach in which they are associated with specific characteristics, to a perspective in which they are viewed as individuals working together within varied and situated contexts.

Terminology

As noted though, issues of space and place are not always explicit or referred to with the same terminology as in urban and human geography or anthropological studies. In the research on Mexican heritage families' socialization practices, socioculturalists are concerned about accounting for the situatedness—both the relational- and negotiated meaning—of activities (Lave and Wenger, 1991). Prior to the shift from a focus on the individual, and the influences of external context as the unit of analysis to studying how person(s) and context(s) mutually constitute each other, the study of Mexican heritage families' practices on childrearing, for example, had been limited to the study of parents' values and goals, or cultural expectations, for their children. Parents of Mexican heritage were known to value that their children have a sense of right and wrong, and that children become good students, obedient, responsible, and respectful (e.g. Arcia and Johnson, 1998; Valdés, 1996). It was argued that parents desired that their children develop family closeness, and become "bien educados" (moral, respectful, responsible to community and self, e.g. Delgado and Ford, 1998; Valdés, 1996). Parents of

Mexican heritage values and beliefs were assessed and compared to those of parents labeled *American*.[6] Parents classified as American were believed to value consistency, praise, love, and reward (Reid and Valsiner, 1986) and to stress the development of children's cognitive abilities over other type of abilities and goals (Harkness and Super, 2006).

However, with the advent of socioculturally driven studies, the parenting practices of families of Mexican heritage have emerged in a different light. Family practices have been examined in their own right and not necessarily in comparison to an American model. With *funds of knowledge* studies, for example, families' use of resources in specific contexts and their resourcefulness has been highlighted (Gonzalez *et al.*, 2001; Moll *et al.*, 1992). Funds of knowledge refer to families' strategies and devices to respond to the daily challenges of living. The approach or methods used in these studies included a teacher-as-researcher stance, whereby teachers visited homes to learn about families' practices, and documented what they learned to share later with other teachers in order to expand their understandings of families' repertoire of practices. The purposes of these activities included using such knowledge in the classroom with students. In this manner, the socially produced space of children's daily family routines was taken into account in order to translate understandings and perceptions of the relational dimensions of home activities to classroom activities. Funds of knowledge studies have replaced a deficit perspective (or a view of how families fall short—see Arzubiaga, 2007), with a perspective that capitalizes on the strengths inherent in families' daily practices.

Additionally, the Latino Diaspora, ethnographic studies, have also contributed to our understandings of how cultural models, such as the model of educación, are enacted and contested in non-traditional settlement areas (Murillo, 2002; Villenas, 2002; Wortham, 2002). Cultural models are shared meanings and understandings about how the world is organized and works (D'Andrade and Strauss, 1992). The concept of *educación* represents an important cultural model for immigrants from Mexico (Valdés, 1996). Villenas (2002) studied how mothers were actively engaged in redefining a space for their children to become *bien educados*. She found Latina/o parents, in a community in North Carolina, approached childrearing from a personal responsibility stance, using the concept of personal responsibility to provide a strong moral education and to provide roles of responsibility to family and community. *Buena educación* reaffirmed their cultural integrity in response to cultural denigration and racism, that both structured and reinforced the "public difficulties" they experienced. New immigrants were forging new ideologies tied to place, which ran counter to White natives' ideologies tied to place. With these studies, a situated-in-place and relationally constructed understanding of family practices has emerged.

Families' Contributions

While considering what families bring to the table, such as their funds of knowledge and cultural models, it is important to consider the implications these perspectives have on how families work and play together. In other words, family members share meanings and understandings to carry out the most mundane and vital tasks. These meanings and understandings shape family practices and account for some of the differences that can be observed across groups. Family practices, however, are also constrained by the spatial organization of physical areas. Gaskins (2008), for example, observed the ways African American, European American, and Latin American (Mexican heritage families were included in this category) families interacted with their children in museums. The purpose of her study was to identify groups' ethnotheories about play, and ways they engaged each other and the material artifacts at the museum. She found support for her proposal that family beliefs about whether or not play was a learning activity—and if adults were considered legitimate playmates—was related to if and how families engaged with each other and the material artifacts or props within the museum exhibits; she asked parents about their beliefs about play and observed them while in the museum with their children. Latin American parents, Gaskins found, tended to play in collaboration with their children, but they did not make a connection between play and learning. In contrast, the European American parents endorsed a strong relationship between play and learning, and had the greatest incidence of child-directed play interactions in comparison to both African American and Latin American parents. Gaskins argues that museums need to accommodate for differences in beliefs about play by restructuring their exhibits to allow for different interpretations of how space is utilized and envisioned by its visitors. Seating arrangements both as part of the exhibits and on the periphery, for example, would allow for different forms of participation.

In line with taking into account diverse forms of participation, sociocultural studies have been increasingly interested in creating learning spaces that acknowledge such differences. For example, studies aimed at transforming the spaces of learning for non-dominant groups include those conducted in after-school clubs known as the Fifth Dimension (for example, see http:// lchc.ucsd.edu). In the Fifth Dimension clubs children's participation is mediated by socially organized activities, which are purposefully based on sociocultural principles of learning. For example, children are not separated into age-segregated groups, but rather are encouraged to work with other children and adults interested in solving the same problems. In this manner, by arranging relational dimensions, the socially constructed space affords children opportunities to display their knowledge and expertise in new ways. The structural and social organization leads participants to engage in problem solving and literacy learning. In the same vein, Gutiérrez (2008) argues for a transformation of space through critical literacies that lead the institutional space to become a place of hybrid spaces (Gutiérrez et al., 2009). As mentioned earlier, a key concept related to issues of space and place is third space. In earlier work, Gutiérrez et al., (1995) conceptualized third space as the moments when both scripts and counterscripts in classrooms are afforded a place, and work together in transforming the learning space for teachers and students. Through transformations, third spaces—which include the knowledge and practices of both dominant and non-dominant groups—emerge. These spaces are called hybrid spaces because they include knowledge and practices that are often relegated to other spaces.

Space Creation

A study by Dworin (2006) is an interesting example of how a classroom was purposefully designed to afford children opportunities to engage in hybrid spaces, even though the author does not use the term hybridity. A sample of 4th grade students whose parents were Mexican immigrants were initially asked to tell a true story of a family member and to write it in the language of their choice. The multiple social spaces were created through the processes of collecting and recollecting memories, writing these into narratives, and sharing and revising text. Social spaces included peer groups, where suggestions and questions to make the story accessible to readers were provided. More importantly, however, students were encouraged to work on their stories with their parents or a family member. The process became a recursive cycle of discovery, purposefully orchestrated to create multiple intersections of social space, such as the intersections of the social spaces of the classroom, communities, and homes.

Another of these intersections was the use of different languages within and across locations. Machado-Casas (2009) argues that languages create borders in much the same manner that physical borders keep people in or out of their perimeters. In Dworin's (2006) study, processes of interpretation and translation in both English and Spanish created social spaces where hybrid practices allowed navigation through language barriers. Students translated their stories into a second language. In Dworin's study fifteen of the eighteen students had written their original story in Spanish. Visual examples (such as using an overhead projector) were used to translate text as a group. The students translated text (both oral and written) from Spanish to English and English to Spanish, and did not translate their own stories, but rather worked with a partner and translated other's stories, which were illustrated in black and white by the student authors then typed up and printed into two books, one in English, one in Spanish. Each student received two copies of the book which they shared with their families. Prior to Dworin's study, usual instances of interpretation in the classroom had been limited to a single word. However, because the students had the opportunity to work in peer review groups to examine their translations and the stories, they were able to perform in-depth interpretations and translations of ideas. This process brought to the classroom a practice which language brokers often engage in their everyday lives. Though Dworin stresses the aspect of how such funds of knowledge were accessed, we stress how their use created explicitly hybrid social spaces.

As mentioned previously, space is, at times, not explicitly referenced in sociocultural studies of learning and development. However, a close examination of the approaches and methods used in socioculturally driven studies reveals that spatialization has been a central concern of the research. A particularly relevant article by Angelillo *et al.*, (2007) unpackages or explains researchers' efforts to develop visual representations of collaboration amongst participants, with an understanding that representations of collaboration also provide examples of processes that lead to changes or transformations of cognitive configurations over time. These representations of collaboration identified by Angelillo (and colleagues) capture families' socially constructed space. The researchers also convey the different participants' organization around a family task, and provide us with a view of the socially produced space of the research team.

In another study, Machado-Casas (2009) gathered life stories of indigenous parents from Mexico, Guatemala, and El Salvador. In the study, space is conceptualized as a social space with borders that place constraints on how—when, where, and with whom—participants speak the language. How participants used languages created social spaces for them and their children. Parents argued they used languages as a *coyote tool*, to help them cross borders (*coyote* is the term informally used to refer to people who smuggle others across national borders). Machado-Casas found the use of multiple languages, particularly English, facilitated access to colonized spaces such as the school. The notion of the school as a colonized space is reminiscent of Gutiérrez's description of institutional spaces (Gutiérrez, 2008). At the same time, use of languages created social spaces or *transnational* mobility for participants who were unable to move physically across physical borders. For example, Machado-Casas (2009) describes a report by one participant who said that by purposefully maintaining ties with the sending country through use of communication in all languages available to him, he was able to maintain his position in both spaces of the receiving country and home country. However, we want to emphasize that at the same time, new spaces were being created, spaces with a transnational[7] character.

Maintaining Historical Links

Maintaining ties with the sending country while living elsewhere implies that the spaces created, and in which participants live, also have transnational dimensions. As the first author has written elsewhere (Arzubiaga *et al.*, 2009), transnationalism has been more often related to the first immigrant generation, who actively maintain ties with the sending country by, for example, participating in political processes of their native country (Portes *et al.*, 2008). Nonetheless, the concept of transnationalism is important for children in immigrant families because it emphasizes the connections and presence of the sending country in their lives.

Children within families that are embedded in *transnational social fields* are the focus of another ethnographic study (Orellana *et al.*, 2001). Transnational social fields are multi-stranded social relations that link places of origin and settlement. Orellana and colleagues argue for the variation in the structure and dynamics of transnational social fields of children from Mexico, Central America, Korea, and Yemen. Parenting strategies to educate their children are discussed, such as Korean parents who send their young children (parachute kids) to study in the United States. In contrast, parents of Mexican heritage send their children back to Mexico to protect them from gangs. In the Orellana *et al.* (2001) study families are conceptualized as field builders, as they do relational work across borders. The children are conceptualized as pivotal points in these field constructions as, for example, when they yearn to leave countries of origin—and actually do—to be with their parents.

Summary

The preceding review discussed studies that illustrated both the need for a consideration of space in the study of the particular realities of Mexican heritage families, and studies that suggest directions for future research. The studies discussed were chosen to illustrate some of the issues involving Mexican heritage families. Additionally, the review offers perspectives on how a focus on the social production of space might contribute to understandings about the situated realities of Mexican heritage families.

Future Directions and Challenges

The challenges ahead include understanding that different ideologies and political stances towards immigrants will matter for our comprehension of the spaces Mexican immigrant families inhabit. One of the important ideas in the review is that shifts towards sociocultural approaches has moved the research focus from preordained categories or classifications, to repertoires of practice and the relational dimensions of these practices. Further, by approaching families from a non-deficit perspective, with the intent of learning rather than teaching families, funds of knowledge research has revealed a wealth of practices (Moll *et al.*, 1992). Teacher–Researchers identified practices that reflected the different relational dimensions of family tasks. Through ethnography we have also learned about the different spaces created, based on ideological and political dimensions within new settlement areas, and how families innovate using their cultural models to counter anti-immigrant rhetoric and policies (Villenas, 2002). New spaces of possibilities have emerged through revised cultural models meant to instill heritage values within politically charged settlement areas.

Further, our discussion of Gaskins' 2008 study allows us to take into account different uses of the same physical spaces, and the relationship between ethnotheories and the social production of space. Additionally, study of the promotion of third spaces—which are hybrid spaces, or spaces which reflect innovative uses of shared knowledge and practices—have provided insight on the range of possibilities both for teaching and learning (5th Dimension). In the same vein, we discussed transformations of space through critical literacies (e.g. Dworin, 2006). Dworin's study is an example of how to access funds of knowledge, and we stressed that at the same time there was the creation of hybrid social spaces. Another aspect related to the conceptualization of space was discussed in regard to the visualization and representation of collaborations (Angelillo, *et al.*, 2007). Angelillo and colleagues' study implies for us that engagement in such representations of collaboration is potentially useful. In addition, we find useful the notions related to conceptualizing language as a tool that creates social spaces. Machado Casas' 2009 participants had described language as a coyote tool. Finally, we discussed the importance of transnational spaces, which makes explicit the notion that spaces traverse the limitations of physical presence. Transnational spaces, which in this case referred to spaces across country or national boundaries, are increasingly playing a role within a globalized world.

Examples of Families' Social Spaces in The Southeast of The United States

We now turn to some examples to illustrate the importance of space and place that are drawn from a study of families who had recently settled in a US Southeastern non-traditional settlement area. The practices families engaged in included literacy and socialization goals, and were observed in everyday routines. Through the examples, we aim to illustrate how spatializations can add to our understandings of the practices of families of Mexican heritage. We also studied what our participants said about their parental involvement with school, including school visits, and related practices, such as reading and doing homework. The following observer notes reveal what happened to one of the mothers, Carolina Calle (pseudonym), when she visited her child's school with the intent of observing his classroom.

During a visit with a family, while in their home, the mother, Carolina stated:

> *Quiero estar en el salón de Alejandro otro rato para ver . . . Un día yo fui . . ., Me quedé ahí sentada (oficina principal), no, no pude entrar ni pude ir para allá, no mas los maestros me decían que si a qué iba que si qué necesitaba (. . .).*

> I want to be in Alejandro's classroom another time to see . . . One day I went . . . I ended up just sitting there (main office), no, I couldn't go in or go inside, only the teachers were asking why I was there, that if I needed something (. . .)

Mrs. Calle had sat and waited to visit her third child's classroom until she realized she was not going to be invited. As she crossed the street, two blocks from the elementary, to her one floor modest home, she told us she had thought about previous experiences visiting her children's schools. What had just transpired was in sharp contrast to her visits in California where she regularly attended the classrooms, the cafeteria, and the recess areas with her toddler astride. Though her two younger children were now completing their second year of school she had not been able to "find out how they're doing, what the kids are doing, [and] that they see [me]."

Analysis

What happened at the school had occurred despite the fact that it had been eleven years since the Calle family immigrated from Jalisco, Mexico. By the time of our meeting, five of their six children had been born in the US. Yet, Carolina was struggling with her identity as a supportive and involved parent. At the same time, we knew Carolina had been able to find many opportunities for her children, outside of school and home, which supported her beliefs about learning and the importance of using Spanish and English. These opportunities included practices at church where she explained her son Alex was quickly learning to identify letters and expanding his vocabulary. She had shared with us many times how much her young sons had learned. She had also noticed during a trip in Mexico that Andrés, one of her sons, had been interested in reading urban environmental print, as he read out loud for his siblings.

Why was there such a contrast between her experience in schools in California and Tennessee? Why was Carolina struggling with her identity as a supportive and involved parent in her children's school? We believe a spatial lens can afford us ways to begin to address such questions. We need to focus on the discrepancies between the different ways space is socially constructed and the multiple spatializations in the everyday lives of parents of Mexican heritage. With another family, the Rosas, we compared the different spaces where their child learned to read (Gutiérrez and Arzubiaga, 2011). The home afforded the child spaces where reading was about meaning-making, in collaboration with siblings and parents. In contrast, the school rewarded the child for her identification of words and encouraged her to work by herself. We were able to identify such discrepancies by examining how the practices were socially enacted and embodied: In the school the spatialization of reading was related to performing at great speed, whereas in the home the spatialization of reading related to understanding text. We argue for studies that consider several locations and spatializations of such places. Each location can hold several competing spatializations on how to read, as in the aforementioned example.

In summary, utilizing a spatial lens and discussion of issues of space and place brings to the foreground the notion that we and the people we study with or study about are spatialized beings, always embodied, contextualized and identified (not bodies or contexts or identities— Van Loon, 2002). We recommend keeping in mind that everyone is a spatialized being. That is, in addition to people being embedded in social and historical worlds, these worlds are always embodied, lived in, and experienced.

Policy Implications

Consideration of the particular, or individual, and the local realities—the situated realities—of Mexican heritage families is perhaps the most salient implication when bringing to the foreground the notion of socially produced space to policy. In this sense it will be necessary to consider how the same physical locations may hold widely different spaces or spatializations— conceptualizations of space—for individuals. For example, when constituting a health policy, it will be important to consider what, if any, anti-immigrant policies are in place. It will not suffice to merely examine policies that have been approved and are being enforced. Fears about the consequences of proposed-but-not-approved, approved, and imagined ramifications of such polices will have an impact on individual's spatializations.

To explain this: Anti-immigrant policies may keep people who fear deportation from going to local clinics for general population vaccines. Spatializations, or the conceptualization of space, of the clinic may vary, by beliefs related to both *imagined* actual, and policies in place. For some, the clinics may represent a haven for protection from an epidemic, whereas for others the clinics might be seen as locations where repressive measures against lack of legal status will be sanctioned. Another example includes parents' hesitation to participate in schools when legal status is also at issue: Family members may stay away from school if they fear their status may be questioned. In this sense, there need to be policies in place, which are responsible for reaching out to communities to explain whether or not there will be consequences associated with lack of legal status.

Perhaps the most glaring implication for policy is that regulations have differing consequences and implications for people. The different implications depend on both the intersections of each individual's characteristics, such as legal status, age, educational level, and gender, and the contexts where such policies will be in effect. For example, a father who is undocumented would hold spatializations about driving in the city when a broadcast emergency response is issued, that would be different from his documented neighbor's spatializations. The former would be more likely to change his family's routine while the emergency response was in effect, in order to avoid a brush with the law. Additionally, it will be necessary to take into account how new policies fit with explicit and implicit policies already in place. These dimensions will make for important differences related to the spaces and spatializations, or conceptualizations of space, operating for and about Mexican heritage families.

Following are some of the implications for future research. Our review suggests that legal status needs to be taken into account in order to understand repercussions for family members' differential spaces. As noted, Mangual Figueroa's (2011) study revealed differences within mixed status families. We also noted that parenting is context dependent, or in other words, that parenting practices develop within varied spaces which have ranges in how they both constrain and afford opportunities for children, thereby shaping parents' practices (Arzubiaga *et al.*, 2000). In this sense, we argue there is a need to understand different contexts and parents' perceptions of these contexts, since they are associated to families' practices.

Future research on the parenting practices of parents of Mexican heritage needs to address the organization and meaning of everyday practices as space that is lived in, experienced, and changing. There is much work to be done. Work in the areas of visual representations of different forms of collaboration as discussed by Angelillo and colleagues (2007), for example, needs to include families', communities', and researchers' cultural activities related to perceiving space. For example, visual representations of family collaborations, which capture moment to moment changes in engagement, such as when a mother turns to talk to her youngest, can be further studied by including parents' and communities' explanations of such actions.

The articles we reviewed were mostly from traditional settlement areas, including cities and states where immigrants have historically stayed. There is a need for more studies in non-traditional settlement areas—areas new to immigration settlement. More importantly, however, we need to be able to compare and contrast studies in traditional, non-traditional, enclave—communities with a preponderance of an immigrant group, and the diaspora— dispersed groups of co-nationals or co-ethnics. The social construction of space is likely to have certain regularities bound to the history of the location.

There is a need for furthering our understanding of the relational work that is part of everyday lives, and that determines whether or not mothers such as Carolina can exercise the parenting practices they desire for their children. In addition, we need to continue to identify the areas and the important relational work that need to be studied. We need also to consider other ways of examining important relational work, such as strategies that are particular to the transnational social fields of parents and children who are of Mexican heritage and are also immigrants. Clearly, high stake language encounters, such as parent meetings or Individualized Education Programs (IEP), lend themselves to the study of languages as borders, and how the social spaces constructed can either afford families opportunities or close doors. By focusing on space and place issues related to the parenting of Mexican heritage families, we hope to promote new social constructions and new ways of representing in research and in our related discourses about Mexican heritage families, diverse ways of sensing space and making place.

Notes

1 Theme parks are examples of spaces more explicitly bound to specific ideologies. For example, Disneyland is promoted as a magical place for kids of all ages. However, while it conjures childhood for many, it also represents for some at the global level, an unwelcome imposition of *American* values.
2 Anzaldúa (1999) and Gutiérrez (2008) use third space (two words) and Soja (1996) uses thirdspace (one word).
3 Lifeworlds is used to refer to shared understandings amongst people about the way the world is experienced. Lifeworlds include assumptions about identity and social groups, families and communities' values.

4   Anchoristic refers to a lack of notions of both space and time. Anchoristic representations occur when persons are studied without consideration of their spatial location and the time of the research. For example, the study of an undocumented family's practices is more informed when it is taken into account that they were living in Arizona in 2010. Both where the study was conducted and the historical time have implications, because Arizona Senate Bill 1070 was passed in 2010. The controversial bill proposed to enforce regulations that limit the freedom to work and transit for undocumented persons.

5   We use the term non-dominant to refer to communities or individuals who have less power—historically as well as in the present—vis-à-vis the dominant community, e.g. economically, socio-politically, educationally. A focus on power differential is more accurate than using descriptors such as "minority" or "communities/persons of color," for example (Gutiérrez and Arzubiaga, 2011).

6   The term *American* is used in the sense researchers, at times unaware, have used it in the past, as representing the dominant white middle class.

7   Transnationalism refers to people's engagements between their sending and receiving communities.

References

Angelillo, C., Rogoff, B., and Chavajay, P. (2007). Examining shared endeavors by abstracting video coding schemes with fidelity to cases. In R. Goldman, R. Pea, B. Barron, and S. Derry (Eds.), *Video research in the learning sciences*. Mahwah, NJ: Lawrence Erlbaum Associates.

Anzaldúa, G. (1999). *Borderlands La Frontera*. San Francisco: Aunt Lute.

Arcia, E., and Johnson, A. (1998). When respect means to obey: Immigrant Mexican mothers values for their children. *Journal of Child and Family Studies*, 7(1), 79–95.

Artiles, A. J. (2008). Special education's changing identity: Paradoxes and dilemmas in views of culture and space. *Harvard Educational Review*, 73(2), 164–202.

Arzubiaga, A. (2007). Deficit perspectives: Transcending deficit thinking about Latina/o Parents. In L. Diaz Soto (Ed.), *The Praeger handbook of Latino education in the U.S.* (pp. 102–105) [Two Volumes]. Westport, CT: Praeger Publishers.

Arzubiaga, A., Ceja. M., and Artiles, A. J. (2000). Transcending deficit thinking about Latinos' parenting styles: Toward an ecocultural view of family life. In C. Tejeda, C. Martinez, Z. Leonardo, and P. McLaren (Eds.), *Charting new terrains of Chicana(o)/ Latina(o) education.* (pp. 93–106). Cresskill, NY: Hampton Press.

Arzubiaga, A., Noguerón, S., and Sullivan, A. (2009). The education of children in im/migrant families. *Review of Research in Education 33*, 246–271.

Arzubiaga, A., Rueda, R., and Monzó, R. R. (2002). Family matters related to the reading engagement of Latino children. *Journal of Latinos and Education*, 1(4), 231–243.

Basso, K. (1996). *Wisdom sits in places: Notes on a western Apache landscape*. Albuquerque: University of New Mexico Press.

Bhabha, H. K. (1995). Signs taken for wonders. In B. Ashcroft, G. Griffiths, and H. Tiffin (Eds.), *The post-colonial studies reader* (pp. 29–35). London: Routledge.

D'Andrade, R., and Strauss, C. (Eds.) (1992). *Human motives and cultural models*. Cambridge University Press.

Delgado, B., and Ford, L. (1998). Parental perceptions of child development among low-income Mexican American families. *Journal of Child and Family Studies*, 7(4), 469–481.

Dworin, J. E. (2006). The family stories project: Using funds of knowledge for writing. *The Reading Teacher*, 59, 510–520.

Gaskins, S. (2008). The cultural meaning of play and learning in children's museums. *Hand to Hand*, 22(4), 1–11.

Gonzalez, N., Andrade, R., Civil, M., and Moll, L. (2001). Bridging funds of knowledge: Creating zones of practices in mathematics. *Journal of Education for Students Placed at Risk*, 6, 115–132.

Gutiérrez, K. D. (2008). Developing a sociocritical literacy in the third space. *Reading Research Quarterly*, 43(2), 148–164.

Gutiérrez, K. and Arzubiaga, A. (2011). An ecological and activity theoretic approach to understanding diasporic and non-dominant communities. In W. Tate and C. C. Yeakey (Eds.), *Research on schools, communities, and neighborhoods: Toward civic responsibility*. Lanham, Maryland: Rowman and Littlefield.

Gutiérrez, K., Hunter, J., and Arzubiaga, A. (2009). Re-mediating the university: Learning through socio-critical literacies. *Pedagogies: An International Journal, 4,* 1–23.

Gutiérrez, K., Rymes, B., and Larson, J. (1995). Script, counterscript, and underlife in the classroom: James Brown versus Brown v. Board of Education. *Harvard Educational Review, 65*(3), 445–471.

Harding, J., (2011). The deaths' map: At the Mexican Border. *London Review of Books, 33*(20), 7–13.

Harkness, S., and Super, C. (2006). Themes and variations: Parental ethnotheories in western cultures. In K. Rubin and O. B. Chung (Eds.), *Parenting beliefs, behaviors, and parent-child relations: A cross-cultural perspective* (pp. 61–79). New York: Psychology Press.

Hooks, B. (1995). *Killing rage: Ending racism.* New York: Henry Holt and Company, LLC.

Lave, J., and Wenger, E. (1991). *Situated learning—Legitimate peripheral participation.* New York: Cambridge University Press.

Low, S. M., and Lawrence-Zúñiga, D. (2000). *On the plaza: The politics of public space and culture.* Austin: University of Texas Press.

Low, S. M., and Lawrence-Zúñiga, D. (2003). The anthropology of space and place: Locating culture. In S. M. Low and D. Lawrence-Zúñiga (Eds.), *Locating culture* (pp. 1–47). Malden, MA: Blackwell.

Machado-Casas, M. (2009). The politics of organic phylogeny: The art of parenting and surviving as transnational multilingual Latino indigenous immigrants in the U. S. *The High School Journal, 92*(4), 82–99.

Mangual Figueroa, A. (2011). Citizenship and education in the homework completion routine. *Anthropology and Education Quarterly, 42,* 263–280. doi: 10.1111/j.1548–1492.2011.01131.x

Moll, L. C., Amanti, C., Neff, D., and Gonzalez, N. (1992). Funds of knowledge for teaching: Using a qualitative approach to connect homes and classrooms. *Theory into Practice, 31*(2), 132–141.

Murillo, E. G., Jr. (2002). How does it feel to be a problem? "Disciplining" the transnational subject in the American South. In S. Wortham, E. G. Murillo Jr., and E. T. Hamann (Eds.), *Education in the new Latino diaspora* (pp. 215–240). Westport, CT: Greenwood Publishing Group, Inc.

Orellana, M. F., Thorne, B., Chee, A., and Eva Lam, W. S. (2001). Transnational childhoods: The participation of children in processes of family migration. *Social Problems, 48*(4), 572–591.

Portes, A., Escobar, C., and Arana, R. (2008). Bridging the gap: Transnational and ethnic organizations in the political incorporation of immigrants in the United States. *Ethnic and Racial Studies, 31*(6), 1065–1090.

Reid, B., and Valsiner, J. (1986). Consistency, praise, and love: Folk theories of American parents. *Ethos, 14*(3), 282–304.

Rogoff, B., and Chavajay, P. (1995). What's become of research on the cultural basis of cognitive development? *American Psychologist, 50,* 859–877.

Soja, E. W. (1989). *Postmodern geographies: The reassertion of space in critical social theory.* London; New York: Verso.

Soja, E. (1996). *Thirdspace: Journeys to Los Angeles and other real and imagined places.* Malden, MA: Blackwell Publishing.

Tejeda, C. (2000). Spatialized understandings of the Chicana(o)/Latina(o) educational experience: Theorizations of space and the mapping of educational outcomes. In C. Tejeda, C. Martinez, Z. Leonardo, and P. McLaren (Eds.), *Charting new terrains of Chicana(o)/Latina(o) education* (pp. 93–106). Cresskill, NY: Hampton Press.

Valdés, G. (1996). *Con Respeto: Bridging the Distances between Culturally Diverse Families and Schools—An Ethnographic Portrait.* New York, NY: Teachers College Press.

Van Loon, J. (2002). Social spatialization and everyday life. *Space and Culture, 5*(2), 88–95.

Villenas, S. (2002). Reinventing education in new Latino communities: Pedagogies of change and continuity in North Carolina. In S. Wortham, E. G. Murillo Jr., and E. T. Hamann (Eds.), *Education in the new Latino diaspora: Policy and the politics of identity* (pp. 17–36). Westport, CT: Greenwood Publishing Group, Inc.

Wortham, S. (2002). Gender and school success in the Latino diaspora. In S. Wortham, E. G. Murillo Jr., and E. T. Hamann (Eds.), *Education in the new Latino diaspora: Policy and the politics of identity.* (pp. 117–141). Westport, CT: Greenwood Publishing Group, Inc.

PART III

School and Community Contexts

8

ISSUES IN EDUCATING MEXICAN AMERICAN ENGLISH LANGUAGE LEARNERS

Eva Midobuche, Alfredo H. Benavides, and Fatih Koca

Introduction

The issues faced by Mexican American[1] students in American schools over the past fifty years or more have continued to worsen without adequate responses by K–12 school districts, or by colleges and universities. The public schools have done little more than ignore the under-performance of this group of minority students, as was highlighted by the NEA-Tucson Report (NEA, 1966). Carter (1970) used the term *benign neglect* to characterize the attention and effort that American education systems had given to this population. And this characterization was written in 1970—44 years ago. It seems that schools have always been too preoccupied with other issues to pay much attention to Mexican Americans, who have had a history of neglect. While some Mexican American scholars, such as George I. Sánchez (1940), attempted to shed light on this population, American schools did not seem to respond in any significant manner.

The Pew Hispanic Center (Motel and Patten, 2011) reports the population of *Hispanics*[2] in the United States at 51,927,158. Mexican Americans account for 33,539,000 of this population, or approximately 65 percent. By contrast, the U.S. Census Bureau Decennial Censuses Report (2008) counted only 9.1 million Hispanics in 1970. The Bureau's projection of 52,000,000 for 2010 was extremely close to the Pew Center count. These statistics on Hispanic population growth demonstrate an almost 82.5 percent increase in the US Hispanic population over the past forty years. However, educational progress among Hispanics has been slow for years (NEA, 1966).

One of the states with a large Mexican American student population is Texas. According to the Texas Education Agency (TEA, 2013), of the 4,978,120 students in Texas schools during the 2011–2012 academic year, Mexican Americans accounted for 50.8 percent or 2,530,789 students. This makes Texas a "majority-minority state." Non-Hispanic white students number 1,520,320, or 30.5 percent, of the student population. Students classified as English language learners (ELLs) totaled 837,536, or 16.8 percent, of the total K–12 population. Obviously the large number of ELLs has much to do with the fact that Texas shares a long border with Mexico. However, this is nothing new. Texas has always shared this border and the problematic issues for Mexican Americans in the Texas educational system have persisted through the years. To exacerbate the concern, the TEA also reported that 60.4 percent of all students were considered to be economically disadvantaged (TEA, 2013). This would include a very large number of Mexican American students. Although issues associated with poor school performance among

Mexican Americans can be generalized to many parts of the country, this discussion will stress the factors and issues that seem to be prevalent in Texas, and perhaps be applicable to other Mexican American enclaves outside of the state.

Literature Review

Issues that affect educational persistence and attainment include some that are common to many different ethnic groups, and others that are unique to Mexican Americans. A comprehensive review of all of these factors is beyond the scope of this chapter, therefore we instead focus on the following five issues: (1) poverty, (2) inadequate programs, (3) unqualified teachers, (4) the lack of English skills and the loss of the native language and culture, and (5) immigration (documented or undocumented status). These issues, as well as others, combine to cause stress among families and individuals alike, thus adding negative pressures that obstruct positive school performance among students.

Poverty

Identifying rates of poverty among Mexican Americans is not easily accomplished due to the aggregated nature of statistical studies that focus on the total number of Hispanics living in the US, including Mexican Americans. Thus to obtain information about the poverty levels of Mexican Americans we must rely on inferences made from statistics on the total numbers of Hispanics living in poverty in the United States. The 2011 Statistical Portrait of Hispanics Living in the United States puts the total number of Hispanics living in poverty at 13,205,049. The rate of poverty for all Americans in 2011 was 15.9 percent. Hispanics, however, had a total poverty rate of 25.9 percent (Motel and Patten, 2011). Lopez and Cohn (2011) report the supplemental poverty rates among Hispanics at 14.7 percent for native born, 25.5 percent for foreign born, and 32.4 percent for those Hispanics who are not citizens. By any measure these are staggering figures. Given that almost 66 percent of Hispanics are of Mexican origin it seems safe to surmise that Mexican Americans figure prominently in these high numbers.

How does poverty affect achievement, and the American idea that anyone can overcome poverty if they try or are persistent enough? Berliner (2014) calls this belief "America's dirty little secret." Berliner expands on the American beliefs that in order to succeed people in this country only need to "pull themselves up by their bootstraps" and that "teachers are the most important factor in determining the achievement of our youth." Berliner's example reasons that these types of beliefs guide American educational policy to the detriment of minority children in particular. He states:

> America's dirty little secret is that a large majority of poor kids attending schools that serve the poor are not going to have successful lives. Reality is not nearly as comforting as myth. Reality does not make us feel good. But the facts are clear. Most children born into the lower social classes will not make it out of that class, even when exposed to heroic educators.
>
> *(Berliner, 2014)*

Berliner concludes that the best way to improve minority children's academic performance, and thus improve schools, is to provide jobs that give families a living wage. The share of Mexicans who live in poverty (27 percent) is slightly higher than the rate for Hispanics overall (25 percent). US-born Mexicans are slightly less likely to live in poverty than their foreign-born counterparts—26 percent vs. 29 percent respectively (Gonzalez-Barrera and Lopez, 2013).

Stephen Krashen (2011) also is of the belief that poverty is a major impediment to our nation's poor children. Krashen maintains that there is no crisis in American education except perhaps for the one that has been manufactured. Krashen states:

> The crisis is 100 percent manufactured . . . what struggling schools need is more resources for children: food, health care, and above all, access to books.
>
> *(Krashen, S., Fordham University, July 7, 2011)*

Inadequate Programs

Historically there have been few programs aimed specifically at the education of Mexican American students. The American educational system struggles with dropout rates well above 50 percent among this group, and these rates continue in many school districts throughout the country. Education for Mexican Americans was not deemed a priority in many parts of the southwest (Sánchez, 1940). Mexican Americans were expected to fill the labor void in agriculture, ranching, and other menial jobs. Open discrimination was practiced and condoned in many communities. Businesses often displayed signs in their windows announcing "No Dogs or Mexicans Allowed" (Midobuche, 1999). Could this type of sentiment and open hostility have adverse effects on Mexican American children or adults?

It was not until the 1960s that the idea of bilingual education began to emerge as a possible solution to the growing educational crisis in the Mexican American community. Led primarily by Mexican American educators, bilingual education and bilingualism were seen as something that made sense. President Lyndon Johnson signed the Bilingual Education Act into law on January 2, 1968 (Crawford, 2004). However, the law did not provide funds for the establishment of bilingual programs during its first year. Complicating matters, very little was known pedagogically about bilingual education at that time. Naturally, the new initiative came under fire from different groups citing many different reasons why bilingual education should not be permitted. Among these were that it was unpatriotic and that it was ineffective, although no evidence was brought forward to support such claims. Texas, an early leader in bilingual education, decriminalized teaching in a foreign language in 1969 (Crawford, 2004). Until then, Mexican American children who were caught speaking Spanish (often the only language they knew), were often severely punished (Arias and Casanova, 1993; Midobuche, 1999).

The charge that bilingual education was ineffective was not necessarily true. However, there was still much that was not known about bilingualism and bilingual education. Researchers were slow to begin the study of program effectiveness. Opponents of bilingual education wanted the maintenance of native languages banned, and succeeded in doing so with the 1978 reauthorization of the Bilingual Education Act (Crawford, 2004). There were various other reports that claimed bilingual education to be a poor program for speakers of other languages. As a result of the 1978 reauthorization, bilingual programs were limited to transitional programs only. Transitional programs were those that "transitioned" children from Spanish to English, usually in the quickest time possible. These kinds of programs were compensatory in nature and were not aimed at enriching the student, whose best asset was the ability to speak another language. This was an attribute that other American children usually did not possess. The knowledge of another language was seen as a handicap instead of as an asset. It was in this atmosphere of doubt and fear that the push for bilingual education research began. While bilingual education researchers were attempting to discover the best ways to educate children who did not speak the English language, others were determined to show that bilingual approaches were ineffective. Thus, program effectiveness dominated the bilingual agenda during the 1980s.

Many approaches to teach English were developed, such as: (1) Submersion (a.k.a. Sink-or-Swim); (2) ESL Pullout (English as a Second Language); (3) Structured Immersion (plus ESL); (4) Transitional Bilingual Education (Early Exit); (5) Developmental Bilingual Education (Gradual/Late Exit); and (6) Two-Way Bilingual Education—Dual Immersion, Dual Language, Two-Way Immersion (Crawford, 2004; Ovando *et al.*, 2006; Thomas and Collier 1997). These programmatic approaches differed in intensity, goals, length of time, and of course, effectiveness. To more fully understand the nature of these programs a quick explanation is in order.

- Submersion—is basically a "sink or swim" program. There is nothing done for the child. They either make it or "sink".
- ESL Pullout—essentially pulls out children from their mainstream classes a few times per week for 20 to 30 minutes to be taught English.
- Structured Immersion—is another form of ESL content teaching within a self-contained classroom.
- Transitional bilingual programs—were the original programs that were to be used in classrooms of ELLs (English language learners). Basically, these programs utilized a bilingual approach, but were intended more as compensatory education (Crawford, 2004), and were also early-exit programs.
- Developmental Bilingual Education—was developed as a late-exit program with strong heritage-language usage, and children from English speaking backgrounds enrolled in the programs. These types of programs were proven to be the most effective.
- Two-Way Bilingual Education (Dual Immersion, Dual Language, Two-Way Immersion)— the sixth option for teaching English that is itself implemented in multiple ways, with the basic strategy being to teach both English and Spanish concurrently.

Therefore, schools have many choices in how to more effectively approach the education of Mexican American students. Unfortunately, many schools often choose to do nothing, or choose programs that are less costly and also less efficient than other programs. This sometimes becomes problematic for some schools that do not have/or want to spend resources on these children, or that refuse to admit that they have a problem educating language-minority students in their schools.

Unqualified Teachers

In order to make sure that Mexican American English language learners are successful in school, they must be taught by teachers who have been prepared well and have positive dispositions towards them. However, there has been a historical shortage of bilingual education and ESL teachers. The shortage of bilingual education teachers has been well documented since before bilingual education was really a programmatic approach (Gándara, 1986; Macías, 1989; Quezada, 1991; Torres-Guzman and Goodwin, 1995). This shortage has remained critical since the early 1980s. Boe (1990) noted that no national database of bilingual education teachers was available to support refined supply and demand research in this area. Gold (1992) referred to this shortage as "the single greatest barrier to the improvement of instructional programs for limited English proficient (LEP) students" (p. 223).

Some districts made trips to Mexico to recruit Mexican teachers for their bilingual education programs (Barbe, 2006). In order to provide schools with the certified bilingual education and ESL teachers needed, Texas only requires that certified mainstream teachers take the required certification exams needed for bilingual and ESL education without any formal preparation in teaching ELLs. Not only are these teachers often unprepared, they also may not have the appropriate dispositions needed to teach ELLs.

Dispositions can be defined as professional judgments and actions based on moral and ethical concerns (Johnson and Reiman, 2007). Teacher dispositions play a key role in all instructional modes. Historically many mainstream teachers have had trouble understanding Mexican American students and as a result form unfavorable dispositions toward them. This was one reason why Mexican Americans performed poorly in American schools. These teachers had a tremendous amount of prejudice and antipathy toward Mexican American students, and their lack of acceptance of students' language and culture has been well documented by the historically negative treatment that Mexican Americans received in schools (Midobuche, 1999). Mayeske (1967), in analyzing the Coleman Report of 1966, found that teachers' characteristics had the most influence on Mexican American students' academic achievement. Samway and McKeon (1999) reported that some teacher candidates believed that the lack of English proficiency among students was a lack of cognitive ability. For teachers of ELLs, dispositions become extremely important, because according to Cline and Necochea (2006) "teachers become better prepared to adapt to the local context, linguistic diversity, and cultural differences . . ." when they understand themselves and their students better (p. 1).

Who prepares teachers to work with English language learners? And, what types of dispositions do they bring to the classroom experience? Do they have preparation in these areas or are they just attempting to be marketable? There is no consensus through research on defining dispositions and there exists no common language to universally describe them (Thornton, 2006; Thompson *et al.*, 2005). As a result, at times, even the university professoriate is not prepared adequately or may also not possess the appropriate dispositions to prepare teachers for these environments (Midobuche and Benavides, 2010; Midobuche *et al.*, 2010). Of equal concern are those teachers who take the bilingual or ESL certification exams through alternative certification processes without any formal preparation, so that whatever dispositions they may possess go completely unchecked. If their dispositions go unchecked and no one intervenes and weak teacher candidates become licensed to teach, many future children could receive less than effective instruction.

When teacher candidates enter a teacher preparation program they come with their own set of beliefs, values, and dispositions. It is understood that not all teacher candidates come to class with an understanding of cultural and linguistic differences, and of white privilege. In teacher preparation programs students examine their attitudes, beliefs, values, and dispositions (Major and Brock, 2003). When the professor asks teacher candidates to reconsider their prejudices and misconceptions and become more critical and reflective, this may lead to a philosophical mismatch (op.cit.; Pajares, 1993). Through this process teachers in training may expand their knowledge base and open new ways of thinking, seeing, and behaving. They may come to question themselves and others regarding their beliefs and practices. They explore and develop new attitudes and understanding. They develop a self-awareness, as well as critical and reflective thinking. However, teacher educators must be concerned with transforming attitudes and dispositions beyond the surface level pedagogical practices, cross-cultural awareness, and field experiences. Otherwise, teacher preparation programs could be reinforcing the negative stereotypes that they are attempting to eradicate (Wiggins and Follo, 1999). It is vital that all teacher education programs prepare new teachers in a manner that exposes them to the diversity that they will have to address as teachers. To not do so would be a disservice to the new teacher and a travesty to any student they will teach.

The Lack of English Skills and the Loss of the Native Language and Culture

Many Mexican American English language learners are US native born, while others are foreign born. The US native-born learners may have been raised in homes and communities where limited English was spoken. Hadaway *et al.*, (2009) found that native-born students may have a weak first language since their caretakers are also losing their primary language due to living away from their home country. The fact that caregivers may have also interspersed their heritage language with English is likely to have affected the modeling of this language to children. Hadaway *et al.*, (op.cit.) also maintain that native-born English language learners usually do not acquire literacy in their first language and that there is inconsistent language modeling in both the native and target languages. These researchers state that the native US-born English language learner may feel ambiguity toward their heritage language and culture, and that these students may also feel confused and marginalized within our American school system.

Hadaway *et al.*, also point out some characteristics of the foreign-born English learners that may be more advantageous than those of the US native-born ELLs. These researchers state that foreign-born students generally have a stronger heritage language model at home. This helps to not only reinforce language concepts, but also to bridge the learning of new language. Foreign-born ELLs may have had schooling in their country and developed literacy in their heritage language. Researchers also find that foreign-born ELLs generally identify with their heritage language and culture. They feel pride in their background experiences and this promotes a positive self-esteem. This is very different from the experiences of many US-born Mexican American students who often perceive their cultural and linguistic differences as negative.

The majority community, the American culture, schools, and sometimes the parents of the ELLs push them toward the target language (English) quickly. According to Schwartz and Sprouse (1996) there is a trend to make the children of immigrants monolingual English speakers. The Mexican American English language learner may enter school and be placed in an English-speaking classroom where they may struggle to understand and master difficult concepts because of the mismatch between their English skills and the English language development program. When many young Mexican American children begin school in the United States without speaking the English language they are at an immediate disadvantage because they are placed in a catch-up mode (Cummins, 2001). As a student progresses through the curriculum they may encounter even greater difficulty in acquiring the target language and could easily become a dropout statistic, never achieving their full potential as a learner or a productive member of society (Midobuche and Benavides, 2002).

Mexican American students in American school systems are often the targets of Americanization attempts by teachers and peers alike. This sometimes takes the form of Americanizing names and the pronunciation of last names. Changing a student's name is a severe disrespect, yet teachers continue to sometimes attempt a total assimilation of the Mexican American student. Bartolemé and Balderama (2001) state:

> The combination of an assimilationist belief system and a deficit ideology proves to be an especially deadly one. It is so because it justifies disrespecting Latino students' native language and culture, mis-teaching them dominant culture and English, and then blaming their academic difficulties on their "pathological deficiencies" (p. 52).

However, many schools would feel that if these students just spoke English they would count as success stories since the role of the school is to teach the student English (Midobuche and Benavides, 2002). Baker (1993) notes that English is the language of power, value, and prestige.

But can it be labeled a success story when a Mexican American student loses his heritage language and culture?

Many Mexican American children enter the American classroom not speaking English. For the majority of educators it seems that nothing is more important than making up this "deficit." The child's culture, traditions, and native language are often viewed as secondary and non-essential to the mastery of English. Often, American public schools view English language learners as "deficient" solely because of their lack of English skills (Midobuche and Benavides, 2002). The student is placed in the category society reserves for those lacking something. They are deficient and missing something within themselves. Generally speaking, society, the national community, and many local schools pressure the Mexican American family and the English language learner to learn English to the exclusion of all else that may be important in their lives. They do it with the single-minded purpose of helping the child mainstream into the American classroom. The overall goal is to ensure that as an adult, the Mexican American child will speak English. The emphasis supposedly is placed on making this child feel that they are no longer deficient or limited in their English proficiency. So much attention (and yet so little time) is given to the child attempting to learn the English language that their native language is often sacrificed and forgotten.

In the past it usually took three generations (the first being the immigrants themselves) to lose a heritage language (Pew Hispanic Center, 2009). Many immigrant parents whose English may have been limited, or who may have suffered discrimination based on their lack of English or accented English, may have insisted that their children speak only English (Hadaway *et al.*, 2009). Perhaps if these parents had been aware of what Fishman describes when a language is lost they may not have been so eager to push for validating only the English language and neglecting the Spanish. Joshua Fishman (1997), wrote:

> The heart of what is lost when you lose a language, is that most of the culture is in the language, and is expressed in that language. Take it away from the culture, and you take away its greetings, its curses, its praises, its laws, its literature, its songs, its riddles, its proverbs, its cures, its wisdom, its prayers. The culture could not be expressed and handed down in any other way. What would be left? When you are talking about the language, most of what you are talking about is the culture. That is, you are losing all those things that essentially are the way of life, the way of thought, the way of valuing, and the human reality that you are talking about" (p. 81).

A parent must realize that if the child's native language is not validated, and if they do not acquire proficiency in English rapidly, they will be viewed by society as an academic failure and quickly be forgotten as a statistic. As an adult, this individual will be frequently asked: "Do you speak Spanish?" If the person replies with a "no," then the inevitable "why not" is next. This can be followed with something like: "After all, you are of Mexican descent, didn't your parents teach you Spanish at home? Didn't you communicate in Spanish? Didn't you live in a Spanish-speaking community?" The implied and usually unspoken questions are: Don't you value your heritage? Are you ashamed of being Hispanic (Midobuche and Benavides, 2002)?

The individual is immediately placed in a situation where they have to defend their "deficiency." It is at this point that the person comes full circle to those feelings of a child attempting to learn English; feelings of powerlessness, frustration, embarrassment, and occasionally shame. They quickly have to make excuses for their apparent inadequacies. They in essence shoulder the entire blame for the situation, never thinking that perhaps the school system and its inadequate programs—and the community's efforts to totally "Americanize" them—might in some way be partially at fault for their feelings. This is truly a "no-win" situation for the individual and demonstrates an attitude of convenience toward language by the majority community (Midobuche and Benavides, 2002).

The validation of one's language and culture is essential. However, in an initial study of teacher reactions to the study of Mexican and Mexican American history, the authors found that American bilingual and ESL teachers were at best ambivalent about teaching this material to their Mexican American students (Benavides and Midobuche, 2001; Midobuche and Benavides, 2010). There was a general feeling of discomfort among many of the respondents when asked to include Mexican, or Mexican American history and culture in their bilingual or ESL classroom; at times they seemed very conflicted. Some thought it was a great idea while others rejected the material as not true history, even when it was emphasized that this was Mexico's version of their history. These teachers seemed to want to "sanitize" the Mexican version of history in order to make it more comfortable for them. While some of these teachers did not want to deviate from the standard American curriculum, others simply refused to acknowledge Mexican history at all.

The Anglo world expects Mexican American individuals to not only speak English, but Spanish as well. Conversely, the Mexican American community expects them to retain their native language and be especially proud of their heritage. Why do American schools persist in labeling children and requiring them to change their entire essence in order to survive? Why must society make children feel "incomplete and deficient," and allow some of them to grow into "incomplete and deficient" adults (Midobuche and Benavides, 2002)?

Immigration: Documented or Undocumented Status

The issue of migration and/or immigration is probably one of the most misunderstood issues confronting both immigrants and American citizens alike. Perez *et al.* (2009) reported that migration is one of the most radical transitions and life changes that an individual or a family can endure. For immigrant children this change is a dramatic experience that reshapes their lives. Schools need to sensitize their faculties and staffs to understand students like these in order to better serve them. American law guarantees educational rights for these particular students (*Plyler v. Doe*, 1982).

Migration produces stressors related to the loss of close relationships; housing problems; a sense of isolation; obtaining legal documentation; going through the acculturation process; learning the English language; negotiating ethnic identity; changing family roles; and adjusting to the schooling experience (Garza *et al.*, 2004; Perez *et al.* 2009; Portes and Rumbaut, 2001; Suarez-Orozco and Suarez-Orozco, 2001; Zhou, 1997). Acculturation stressors would include leaving relatives and friends behind when moving; feeling pressured to speak only Spanish at home; living at home with many people; and feeling that other kids make fun of the way they speak English (Padilla *et al.*, 1988; Perez *et al.* 2009). Stress may also be created in selecting which set of cultural norms and expectations to follow. Mexican American children and their families either have to select expectations from their culture of origin or that of the mainstream culture. The differences in their value may create pressure (Perez *et al.* 2009).

Immigrant college-age students are not spared the problems of trying to obtain an American education. Perez *et al.* (2009) also report that there are only a handful of studies on undocumented college students. De Leon's (2005) study reported that these students remember: isolation, fear, and those teachers who treated them negatively. Dozier (1993) found three central emotional concerns for undocumented college students. These are fear of deportation, loneliness, and depression. Fear of deportation is very central to undocumented students. It influences every aspect of their lives. They are afraid to go to hospitals and this fear makes it impossible to obtain work authorization or they are forced to stay in bad work conditions. They are also reluctant to develop close emotional relationships with others (Dozier, 1993). All of the respondents in the study by Buriel *et al.*, (1998) reported frustration, helplessness, shame, and fear—due to their undocumented status. They also reported that language brokering was seen as a positive experience while ethnic identity formation, stereotypes about Mexicans and negotiating gender role expectations with their parents were stressors. How can students be expected to learn in this climate of fear (Midobuche and Benavides, 2012)?

Garza *et al.* (2004) stated that the image that has been constructed for Mexican American migrant children is one of a perpetuating cycle of failure. Consequently, many educators are convinced that the children of farm workers ("the ghost workers") will never be able to transition to high achieving positions. Sadly, many of these students are led to believe that they are intrinsically inferior, or that their fate is to follow the path of hopelessness that has been imposed on them for generations.

Olivarez (2006) reported that families seemed to support students' aspirations to attend college, but the home environments were not always conducive to college preparation. Students had to care for younger siblings and often did their homework away from home because it was crowded in the family's small rented apartment, or they secluded themselves in a corner or waited until everyone was asleep to get their work done. None of the students had a separate room in their homes where they could find a quiet space to study. Sixty percent of these students lived in crowded homes with six or more people, and 90 percent lived in single studio apartments where everyone slept in the same room (Olivarez, 2006). Some students attributed their lack of academic success to not having enough time or being too busy to complete their schoolwork to the best of their ability, and others felt their jobs sometimes left them too tired to focus on school. Again, 60 percent reported working after school or on the weekends, between 16 and 40 hours per week, and 60 percent also participated on athletic teams (Olivarez, 2006). High school employment was considered a risk factor if students worked more than 20 hours per week (Perez *et al.*, 2009; Steinberg and Cauffman, 1995).

In a report by the Pew Center, Lopez (2009) states that the main reasons given by 16 to 25-year-old Latinos for dropping out of school were economic (74 percent), poor English skills (40 percent), and a general dislike of school (40 percent). These types of statistics and reasons for low achievement have perplexed educators for decades. Mexican American schooling in the US has long been characterized by high dropout rates and low college completion rates. Both problems have moderated over time, but a persistent educational attainment gap remains between Hispanics and non-Hispanic whites (Lopez, 2009). Length of time in the US also seemed to play a role in academic success. Those who had spent 10 years or more in the US had lower GPAs than those who had been in the US from 3 to 8 years (Olivarez, 2006). Does this mean that the longer Mexican American immigrant students attend US schools, the less learning is taking place among these students? What factors and conditions are responsible for these dropout rates? How can they be addressed by the educational system?

The educational experience of Mexican Americans normally has been characterized by high dropout rates, and this is especially true among foreign-born Latino students. Foreign-born Latino students also suffer low college completion rates (Chapman *et al.*, 2011). Hadaway *et al.*, (2009), point out that native-born and foreign-born Latino students have major differences in their lives and that these impact their schooling. For example, students born in the US may have a weak first language model at home while foreign-born students generally have a strong first language model in their homes. Strong first language skills help to reinforce language concepts and structures and therefore can serve as a bridge to learning another language. US-born Mexican American students may also experience difficulty in acquiring another language due to the pressures of assimilation or learning English, that soon there is inconsistent modeling in one or both home languages. Because US-born Latinos inhabit two worlds, they are often at odds with fitting into either or both. This may lead to confusion and perhaps marginalization (Hadaway *et al.*, 2009).

There are many sides to the issue of immigration and the issues thus created in the field of education. While it is not up to educators to solve the problem of immigration, they do need to look deeply into the issues surrounding the education of these students. With immigration, the problem is very close to home. It is imperative that all educators look at themselves and see how these issues affect not only them but also these particular children and their extended families.

Summary

There are many issues involved in the education of Mexican American students in today's schools, especially for those students that are English language learners. The issues and their corollaries discussed here have been present in American education since Mexican Americans were made part of the American landscape in the 1800s. For many decades Mexican Americans were neglected and their educational needs were never considered essential to the future of their country. The changing demographics and the need to be inclusive in the approach to educating all students and making them contributing members to society have changed those particular sentiments. The United States can no longer continue to squander its personal capital as it did in past years. It is important to seriously study the needs of these particular children and find ways to make them contributing members of our overall social system. American schools and universities must find ways to understand, include, and celebrate the linguistic and cultural differences that many of our Mexican American students bring to the educational experience. To continue to neglect this growing segment of our population is a strategy that puts our entire nation at risk.

It is not in the best interests of our country to continue to ignore the issues of poverty, language and cultural differences, inadequate schools and programs, as well as shortages of qualified teachers and administrators, that contribute to poor educational outcomes among the Mexican American population and the growing numbers of English language learners. Mexican Americans have been a great part of the growth of this nation and have contributed in ways that would make any nation proud to include them in their family. The American educational system should be concerned with providing an equal educational opportunity to all of its children. Mexican Americans have been, and will continue to be, a large part of our country. Only with equal opportunities, respect, and validation will this population be able to contribute in positive ways.

Ending our country's impoverished view of Mexican Americans should be a top priority. These children are not validated linguistically, nor are they taught to value their culture and history. This treatment of Mexican American children decidedly worsens their opportunities to improve, contribute more, and become a part of the American mosaic that is so critical in leading our country into the new century. Bringing these students successfully into the realm of education will help to break the cycle of poverty and low educational attainment. All of these children, including English language learners, need to be educated by teachers and teacher preparation programs that address the dispositions needed in order to understand and respect their students. These teachers and teacher preparation programs need to go beyond platitudes to ensure that these children succeed.

Future Directions and Challenges

Teaching culturally and linguistically diverse students can be a challenge. Perhaps what is needed is what Midobuche and Benavides (2010) refer to as the catalysts for change. These catalysts are referred to as the 4Rs and 4Cs. They are meant as a set of indicators to guide educators when working with Mexican American students or other language-minority children.

THE 4 Rs

Recognition—the first of the 4 Rs—on the part of the American public school system and the larger US community that people come in different languages. Therefore, social institutions and individuals in general must recognize, acknowledge, and validate a child's language. Language, culture, and the child are after all, inseparable.

Respect—the second R—for another person's language (and by association their culture), manifested by an acceptance of individual and group differences and attributes. This value will help ensure that individuals promote and defend each other's rights and privileges. Respect for children in the classroom and their families in the community will lead to mutual respect and acceptance.

Retention—the third R—should capture the idea that by recognizing and respecting an individual's language, we should help them to *retain* and maintain it in order to not lose it. As Fishman (1997) has pointed out, losing one's language entails losing the culture as well, leading to a loss of direction in life.

Responsiveness—the fourth R—stands for the appropriate action/s of teachers, administrators, and schools to ensure the success of all students. It is especially critical that effective schools maintain high student expectations and academic rigor in order to allow the student to acquire the academic skills necessary to succeed. Responsiveness also refers to the specific adaptations and modifications needed in developing a quality curriculum in order to meet the educational needs of culturally and linguistically diverse students.

THE 4 Cs

Caring—the first C—is an "action" that encompasses involvement and participation in the meaningful education of students.

Courage—in a teacher, refers to having the courage to advocate for the linguistic, cultural, and educational needs of English language learners. This is especially important in a time when the field of bilingual education is experiencing backlashes against immigrant students and bilingual education programs.

Conocimiento—in Spanish, refers to understanding the cultural, linguistic, and content knowledge of the areas involved in the education of ELLs. Conocimiento also refers to a thorough understanding of procedures, policies, court decisions, laws, and legislation affecting the education of ELLs. Every state should have a well-prepared and highly qualified teacher in every classroom who knows what to teach, how to teach, and has command of the subject matter being taught.

Commitment—the fourth C—is required of teachers of ELLs, characterized by a dedication to the education of the child, professional development, and the advocacy for ELLs and their families and communities, in order to ensure that their linguistic and educational rights are protected, respected, and enforced. This commitment is crucial because those that subscribe to it are frequently the only advocates that these children will have (Midobuche, 2011; Midobuche and Benavides 2002; 2010).

Policy Implications

The implications for practice, policy, and research are extremely important to all. The history of neglect afforded Mexican Americans in all three of these areas means that neglect is likely to continue into the future unless concentrated efforts are made to ameliorate this historical trend. Demographic predictions concerning the increasing number of Mexican Americans indicate that the future educational needs of this population will have a profound impact on US schools— and society as well. Therefore teacher education programs within universities will need to take much of the responsibility and leadership for creating meaningful programs to prepare teachers who, through a process of heightening their own dispositions, can recognize and understand Mexican American students. These preparation programs must ensure that Mexican American students receive the education that will allow them to contribute to our economic and social well-being. The overall policy needs to be one of inclusion and not of neglect. Research can strengthen the development of better dispositions emphasizing the entire field, in order to assure the development of a teaching force that is prepared for the future.

Preparing better teachers will in turn give school administrators the ability to hire better teachers for their programs, thus helping to alleviate the constant shortage of teachers in this field. The State government should assist universities in their leadership role by providing adequate funding, and universities should create bilingual and ESL preparation programs, as well as a better type of leadership within local school districts. Leaders in local districts (as well as in Colleges of Education within universities), will need to learn about ELLs; together, these entities should enable the building of sustainable programs within their schools and universities—and this should assist schools in hiring better teachers, because the schools will be stakeholders in the future of these children and their communities. Universities, state government, and the private sector will also benefit from a better-educated citizenry.

Notes

1   The authors have chosen to use the term Mexican American(s) to refer specifically to a subsection of the US Hispanic population that derives its ethnic and cultural roots from Mexico.
2   The term Hispanic or Latino refers to all other populations from other parts of Central and South America as well as Spain, Cuba, Puerto Rico, Mexico, and/or other Caribbean countries.

References

Arias, M. B., and Casanova, U. (1993). *Bilingual education: Politics, practice, and research*. Chicago: University of Chicago Press.

Baker, C. (1993). *Foundations of bilingual education and bilingualism*. Clevedon, Philadelphia: Multilingual Matters.

Barbe, A. (2006, January 21). JISD heads to Mexico to recruit bilingual teachers. *Jacksonville Daily Progress* (TX). Retrieved July 29, 2008 from: http://www.jacksonvilleprogress.com/homepage/local_story_021155148.html?keyword=leadpicturestory

Bartolomé, L. L., and Balderama, M. V. (2001). The need for educators with political and ideological clarity: Providing our children with "the best." In M. de la Luz Reyes and J.J. Halcon (Eds.), *The best for our children: Critical perspectives on literacy for Latino students* (pp. 48–64). New York: Teachers College, Columbia University.

Benavides, A., and Midobuche, E. (2001, April). "Bilingual and ESL teachers and the social studies classroom: A study of attitudes and perceptions". Paper Presentation, American Educational Research Association (AERA), Seattle, Washington.

Berliner, D. (2014). Effects of inequality and poverty vs. teachers and schooling on America's youth. *Teachers College Record, 116*, from: http://www.tcrecord.org

Boe, E. E. (1990). Demand, supply, and shortage of bilingual and ESL teachers: Models, data, and policy issues. In *Proceedings of the first annual research symposium on limited English proficient students' issues.* Washington, DC: U.S. Department of Education, OBEMLA.

Buriel, R., Perez, W., De Ment, T., Chavez, D., and Moran, V. (1998). The relationship of language brokering to academic performance, biculturalism, and self-efficacy among Latino adolescents. *Hispanic Journal of Behavioral Sciences, 20,* 283–287.

Carter, T. P. (1970). *Mexican Americans in schools: A history of educational neglect.* College Entrance Examination Board, New York.

Chapman, C., Laird, J., Ifill, N., and Kewal, R. A. (2011). Trends in high school dropout and completion rates in the United States: 1972–2009 (NCES 2012-006). U.S. Department of Education. Washington, DC: National Center for Education Statistics. Retrieved April 5, 2012, from: http://nces.ed.gov/pubsearch

Cline, Z., and Necochea, J. (2006). Teacher dispositions for effective education in the borderlands. *The Educational Forum.* Retrieved July 25, 2008 from: http://findarticles.com/p/articles/mi_qa4013/is_200604/ai_n17178245/pg_1

Crawford, J. (2004). *Educating English learners: Language diversity in the classroom* (5th edn.). Los Angeles, CA: Bilingual Educational Services, Inc.

Cummins, J. (2001). Assessment and intervention with culturally linguistically diverse learners. In S. R. Hurlely and J. V. Tinajero (Eds.), *Literacy assessment of second language learners* (pp. 115–129). Boston, MA: Allyn and Bacon.

De Leon, S. (2005). *Assimilation and ambiguous experience of the resilient male Mexican immigrants that successfully navigate American higher education.* Austin: Unpublished doctoral dissertation, University of Texas.

Dozier, S. B. (1993). Emotional concerns of undocumented and out-of-status foreign students. *Community Review, 13,* 29–33.

Fishman, J. (1997). What do you lose when you lose your language? In G. Cantoni (Ed.), *Stabilizing indigenous languages.* Flagstaff: Center for Excellence in Education, Northern Arizona University. Retrieved November 14, 2013, from: http://jan.ucc.nau.edu/jar/SIL.pdf

Gándara, P. (1986). *Bilingual education: Learning English in California.* Sacramento: Assembly Office of Research.

Garza, E., Reyes, P., and Trueba, E. (2004). *Resiliency and success: Migrant children in the United States.* Boulder, CO: Paradigm.

Gold, N. C. (1992). Solving the shortage of bilingual teachers: Policy implications of California's staffing initiative for LEP students. *Proceedings of the third national research symposium on limited English proficient students issues.* Vol.1, pp. 223–278. Washington, DC: U.S. Department of Education, Office of Bilingual Education and Minority Language Affairs.

Gonzalez-Barrera, A., and Lopez, M. H. (2013). A demographic portrait of Mexican-Origin Hispanics in the United States. Pew Research Center, Hispanic Trends Project. Retrieved November, 14, 2013, from: http://www.pewhispanic.org/2013/05/01/a-demographic-portrait-of-Mexican-origin-Hispanics-in-the-united-states/

Hadaway, N. L., Vardell, S. M., and Young, T. A. (2009). *What every teacher should know about English language learners.* Boston: Pearson Education Inc.

Johnson, L., and Reiman, A. (2007). Beginning teacher disposition: Examining the moral/ethical domain. *Teaching and Teacher Education, 23*(5), 676–687.

Krashen, S. D. (2011). *To Improve Schools, Fight Poverty, Education Expert Says,* Lecture at Fordham University, Campus Resources, Newsroom, from: http://www.fordham.edu/Campus_Resources/enewsroom/topstories_2153.asp

Lopez, M. H. (2009). *Latinos and education: Explaining the attainment gap.* Pew Hispanic Center, from: http://pewhispanic.org/reports/report.phb?ReportID=115

Lopez, M. H., and Cohn, D. (2011). *Hispanic poverty rate highest in new supplemental census measure.* Pew Research Center, Hispanic Trends Project, from: http://www.pewhispanic.org/2011/11/08/hispanic-poverty-rate-highest-in-new-supplemental-census-measure/

Macías, R. F. (1989). *Bilingual teacher supply and demand in the United States.* Los Angeles: University of California Center for Multilingual, Multicultural Research. Claremont, CA: The Tomas Rivera Center.

Major, E. M., and Brock, C. H. (2003). Fostering positive dispositions toward diversity: Dialogical explorations of a moral dilemma. *Teacher Education Quarterly, 30*(4), 7–26.

Mayeske, G. W. (1967). Educational achievement among Mexican Americans: A special report from the Educational Opportunities Survey, an unofficial analysis of Coleman *et. al.*, 1966. Washington, DC: National Center for Educational Statistics, U.S. Office of Education, Technical Note 22, Jan 9, 1967.

Midobuche, E. (1999). Respect in the classroom: Reflections of a Mexican American educator. *Educational Leadership, 56*(7), 80–82.

Midobuche, E. (2011). Becoming a dream catcher for English language learners: Implications for teachers, students, and self. In A. Benavides, E. Midobuche, and P. Carlson (Eds.), *Hispanics in the Southwest: Issues in immigration, education, health, and public policy*. Tempe, AZ: Bilingual Review Press.

Midobuche, E., and Benavides, A. H. (2002). Language attitudes and the educational culture of convenience: Placing students in a no win situation. *National Forum of Applied Education Research Journal, 15*(4), 73–80.

Midobuche, E., and Benavides, A. (2010). Preparing teachers for English language learners: Meeting the challenges of teacher shortages, transitions, dispositions, and partnerships. In M. Cowart and P. Dam (Eds.), *Teaching English language learners: Paths to success*. Texas Woman's University: Canh Nam Publishers, Inc.

Midobuche, E., and Benavides, A. (2012). Mexican American English language learners: Learning in a climate of politics, curriculum reform, immigration, and fear. In M. Cowart and L. Anderson (Eds.), *English language learners in the 21st century classroom: Challenges and expectations* (pp. 258–281). Texas Woman's University: Canh Nam Publishers, Inc.

Midobuche, E., Benavides, A., and de Rasez de Guyenne, W. (2010). Perceptions, attitudes and the identification of dispositions: Creating a model for teaching English language learners. *Teacher Education and Practice Journal, 23*, 181–193.

Motel, S., and Patten, E. (2011). *Statistical portrait of Hispanics in the United States, 2011*. Hispanic Trends Project, Pew Research Center. from: http:// www.pewhispanic.org/2013/02/15/statistical-portrait-of-hispanics-in-the-united-states-2011/

National Education Association, The invisible minority, (1966). Report of The NEA-Tucson Survey on the Teaching of Spanish to the Spanish-Speaking, National Education Association, Washington, D.C., from: http://eric.ed.gov/?id=ED017222

Olivarez, P. M. (2006). *Ready but restricted: An examination of the challenges of college access and financial aid for college-ready undocumented students in the U. S.* Unpublished doctoral dissertation, University of Southern California.

Ovando, C. J., Combs, M. C., and Collier, V. P. (2006). *Bilingual and ESL classrooms: Teaching in multicultural contexts*. New York, NY: McGraw Hill.

Padilla, A. M., Cervantes, R. C., Maldonado, M., and Garcia, R. E. (1988). Coping responses to psychosocial stressors in Mexican and Central American immigrants. *Journal of Community Psychology, 16*, 418–427.

Pajares, F. (1993). Preservice teachers' beliefs: A focus for teacher education. *Action in Teacher Education, 15*(2), 45–54.

Perez, W., Espinoza, R., Ramos, K., Coronado, H., and Cortes, R. (2009). Academic resilience among undocumented Latino students. *Hispanic Journal of Behavioral Sciences, 31*, 149–181.

Pew Hispanic Center, (2009, December 11). "Between two Worlds: How young Latinos come of age in America." Washington, DC: Pewhispanic.org. From: http://www.pewhispanic.org/2009/12/11/between-two-worlds-how-young-latinos-come-of-age-in-america/

Plyler v. Doe, (No. 80-1538), 457 202, U.S. Supreme Court, 1982.

Portes, A., and Rumbaut, R. G. (2001). *Legacies: The story of the immigrant second generation*. Berkeley, CA: University of California Press.

Quezada, M. (1991). *District remedies to eliminate the shortage of qualified teachers of limited English proficient students in California*. Doctoral dissertation, University of Southern California.

Samway, K., and McKeon, D. (1999). *Myths and realities: Best practices for language minority students*. Portsmouth, NH: Heinemann.

Sánchez, G. I. (1940). *Forgotten people*. Albuquerque, NM: The University of New Mexico Press.

Schwartz, B. D., and Sprouse, R. A. (1996). L2 cognitive states and the full transfer/full access model. *Second language research, 12*(1), 40–72.

Steinberg, L., and Cauffman, E. (1995). The impact of employment on adolescent development. *Annals of Child Development, 33*, 131–166.

Suarez-Orozco, C., and Suarez-Orozco, M. M. (2001). *Children of Immigration.* Cambridge, MA: Harvard University Press.

Texas Education Agency, Division of Performance Reporting, Academic Excellence Indicator System (AEIS) (2013). *2011–2012 State Performance Report, Section 1, p. 2.* from: http://ritter.tea.state.tx.us/perfreport/aeis/2012/state.html

Thomas, W. P., and Collier, V. P. (1997). *A national study of school effectiveness for language minority students' long-term academic achievement.* Center for Research on Education, Diversity and Excellence, UC Berkeley. From: http://www.usc.edu/ dept/education/CMMR/CollierThomasComplete.pdf

Thompson, S., Ransdell, M., and Rousseau, C. (2005). Effective teachers in urban school settings: Linking teacher disposition and student performance on standardized tests. *Journal of Authentic Learning, 2*(1), 22–34.

Thornton, H. (2006). Dispositions in action: Do dispositions make a difference in practice? *Teacher Education Quarterly.* Retrieved July 22, 2008, from: http://findarticles.com/p/articles/mi_qa3960/is_200604/ai_n17183802/print

Torres-Guzman, M. E., and Goodwin, A. L. (1995). Mentoring bilingual teachers. NCBE FOCUS. *Occasional Papers in Bilingual Education, 12.*

U.S. Census Bureau (2008). *1970, 1980, 1990, and 2000 Decennial Censuses, July 1, 2011 Population Estimates; 2008 National Population Projections.* From: http://www.census.gov/newsroom/cspan/hispanic/2012.06.22_cspan_hispanics_4.pdf

Wiggins, R. A., and Follo, E. J. (1999). Development of knowledge, attitudes, and commitment to teach diverse student populations. *Journal of Teacher Education, 50*(2), 94–105.

Zhou, M. (1997). Growing up American: The challenge of immigrant children and children of immigrants. *Annual Review of Sociology, 23*, 63–95.

9

BILINGUAL DEVELOPMENT IN EARLY CHILDHOOD

Research and Policy Implications for Mexican American Children

Marlene Zepeda and James L. Rodriguez

Introduction

This chapter focuses on bilingual language development from birth through age five, and its implications for research and policy for Mexican-origin children living in the United States. This particular topic is highly relevant given the implications for school readiness and achievement for Latino children in general (Garcia and Jensen, 2010) and, more specifically, for Mexican Americans—who are the largest Latino sub-population in the US (Lopez *et al.*, 2013).

Though historically and contemporaneously Mexican Americans have been the largest Latino sub-population, much of the published empirical research on bilingual language development among Latino children has tended to focus on Cubans, Puerto Ricans, and Dominicans. Thus, this chapter unveils a notable gap in the literature that also presents a significant research opportunity, since it is unclear whether and to what extent research findings to date are generalizable to Mexican-origin children.

We begin this chapter with an overview of the theoretical basis for bilingual language development, followed by a review of factors that promote and constrain such development. We then proceed to describe research on bilingual language development chronologically (birth to three and preschool-age). The final section of the chapter provides our recommendations, along with considerations and implications for practice, policy, and research.

Literature Review

Theoretical Basis

From an international perspective, bilingual development is considered normative. According to Grosjean (2010) it is estimated that half of the world's population knows two or more languages. A number of experts (García and Kleifgen, 2010; Genesee *et al.*, 2004) suggest that bilingualism should be considered a particular case of language acquisition that is normative and can impart cognitive advantages. But what are some of the general processes involved in the development of bilingualism and how does it proceed across the early childhood years? Is the developmental trajectory of bilingualism similar or different from that of monolingualism?

In the context of early childhood, bilingualism refers to learning two or more languages at the same time, as well as learning a second language while continuing to develop a first (or home) language (Office of Head Start, 2009). For young children, there are two possible routes to bilingualism: simultaneous and sequential/successive. In simultaneous bilingualism, the child is exposed to two languages from birth, and in sequential—sometimes termed successive—children are exposed to a second language after they have learned the first (Paradis, 2007). Among Mexican-origin children, simultaneous bilinguals are children who are exposed to both Spanish and English prior to school entry, whereas sequential bilinguals are those children who have primarily been exposed to Spanish and encounter English for the first time in a formal school setting.

The characterization of the developmental trajectory of bilingualism as simultaneous or sequential, generally drawn from work with older children, has been criticized for not unpacking the timing of simultaneous bilingualism in early childhood. According to Genesee (2006) the confusion lies in the age in which a child is first exposed to a second language. Various ages of introduction of the second language have been posited as constituting a simultaneous bilingual (de Houwer, 1995). The issue of when a second language is introduced and used with the developing child has practical implications for our understanding of how and when to begin supporting bilingual language development.

An important theoretical underpinning of bilingualism is the notion that the first language provides a foundation for development of the second language (August and Shanahan, 2006). When a child is learning a second language the process of *cross-linguistic* influence or *transfer* occurs. This process describes how aspects of the first language, such as knowledge of vocabulary and grammar, are applied in the development of the second language. There are two mechanisms that have been advanced to explain how cross-linguistic influence or transfer occurs (op.cit.). The first is *interdependence* in language proficiency and the second is *contrastive influence*, that operates between the two languages. In *interdependence*, it is posited that a centralized language system exists that allows the developing bilingual child to draw information from one language to inform their understanding of another language (Cummins, 1979). In *contrastive influence*, structural similarities between languages, such as word order, are stressed, allowing the bilingual child to borrow grammar from one language to transfer to another (Odin, 1989). Based on contrastive analysis, a speaker of Spanish would place an adjective after the noun in English since that is the typical word order in Spanish (e.g. "the car blue"). The degree to which particular elements of a language can be easily transferred is contingent upon the alphabetic or ideographic similarity of the two languages.

In addition to alphabetic or ideographic similarity, the extent of language transfer may also depend upon the complexity of the language components considered. In a meta-analysis of oral language and phonology in bilinguals at various age levels, Melby-Lervag and Lervag (2011) found moderate to large associations between first and second language transfer on the language component of phonological awareness and decoding, whereas there was only a small relationship between first and second language transfer on the language component of orality. These researchers conclude that because learning the sounds of a language is easier than speaking the language, stronger associations exist for phonology than they do for oral language development. Another factor in the transfer of knowledge from one language to another is the strength of the child's phonology, semantics, and syntax in the first language. Research has shown that children who show greater ability in their second language have established a foundation in their first language (Genesee *et al.*, 2006). For example, in a study of the language and literacy skills of Spanish-speaking kindergarten children, Cardenas-Hagen *et al.*, (2007) found that children with strong Spanish letter-name and sound knowledge showed higher levels of English letter-name and sound knowledge when compared to Spanish–English bilinguals with lower levels of knowledge in their first language. These findings support the idea advanced by Cummins (1979) that a certain level of proficiency or "threshold" needs to exist in the development of the first language before an adequate level of proficiency can develop in the second language.

Contextual Factors that Promote and Constrain Bilingual Language Development

There are a number of important factors that influence the level of bilingualism that a child can achieve. For monolinguals, it has been noted that the degree to which they will learn language is contingent on the quality and quantity of their language input (Hart and Risley, 1995). This presumption of language input holds true for bilingual language development as well. However, in bilingual development, language input is influenced by a host of individual and contextual factors that affect language maintenance and loss (Pearson, 2007). These factors include the age of first exposure, familial attitudes towards bilingualism, familial use of the primary language, familial socio-demographic factors, such as generational level, and maternal education, and societal context factors, such as the status of the minority language (see also Quintana *et al.*, Chapter 2).

For a child to learn a language they must have systematic exposure to it and opportunities to practice speaking it. Studies with non-Latino children have demonstrated that the relationship between the amount of language input is critical to subsequent language development (Hoff, 2003). However, for bilingual children the role of language input is more complicated and the quantity of exposure in any one language by necessity will be less when compared to monolinguals. Thus, depending on the amount of language exposure in any particular language, bilingual children will demonstrate differential development in each of their languages (Hammer *et al.*, 2004).

In addition to systematic language exposure, the age at which a child is first exposed to a second language may play a role in their ultimate proficiency in that language. In general, it is thought that children who receive early bilingual exposure, prior to age 3, will achieve greater bilingual mastery than children exposed later in life, due their greater brain plasticity (Petitto, 2009). Support for this argument comes from an interesting study by Kovelman *et al.*, (2008) examining reading development in relation to the timing of second language learning, that found that early bilinguals (before the age of 3) outperformed later exposed bilinguals (ages 3 to 6) across a number of reading skills. However, rates of language growth on such variables as vocabulary (Jia and Fuse, 2007) and morphology (Goldberg *et al.*, 2008) favor older children learning a second language over younger children exposed to two languages simultaneously. It is conjectured that older children have higher levels of cognitive and linguistic readiness that help them learn language more easily (Paradis, 2008). Thus, there are currently two perspectives on the timing of second language exposure and its later effects. In the first, humans are considered to have a "sensitive period" for language development that occurs prior to age 3. The second perspective argues that maturational changes associated with increased language and cognitive abilities allow for greater growth in the second language as a child grows older.

Whether a child develops bilingually may also depend upon individual factors that emanate from the child. According to Pearson (2007), if the developing bilingual child does use their home language, that action invites further development in the child's second language leading to increased proficiency. However, if the child chooses to use English then it is likely that they will receive less input in their home language leading to decreased proficiency.

In the US, Spanish is viewed as a low status language as it is often associated with individuals who are poor and immigrant, whereas the dominant language, English, is perceived as having greater sociocultural status. Thus, immigrant families often perceive the acquisition of English as an important tool to access the educational and economic benefits of the dominant culture. Although the acquisition of English is deemed important, research suggests that many Spanish speaking and Spanish/English speaking parents desire that their children develop fluency in both languages (Farrugio, 2010). In actual practice, however, this objective is often thwarted. For example, in a study of bilingualism in Miami, Florida, parents of infants reported a desire to maintain Spanish while their child developed English, but parents underestimated the challenge of maintaining strong language input in Spanish by the adults in the child's life (Pearson, 2007).

In light of the strong influence of English, preservation of Spanish is contingent on a variety of factors including parental attitude and use of Spanish with their developing child (see Caldera *et al.*, Chapter 1). Adult attitudes towards language maintenance have been posited to be influential in preserving the home language (Shin, 2000); however, the demonstrated connections between attitudes or beliefs towards language maintenance and parental language behavior has not been well documented in research with young children of Mexican origin. A negative relationship between parental attitudes towards Spanish language maintenance and children's preference for the use of English over Spanish was found in the Miami bilingualism study with a sample of Cuban and Puerto Rican families (Eilers *et al.*, 2006). Specifically, researchers found that, regardless of the type of language instruction the children received (e.g. one-way, English-only, or two-way dual language programs in Spanish and English), the majority of Spanish–English bilinguals preferred to use English across the elementary school years.

Whether children become bilingual depends to a large extent on their generational status. Previous waves of immigrants have followed a pattern where the home language is lost by the third generation (Fishman, 1966). In this model, immigrant parents speak their primary language to their children, many of whom become bilingual. However, by the third generation, the grandchildren of the original immigrant family are basically monolingual English speakers. A report from the Pew Hispanic Center (2009) documents that language use among Latinos follows the third generation pattern exhibited by other immigrant groups to the US. However, the same report indicates that Spanish persists in daily use among third generation individuals when they engage in activities such as listening to music or watching television.

Studies have shown that social class has an effect on monolingual children learning English (Hoff, 2003), but its role in learning Spanish among bilinguals is not clear. In the Miami study of bilingualism (Pearson, 2007), SES (socioeconomic status) showed a similar pattern of relationship to language development as that found in other studies when the outcomes were measured in English; however, researchers found no clear profile of associations for SES when outcomes were measured in Spanish. Results suggested that children from working class families did better in speaking Spanish than did children from professional families. Pearson (2007) concluded that although the higher SES families reported valuing Spanish maintenance, they provided more English language input than did lower SES families, who valued English language development but provided more Spanish input.

One important correlate of SES is a mother's level of education. Research with non-bilingual populations has found clear connections between maternal education and children's receptive and expressive language (Magnuson *et al.*, 2009). In fact, children from low SES backgrounds demonstrate lower levels of performance across a variety of language measures from infancy to secondary school (Fernald *et al.*, 2013). Investigations with bilingual Latino children have found similar patterns. Specifically 4- and 5-year-olds score one to two standard deviations below monolingual norms on receptive, expressive, and auditory comprehension in English (Hammer *et al.*, 2008). The amount of maternal education likely influences mothers' ideas about child growth and development—and the importance of language stimulation, which in turn, influences child language outcomes.

Developmental Changes in Language

Children display rapid growth and development in language between the ages of zero to five. Although bilingual children will follow a similar general language trajectory as monolingual children, their development manifests unique characteristics as a function of learning two languages. These include code-mixing, smaller vocabulary inventories in each language, and differences in how linguistic elements emerge. There is a growing body of research demonstrating that bilingual children process information differently than monolingual children, leading to increased brain activity that may have cognitive benefits.

Birth to Age Three

Theorists have debated whether children develop one linguistic system or two before the age of three. In the Unitary Language System Hypothesis posited by Volterra and Taeschner (1978) the child is considered to have one lexical system comprised of words from each language. These authors argue that bilingual children have a fused linguistic representation and are unable to differentiate languages until age three. Because of this fused representation, bilingual children will mix languages. In contrast, the Dual Language System Hypothesis posits that children have a separate system for their first and second languages, and that both languages can be developed simultaneously (de Houwer, 1995). Arguing that young bilingual children can and do differentiate between their two languages from an early age, Genesee (1989) found that language mixing is a result of the child's need to communicate in their bilingual environments. In the Dual Language Hypothesis, young bilingual children learn two different words for the same concept (e.g. ball) while understanding that the concept has the same meaning.

Bilingual children go through the same developmental progression as monolingual children. They babble at the same time, say their first words at the same time, and combine words into phrases at about the same time (Genesee, 2008). However, young bilinguals may appear to have some delay in language development due to the distribution of vocabulary words across two languages (Bedore *et al.*, 2005), resulting from the necessity of using different languages in different situations, such as home and school (Grosjean, 2008). Assessment of bilingual children's vocabulary inventories only in one language (usually English) will underestimate their understanding. The work of Pearson and her colleagues (Pearson and Fernandez, 1994; Pearson *et al.*, 1993) revealed that when middle-income Spanish–English bilingual children's scores were considered only in one language their scores were lower when compared to established monolingual norms. These researchers also determined that about 30 percent of vocabulary equivalents were similar in Spanish and English, suggesting that the majority of the developing bilingual infant's vocabulary occurs in separate languages.

Emerging research suggests that bilingual infants process information differently than monolinguals. This distinction in information processing leads to enhanced attention to visual (Sebastian-Galles *et al.*, 2011) and sound (Kovács and Mehler, 2009a) cues during speech processing, earlier detection of language switching (Kovács and Mehler, 2009b), and greater advantage in executive control tasks (Carlson and Meltzoff, 2008; Poulin-Dubois *et al.*, 2011).

Bilingual infants, as young as 12 months, have been found to distinguish structural irregularities in speech sounds better than monolingual infants. Specifically, Kovács and Mehler (2009a) found that bilingual infants were superior in differentiating alternating sound patterns than were monolingual infants. These researchers suggest that because bilinguals must learn two languages at the same time as monolinguals learn one, bilinguals, by necessity, are more flexible learners. These results illustrate that the cognitive advantage of bilingualism can be detected in infancy. It should be noted, however, that much of this research has not been conducted in the United States. Thus, the question of generalizability to young US Latino children persists.

An important contributor to very young children's acquisition of English as a second language is whether they have an older sibling who speaks English with them. In a study conducted with Latino origin families in the Miami area, investigators found that toddlers who had school-age siblings scored higher on measures of English language development than did toddlers with siblings who were not school age (Bridges and Hoff, 2013). In these households, the presence of a school-age sibling also increased the amount of English that the mother used. Research with non-Spanish speaking bilingual populations confirms that once an older sibling enters the formal school setting, they prefer to speak the language of the school and will use that language with their younger sibling (Barron-Hauwaert, 2004).

Age Three to Five

Much of the empirical data on bilingual development in Spanish speaking three- and four-year-olds is drawn from samples in preschool settings. Because early childhood education is viewed as an important contributor to closing the achievement gap for Latinos (Magnuson and Waldfogel, 2005), and particularly for children who come to school speaking Spanish, preschool as an intervention has received much attention. However, much of the research from these contexts favors a focus on English language acquisition, rather than language development in both Spanish and English. Thus, the majority of research on child outcomes focuses on language and literacy development in English, not Spanish.

In her work on how preschool children acquire English as a second language, Tabors (2008) describes how young children follow a sequence of language acquisition stages. In the first stage, children attempt to use their home language. When the child realizes that the home language proves ineffective, they move to stage 2 where they become quiet and observe their environment to gain information. After they have observed for a period of time, the child moves into stage 3 where they "go public" with a few words and phrases. Finally, in the last stage, the child becomes more comfortable producing new words, phrases, and sentences. How long it takes a bilingual preschool child to pass through these stages remains an open question.

Language development experts have studied the language trajectory of bilingual preschool children in relation to how well they understand the sound system of the language or phonology, their language's grammar or syntax, and the social rules associated with language use or its pragmatics. Because phonological development among monolingual English speakers has been linked to future literacy abilities such as decoding, reading comprehension, and spelling (Report of the National Early Literacy Panel, 2008), phonological development among young bilingual children may have important implications for their success in school (see also Aldoney et al., Chapter 4). Research on Spanish–English bilingual preschoolers suggests that they have phonetic inventories that differ in degree of complexity (Fabiano-Smith and Barlow, 2009). In addition, research has demonstrated that bilingual children may have slower rates of acquisition when compared to monolinguals (Fabiano-Smith and Goldstein, 2010), but that this discrepancy may be a temporary phenomenon that dissipates with additional language exposure and practice (Gildersleeve-Neumann *et al.*, 2008). As noted with younger children, phonological abilities in preschool children's first language, transfer to phonological abilities in children's second language (Lopez and Greenfield, 2004). However, accuracy in either language is influenced by whichever language predominates in the child's home. Hammer *et al.*, (2009) found that Spanish-speaking preschool children exposed to English prior to school entry scored higher on a phonological task in English compared to children who came from homes where Spanish predominated, but the groups did not differ on a similar phonological task in Spanish.

With regard to grammatical development, there is a general consensus that children learning two languages use the grammatical patterns characteristic of each of their languages (Genesee *et al.*, 2004). According to Bedore and Peña (2008) comparable grammatical forms across two languages will be acquired earlier by bilingual children because they have more experience with these forms. Interestingly, work by Hammer *et al.*, (2011) indicates that the order in which bilingual Spanish–English preschoolers develop morphemes in English differs from the order shown by English monolinguals, and that bilingual children who are exposed to more English in the home prior to preschool initially demonstrate better mastery of morphemes in English. In contrast, by the end of their second year in preschool, children coming from predominantly Spanish speaking homes catch-up to their bilingual peers who were exposed to more English in the home (Davison and Hammer, 2012).

Pragmatic sensitivity in bilingual children is the capacity to use each of their languages appropriately with different individuals. Although toddlers exposed to two languages begin to accommodate to the language of the adult with whom they interact (Nicoladis and Genesee, 1996), it is believed that pragmatic differentiation develops more fully during the preschool period (Tare and Gelman, 2010). How skillful a child is in switching from one language to another may be related to their metalinguistic awareness or their ability to attend to and reflect upon properties of their two languages. Research suggests that bilingual children may have enhanced metalinguistic capacity due to increased awareness of their two languages (Kovács, 2009), as well as increased ability to understand other people and what they are thinking (Goetz, 2003).

It is important to note that throughout the preschool period bilingual children will exhibit code-mixing, that is, the use of two languages when speaking. Research suggests that the developing bilingual child combines languages to fill in gaps in their word knowledge, uses code-mixing to show sensitivity towards the individual with whom they are speaking, and code-mixes to demonstrate differential identities through their word choice (Hoff and Shatz, 2009). Code-mixing is a common strategy used to bridge knowledge between two languages, but the rates of code-mixing vary by individual differences in children, such as their language dominance (Nicoladis and Genesee, 1997) or risk status (Greene *et al.*, 2013). Code-mixing should not be viewed as a deficiency in a child's language development, but rather is evidence of intelligent behavior, as children are integrating two language systems (Hughes *et al.*, 2006).

Summary

Our aim in this chapter was to provide an overview of bilingual language development in young children, particularly for Spanish–English bilinguals from birth through early child-hood. This overview was largely based on research published during the last decade, although some of the research cited was from the 1990s and earlier. Given our review of the published research, we would like to share challenges and recommendations and discuss implications for research, policy, and practice in the following sections.

Future Directions and Challenges

The most notable challenge at this time is the paucity of published empirical research on bilingual language development among Mexican-origin children between the ages of zero to five. The majority of the published research cited in this chapter is based upon studies with children from non-Latino bilingual populations or Latino populations other than Mexican Americans (e.g. Cubans, Dominicans, Puerto Ricans). As a result, there is a significant need and opportunity for research to better understand bilingual language development among young Mexican American children. A second notable challenge we'd like to highlight is that the volume of published research increases with a child's age. In general, research on bilingual language development has been largely focused on preschool- and elementary-aged children. This trend reveals an opportunity for researchers to focus on bilingual language development among children from zero to three years of age. A third challenge is related to the current sociopolitical climate in the United States in which anti-immigrant sentiment and language policy often converge, resulting in educational policies and programs that embrace a subtractive approach to bilingualism in which English language proficiency is acquired at the expense of Spanish language proficiency. As we discuss in the following section on implications for research, policy, and practice, these policies have multiple educational impacts.

Given these challenges, we offer the following recommendations:

- Researchers and those who fund empirical research should prioritize research on the bilingual language development of Mexican-origin children from the ages of zero to five in the United States.
- Since there is a greater volume of published empirical research on bilingual language development among preschool- and school-aged children in general, greater emphasis should be placed on research that increases our understanding of bilingual language development among Mexican-origin infants and toddlers leading up to the preschool and elementary school years.
- Given that Mexican Americans are the largest Latino sub-population in the United States—and the importance of early childhood experiences in high quality childcare settings and preschools has been noted by researchers—it is important that policies be enacted that (a) ensure greater participation in high quality childcare settings and preschools, (b) embrace and promote the cultural and linguistic assets associated with bilingualism, including support for the home language, and (c) provide for the preparation and professional development of high quality early childhood practitioners.

A significant contribution of this chapter is a detailed overview of bilingual language development and related issues among children between the ages of zero to five. While the focus of the chapter is Mexican American children in the US, the review of the literature reveals a significant need for research on bilingual language development among young Mexican-*origin* children, particularly from birth to age three. While, the research findings on other Latino populations may be generalizable to Mexican-origin children, it should not be assumed this is the case, given the within-group diversity among Mexican Americans and the between-group diversity among Latino populations. Future research must continue to explore similarities and differences in bilingual language development among Mexican American children and children from other Latino subgroups.

Another significant research implication pertains to the reporting of empirical data. There are two aspects to this implication. First, outcomes are generally reported for English only, as opposed to outcomes in both English and Spanish. It is critical that future empirical research reports on both English and Spanish language development, given that the research is clear that each language influences the other. Second, because many studies of bilingual language development conducted with Latino children report aggregated data across ethnic sub-populations, it is imperative that future empirical research include a clear description of the ethnic background of participants and, if possible, that the analysis and reporting of data be disaggregated by ethnic sub-population.

Policy Implications

Researchers and educators such as Garcia and Jensen (2010) have drawn attention to the relation between young Latino children's language development and its longer-term implications for academic achievement. For example, the National Assessment of Educational Progress shows significantly lower reading scores among 9-year old Latino students when compared to White students (U.S. Department of Education, National Center for Education Statistics, 2013). This gap in reading persists on assessments for 13- and 17-year-old students. While the disparity in reading scores has narrowed in the past decade, it remains a significant issue for Latino students and one that merits concerted attention.

It is worth noting that bilingual language development occurs within sociopolitical and sociocultural contexts over time and that the role of bilingual instruction in US schools has been influenced by restrictive language policies not premised on theory and research (Gandara and Hopkins, 2010). Bilingualism can be viewed as either an additive or subtractive process (Lambert, 1981). In the subtractive process, a child acquires increasing language proficiency in one language, while proficiency in the other language decreases. The subtractive process emphasizes the replacement of the primary language with another language. In the additive process, the goal is to increase proficiency in the second language while maintaining or further developing proficiency in the child's primary language. In the US, the tendency is for schools to focus on subtractive bilingualism especially for those whose primary language is seen as an obstacle to academic achievement (Gandara and Contreras, 2009).

Recent research demonstrates that bilingualism confers cognitive advantages (see Bialystok, 2001; Bialystok and Hakuta, 1994). Paradoxically, many educational policies and programs do not view bilingualism as a desirable outcome, and in some states bilingual education programs have been dismantled. In Arizona and California (states with significantly large numbers of Mexican American children who are English learners) the implementation of state laws and policies have resulted in the decline of bilingual education programs and the decimation of bilingual teacher preparation programs (Cadiero-Kaplan and Rodriguez, 2008; Gandara and Orfield, 2012).

An important related issue is that of school financing. In California, for example, funding augmentations target schools with majority concentrations of Dual Language learners and low-income students, a practice that will predominately, although not exclusively, impact Mexican American students (State of California, Department of Finance, 2013). School finance policy and its relation to teacher preparation, professional development, curriculum, and pedagogy for Dual Language learners, the majority of whom are Mexican American children, has been a major focus of researchers (Cadiero-Kaplan and Rodríguez, 2008; Gandara and Rumberger, 2008; Jimenez-Castellanos and Topper, 2012). School finance policy and its implementation must be connected to curriculum, programs, and practices that promote the advancement of Mexican American children, while taking into account group diversity, and building upon what is generally known about bilingual language development.

In the absence of continuity between research and policy, dual immersion programs—in which all children simultaneously gain academic proficiency in two languages—have arisen as an alternate educational platform. Dual immersion programs that promote dual language learning are also prevalent for preschool-aged children, and may serve as a bridge between research, policy, and practice, and between preschool and K–12 education. An example of an opportunity to do this, is the adoption of the Common Core Standards by forty-five states. Researchers have led efforts to ensure the consideration of Dual Language learners in policy created at both the federal and state levels (Hakuta *et al.*, 2013; Hopkins *et al.*, 2013). However, concerns remain, given that only a handful of states that have adopted the Common Core Standards have also implemented practices and provisions geared towards children who are English learners (Castro *et al.*, 2013).

Clearly, challenges to bilingual education remain within the greater sociopolitical context, including unfavorable attitudes toward immigrant populations (particularly Latinos), negative perceptions of bilingualism, and monolithic, one-size-fits-all approaches toward the education of Latinos. However, opportunities also exist. It is important for researchers, policy-makers, and practitioners to align efforts to serve the ever-growing population of Mexican American children. As research increasingly focuses on bilingual language development among young Mexican American children and related developmental and academic outcomes, we must be ready to develop, implement, and assess policies, programs, and practices that are linguistically responsive.

References

August, D., and Shanahan, T. (2006). *Developing literacy in second-language learners: A report of the National Literacy Panel on language minority children and youth*. Mahwah, NJ: Erlbaum.

Barron-Hauwaert, S. (2004). *Bilingual siblings: Language use in families*. Bristol: Multilingual Matters.

Bedore, L. M., and Peña, E. D. (2008). Assessment of bilingual children for identification of language impairment: Current findings and implications for practice. *International Journal of Bilingual Education and Bilingualism, 11*, 1–29.

Bedore, L. M., Peña, E. D., Garcia, M., and Cortez, C. (2005). Conceptual versus monolingual scoring: When does it make a difference? *Language, Speech and Hearing Services in Schools, 36*, 188–200.

Bialystok, E. (2001). *Bilingualism in development: Language, literacy, and cognition*. New York: Cambridge University Press.

Bialystok, E., and Hakuta, K. (1994). *In other words: The psychology and science of second language acquisition*. New York: Basic Books.

Bridges, K., and Hoff, E. (2013). Older sibling influences on the language environment and language development of toddlers in bilingual homes. *Applied Psycholinguistics, 1*(1), 1–17.

Cadiero-Kaplan, K., and Rodríguez, J. L. (2008). The preparation of highly qualified teachers for English learners: Educational responsiveness for unmet needs. *Equity and Excellence in Education, 41*, 372–387.

Cardenas-Hagen, E., Carlson, C. D., and Pollard-Durdola, S. D. (2007). The cross-linguistic transfer of early literacy skills: The role of initial L1 and L2 skills and language of instruction. *Language, Speech and Hearing Services in Schools, 38*(3), 219–257.

Carlson, S. M., and Meltzoff, A. (2008). Bilingual experience and executive functioning in young children. *Developmental Science, 11*(2), 282–298.

Castro, D. C., Garcia, E. E., and Markos, A. M. (2013). *Dual language learners: Research informing policy*. Chapel Hill: The University of North Carolina, Frank Porter Graham Child Development Institute, Center for Early Care and Education—Dual Language Learners.

Cummins, J. (2000). *Language, power and pedagogy: Bilingual children in the crossfire*. Clevedon: Multilingual Matters.

Davison, M. D., and Hammer, C. S. (2012). Development of 14 English grammatical morphemes in Spanish–English preschoolers. *Clinical Linguistics and Phonetics, 26*(8), 728–742.

de Houwer, A. (1995). Bilingual language acquisition. In P. Fletcher and B. MacWhinney (Eds.), *The handbook of child language* (pp. 219–250). Oxford, UK: Blackwell.

Eilers, R. E., Oller, D. K., and Cobo-Lewis, A. B. (2006). Social factors in bilingual development: The Miami experience. In P. McCardel and E. Hoff (Eds.), *Childhood bilingualism: Research on infancy through school age* (pp. 68–90). Clevedon: Multilingual Matters.

Fabiano-Smith, L., and Barlow, J. (2009). Interaction in bilingual phonological acquisition: Evidence from phonetic inventories. *International Journal of Bilingual Education and Bilingualism, 13*(1), 81–97.

Fabiano-Smith, L., and Goldstein, B. A. (2010). Phonological acquisition in bilingual Spanish–English speaking children. *Journal of Speech, Language, and Hearing Research, 53*(1), 160–178.

Farrugio, P. (2010). Latino immigrant parents' views of bilingual education as a vehicle for heritage preservation. *Journal of Latinos and Education, 9*(1), 3–21.

Fernald, A., Marchman, V. A., and Weisleder, A. (2013). SES differences in language processing skill and vocabulary are evident at 18 months. *Developmental Science, 16*, 234–248.

Fishman, J. (1966). *Language loyalty in the US: The maintenance and perpetuation of non-English mother tongues by American ethnic and religious groups.* The Hague: Mouton.

Gandara, P., and Contreras, F. (2009). *The Latino educational crisis: The Consequences of failed social policy.* Cambridge, MA: Harvard University Press.

Gandara, P., and Hopkins, M. (2010). *Forbidden language: English learners and restrictive language policies.* New York: Teachers College Press.

Gandara, P., and Orfield, G. (2012). Why Arizona matters: The historical, legal, and political contexts of Arizona's instructional policies and U.S. linguistic hegemony. *Language Policy, 11*(1), 7–19.

Gandara, P., and Rumberger, R. (2008). Defining an adequate education for English learners. *Education Finance and Policy, 3*(1), 130–148.

Garcia, E. E., and Jensen, B. (2010). Language development and early education of young Hispanic children in the United States. In O. N. Saracho and B. Spodek (Eds.), *Contemporary perspectives on language and cultural diversity in early childhood education* (pp. 43–64). Charlotte, NC: IAP, Inc.

García, O., and Kleifgen, J. (2010). *Educating emergent bilinguals. Policies, programs and practices for English language learners.* New York: Teachers College Press.

Genesee, F. (1989). One language or two? *Journal of Child Language, 16*, 161–179.

Genesee, F. (2006). Bilingual first language acquisition in perspective. In P. McCardle and E. Hoff (Eds.), *Childhood bilingualism: Research on infancy through school age* (pp. 45–67). Clevedon: Multilingual Matters.

Genesee, F. (2008). Early dual language learners. *Zero to Three, 29*(1), 17–22.

Genesee, F., Paradis, J., and Crago, M. B. (2004). *Dual language development and disorders: A handbook on bilingualism and second language learning.* Baltimore: Brookes.

Genesee, F., Lindholm-Leary, K., Sanders, W. M., and Christian, D. (2006). *Educating English language learners: A syntheses of research evidence.* NY: Cambridge University Press.

Gildersleeve-Neumann, C., Kester, E., Davis, B., and Peña, E. (2008). English speech sound development in preschool-aged children from bilingual Spanish-English environments. *Language, Speech and Hearing Services in Schools, 39*, 314–328.

Goetz, P. J. (2003). The effects of bilingualism on theory of mind development. *Bilingualism: Language and cognition, 6*(1), 1–15.

Goldberg, H., Paradis, J., and Crago, M. (2008). Lexical acquisition over time in minority L1 children learning English as a L2. *Applied Psycholinguistics, 29*, 1–25.

Greene, K. J., Peña, E. D., and Bedore L. M. (2013). Lexical choice and language in bilingual preschoolers. *Child Language Teaching and Therapy, 29*, 27–39.

Grosjean, F. (2008). *Studying bilinguals.* Oxford: Oxford University Press.

Grosjean, F. (2010). *Bilingual life and reality.* Cambridge, MA: Harvard University Press.

Hakuta, K., Santos, M., and Fang, Z. (2013). Challenges and opportunities for language learning in the context of the ccss and the ngss. *Journal of Adolescent and Adult Literacy, 56*(6), 451–454.

Hammer, C. S., Lawrence, F. R., and Miccio, A. W. (2008). The effect of summer vacation on bilingual preschoolers' language development. *Clinical Linguistics and Phonetics, 22*, 687–702.

Hammer, C. S., Miccio, A. W., and Rodriguez, B. I. (2004). Bilingual language acquisition and the child socialization process. In B. A. Goldstein (Ed.), *Bilingual language development and disorders in Spanish-English speakers* (pp. 21–50). Baltimore: Brookes.

Hammer, C. S., Scarpino, S., and Davison, M. D. (2011). Beginning with language: Spanish-English bilingual preschoolers' early literacy development. In D. Dickinson and S. Neuman (Eds.), *Handbook in early literacy (vol 3)* (pp. 118–135). NY: Guilford.

Hammer, C. S., Davison, M. D., Lawrence, F. R., and Miccio, A. W. (2009). The effect of home language on bilingual children's vocabulary and emergent literacy development during Head Start and kindergarten. *Scientific Studies of Reading, 13*(2), 99–121.

Hart, B., and Risley, T. (1995). *Meaningful differences in the everyday experience of young Americans.* Baltimore: Brookes.

Hoff, E. (2003). The specificity of environmental influence: Socioeconomic status affects early vocabulary development via maternal speech. *Child Development, 74*(5), 1368–1378.

Hoff, E., and Shatz, M. (2009). *Blackwell handbook of language development.* MA: Wiley-Blackwell.

Hopkins, M., Thompson, K., Linquanti, R., Hakuta, K., and August, D. (2013). Fully accounting for English learner performance: A key issue in ESEA reauthorization. *Educational Researcher, 42*(2), 101–108.

Hughes, C. E., Shaunessy, E. S., Brice, A. R., Ratliff, M. A., and McHatton, P. A. (2006). Code switching among bilingual and limited English proficient students: Possible indicators of giftedness. *Journal for the Education of the Gifted, 30*(1), 7–28.

Jia, G., and Fuse, A. (2007). Acquisition of English grammatical morphology by native Mandarin-speaking children and adolescents: Age related differences. *Journal of Speech, Language and Hearing Research, 50,* 1280–1299.

Jimenez-Castellanos, O., and Topper, A. (2012). The cost of providing an adequate education to English language learners: A review of the literature. *Review of Educational Research, 82*(2), 179–232.

Kovács, Á. M. (2009). Early bilingualism enhances mechanisms of false-belief reasoning. *Developmental Science, 12*(1), 48–54.

Kovács, Á. M., and Mehler, J. (2009a). Cognitive gains in 7-month-old bilingual infants. *Proceedings of the National Academy of Sciences, 106*(16), 6556–6560.

Kovács, Á. M., and Mehler, J. (2009b). Flexible learning in multiple speech structures in bilingual infants. *Science, 325,* 611–612.

Kovelman, I., Baker, S. A., and Petitto, L. A. (2008). Age of bilingual language exposure as a new window into bilingual reading development. *Bilingualism, Language and Cognition, 11,* 203–223.

Lambert, W. E. (1981). Bilingualism and language acquisition. *Annals of the New York Academy of Sciences, 379,* 9–22. doi: 10.111/j.1749-6632.1981.tb41993.x/pdf

Lopez, L. M., and Greenfield, D. B. (2004). The cross-language transfer of phonological skills in Hispanic Head Start children. *Bilingual Research Journal, 28*(1), 1–18.

Lopez, M. H., Gonzalez-Barrera, A., and Cuddington, D. (2013). *Diverse origins: The Nations 14 largest Hispanic-origin groups.* Pew Hispanic Center. Washington, DC.

Magnuson, K., and Waldfogel, J. (2005). Early childhood care and education: Effects on ethnic and racial gaps in school readiness. *The Future of Children, 15*(1), 169–196.

Magnuson, K., Sexton, H. R., Davis-Kean, P. E., and Huston, A. C. (2009). Increases in maternal education and young children's language skills. *Merrill Palmer Quarterly, 55,* 319–350.

Melby-Lervag, M., and Lervag, A. (2011). Cross linguistic transfer of oral language, decoding, phonological awareness and reading comprehension: A meta-analysis. *Journal of Research in Reading, 34*(1), 114–135.

National Early Literacy Panel. (2008). *Developing early literacy: A scientific synthesis of early literacy development and implications for intervention.* Jessup, MD: National Institute of Literacy. http://incs.ed.gov/publications/pdf/NELPReport09.pdf

Nicoladis, E., and Genesee, F. (1996). A longitudinal study of pragmatic differentiation in young bilingual children. *Language Learning, 46,* 439–464.

Nicoladis, E., and Genesee, F. (1997). Language development in preschool bilingual children. *Journal of Speech-Language Pathology and Audiology, 21,* 258–270.

Odin, T. (1989). *Language transfer: Cross-linguistic influence on language learning.* Cambridge: Cambridge University Press.

Office of Head Start (2009). *Dual language learners: What does it take?* Washington, DC: Administration of Children and Families.

Paradis, J. (2007). Second language acquisition in childhood. In E. Hoff and M. Shatz (Eds.), *Handbook of language development* (pp. 387–405). Oxford, UK: Blackwell.

Paradis, J. (October, 2008). *Are simultaneous and early bilingual acquisition fundamentally the same or different?* Paper presented at Models of Interaction in Bilinguals. University of Wales, Bangor.

Pearson, B. Z. (2007). Social factors in childhood bilingualism in the United States. *Applied Psycholinguistics, 28,* 399–410.

Pearson, B. Z., and Fernandez, S. C. (1994). Patterns of interaction in the lexical growth in two languages of bilingual infants and toddlers. *Language Learning, 44,* 617–653.

Pearson, B. Z., Fernandez, S. C., and Oller, D. K. (1993). Lexical development in bilingual infants and toddlers: Comparison to monolingual norms. *Language Learning, 43,* 93–120.

Petitto, L. (2009). New discoveries from the bilingual brain and mind across the life span: Implications for education. *Mind, Brain and Education, 3*(4), 185–197.

Pew Hispanic Center. (2009). *Between two worlds: How young Latinos come of age in America.* Washington, DC.

Poulin-Dubois, D., Blaye, A., Coutya, J., and Bialystok, E. (2011). The effects of bilingualism on a toddler's executive functioning. *Journal of Experimental Child Psychology, 108,* 567–579.

Sebastian-Galles, N., Albareda-Castellot, B., Weikum, W. M., and Werker, J. F. (2011). A bilingual advantage in visual language discrimination in infancy. *Psychological Science, 23*(9), 994–999.

Shin, F. H. (2000). Parent attitudes towards the principles of bilingual education and their children's participation in bilingual programs. *Journal of Intercultural Studies, 21*(1), 93–99.

State of California, Department of Finance. (2013). California State Budget 2013–2014. Sacramento, CA: Department of Finance.

Tabors, P. O. (2008). *One child, two languages: A guide for early educators of children learning English as a second language.* Cambridge: Brookes.

Tare, M., and Gelman, S. A. (2010). Can you say it another way? Cognitive factors in bilingual children's pragmatic language use. *Journal of Cognition and Development, 11*(2), 137–158.

U.S. Department of Education, National Center for Education Statistics. (2013). NAEP 2012: Trends in Academic Progress (NCES Report No. 2013-456). Washington, DC: National Center for Education Statistics.

Volterra, V., and Taeschner, T. (1978). The acquisition and development of language by bilingual children. *Journal of Child Language, 5*(2), 311–326.

10

MEXICAN AMERICAN PARENTS' INVOLVEMENT IN THEIR CHILDREN'S SCHOOLING

Marie-Anne Suizzo

Introduction

Mexican American Parents' Involvement in Their Children's Schooling

> *I try to tell him what is best for him, how to live, how to live better. I tell him school is the most important thing. I tell him to better himself so that he can be something in this life. I tell him, not like me, since I am nothing in this life.*
>
> *Mexican-origin mother of 12-year-old son*

Many Mexican American parents have sacrificed, or seen their parents sacrifice, their most fundamental human needs for the promise of a better life for their children (Suarez-Orozco and Suarez-Orozco, 1995). And yet, these parents are perceived as not caring about their children's education because they do not volunteer at their child's school, or because their child sometimes comes to school with unfinished homework or unsigned forms (Quiocho and Daoud, 2006). There can no longer be any doubt that the deficit perspective that Mexican American parents are not concerned with their children's education is wrong (Valencia and Black, 2002). We now have a large body of evidence from quantitative, qualitative, and ethnographic studies demonstrating the opposite reality: Mexican American parents are passionately determined to support their children's learning (Okagaki *et al.*, 1995; Suizzo *et al.*, 2012).

In this chapter I first present, from various disciplinary perspectives, the main theories proposed to explain the construct of parental involvement. I then present the ecocultural framework and describe the cultural models of parenting specific to Mexican Americans. I review existing research on Mexican American parental involvement, summarize the challenges to their involvement, and offer recommendations for addressing those challenges. I then highlight policies and programs that have proven effective in helping Mexican American parents realize their goals with regard to their children's schooling. Finally, I suggest directions for future research to expand and deepen our knowledge of Mexican American parental involvement.

Literature Review

Theories of Parental Involvement

Parental involvement is defined as the ways that parents support and facilitate their children's educational experiences (Fantuzzo *et al.*, 2004). Because parental involvement is a broad construct that crosses disciplinary boundaries, scholars have identified multiple dimensions and categories to codify its complexity. Several models have been suggested, but as a whole, most parental involvement frameworks contain three broad categories: parental beliefs (educational values, long-term aspirations), parental behaviors or practices engaged in either at home or at school, and parental resources (financial, time, social networks).

One of the most frequently utilized frameworks is that proposed by Epstein and Sanders (2002). They divide parental involvement into six types, focusing on behaviors and practices:

1. Basic obligations of families and parenting;
2. Basic obligations of schools to communicate with parents;
3. Parents' involvement at school;
4. Learning activities at home;
5. Decision making in organizations, and
6. Collaborating with the community.

Another framework that focuses on practices is that of Ho and Willms (1996), who propose four dimensions:

1. Home discussions;
2. School communication;
3. Home supervision, and
4. School participation.

Singh *et al.*, (1995) also propose four dimensions, but include parental beliefs such as academic aspirations for children in their framework.

Other frameworks take a more intrapsychic focus including not only behaviors, but also cognitive and emotional aspects of parental involvement. For example, Grolnick and Slowiaczek (1994) propose three parental involvement categories along the lines of individual domains: (1) behavioral involvement, including both school- and home-based strategies, (2) cognitive-intellectual involvement, including home-based practices such as learning stimulating activities, and (3) personal involvement, including attitudes and expectations about school, education, and learning. Hoover-Dempsey and Sandler (1997) propose that the extent to which parents become involved in their children's schooling depends on three factors: (1) their beliefs about what should be their role or responsibility in their children's education, (2) their self-efficacy, or confidence in their ability and power to help their children succeed in school, and (3) invitations and opportunities they receive from the child and from the school.

Within psychology, *parental academic socialization* (PAS) is a theoretical framework for studying parental involvement from the perspective of children's socialization (Taylor *et al.*, 2004). Accordingly, parents hold goals and values for their children's intellectual development and are motivated to interact with them in specific ways to promote the internalization of those goals and values (Grusec *et al.*, 1997). PAS is a multidimensional construct that includes the processes, such as communicating expectations for academic performance and providing a stimulating and supportive home environment, through which parents shape children's academic development

(Bradley, 2002; McWayne *et al.*, 2004). The two types of PAS that most frequently predict children's academic attitudes and behaviors are (1) holding high educational expectations and aspirations, and (2) discussing the importance of school and education (Davis-Kean, 2005; Englund *et al.*, 2004). Several meta-analyses have consistently revealed PAS as the best predictor of academic achievement across ethnic groups (Fan and Chen, 2001; Hill and Tyson, 2009; Jeynes, 2007).

Within sociology, parental involvement scholars focus on the personal, financial, and social resources provided by parents and the effects of these resources on children's learning and development. According to social capital theory (Coleman, 1988), parents contribute financial, human, and social capitals to their children's education and intellectual development. Social capital includes the time and attention that parents give their children as well as the benefits afforded them by their parents' social networks. Regardless of their educational background and skills (human capital), parents who invest time and effort in their children's education (social capital) will positively impact their achievement. Status attainment theory (Sewell and Hauser, 1980) explains how parents' socioeconomic status (SES), including their income, occupational status, and education level, affects their expectations of their children's educational attainment, which in turn impact children's achievement and later occupational status.

The vast majority of research on parental involvement has been conducted on school-aged children, and has focused on school-based practices (Carranza *et al.*, 2009). Racial/ethnic minority parents, including Mexican-origin parents, are less likely than European American parents to visit schools due to personal and social barriers (Hill and Taylor, 2004). Consequently, teachers and administrators often view them as less involved or less concerned with their children's education. Yet, research demonstrates that these parents are highly supportive of their children's schooling, and engage in a wide variety of home-based involvement practices that positively affect their children's academic achievement.

Mexican American Cultural Models of Parenting

Ecocultural and ecological theories of human development propose that children develop by adapting to the multiple, intersecting environments within which they live, the most proximal being their families and parents (Garcia Coll *et al.*, 1996; Super and Harkness, 1986; Weisner, 2002). *Cultural models* are theoretical constructs composed of the interconnected ideas, beliefs, goals, and practices shared by members of a cultural group that guide their actions and interpretations of phenomena (Holland and Quinn, 1987), and offer a means of mapping the complexity and interrelatedness of various ethnic groups' beliefs and practices with regard to childrearing and education (Gallimore and Goldenberg, 2001). Examining parental academic socialization in a specific cultural or ethnic group from a cultural model's perspective provides insights into how goals and practices are uniquely related in that group.

The cultural models of parenting associated with Mexican Americans that have received the most attention in research on parental involvement are *educación, familismo, respeto,* and *consejos* (Valdés, 1996). *Educación,* is a multidimensional construct that includes teaching children academic skills as well as teaching proper manners, morality, and responsibility (Reese *et al.*, 1995; Delgado and Ford, 1998). Mexican American children are expected to behave in accordance with standards of *bien educado,* or proper rearing, which includes *respeto,* or respect (Arcia and Johnson, 1998).

Familismo is another Mexican American parenting cultural model that contains at least two dimensions. The first dimension is a high value placed on maintaining a strong attachment to one's family, and includes feelings of reciprocity, loyalty, solidarity, and living near family (Santiago-Rivera *et al.*, 2002). The second dimension reflects feelings of duty and obligation to one's family and conforming to traditions and rules established by elders. Steidel and Contreras (2003) developed a questionnaire that measures these two dimensions of *familismo* using four subscales: familial support, family interconnectedness (reflecting attachment), family honor, and subjugation of self for the family (reflecting duty). Using this scale, Esparza and Sánchez (2008) found that overall *familismo* predicted higher school attendance and academic effort of Latino twelfth-graders, of whom about half were Mexican origin, and that for students whose mothers had less than a high school diploma, *familismo* was positively related to grades.

This dimension is also reflected in the cultural model of *respeto*—or obedience to, and high regard for, adults and elders (Arcia and Johnson, 1998). Mexican American mothers have been found to value conformity, politeness, and obedience, more than European Americans (Rodriguez and Olswang, 2003). Some researchers suggest that *respeto* is a component of a larger cultural value, *simpatía*—a set of interpersonal qualities that include empathy, agreeableness, concern for others, and conflict-avoidance, which are associated with maintaining harmonious relationships (Griffith *et al.*, 1998).

The cultural model of *consejos* is directly linked to Mexican American parental involvement. *Consejos* are stories, advice, and encouragement that parents offer their children to motivate them to study hard, achieve in school, and obtain a higher level of education (Delgado-Gaitan, 1994). These cultural narratives are often presented as reminders of the parents' own struggles to provide opportunities for their children, or warnings about the negative consequences of not studying and finishing school. Parents may point out others in the family, or may point to themselves as negative models of what they do not want their children to become.

Mexican American Parental Involvement

Much research on Mexican American parental involvement is mixed with research on Latinos or Hispanics as a group. In these studies, Mexican Americans frequently constitute the greatest proportion of the sample; however, they are not analyzed separately, thereby preventing an understanding of how parental involvement may manifest uniquely within this group. Although the following review includes studies of Latino parents, I select only those in which a majority are of Mexican origin, the proportion specified whenever possible.

Preschool-age Children

The limited research on parental involvement in the education of preschool children has examined home-based activities that support or encourage learning. Much of this research has examined *parenting styles*, which are the ways in which parents combine responsiveness and demandingness in their interactions with their children (Baumrind, 1966). Depending on the amount of responsiveness and demandingness that parents utilize in their interactions, four parenting styles have been identified: authoritarian (high on demandingness, low on respons-iveness), authoritative (high on both), permissive or indulgent (low on demandingness, high on responsiveness), and indifferent (low on both) (Maccoby and Martin, 1983).

Research on Mexican Americans has revealed parenting practices and styles that are not easily categorized within the above framework. Because Mexican American parents utilize unique cultural models in their interactions with their children, studies attempting to describe their styles using existing theories have yielded inconsistent findings. Some research has found that Mexican Americans use a more authoritarian parenting style (high in demandingness) than European Americans (Varela *et al.*, 2004), possibly due to the cultural models of *respeto* and *educación* (Halgunseth *et al.*, 2006). Although Mexican American mothers are very warm and affectionate with their children (Suizzo *et al.*, 2014), studies of their interactions either do not include this dimension or measure it in ways that do not reflect Mexican American cultural models. To address this theoretical limitation, Rodríguez *et al.* (2009) observed parent–child interactions with four- to nine-year-olds and coded for warmth, demandingness, and autonomy-granting. By adding a third dimension, they identified eight parenting styles, and found that Latino parents (mostly of Mexican origin) were classified as *protective parents*: highly demanding, low on autonomy granting, but very high on warmth.

Indeed, several studies of parents of young children have shown that Mexican Americans favor control and conformity over autonomy. In their study of mothers' values for children, Rodriguez and Olswang (2003) found that the Mexican American mothers valued conformity, politeness, and obedience—which are aspects of the cultural model of *educación*—more than self-direction, while the European American mothers valued self-direction over conformity. Mexican American mothers use more structured, direct instruction teaching styles, such as modeling and directives, also indicating a preference for conformity (Gallimore and Goldenberg, 2001) in contrast with European American mothers who provide their children with stimulating experiences and encourage their autonomy (Hess *et al.*, 1984). In her ethnographic study of Mexican American families in Texas, Valdés (1996) found that young children learned to do chores by observing an adult expert and trying to do the chore themselves.

In contrast to these studies, some research has found that Mexican Americans combine agency and conformity in their cultural models of parenting, especially when they are more acculturated to mainstream American culture. For example, in a study of preschool-age children learning to tie their shoes, Moreno (1997) found that more acculturated Mexican American mothers used fewer controlling practices, such as correction and commands, than did the European American mothers. Interestingly, the two techniques, use of commands and use of conceptual questions, were negatively associated among the European American mothers but were positively associated among Mexican American mothers. Savage and Gauvain (1998) found that more acculturated Mexican American parents believed their young children capable of engaging in planning at earlier ages than did less acculturated parents.

Maternal education level also distinguishes Mexican American parents' cultural models. In our study of middle-class Mexican American mothers of preschoolers (Suizzo *et al.*, 2008), we found that these mothers utilize a variety of approaches to help their children learn. These strategies include direct teaching, encouraging persistence and practice, providing incentives and rewards, suggesting an alternative way to do a task, and offering encouragement and physical affection. In an observational study of 43 Chicano mothers, Laosa (1978) found that those with more education used inquiry and praise more than those with less education who used modeling more frequently in teaching their five-year-olds. Similarly, Eisenberg (2002) found that middle-class Mexican-descent mothers discussed more complex issues with their four-year-olds when teaching them baking and block-building than did working-class mothers. These studies provide evidence that Mexican American parents' cultural models of teaching and supporting children's learning are distinct. Fostering autonomy while expecting conformity are not contradictory, especially as parents gain more education and exposure to mainstream American culture.

School-age Children

Research on Mexican American parental involvement has consistently shown positive effects on children. Using National Education Longitudinal Study (NELS) data of which 65 percent of the Latinos are Mexican origin, Fan *et al.* (2012) found that parental advising and parent–school communication were positively related to tenth-grade Latino students' intrinsic motivation and academic self-efficacy in English. LeFevre and Shaw (2012) studied eighth-grade Latinos in the NELS, and found that informal, home-based parental support (discussing education, establishing rules about education) predicted academic achievement nearly as strongly as did formal, school-based support. Only two studies have used the NELS to investigate specifically Mexican Americans. The first, by Trusty *et al.* (2003) found that home-based parental involvement during eighth grade, such as holding high educational expectations and discussing school, was the strongest predictor of adolescents' own expectations two years after high school. The second study by Altschul (2012) found that discussing school, investing in educational resources, providing enriching activities, and becoming involved in their children's schools positively affected Mexican American children's academic achievement.

Parental aspirations and expectations for their children's achievement, and their encouragement and communication of those expectations, have consistently been found to predict academic achievement and motivation. In their longitudinal study of eighth-, tenth-, and twelfth-graders, Hong and Ho (2005) found that among Latinos (about 65 percent Mexican origin), higher parent–child communication and higher parental educational aspirations were linked to higher perceived control by students, which predicted higher academic achievement. In their meta-analysis, Fan and Chen (2001) also identified parental aspirations for their children's education and parental communication about school activities as the strongest predictors of grades and test scores across ethnic groups. There is evidence that Mexican American parents' aspirations may decline as their children begin middle school or later. Azmitia and colleagues (1996) found that the educational and occupational aspirations of Mexican American parents of seventh graders were lower than those of the parents of fifth and third graders.

One of the challenges in drawing conclusions about the specific effects of various dimensions of parental involvement is the variety of instruments used to measure parental involvement. Some measures combine home-based practices, home–school communication, and school involvement in a single scale. Others are short, containing only a few items that may reflect only a single dimension—which cannot capture the complexity of parental involvement. Studies that do not assess home- and school-based parent involvement as separate dimensions, but rather combine them into a single construct, have found that parental involvement positively affects students' achievement. For example, in their study of Hispanic youth in the US–Mexico borderlands, using a five-item measure of parental involvement that combines home- and school-based practices, Chun and Dickson (2011) found that parental involvement affected seventh-grade adolescents' grades through the mediator of academic self-efficacy. Using differentiated measures of parental involvement, however, may provide more useful knowledge of the specific practices that contribute most to motivation and achievement.

A handful of studies have compared the effects of home- and school-based involvement on adolescents' achievement. For example, Martinez *et al.* (2004) conducted a study of 278 Latino adolescents and 73 Latino parents in Oregon, where 78 percent of Latinos are of Mexican origin. Despite institutional barriers and frequent discriminatory experiences, adolescents benefitted from both home- and school-based involvement. Home involvement, such as encouraging academics and discussing important life issues, positively predicted homework completion which in turn predicted higher grades. Although school involvement did not predict higher grades, adolescents whose parents were involved in their schools were less likely to report that they would drop out. In another study of Mexican American families, Dumka *et al.* (2009) found that home-based parental practices, including monitoring, harshness, and warmth, predicted seventh-graders' school outcomes (grades, classroom behaviors, peer associations); however, school involvement had no effect on these outcomes.

Research on only home-based parental involvement has demonstrated the effects of several practices on adolescent academic motivation, achievement, and aspirations. In our study of Mexican American sixth-graders, we measured three dimensions of home-based parental involvement: communicating high expectations for school success, conveying the importance of hard work, and creating a home environment supportive of learning (Suizzo et al., 2012). We found that parental expectations predicted higher levels of determination on schoolwork, which in turn predicted higher grades. Maternal warmth moderated this relation such that adolescents who felt greater warmth reported even higher levels of determination. Finally, the desire to repay and honor their families for their struggles and sacrifices mediated relations between parental involvement and students' achievement. Plunkett and Bámaca-Gómez (2003) asked Mexican American high school students to report on their parents' academic support behaviors such as assisting with homework, monitoring, and offering support. Both mothers' and fathers' help with homework and mothers' monitoring were related to higher academic motivation for these youth. Also, parents' education levels predicted adolescents' educational aspirations.

Summary

In summary, research on Mexican American parents' involvement in their children's education provides ample evidence that these parents hold high aspirations and utilize a variety of methods to support their children. They engage in explicit, direct teaching, and expect compliance with rules and commands; however, they also offer emotional support and encourage reflection and open discussions about children's options. These parental beliefs and practices promote achievement and school adjustment in children by directly affecting their motivation, academic self-concept, and their teachers' expectations. This increased motivation and self-confidence translate to persistence on challenging tasks, completion of homework, and greater feelings of belonging in their schools. Finally, these studies describe a unique Mexican American model of parental involvement that combines promoting agency with maintaining strong family ties and teaching respect, in accordance with the cultural values of *educación* and *familismo*.

Within-group Differences in Mexican-origin Parental Involvement

The research on generation and acculturation differences in Mexican American parental involvement is growing but remains quite scarce, and consequently, inconclusive. The main reason for these inconclusive findings is the paucity of studies that compare similar constructs across similar samples. In some cases, researchers measure a specific dimension of a broad construct, yet label it as a measure of the broader construct. For example, although family support, a dimension of *familismo*, is highly valued across generations of Mexican Americans (Umaña-Taylor et al., 2009; 77 percent Mexican origin), family interconnectedness, a different dimension, has not been shown to vary across generations.

The limited amount of research on sex differences in effects of Mexican American parental involvement has also yielded equivocal results. For example, Alfaro et al. (2006) found that Latina (half of Mexican origin) ninth- and tenth-grade girls who perceived their mothers as supporting them academically, reported higher academic motivation, while boys showed higher motivation when they perceived their fathers' academic support. Plunkett and colleagues (2008), however, found cross-sex influence in their study of ninth-grade Mexican Americans, where fathers' academic support explained more variation in girls' motivation, and mothers' academic support explained more variation in boys' motivation.

Research on within-group differences by socioeconomic status (SES) has been somewhat more conclusive. Across cultures, more-educated mothers promote their children's cognitive development and engage in teaching and verbal interactions in the home more than less-educated mothers (LeVine *et al.*, 2001). In particular, Mexican American parents with more economic resources and higher education levels invest greater financial and human capital in their children's schooling (Altschul, 2012). Roosa *et al.* (2012) found that human capital, operationalized as parental education level of high school or higher, positively predicted academic performance in Mexican American adolescents.

Future Directions and Challenges

The evidence that Mexican American parents care about their children's education and utilize various means to actively promote their achievement is abundant. Yet, teachers and administrators continue to assert that because these parents are not as frequently present in schools, they do not care (Quiocho and Daoud, 2006). To address this misunderstanding, growing research has investigated the challenges and barriers to participation that may help explain Mexican American parents' less frequent school involvement.

Hornby and Lafaele (2011) propose a model of potential barriers to parental involvement. The model categorizes barriers into four types of factors:

- Individual parental and family characteristics—including parents' beliefs about parental involvement, their perceptions of invitation for parental involvement, their current life contexts, and their class, race, and ethnicity.
- Child factors—including for example, the child's age, learning difficulties and disabilities, gifts and talents, and behavioral problems.
- Parent–teacher factors—including differing goals and strategies, differing attitudes, and differing languages used.
- Societal factors—including historical and demographic aspects, political and economic factors.

This theoretical model may serve as a useful guide for the design of future studies identifying barriers at multiple levels.

Several qualitative researchers have conducted in-depth case studies, ethnographic studies, or interview studies of Mexican-origin parents, and have proposed alternative perspectives to conceptualize parental involvement. Auerbach (2007) conducted an ethnographic study of 16 working class parents, 13 of whom were Latino (some Mexican-origin). She identified three types of parents in terms of how they viewed their role in supporting their children's education: *moral supporters, struggling advocates*, and *ambivalent companions*. *Advocates* took more active roles, not trusting that their children would achieve their aspired education without their intervention. *Ambivalent companions*—all single mothers of girls—offered their children strong emotional support and open communication. Their ambivalence was only about whether they wanted their daughters to go to college. Finally, the *moral supporters* were all Latino immigrants with the lowest levels of education, and the lowest English fluency. They provided home support by stressing the importance of education, hard work, and the will to achieve. They tended to trust both their children and the school system and used *consejos* (advice and encouragement) to motivate their children.

Carreón *et al.* (2005) conducted case studies of three Latino immigrant parents, including two from Mexico, and propose *parental engagement* as an alternative to the construct of parental involvement. They describe parental engagement as parents' desire to be "present" in their children's schooling, if not in the actual physical space of the school. Each parent tried to establish relationships with teachers or principals on behalf of their children, sometimes struggling to be heard, sometimes succeeding. In general, researchers who have interviewed Mexican-origin parents report a passionate desire to support their children's education, along with frustration at not having adequate resources and not feeling understood, or disagreeing with the teacher or school's rules or policies (Ramirez, 2003; Suizzo *et al.*, 2012).

Plata-Potter and de Guzman (2012) asked eight Mexican immigrant parents about their experiences of trying to support their children in school. They identified several challenges, including language barriers, misunderstandings about school procedures, and feelings of incompetence or ineptness. A resource that the parents mentioned was giving their children advice or *consejos* (Valdés, 1996) in the form of warnings and encouragement. Behnke *et al.* (2004) interviewed ten families, including nine from Mexico, and heard similar barriers of lack of time, lack of understanding of pathways to reach their aspirations, lack of access to information, and low English proficiency.

Recommendations for reducing barriers and encouraging greater parental involvement in schools have been proposed by an increasing number of scholars. LaRocque, Kleinman, and Darling (2011) suggest addressing emotional, language, and physical barriers as well as cultural differences. For example, schools can provide transportation and child care for events such as Back-To-School-Night. They can work to build trust with immigrant parents by learning about their cultural values, and how to demonstrate respect in their communications with them. Finally, teachers can recognize and encourage the contributions parents are able to make at home, even if they are not able to assist children with academic tasks.

Directions for Future Research

Although our knowledge of Mexican-origin parental involvement has expanded greatly in the past decade, there is much yet to learn. First, and perhaps most importantly, scholars should specify the country of origin and generation level(s) of their participants, even if they cannot— or choose not to—focus on a single group in their analyses. The first difficulty with this suggestion is that an increasing number of Mexican-origin parents and children will be bicultural and/ or biracial, and will self-identify as such. Even as we seek to focus more exclusively on a single group to better understand its context, history, culture, and practices, we should not force ethnic or racial identities on people who view themselves in a more complex way. This trend will present new challenges and opportunities for cultural researchers in the coming years.

Secondly, researchers should make every attempt to include reports from multiple informants, especially from parents, in their studies on parental involvement. Many studies reviewed in this chapter relied exclusively on children's report of their parents' involvement (e.g. Carranza *et al.*, 2009; Kuperminc *et al.*, 2008). Although children's perceptions are crucial to understanding how they experience and are affected by parental involvement, if we wish to learn about parents' perspectives, we need to ask parents. Along these lines, we need to include fathers' and other caregivers' perspectives in a broader conceptualization of parental involvement. Fathers have an important presence within Mexican-origin families, yet they continue to be nearly absent from research on family involvement. There are challenges to overcome when including fathers who may not be as accessible if they are the sole provider or may not live in the same household. Research on fathering across ethnic groups has increased dramatically over the past few years, demonstrating fathers' unique contributions to the academic achievement and development of both girls and boys (see Lowe and Dotterer, 2013; Rodríguez *et al.*, 2013).

Thirdly, we need to continue including ethnographic and qualitative research within our investigations of Mexican-origin families. These studies provide the foundation for constructing more culturally sensitive questionnaires for large-scale studies that measure the beliefs and perspectives native to Mexican culture, rather than impose beliefs and theoretical constructs built with research on non-Mexicans. This knowledge is essential to eradicate the deficit perspective that has dominated much research on ethnic minority groups in the past. If we use instruments that capture beliefs and behaviors of *European* Americans to measure the beliefs and behaviors of *Mexican* Americans, we may overlook those unique to Mexican Americans and draw inaccurate conclusions. For example, in our qualitative study of mothers, Mexican American mothers reported using singing and rhyming to teach verbal skills to their preschool children; but none of the European Americans mentioned this practice (Suizzo *et al.*, 2014). Qualitative research is crucial to expanding and deepening our understanding of Mexican cultural models of parental involvement and to eroding the walls of stereotypes between schools and families.

And fourth, we need to broaden our focus in studies of Mexican American parental involvement to include teacher beliefs and school factors. A substantial body of research has shown that teachers' expectations of their students affect those students' performance and grades (Jussim and Harber, 2005). Further, a recent meta-analysis of teacher expectations studies concluded that teachers have lower expectations of Latino students than of European American students (Tenenbaum and Ruck, 2007). Teachers who are not Mexican-origin may hold misconceptions and stereotypes about their students' families that negatively influence their expectations. Increasing our knowledge of stereotypes and how they are constructed may help us address them more directly and effectively in teacher education programs and policies.

One of the barriers to Mexican American parental school involvement is low trust of parents in their children's schools (Hill and Torres, 2010). Research examining parents' trust in their children's schools is extremely sparse, but the few studies conducted have shown that when parents believe they have some influence on school decisions, they are more likely to trust that the school personnel will work on behalf of their children (Adams *et al.*, 2009). Mexican-origin parents who have experienced racism either as adults or during their own school experiences may be more hesitant to trust that their children's schools are treating their children fairly and investing in their education. More research is needed to identify the school factors and parent–school interactions that contribute to parents' trust in their children's schools.

Policy Implications

Several intervention and educational programs aimed at increasing parental involvement and student achievement among Mexican-origin children and adolescents have shown positive results in evaluations. Two such programs in North Carolina are the Latino Parent and Family Advocacy and Support Training (LPFAST) for parents of kindergarten through 8th grade children, and Juntos Para Una Mejor Educaccion (Together for a Better Education) for parents of 6th through 12th grade students. Both programs consist of six weekly two-hour sessions for parents, and the second program also includes youth participants. These programs provide onsite childcare and dinner for participants, and offer transportation to and from the meeting (Behnke and Kelly, 2011). Sessions are led by two Spanish-speaking facilitators and are held in various locations in the community. Topics covered include gaining skills for effective parent–school communication, understanding standards and testing, and preparing college applications. Both parents and youth participants showed significant pre- to post-test increases in knowledge and skills.

Another parental involvement intervention program used in Latino populations is the Home Instruction of Parents of Preschool Youngsters (HIPPY). HIPPY is a 30-week program consisting of weekly home visits by facilitators who are peers of the mothers in terms of educational level and ethnicity. During each visit, mothers receive a packet with developmentally appropriate games and activities for use in teaching their children math, science, language, literacy, motor skills, and social competence. The facilitator engages in role-playing with the mother to demonstrate and practice strategies for teaching children using these activities. In addition, program facilitators hold larger group meetings to share knowledge with mothers about the school system and community resources. During these meetings, mothers have opportunities to exchange their experiences, thereby building relationships and networks. A recent study of the program's effectiveness with a Latino population (majority Mexican-origin) showed favorable and lasting outcome effects on both mothers and children (Nievar *et al.*, 2011). Notably, mothers' parenting self-efficacy or perceived control over areas of their children's lives, increased during the program. The authors suggest that role-playing and repeated practice build confidence in mothers, who then feel empowered to teach their children.

These programs are effective in part because their design and implementation reflect key Mexican American cultural values such as *familismo, respeto, educación*, and *simpatía*. First, facilitators speak Spanish, are members of the same communities as the parents, and are often graduates of the program. Feeling validated by leaders who share their cultural values and experiences likely increases feelings of *simpatía* and warmth in participants. Second, interventions are held in parents' homes during times that are convenient for them. When meetings are held elsewhere, transportation, childcare, and meals are provided. This aspect demonstrates respect for parents' desire to stay connected with their family in the evenings rather than be separated, and for parents' obligations to provide for their families. Also, holding interventions at parents' homes may increase their level of comfort and feelings of investment in the program. It is important to remain open to alternative meeting sites, however, as some parents, especially from low-SES families, may feel embarrassed or burdened by hosting visitors in their homes. Culturally sensitive program staff from the same backgrounds as the families may be best suited to make these determinations. Third, parents receive valuable information about their children's schools and about the resources available to them in their communities. Although available through other means, this information is translated in Spanish and delivered in ways that are specifically tailored to the needs of Mexican-origin families. Finally, parents have opportunities to share with each other at group meetings so that they may build lasting relationships and social capital upon which to rely when the intervention is completed. These relationships mirror the important cultural value of *simpatía* and serve to empower families.

In conclusion, Mexican origin parents hold high educational aspirations for their children and engage in a variety of practices to support their learning and achievement. These practices are shaped by their beliefs and ideas about family, inter personal relationships, and what it means to educate a child. We have begun to examine more closely the unique and specific ways that these parents participate in their children's education, but there is a great deal more to learn. In taking the next steps, we need to broaden our conceptualization of parental involvement by integrating a wider range of psychological constructs and cultural practices, and by focusing not just on parents, but on families and communities.

References

Adams, C. M., Forsyth, P. B., and Mitchell, R. M. (2009). The formation of parent-school trust: A multilevel analysis. *Educational Administration Quarterly*, *45*(1), 4–33.

Alfaro, E. C., Umaña-Taylor, A. J., and Bámaca, M. Y. (2006). The influence of academic support on Latino adolescents' academic motivation. *Family Relations, 55,* 279–291.

Altschul, I. (2012). Linking socioeconomic status to the academic achievement of Mexican American youth through parent involvement in education. *Journal of the Society for Social Work and Research, 3*(1), 13–30.

Arcia, E., and Johnson, A. (1998). When respect means to obey: Immigrant Mexican mothers' values of their children. *Journal of Child and Family Studies, 7*(1), 79–95.

Auerbach, S. (2007). From moral supporters to struggling advocates. *Urban Education, 42*(3), 250–283.

Azmitia, M., Cooper, C. R., Garcia, E. E., and Dunbar, N. D. (1996). The ecology of family guidance in low-income Mexican-American and European-American families. *Social Development, 5*(1), 1–23.

Baumrind, D. (1966). Effects of authoritative parental control on child behavior. *Child Development, 37,* 887–907.

Behnke, A. O., and Kelly, C. (2011). Creating programs to help Latino youth thrive at school: The influence of Latino parent involvement programs. *Journal of Extension, 49,* 1–11.

Behnke, A. O., Piercy, K. W., and Diversi, M. (2004). Educational and occupational aspirations of Latino youth and their parents. *Hispanic Journal of Behavioral Sciences, 26*(1), 16–35.

Bradley, R. H. (2002). Environment and parenting. In M. H. Bornstein (Ed.), *Handbook of parenting: Vol. 2: Biology and ecology of parenting* (pp. 281–314). Mahwah, NJ: Erlbaum.

Carranza, F. D., You, S., Chhuon, V., and Hudley, C. (2009). Mexican American adolescents' academic achievement and aspirations: The role of perceived parental educational involvement, acculturation, and self-esteem. *Adolescence, 44*(174), 313–333.

Carreón, G. P., Drake, C., and Barton, A. C. (2005). The importance of presence: Immigrant parents' school engagement experiences. *American Educational Research Journal, 42*(3), 465–498.

Chun, H., and Dickson, G. (2011). A psychoecological model of academic performance among Hispanic adolescents. *Journal of Youth and Adolescence, 40*(12), 1581–1594.

Coleman, J. S. (1988). Social capital in the creation of human capital. *American Journal of Sociology,* S95–S120.

Davis-Kean, P. E. (2005). The influence of parent education and family income on child achievement: The indirect role of parental expectations and the home environment. *Journal of Family Psychology, 19*(2), 294–304.

Delgado, B. M., and Ford, L. (1998). Parental perceptions of child development among low-income Mexican American families. *Journal of Child and Family Studies, 7*(4), 469–481.

Delgado-Gaitan, C. (1994). *Consejos:* The power of cultural narratives. *Anthropology and Education Quarterly, 25*(3), 298–316.

Dumka, L. E., Gonzales, N. A., Bonds, D. D., and Millsap, R. E. (2009). Academic success of Mexican origin adolescent boys and girls: The role of mothers' and fathers' parenting and cultural orientation. *Sex Roles, 60,* 588–599.

Eisenberg, A. R. (2002). Maternal teaching talk within families of Mexican descent: Influences of task and socioeconomic status. *Hispanic Journal of Behavioral Sciences, 24*(2), 206–224.

Englund, M. M., Luckner, A. E., Whaley, G. J. L., and Egeland, B. (2004). Children's academic achievement in early elementary school: Longitudinal effects of parental involvement, expectations, and quality of assistance. *Journal of Educational Psychology, 96*(4), 723–730.

Epstein, J. L., and Sanders, M. G. (2002). Family, school, and community partnerships. In M. H. Bornstein (Ed.), *Handbook of parenting: Vol. 5: Practical issues in parenting* (pp. 407–437). Mahwah, NJ: Erlbaum.

Esparza, P., and Sánchez, B. (2008). The role of attitudinal familism in academic outcomes: A study of urban Latino high school seniors. *Cultural Diversity and Ethnic Minority Psychology, 14*(3), 193–200.

Fan, W., Williams, C. M., and Wolters, C. A. (2012). Parental involvement in predicting school motivation: Similar and differential effects across ethnic groups. *The Journal of Educational Research, 105,* 21–35.

Fan, X., and Chen, M. (2001). Parental involvement and students' academic achievement: A meta-analysis. *Educational Psychology Review, 13*(1), 1–22.

Fantuzzo, J., McWayne, C., Perry, M. A., and Childs, S. (2004). Multiple dimensions of family involvement and their relations to behavioral and learning competencies for urban, low-income children. *School Psychology Review, 33*(4), 467–480.

Gallimore, R., and Goldenberg, C. (2001). Analyzing cultural models and settings to connect minority achievement and school improvement research. *Educational Psychologist, 36*(1), 45–56.

Garcia Coll, C., Lamberty, G., Jenkins, R., McAdoo, H. P., Crnic, K., Wasik, B. H., and Garcia, H. V. (1996). An integrative model for the study of developmental competencies in minority children. *Child Development, 67*, 1891–1914.

Griffith, J. D., Joe, G. W., Chatham, L. R., and Simpson, D. D. (1998). The development and validation of a *Simpatía* scale for Hispanic entering drug treatment. *Hispanic Journal of Behavioral Sciences, 20*(4), 468–82.

Grolnick, W. S., and Slowiaczek, M. L. (1994). Parents' involvement in children's schooling: A multidimensional conceptualization and motivation model. *Child Development, 65*, 237–252.

Grusec, J. E., Rudy, D., and Martini, T. (1997). Parenting cognitions and child outcomes: An overview and implications for children's internalization of values. In J. E. Grusec and L. Kuczynski (Eds.), *Parenting and children's internalization of values: A handbook of contemporary theory* (pp. 259–282). Hoboken, NJ: John Wiley and Sons.

Halgunseth, L., Ispa, J., and Rudy, D. (2006). Parental control in Latino families: An integrated review of the literature. *Child Development, 77*(5), 1282–1297.

Hess, R. D., Holloway, S. D., Dickson, W. P., and Price, G. G. (1984). Maternal variables as predictors of children's school readiness and later achievement in vocabulary and mathematics in sixth grade. *Child Development, 55*(5), 1902–1912.

Hill, N. E., and Taylor, L. C. (2004). Parental school involvement and children's academic achievement: Pragmatics and issues. *Current Directions in Psychological Science, 13*, 161–164.

Hill, N. E., and Torres, K. (2010). Negotiating the American dream: The paradox of aspirations and achievement among Latino students and engagement between their families and schools. *Journal of Social Issues, 66*(1), 95–112.

Hill, N. E., and Tyson, D. F. (2009). A meta-analytic assessment of the strategies that promote achievement. *Developmental Psychology, 45*, 740–763.

Ho, E. S., and Willms, J. D. (1996). Effects of parental involvement on eighth-grade achievement. *Sociology of Education, 69*, 126–141.

Holland, D., and Quinn, N. (1987). *Cultural models in language and thought*. NY: Cambridge.

Hong, S., and Ho, H.-Z. (2005). Direct and indirect longitudinal effects of parental involvement on student achievement: Second-order latent growth modeling across ethnic groups. *Journal of Educational Psychology, 97*(1), 32–42.

Hoover-Dempsey, K. V., and Sandler, H. M. (1997). Why do parents become involved in their children's education. *Review of Educational Research, 67*(1), 3–42.

Hornby, G., and Lafaele, R. (2011). Barriers to parental involvement in education: An explanatory model. *Educational Review, 63*(1), 37–52.

Jeynes, W. H. (2007). The relationship between parental involvement and urban secondary school student academic achievement: A meta-analysis. *Urban Education, 42*(1), 82–110.

Jussim, L., and Harber, K. D. (2005). Teacher expectations and self-fulfilling prophecies: Knowns and unknowns, resolved and unresolved controversies. *Personality and Social Psychology Review, 9*(2), 131–155.

Kuperminc, G. P., Darnell, A. J., and Alvarez-Jimenez, A. (2008). Parent involvement in the academic adjustment of Latino middle and high school youth: Teacher expectations and school belonging as mediators. *Journal of Adolescence, 31*(4), 469–483.

Laosa, L. M. (1978). Maternal teaching strategies in Chicano families of varied educational and socioeconomic levels. *Child Development, 49*, 1129–1135.

LaRocque, M., Kleinman, I., and Darling, S. M. (2011). Parental involvement: The missing link in school achievement. *Preventing School Failure, 55*(3), 115–122.

LeFevre, Ann L., and Shaw, Terry V. (2012). Latino parent involvement and school success: Longitudinal effects of formal and informal support. *Education and Urban Society, 44*(6), 707–723.

LeVine, R. A., LeVine, S. E., and Schnell, B. (2001). "Improve the women": Mass schooling, female literacy, and worldwide social change. *Harvard Educational Review, 71*(1), 1–50.

Lowe, K., and Dotterer, A. M. (2013). Parental monitoring, parental warmth, and minority youths' academic outcomes: Exploring the integrative model of parenting. *Journal of Youth and Adolescence, 42*(9), 1413–1425.

Maccoby, E. E., and Martin, J. A. (1983). Socialization in the context of the family: Parent–child interaction. In P. H. Mussen (Series Ed.) and E. M. Hetherington (Vol. Ed.), *Handbook of child psychology: Vol. 4. Socialization, personality, and social development* (pp. 1–101). New York: Wiley.

Martinez, C. R., Jr., DeGarmo, D. S., and Eddy, J. M. (2004). Promoting academic success among Latino youth. *Hispanic Journal of Behavioral Sciences*, *26*(2), 128–151.

McWayne, C., Hampton, V., Fantuzzo, J., Cohen, H., and Sekino, Y. (2004). A multivariate examination of parent involvement and the social and academic competencies of urban kindergarten children. *Psychology in the Schools*, *41*(3), 363–377.

Moreno, R. P. (1997). Everyday instruction: A comparison of Mexican American and Anglo mothers and their preschool children. *Hispanic Journal of Behavioral Sciences*, *19*(4), 527–539.

Nievar, M., Jacobson, A., Chen, Q., Johnson, U., and Dier, S. (2011). Impact of HIPPY on Home Learning Environments of Latino Families. *Early Childhood Research Quarterly*, *26*(3), 268–277.

Okagaki, L., Frensch, P. A., and Gordon, E. W. (1995). Encouraging school achievement in Mexican American children. *Hispanic Journal of Behavioral Sciences*. *17*(2), 160–179.

Plata-Potter, S. I., and de Guzman, M. R. (2012). Mexican immigrant families crossing the education border: A phenomenological study. *Journal of Latinos and Education*, *11*(2), 94–106.

Plunkett, S. W., and Bámaca-Gómez, M. Y. (2003). The relationship between parenting, acculturation, and adolescent academics in Mexican-origin immigrant families in Los Angeles. *Hispanic Journal of Behavioral Sciences*, *25*(2), 222–239.

Plunkett, S. W., Henry, C., Houltberg, B., Sands, T., and Abarca-Mortensen, S. (2008). Academic support by significant others and educational resilience in Mexican-origin ninth grade students from intact families. *The Journal of Early Adolescence*, *28*(3), 333–355.

Quiocho, A. M. L., and Daoud, A. M. (2006). Dispelling myths about Latino parent participation in schools. *Educational Forum*, *70*(3), 255–267.

Ramirez, A. Y. F. (2003). Dismay and disappointment: Parental involvement of Latino immigrant parents. *The Urban Review*, *35*(2), 93–110.

Reese, L., Balzano, S., Gallimore, R., and Goldenberg, C. (1995). The concept of educación: Latino family values and American schooling. *International Journal of Educational Research*, *23*, 57–81.

Rodriguez, B. L., and Olswang, L. B. (2003). Mexican-American and Anglo-American mothers' beliefs and values about childrearing, education, and language impairment. *American Journal of Speech-Language Pathology*, *12*, 452–462.

Rodríguez, M. M. D., Donovick, M. R., and Crowley, S. L. (2009). Parenting styles in a cultural context: Observations of "protective parenting" in first-generation Latinos. *Family Process*, *48*(2), 195–210.

Rodríguez, S. A., Perez-Brena, N. J., Updegraff, K. A., and Umaña-Taylor, A. J. (2013). Emotional closeness in Mexican-origin adolescents' relationships with mothers, fathers, and same-sex friends. *Journal of Youth and Adolescence*, *42*, 1–16.

Roosa, M. W., O'Donnell, M., Cham, H., Gonzales, N. A., Zeiders, K. H., Tein, J.-Y., Knight, G. P., and Umaña-Taylor, A. (2012). A prospective study of Mexican American adolescents' academic success: Considering family and individual factors. *Journal of Youth and Adolescence*, *41*(3), 307–319.

Santiago-Rivera, A. L., Arredondo, P., and Gallardo-Cooper, M. (2002). *Counseling Latinos and la familia: A practical guide*. Thousand Oaks, CA: Sage.

Savage, S. L., and Gauvain, M. (1998). Parental beliefs and children's everyday planning in European-American and Latino families. *Journal of Applied Developmental Psychology*, *19*(3), 319–340.

Sewell, W., and Hauser, R. (1980). The Wisconsin longitudinal study of social and psychological factors in aspirations and achievements. In A. Kerckhoff (Ed.), *Research in the sociology of education and socialization* (Vol. 1, pp. 59–100). Greenwich, GT: JAI.

Singh, K., Bickley, P. G., Keith, T. Z., Keith, P. B., Trivette, P., and Anderson, E. (1995). The effects of four components of parental involvement on 8th grade student achievement: Structural analysis of NELS-88 data. *School Psychology Review*, *24*(2), 299–317.

Steidel, A. G. L., and Contreras, J. M. (2003). A new *familism* scale for use with Latino populations. *Hispanic Journal of Behavioral Sciences*, *25*(3), 312–330.

Suarez-Orozco, C., and Suarez-Orozco, M. M. (1995). *Transformations: Immigration, family life, and achievement motivation among Latino students*. Stanford, CA: Stanford University Press.

Suizzo, M.-A., Pahlke, E., Yarnell, L. M., Chen, K., and Romero, S. (2014). Home-based parental involvement in young children's learning across U.S. ethnic groups: Cultural models of academic socialization. *Journal of Family Issues, 35,* 254–287.

Suizzo, M.-A., Jackson, K., Pahlke, E., Marroquin, Y., Martinez, A., and Blondeau, L.A. (2012). Pathways to achievement: How low-income Mexican-origin parents promote their children through school. *Family Relations, 61,* 533–547.

Suizzo, M.-A., Chen, W.-C., Cheng, C.-C., Liang, A., Contreras, H., Zanger, D., and Robinson, C. R. (2008). Parental beliefs about young children's socialization across U.S. ethnic groups: Coexistence of independence and interdependence. *Early Child Development and Care, 178*(5), 467–486.

Super, C. M., and Harkness, S. (1986). The developmental niche: A conceptualization at the interface of child and culture. *International Journal of Behavioral Development, 9*(4), 545–569.

Taylor, L. C., Clayton, J. D., and Rowley, S. (2004). Academic socialization: Understanding parental influences on children's school-related development in the early years. *Review of General Psychology, 8*(3), 163–178.

Tenenbaum, H. R., and Ruck, M. D. (2007). Are teachers' expectations different for racial minority than for European American students? A meta-analysis. *Journal of Educational Psychology, 99*(2), 253–273.

Trusty, J., Plata, M., and Salazar, C. F. (2003). Modeling Mexican Americans' educational expectations: Longitudinal effects of variables across adolescence. *Journal of Adolescent Research, 18*(2), 131–153.

Umaña-Taylor, A. J., Alfaro, E. C., Bámaca, M. Y., and Guimond, A. B. (2009). The central role of familial ethnic socialization in Latino adolescents' cultural orientation. *Journal of Marriage and Family, 71,* 46–60.

Valdés, G. (1996). *Con Respeto: Bridging the distances between culturally diverse families and schools.* New York: Teachers College.

Valencia, R. R., and Black, M. S. (2002). "Mexican Americans don't value education!"—On the basis of the myth, mythmaking, and debunking. *Journal of Latinos and Education, 1*(2), 81–103.

Varela, R. E., Vernberg, E. M., Sanchez-Sosa, J. J., Riveros, A., Mitchell, M., and Mashunkashey, J. (2004). Parenting style of Mexican, Mexican American, and Caucasian-Non-Hispanic families: Social context and cultural influences. *Journal of Family Psychology, 18*(4), 651–657.

Weisner, T. S. (2002). Ecocultural understanding of children's developmental pathways. *Human Development, 45*(4), 275–281.

PART IV

Perspectives on Mental Health

11

MEXICAN AMERICANS' HELP-SEEKING OF COUNSELING SERVICES

Removing Barriers to Access and Focusing on Strengths

Lucila Ramos-Sánchez

Introduction

Psychiatric epidemiology and psychological studies indicate that Mexican Americans in general experience a significant amount of mental health problems as a result of psychological stressors (Lopez *et al.*, 2012; Tran *et al.*, 2010). Some of the stressors include, but are not limited to, poverty or low socioeconomic status, immigration status, trauma during migration, discrimination, and acculturation (Abreu and Sasaki, 2004). These experiences can result in stress leading to interpersonal conflicts and intrapersonal disorders (Coker *et al.*, 2009; Gloria and Segura-Herrera, 2004; Santiago–Rivera *et al.*, 2002). Among the intrapersonal disorders found in the literature are anxiety, adjustment, and substance dependence disorders (Pérez and Fortuna, 2005). These stressors and psychiatric disorders present a clear need for counseling, to alleviate psychological distress and reduce mental illness for Mexican Americans. However, despite the need for mental health services, there is evidence that Mexican Americans continue to underutilize psychological services (Abreu and Sasaki, 2004; Atdjian and Vega, 2005; Bender *et al.*, 2007; Cummings, 2011; Perron *et al.* (2009); Sullivan *et al.*, 2007; Vega *et al.*, 1999). Of those Mexican Americans who utilized services many reported that they received less individual therapy and a narrower range of services, even though they presented with more severe psychiatric disorders than their white counterparts (Bender *et al.*, 2007).

Research examining Mexican Americans' utilization of mental health services has focused primarily on barriers to access (Leong *et al.*, 1995; Prieto *et al.*, 2001). Other research has indicated that an insufficient number of Mexican American mental health providers exist to meet the needs of the Mexican American population (Ruiz, 2002). Unfortunately, underutilization continues to exist, suggesting that identifying barriers may not be enough to ameliorate the problem (Romero *et al.*, 2013). What may be necessary is to redirect research efforts to focus on areas other than barriers. For example, researchers could investigate the strengths that Mexican Americans bring to counseling and ways in which mental health professionals can utilize those strengths to encourage utilization and persistence in therapy.

Therefore, the overarching goal of the chapter is to identify strengths in the Mexican American culture that Mexican Americans bring to counseling. In order to understand the progress of the literature, the chapter will begin with a review of the early research on barriers to mental health access and utilization for Mexican Americans in order to provide a historical perspective. This will be followed by research aimed at clinical training to decrease mental health disparities. Current research and the direction it has taken toward addressing help-seeking intentions and counseling process will also be reviewed. The chapter will conclude with recommendation for clinicians that outline ways to conceptualize Mexican American culture as a strength to inform clinical practice, clinical training, development of social policy, and future research.

Literature Review

Early Research on Mexican Americans Utilization of Mental Health Services

In review of the literature, research prior to 1995 proposed reasons for underutilization of mental health services that usually fell within two domains: (1) institutional barriers and (2) the deficit perspective. Institutional barriers were considered agency policies, availability, or structural incongruities that served as obstacles to mental health services for Mexican Americans. Whereas, the deficit perspective referred to inherent characteristics of the person that kept them from seeking services.

Institutional-barriers Research

In a comprehensive review of early research on underutilization among ethnic minorities in general, and Mexican Americans in particular, Leong *et al.* (1995) hypothesized that the following served as institutional barriers to mental health services: (a) lack of Spanish-speaking counselors, (b) lack of ethnically similar counselors, (c) culturally irrelevant therapeutic approaches, (d) location of mental health clinics outside of Latino communities, and (e) inadequate financial resources.

Some of the first studies regarding underutilization found that language of the counselor seemed to be a significant obstacle to mental health (Barrera, 1978; Padilla *et al.*, 1976). These studies asserted that Spanish-speaking Mexican American clients did not use mental health services because few if any clinicians existed that could provide linguistically congruent therapeutic services. Lack of bilingual counselors was one aspect, other research found that providing therapy in one's nondominant language negatively affected the therapeutic process (Marcos and Urcuyo, 1979; Pitta *et al.*, 1978). These case studies examined the effectiveness of bilingual counselors compared with monolingual English-speaking counselors, with bilingual clients. Findings indicated that with bilingual counselors, clients disclosed more and were able to access their feelings more compared to clients with monolingual English speaking counselors. More recent studies have also looked at the impact of bilingual counselors on the counseling process; however, those will be reviewed further in the chapter.

Early research also focused on the availability of ethnically similar counselors and its relationship to underutilization of mental health services. The preponderance of evidence indicated that ethnic minorities, including Mexican Americans, expressed a greater willingness to see and perceive as more credible, an ethnically similar counselor, rather than an ethnically dissimilar one (Coleman *et al.*, 1995; Escobar and Randolph, 1982; Lopez *et al.*, 1991; Sanchez and Atkinson, 1983). Most studies indicated that Mexican American clients would be more willing to see an ethnically similar counselor because they would feel understood or more comfortable than with an ethnically dissimilar counselor. Therefore, the lack of Mexican American counselors available in the community may inhibit initial help-seeking intentions. However, in one of the only studies of its kind, Fraga *et al.*, (2004) found that ethnically similar counselors were very low on the list when ranked against other counselor traits. The authors concluded that when asked to choose between only an ethnically similar and dissimilar counselor, participants had the tendency to choose an ethnically similar counselor. However, if given the option to choose among a range of counselor characteristics, counselor ethnicity was not the most important factor. What these findings suggest is that, even though counselor ethnicity may be important, other counselor characteristics may be just as, if not more important, for selection of a counselor.

Studies on ethnically similar counselors has helped identify barriers to utilization for Mexican Americans. However, one of the major gaps in this early research is looking at whether enough Mexican American counselors exist. Ruiz (2002) alluded to the shortfall, though few other studies take a comprehensive examination at availability. Even if Mexican Americans prefer ethnically similar counselors, it has little clinical relevance if there are insufficient numbers of Mexican American counselors to meet the needs of the community.

Similarly, research is scarce for the other barriers to mental health services, namely: culturally irrelevant therapeutic approaches, location of mental health clinics outside of Latino communities, and inadequate financial resources. In a review of utilization of health care services, Marín *et al.*, (1983) found that financial difficulty was the most significant reason for underutilization. There is evidence to suggest that cultural disparity between the counselor and the client also negatively affected utilization (Padilla *et al.*, 1976). Even though location of services was included in the review by Leong *et al.* (1995), no early studies were found that specifically addressed location. The assertion seemed to be extrapolated from findings of general health-care utilization research. However, a later study (Vega *et al.*, 1999) found location of services compounded other reasons for underutilization.

Deficit Perspective Research

The remaining reasons for underutilization of mental health services are generally believed to be characteristics inherent to the individual or the individual's culture. For example, factors related to culture have been used to explain underutilization of mental health services (Leong *et al.*, 1995; Padilla *et al.*, 1976). Leong *et al.* asserted that various aspects of Mexican culture predisposed members not to seek professional services. These factors were identified as: alternative resources, lack of acculturation, and traditional Mexican values. Examples of alternative resources included family and spiritual- or folk healers (Heathcote *et al.*, 2011; Sue and Sue, 2008).

Family is considered central to the Mexican American culture, a place where members receive primary emotional, social, and economic support (Escobar and Randolph, 1982; Gloria and Peregoy, 1996; Ruiz and Padilla, 1977; Sandoval and De La Roza, 1986; Vazquez-Nuttal *et al.*, 1984; Vega *et al.*, 1991). The Mexican American culture does not limit the family to the immediate nuclear unit or biological relations, but includes extended family as well (Zinn, 1982). For example, close family members could consist of uncles, aunts, grandparents, cousins, *compadres* (extended kin), and friends. An example of resources within extended family is evident with compadres, who are esteemed friends or family members that assume parental responsibility of the children, in the event of the untimely passing of the parents. Ruiz and Padilla (1977) found that reliance on extended family for support was utilized more frequently than services from public agencies. Similarly, Padilla *et al.* (1976) reported that relatives, friends, and clergy were the most significant reasons for underutilization of mental health services for emotional problems. Therefore, family may be one of the first resources Mexican Americans turn to in times of emotional need.

Another alternative resource utilized by Mexican Americans and found in the early literature was spiritual leaders (priests) or folk healers. In a study of cultural values, Zea *et al.* (1994) found that because of the importance of religion, many Mexican Americans likely sought out the guidance of a priest (spiritual) rather than counseling services. Similarly, Leong *et al.* (1995) asserted that Mexican Americans sought out spiritual/folk healers because of similar beliefs regarding the causes of mental illness. For example, some Mexican Americans may believe that their symptoms result from conditions such as *mal de ojo* (evil eye), which necessitates a *curandero/a* for healing. In some regions, folk healers such as *curanderos* were considered to be the psychotherapist of the Mexican American population (Keefe and Casas, 1978). Gomez (1987) contended that Mexican Americans, because of their Indian traditions and beliefs in folklore, would not hesitate to use a curandero to resolve their health problems. However, Nall and Spielberg (1967) found no significant difference between adherence to folk beliefs and utilization rates; the study concluded that Mexican Americans used folk healers and mental health services together—it was not an either/or decision. However, few other studies have empirical evidence regarding utilization of folk healers or priests over counseling services.

Nonetheless, along with other alternative resources folk healers and spiritual leaders were considered a barrier in the literature rather than a resource. Interestingly, the direction of the research was to find fault with what Mexican Americans utilized in times of stress, when they chose something other than mental health services. This area of study might have been better served had they examined how services were delivered. The goal seemed aimed at changing the perspective of the client instead of how approaches could be delivered differently or how traditional methods of healing could be incorporated into therapy.

The relationship between acculturation and utilization also received a lot of attention in the early literature. Some of the earlier research findings on acculturation indicated that less acculturation negatively influenced utilization of mental health services and help-seeking intentions (Atkinson *et al.*, 1990; Keefe and Casas, 1978; Leong *et al.*, 1995; Rogler *et al.*, 1989; Sanchez and Atkinson, 1983; Wells *et al.*, 1987). Meaning, individuals who were less acculturated were less likely to utilize mental health services than individuals who were more acculturated. However, other studies contradicted the above findings for acculturation and found no significant relationship between acculturation and utilization or help-seeking intentions (Atkinson *et al.*, 1992; Cuellar *et al.*, 1980; Hess and Street, 1991; Ponce and Atkinson, 1989). In one of the most seminal studies regarding utilization, Reeves (1986) reported that two-thirds of the clients who used a local clinic were unacculturated, of immigrant status, less educated, and monolingual Spanish speakers. The author indicated that when culturally relevant services were available, they were utilized. Moreover, this finding suggests that service delivery not the individual should be scrutinized.

Mexican American values were also identified as contributing to underutilization of mental health services. The majority of research assumed that traditional Mexican American values contradict the focus of more individually oriented psychotherapeutic approaches. For example, Leong *et al.* (1995) indicated that the expansive support provided by the value of familism reduced the need for mental health services. Zea *et al.* (1994) asserted that family members may discourage seeking help outside so as not to dishonor the family. Similarly, other research identified fatalism, religiosity, and machismo (Magaña and Clark, 1995; Shapiro and Simonsen, 1994; Vazquez-Nuttal *et al.*, 1984), as values that discouraged Mexican Americans from utilizing mental health services. In contrast, Flores (1978) found that lack of acceptance by the community not traditional values of Mexican Americans impeded utilization. Flores indicated that acceptance of the agency that provided the services was central to utilization. Moreover, no empirical studies were found that supported the negative relationship between cultural values and mental health utilization. Most of the literature hypothesized this to be the case, but with little evidence.

Multicultural Counseling Training

Efforts to remedy underutilization, as well as other issues of diversity, have come primarily through multicultural training in masters and doctoral counseling programs (Robertson and Morris, 2000). Prior to the mid-1980s few if any graduate counseling students were exposed to multicultural training in their course work (Allison *et al.*, 1994). Training programs attempted to address underutilization and diversity by increasing cultural competence course work in graduate counseling programs. This was evident in the proliferation of multicultural and/or cross-cultural courses at the graduate level by the late 1980s and early 1990s (Quintana and Bernal, 1995). Unfortunately, no studies were found that examined multicultural counseling training and an increase in utilization of mental health services.

Recent Research on Mexican American Utilization of Mental Health Services

Recent research of Mexican American mental health utilization will consist of any research after 1995. The distinction comes from a shift in the direction of the research away from the deficit perspective. It is possible that the direction of the research may have shifted because of greater cultural and sensitivity training in working with Mexican Americans and other populations. Interestingly, Mexican American utilization of mental health services has increased over the years (Romero *et al.*, 2013). However, no research exists that links increases in cultural- and sensitivity training, to the increase in Mexican Americans' use of mental health services.

Barriers such as institutional barriers continue to be an issue for accessing services (Atdjian and Vega, 2005; Bridges *et al.*, 2012; Ruiz, 2002; Vega *et al.*, 1999). In an attempt to focus away from the deficit perspective it seems more studies have tried to examine personal characteristics that could increase help-seeking intentions. Help-seeking intentions are a person's stated intent that they would seek counseling if a problem were to arise (Ruelas *et al.*, 1998). Research has also attempted to study strategies and interventions that clinicians can employ with Mexican Americans who use mental health services, to increase client persistence in following the treatments clinicians offer (Ramos-Sánchez and Atkinson, 2009). As a result, this section was ordered differently to accommodate the new direction.

Institutional Barriers

Even though Mexican Americans have increased utilization of mental health services, institutional barriers continue to exist (Romero *et al.*, 2013). However, fewer studies were conducted that addressed institutional barriers as this was well established in the early research. Of the studies that did address institutional barriers, Vega *et al.* (1999) reported that location served as a significant deterrent in rural areas. Access to health insurance seemed to significantly impair utilization of services (Romero *et al.*, 2013). As high as 31 percent of Mexican Americans are without health insurance, and the percentage is higher for foreign-born. Thus, Mexican Americans who do not have the means to pay "out of pocket" and also do not have insurance, remain without services. It is possible that uninsured individuals may not consider counseling an option because of the cost. Early research examined the lack of ethnically similar counselors; later and recent research has focused more on the lack of bilingual counselors to address the linguistic needs of the client (Bridges *et al.*, 2012; Ruiz, 2002).

Adherence to Culture

Recent research has found that enculturation—strong adherence to one's culture of origin—was positively related to help-seeking intentions (Ramos-Sánchez et al., 1999; Ruelas et al., 1998). Positive help-seeking intentions of counseling indicate a greater willingness to utilize mental health services. Ruelas et al. found that less acculturated (more enculturated) Mexican Americans perceived counselors as more credible than more acculturated (less enculturated) Mexican Americans. Ramos-Sánchez and Atkinson (2009) extended these findings in their research of Mexican Americans' help-seeking intentions and cultural values. Based on the results of the study, the researchers concluded that as Mexican Americans lost their culture of origin (more acculturated), their attitudes toward help-seeking became less favorable, resulting in less utilization. Similarly, Shim et al., (2009) reported that client ethnicity predicted positive attitudes toward help-seeking. Mexican American clients reported more positive help-seeking intentions and less embarrassment in seeking services than their non-Hispanic white counterparts.

Enculturation or adherence to one's culture of origin suggests an individual strongly maintains the values and beliefs of their culture. Therefore, it would follow that both enculturation and Mexican cultural values have a positive impact on help-seeking intentions. As such, the findings for enculturation and help-seeking refute claims that Mexican values contribute to underutilization of mental health services (Ramos-Sánchez and Atkinson, 2009). Recent findings for help-seeking intentions suggest that theorists and clinicians should move away from the culture-blaming that has permeated the literature. These studies have found that traditional Mexican American cultural values or adherence to traditional culture (enculturation) may actually encourage help-seeking among certain individuals (Ramos-Sánchez and Atkinson, op. cit.; Ruelas et al., 1998). Specifically, Ramos-Sánchez and Atkinson (op. cit.) reported that the value of *personalismo* and religiosity were positively related to Mexican Americans' help-seeking intentions. Unfortunately, few studies have framed adherence to cultural values as an asset or strength, rather they have been viewed as a deficit toward utilization and help-seeking intentions.

Further evidence of the positive impact of enculturation (less acculturation) to traditional Mexican American culture was found with incidence of psychiatric disorders (Vega et al., 2003; Vega et al., 2004; Vega and Sribney, 2011). Vega et al. (2003) concluded that strong adherence to Mexican American culture corresponded with strong familial social support, that in turn, mitigated major stressors that impacted psychological well-being. In their study of migrant individuals and Mexican Americans, Alderete et al. (2000), reported length of time in the US was positively associated with a rise in psychiatric disorders. Alderete (op.cit.) concluded that protective sociocultural factors diminished as individuals become more established in society. Sociocultural protective factors included social support, strong family cohesion, and group identity.

Vega et al. (2004) found that greater social assimilation, closely related to acculturation by Mexican Americans, was associated with higher rates of clinically diagnosed mental health disorders. Mexican Americans who were less socially assimilated had stronger marital and family support, making them less vulnerable to developing mood, anxiety, and substance disorders than more socially assimilated Mexican Americans. The most vulnerable were Mexican Americans who had spent a significant amount of their childhood and adolescence in the US. Other recent studies have also found the deleterious effects of social assimilation on family composition, stability, cohesiveness, and parental control of children and adolescents (Portes and Rumbaut, 2001; Vega and Gil, 1998; Vega et al., 2003). An explanation of this relationship was provided by Vega and Sribney (2011) who suggested that Mexican Americans make adaptive changes in response to their culturally incongruent environment. These adaptive changes may result in some problem behaviors that may increase in magnitude across genera-tions. An example is the use of substances to deal with the stress of being socially uprooted (Falicov, 1998). These findings suggest that remaining enculturated to Mexican American culture could have substantial benefits to Mexican Americans' familial structure.

The research on help-seeking intentions provides a good understanding of what factors contribute to attitudes toward help-seeking. However, uncertainty remains as to whether positive help-seeking attitudes lead to help-seeking behavior. More research is needed to ascertain what factors actually contribute to help-seeking behavior. Nonetheless, these studies did not support the sweeping generalization, that enculturation (less acculturated) was negatively associated with willingness to seek counseling. To the contrary, many of these findings suggest that maintaining one's culture of origin may have a positive impact on the perception of mental health services and subsequent help-seeking intentions. Therefore, enculturation could be viewed as a source of strength. Strengths that Mexican Americans bring to counseling have not been given much attention in the literature. Evaluating underutilization is important; however, identifying strengths that reside within the individual, families, and culture are equally as important.

Adherence to Culture as a Strength

Given the strong evidence for enculturation with both positive help-seeking intentions and lower psychiatric disorders in more recent research, identifying characteristics within the culture such as values would make sense. Cultural values have received some attention in the literature as a source of strength. In their review of Mexican American culture, Sue and Sue (2013) identified *familismo, personalismo*, and religiosity as values that could help clinicians develop a strength-based approach in therapeutic treatment and to increase utilization. *Familismo* refers to familial cohesiveness, interdependence, and loyalty, in addition to putting the needs of friends and family before personal needs (Baumann *et al.*, 2010). Research covered earlier in the chapter reviewed how the literature often framed *familismo* from the deficit perspective, faulting family for underutilization of mental health services. However, *familismo* can be considered a source of strength for many Mexican Americans. As a whole, the family provides identity, perceived security, sense of reference, social, emotional, and economic support, in which all members, regardless of age or gender enjoy a certain status. Family also serves as a buffer against a hostile environment and circulates limited resources (Zinn, 1982). In fact, evidence suggests that Mexican Americans become more vulnerable to psychiatric disorders with the loss of familial cohesion (Alderete *et al.*, 2000).

Personalismo could be another source of strength for Mexican Americans, and refers to a communication style that emphasizes respectful, interdependent, cooperative interactions, and worth and dignity of the individual (Diller, 2010). It is most noted through style of communic-ation that promotes relationships toward people rather than impersonal institutional relation-ships (Cuellar *et al.*, 1995). In American mainstream culture respect is afforded because of achievement, status, and wealth, whereas in Mexican American culture respect is afforded by sheer nature of one's humanity (Diller, 2010). Adherence to this value can actually facilitate the therapeutic alliance between counselor and client, insofar as the counselor treats the Mexican American client with dignity and respect. *Personalismo* may help establish pathways in forming a relationship with a client because of the inherent friendliness and warmth toward others. In addition, the characteristics of *personalismo* are similar to therapists' goals of rapport-building; to this end, it is reasonable to assume that they would complement each other and lead to enhanced attitudes of utilization of mental health services (Ramos-Sánchez and Atkinson, 2009) and promote persistence in therapy.

Finally, religiosity—suggests a belief in a greater power, and that suffrage and healing are linked to this greater power. A fundamental feature of Latino spirituality is its preoccupation with healing the physical, the mental, and the spiritual part of oneself (Heathcote *et al.*, 2011; Magaña and Clark, 1995). Religion or religiosity assumes a large significance in Mexican American culture, as the majority of Mexican Americans (67.6 percent) identify as Roman Catholics, or were at least raised Catholic (Pew Hispanic Center, 2007). Studies support the integration of religious coping and the benefits of religion to Mexican Americans' psychological well-being (Koerner *et al.*, 2013; Lujan, 2006). Religiosity and the aforementioned values would be beneficial if integrated within a clinical context.

Summary

Traditional approaches to counseling Mexican Americans have come under scrutiny as they relate to the deficit perspective and how mental health services are delivered. This deficit perspective only serves to perpetuate the culture- and person-blaming that has permeated the literature for decades. Counselors, agencies, social policies, and training programs need to reexamine how their own practices and ways of service delivery maintain the problem of underutilization of mental health services.

Approaching Mexican American clients from a strength-based approach that focuses on integration of values and culture may encourage persistence in therapy so that treatment can be effective. Also, conceptualizing values and culture as a strength may be empowering to some Mexican American clients who may have had a different experience because of their cultural differences. Moreover, rethinking traditional models of service delivery, from office-based to school-based, may open up access to many Mexican Americans who may not otherwise use services. Overall, thinking creatively at all levels is important and necessary for effective change to occur.

Future Directions and Challenges

Like many other populations, Mexican Americans generally seek counseling for a wide variety of issues. Most often they seem to coincide with some of the major stressors they may be experiencing, such as familial conflict (Suárez-Orozco *et al.*, 2002), stress from parent–child cultural disparity, children's behavioral issues, children's academic issues (Falicov, 1998), substance abuse, trauma, depression, anxiety (Alderete *et al.*, 2000; Vega *et al.*, 2004) and the list continues. Irrespective of issues, most Mexican Americans have some strengths or resilience that can be tapped into and focused on to meet the goals of therapy. The recommendations provided in this section are based on the aforementioned strengths and how to utilize these strengths to improve services, promote help-seeking, and decrease institutional barriers. Recommendations are divided into four sections: clinical practice, training, social policy, and future research. Recommendations for clinical practice are related specifically to traditional Mexican American values.

Clinical Practice

Studies indicate that 60–80 percent of Mexican Americans do not return to therapy after the first session (Cheung and Snowden, 1990). The professional and formal presentation exhibited by many clinicians may actually be a deterrent for Mexican Americans. Some Mexican American clients may find this formality as aloof, distancing, and unfriendly, decreasing their likelihood of returning. This goes counter to the values of *personalismo* inherent in the Mexican American culture. Clinicians could attempt to demonstrate more warmth and be more personable when meeting and working with Mexican American clients. A warm, friendly, and respectful demeanor rather than a formal distant demeanor will go a long way in making some Mexican American clients feel more welcomed and increase their persistence in counseling.

In clinical practice, *familismo* could be a strength used to formulate therapeutic interventions. For example, family connectedness and loyalty among family members can provide significant social and emotional support in times of need (Hays and Erford, 2010; Hernandez *et al.*, 2010; Sue and Sue, 2013). In a therapeutic setting, familial connectedness could be encouraged as a way of bolstering one's support network, especially during times of duress. Systems theorists have long expounded on the virtues of understanding family dynamics in conceptualizing individual problems (Gladding, 2010). Clinicians may find it helpful to invite family members to the session either as sources of support or as part of treatment, to shed light on the complexity of the issue. Either way, family should be at the forefront of the treatment because of their importance in the person's life.

Religiosity is another strength that could be included in treatment. Given the importance of religiosity in the Mexican American community, exploring how religious and spiritual beliefs may influence a client's understanding of the presenting problem may be helpful (Andrés-Hyman *et al.*, 2006). Integrating the use of prayer and encouraging spiritual connectedness into therapy can bring comfort during times of stress (Sue and Sue, 2013). These practices suggest that religiosity should be viewed as a resource that can be accessed for support and problem-solving in a therapeutic setting. In fact, Mexican Americans who expressed greater religiosity reported higher help-seeking intentions than Mexican Americans with lesser religiosity (Ramos-Sánchez and Atkinson, 2009). This supports the idea of cultural values as an asset rather than a deficit in the counseling process.

Policy Implications

Evidence from past research (Atkinson *et al.*, 1989; Marcos and Urcuyo, 1979; Pitta *et al.*, 1978; Sanchez and Atkinson, 1983; Guttfreund, 1990; Ramos-Sánchez *et al.*, 1999) suggests that counselor language ability and ethnicity may contribute to making counseling services more welcoming to this population. A majority of first-generation Mexican Americans speak Spanish in the home, with second and third generation maintaining some level of proficiency (Biever *et al.*, 2002). Thus, more bilingual counselors are needed because language continues to be a barrier to access (Bridges *et al.*, 2012; Ruiz, 2002). Within the counseling process, Ramos-Sánchez (2009) found that Mexican American participants rated the Spanish-speaking counselors higher than the monolingual English-speaking counselors. Santiago-Rivera and Altarriba (2002) indicated increased positive outcomes in therapy when the counselor could speak the bilingual client's primary language. These findings are consistent with previous research that has investigated the relationship between counselor language ability and the therapeutic process (Marcos and Urcuyo, 1979; Pitta *et al.* 1978; Guttfreund, 1990; Ramos-Sánchez *et al.*, 1999). Therefore, bilingual counselors are needed in order to provide effective services and linguistic-congruent counseling to a Spanish-speaking population.

Training

In terms of training, it is important for the field of psychology to train more counselors who are both culturally and linguistically competent to work with the Mexican American population.

Graduate programs could offer specialized courses on how to work with the Mexican American population. Model programs that tailor counseling courses specific to Latino psychology (Mexican Americans specifically) exist at both the doctoral (Biever *et al.*, 2002) and master's level (Ramos-Sánchez and Shapiro, 2009). Specifically, these model programs provide cultural and linguistic training for counseling students who desire to work with Mexican Americans. The curricula at both Our Lady of the Lakes and Santa Clara University, overlap to some extent and generally focus on the psychosocial experience of Mexican Americans, family process and interventions with Mexican American families, interviewing skills with Mexican Americans, and professional Spanish language courses. The subset of courses taught in Spanish (Biever *et al.*, 2002; Ramos-Sánchez and Shapiro, 2009) are distinctive, and attempt to improve counseling services provided to monolingual Spanish-speakers.

Courses taught in Spanish were developed by professors at the institutions because there seemed to be an inaccurate assumption that bilingual counseling students could easily transfer recently acquired professional skills and knowledge in English, to Spanish-speaking clients (Biever *et al.*, 2002). Biever *et al.* indicated that such expectations were unrealistic and left many counseling students feeling incompetent when providing counseling in Spanish. Counselors-in-training did not have the vocabulary or fluidity because their training was language-specific. In addition to lacking competence, lack of supervision of skill development in Spanish could potentially affect the quality of counseling services delivered to the Spanish-speaking community. Therefore, Spanish courses are intended to provide formal counseling training in the language in which the students would be delivering services. Training programs are encouraged to incorporate the aforementioned training models and to recruit bilingual individuals who can effectively work with Mexican Americans.

Social Policy

Traditionally, providers of mental health services used a model of service delivery that was provider driven. If someone wanted mental health services they sought out a clinician and went to the clinician's office. This method required an implicit commitment from the client. Effort was put forth to find a clinician; therefore, the client was taking responsibility for, and making a commitment to therapy. However, such a model of service delivery has narrowed access for some populations, one of them being the Mexican American community. Even though the older model of service is still functional for some, policy surrounding delivery of mental health services can be altered to decrease disparities within the Mexican American population (Aguilar-Gaxiola *et al.*, 2012).

In a review of decreasing mental health disparities, Aguilar-Gaxiola *et al.*'s (2012) study recommended policy changes that focused on therapist capacity, and academic and school-based mental health programs. In terms of therapist capacity, having therapists who are culturally and linguistically capable of providing culturally competent services is a must. Cultural competence training for working with Mexican Americans was addressed previously, and general multicultural competence is an ongoing process in clinician training programs; however, second language ability is often overlooked. Licensing boards could require that graduate counseling programs incorporate specialized competency training addressing mental health needs of Mexican Americans into the academic curriculum. Students would be required to complete the coursework to be license eligible. Licensing boards could also require graduate programs to provide Spanish-language clinical courses. Students would not be required to complete these courses, but they would be offered an opportunity for this training. At the same time, states could provide funding to graduate training programs that make a greater effort to recruit Spanish-speaking students into their programs to address the shortage of Spanish-speaking clinicians in the community. University admissions could alter criteria in the selection process to include second language ability, and weight it just as high as standardized test scores or grade point average.

Aguilar-Gaxiola *et al.* (2012) indicated that funding is essential to policy change. The question is, how does this address the larger issue of increasing the numbers of bilingual counselors? Any state or county money that is issued to mental health agencies to serve individuals from a lower socioeconomic status could mandate that the agencies have a certain percentage of bilingual counselors on staff. While state licensing boards may not be able to mandate bilingual capacity of therapists, they can determine who receives funding depending on the make-up of the staff. This would be particularly salient in states where there is a high Mexican American population.

Establishing academic and school-based mental health programs is also essential to increase access and utilization (Aguilar-Gaxiola *et al.*, 2012). Schools are a central location with easy access to many families because of their location in the community. Although, centrality of services is just part of the program. Academic and school-based programs encourage screening to detect and diagnose potential mental health problems of current students for early intervention. Secondary schools could collaborate with agencies or county programs to develop interventions to decrease adolescent-related issues such as drug use, depression, stress, or behavioral problems. Schools could also work with the parents by offering seminars or classes aimed at discussing psychological well-being for their children and families. Finally, schools could expand their services or collaborate with agencies to provide mental health services at the school for both children and families. Agencies should also consider a community-based approach to mental health. Boyd-Franklin and Bry (2000) recommended providing services in the setting in which the client lives, for example, in-home therapy visits rather than having clients go to the agency offices (Slattery and Knapp, 2003). Clinicians going directly to the client may eliminate issues of transportation and childcare. The integration of mental health services within a school setting or within the community would go a long way in decreasing barriers to access.

Influencing policy changes could also occur through sources that provide funding for mental health services (Aguilar-Gaxiola *et al.*, 2012). County, state, and federal funding sources should consider incorporating these recommendations as criteria or requirements for agencies and schools who are applying for funds. For example, state and federal funding could provide grants to training programs that recruit bilingual (English/Spanish) students. Fellowships could also be offered to students who are bilingual and pursue a doctorate or master's level counseling degree. At the program level, only agencies that provide school-based mental health programs and have bilingual therapists would be considered for state and/or federal mental health funds. This would ensure adoption and implementation of recommendations so that Mexican Americans gain access to better mental health services.

Future Research

More research is needed to examine counseling outcomes with a strength-based rather than a deficit-based approach in a clinical setting with Mexican Americans. Two areas would be targeted: persistence and symptoms reduction. First, researchers could develop interventions that integrate Mexican American values and assess their effect on persistence in counseling, as many do not return after the first session. Second, client self-report or counselor assessment could determine symptoms reduction after 10 or 20 sessions. Also, more research should be conducted that focuses on academic and school-based mental health programs to determine their effect on issues such as drug abuse, attrition, and other high-risk behavior that would negatively impact school performance and persistence.

References

Abreu, J. M., and Sasaki, H. M. (2004). Physical and mental health concerns of Hispanics. In D. R. Atkinson (Ed.), *Counseling American Minorities* (6th ed.) (pp. 300–316). New York, NY: McGraw-Hill.

Aguilar-Gaxiola, S., Loera, G., Méndez, L., Sala, M., Latino Mental Health Concilio, and Nakamoto, J. (2012). *Community-defined solutions for Latino mental health care disparities: California reducing disparities project, Latino strategic planning workgroup population report.* Sacramento, CA: UC Davis.

Alderete, E., Vega, W. A., Kolody, B., and Aguilar-Gaxiola, S. A. (2000). Lifetime prevalence of and risk factors for psychiatric disorders among Mexican migrant farmworkers in California. *American Journal of Public Health*, *90*, 608–614.

Allison, K. W., Crawford, I., Echemendia, R., Robinson, L., and Knepp, D. (1994). Human diversity and professional competence: Training in clinical and counseling psychology revisited. *American Psychologist*, *49*, 792–796.

Andrés-Hyman, R. C., Ortiz, J., Añez, L. M., Paris, M., and Davidson, L. (2006). Culture and clinical practice: Recommendations for working with Puerto Ricans and other Latinas(os) in the United States. *Professional Psychology: Research and Practice*, *37*, 694–701.

Atdjian, S., and Vega, W. A. (2005). Disparities in mental health treatment in U.S. racial and ethnic minority groups: Implications for psychiatrists. *Psychiatric Services*, *56*, 1600–1602.

Atkinson, D. R., Casas, A., and Abreu, J. (1992). Mexican-American acculturation, counselor ethnicity and cultural sensitivity, and perceived counselor credibility. *Journal of Counseling Psychology*, *39*, 515–520.

Atkinson, D. R., Jennings, R. G., and Liongson, L. (1990). Minority students' reasons for not seeking counseling and suggestions for improving services. *Journal of College Student Development*, *31*, 342–350.

Atkinson, D. R., Poston, W. C., Furlong, M. J., and Mercado, P. (1989). Ethnic group preferences for counselor characteristics. *Journal of Counseling Psychology*, *36*, 68–72.

Barrera, M. (1978). Mexican-American mental health service utilization: A critical examination of some proposed variables. *Community Mental Health Journal*, *14*, 35–45.

Baumann, A. A., Kuhlberg, J. A., and Zayas, L. H. (2010). Familism, mother-daughter mutuality, and suicide attempts of adolescent Latinas. *Journal of Family Psychology*, *24*, 616–624.

Bender, D. S., Skodol, A. E., Dyck, I. R., Markowitz, J. C., Shea, M. T., Yen, S., Sanislow, C. A., Pinto, A., Zanarini, M. C., McGlashan, T. H., Gunderson, J. G., Daversa, M. T., and Grilo, C. M. (2007). Ethnicity and mental health treatment utilization by patients with personality disorders. *Journal of Consulting and Clinical Psychology*, *75*, 992–999.

Biever, J. L., Castaño, M. T., de las Fuentes, C., González, C., Servín-López, S., Sprowls, C., and Tripp, C. G. (2002). The role of language in training psychologists to work with Hispanic clients. *Professional Psychology: Research and Practice*, *33*, 330–336.

Boyd-Franklin, N., and Bry, B. H. (2000). *Reaching out in family therapy: Home-based, school, and community interventions.* New York, NY: Guilford Press.

Bridges, A. J., Andrews, A. R., and Deen, T. L. (2012). Mental health needs and services utilization by Hispanic immigrants residing in Mid-southern United States. *Journal of Transcultural Nursing*, *23*, 359–368.

Cheung, F. K., and Snowden, L. R. (1990). Community mental health and ethnic minority populations. *Community Mental Health Journal*, *26*, 277–291.

Coker, T. R., Elliott, M. N., Kanouse, D. E., Grunbaum, J. A., Schwebel, D. C., Gilliland, M. J., Tortolero, S. R., Peskin, M. F., and Schuster, M. A. (2009). Perceived racial/ethnic discrimination among fifth-grade students and its association with mental health. *American Journal of Public Health*, *99*, 878–884.

Coleman, H. L. K., Wampold, B. E., and Casali, S. L. (1995). Ethnic minorities' ratings of ethnically similar and European American counselors: A meta-analysis. *Journal of Counseling Psychology*, *42*, 55–64.

Cuellar, I., Arnold, B., and González, G. (1995). Cognitive referents of acculturation: Assessment of cultural constructs in Mexican Americans. *Journal of Community Psychology*, *23*, 339–356.

Cuellar, I., Harris, L. C., and Jasso, R. (1980). An acculturation scale for Mexican American normal and clinical populations. *Hispanic Journal of Behavioral Sciences*, *2*, 199–217.

Cummings, J. R. (2011). Racial/ethnic differences in mental health service use among adolescents with major depression. *Journal of the American Academy of Child Psychiatry*, *50*, 160–170.

Diller, J. V. (2010). *Cultural diversity. A primer for the human services.* (4th Edition). Belmont, CA: Thompson Brooks/Cole.

Escobar, J. I., and Randolph, E. T. (1982). The Hispanic and social networks. In R. M. Becerra, M. Karno, and J. I. Escobar (Eds.), *Mental health and Hispanic Americans.* New York: Grune and Stratton.

Falicov, C. (1998). *Latino families in therapy: A guide to multicultural practice.* NY: Guilford.

Flores, J. L. (1978). The utilization of a community mental health service by Mexican Americans. *International Journal of Social Psychiatry, 24,* 271–275.

Fraga, E. D., Atkinson, D. R., and Wampold, B. E. (2004). Ethnic group preference for multicultural counseling competencies. *Cultural Diversity Ethnic Minority Psychology, 10,* 53–65.

Gladding, S. (2010). *Family therapy: History, theory, and practice.* (5th Edition). Englewood Cliffs, NJ: Merrill/Prentice Hall.

Gloria, A. M., and Peregoy, J. J. (1996). Counseling Latino alcohol and other substance users/abusers. *Journal of Substance Abuse of Treatment, 13,* 119–126.

Gloria, A. M., and Segura-Herrera, T. A. (2004). In D. R. Atkinson (Ed.), *Counseling American minorities* (6th edn.) (pp. 279–299). New York, NY: McGraw-Hill.

Gomez, E. A. (1987). Hispanic Americans: Ethnic shared values and traditional treatments. *American Journal of Social Psychiatry, 7,* 215–219.

Guttfreund, D. G. (1990). Effects of language usage on the emotional experience of Spanish-English and English-Spanish bilinguals. *Journal of Consulting and Clinical Psychology, 58,* 604–607.

Hays, D., and Erford, B. T. (2010). *Developing multicultural counseling competence: A systemic approach.* (2nd Edition). Boston, MA: Pearson.

Heathcote, J. D., West, J. H., Cougar Hall, P., and Trinidad, D. R. (2011). Religiosity and utilization of complementary and alternative medicine among foreign-born Hispanics in the United States. *Hispanic Journal of Behavioral Sciences, 33,* 398–408.

Hernandez, B., Garcia, J. I. R., and Flynn, M. (2010). The role of familism in the relation between parent–child discord and psychological distress among emerging adults of Mexican descent. *Journal of Family Psychology, 24,* 105–114.

Hess, R. S., and Street, E. M. (1991). The effect of acculturation on the relationship of counselor ethnicity and client ratings. *Journal of Counseling Psychology, 38,* 71–75.

Keefe, S. E., and Casas, J. M. (1978). *Family and mental health in the Mexican American community.* Spanish Speaking Mental Health Research Center Monograph Series, University of California, Los Angeles: CA.

Koerner, S., Shirai, Y., and Pedroza, R. (2013). Role of religious/spiritual beliefs and practices among Latino family caregivers of Mexican descent. *Journal of Latina/o Psychology, 1,* 95–111.

Leong, F. T. L., Wagner, N. S., and Tata, S. P. (1995). Racial and ethnic variations in help-seeking attitudes. In J. G. Ponterotto, J. M. Casas, L. A. Suzuki, and C. M. Alexander (Eds.), *The handbook of multicultural counseling.* Thousand Oaks, CA: Sage.

Lopez, S. R., Lopez, A. A., and Fong, K. T. (1991). Mexican Americans' initial preferences for counselors: The role of ethnic factors. *Journal of Counseling Psychology, 38,* 487–496.

Lopez, S. R., Barrio, C., Kopelowicz, A., and Vega, W. A. (2012). From documenting to eliminating disparities in mental health care for Latinos. *American Psychologist, 67,* 511–523.

Lujan, J. (2006). The role of religion on the health practices of Mexican Americans. *Journal of Religion and Health, 45,* 183–195.

Magaña, A., and Clark, N. M. (1995). Examining a paradox: Does religiosity contribute to positive birth outcomes in Mexican American populations? *Health Education Quarterly, 22,* 96–109.

Marcos, L. R., and Urcuyo, L. (1979). Dynamic psychotherapy with the bilingual patient. *American Journal of Psychotherapy, 3,* 331–338.

Marín, B. V., Marín, G., Padilla, A. M., and De La Rocha, C. (1983). Utilization of traditional and non-traditional sources of health care among Hispanics. *Hispanic Journal of Behavioral Sciences, 5,* 65–80.

Nall, F. C., and Spielberg, J. (1967). Social and cultural factors in the responses of Mexican-Americans to medical treatment. *Journal of Health and Social Behavior, 8,* 299–308.

Padilla, A. M., Carlos, M. A., and Keefe, S. E. (1976). Mental health service utilization by Mexican Americans. *Spanish Speaking Mental Health Research Center Monograph Series, 3,* 9–20.

Pérez, M. C., and Fortuna, L. (2005). Psychosocial stressors, psychiatric diagnoses and utilization of mental health services among undocumented immigrants. *Journal of Immigrant and Refugee Services, 3,* 107–123.

Perron, B. E., Mowbray, O. P., Glass, J. E., Delva, J., Vaughn, M. G., and Howard, M. O. (2009). Differences in service utilization and barriers among Blacks, Hispanics, and Whites with drug use disorders. *Substance Abuse Treatment, Prevention, and Policy, 4,* ArtI D3.

Pew Hispanic Center. (2007). *Changing faiths: Latinos and the transformation of American religion.* Washington, DC: Author.

Pitta, P., Marcos, L. R., and Alpert, M. (1978). Language switching as a treatment strategy with bilingual patients. *The American Journal of Psychoanalysis, 38,* 255–258.

Ponce, F. Q., and Atkinson, D. R. (1989). Mexican-American acculturation, counselor ethnicity, counseling style, and perceived counselor credibility. *Journal of Counseling Psychology, 36,* 203–208.

Portes A., and Rumbaut R. G. (2001). *Legacies: The story of the immigrant second generation.* Berkeley, CA: University of California Press.

Prieto, L. R., McNeill, B. W., Walls, R G., and Gómez, S. P. (2001). Chicana/os and mental health services: An overview of utilization, counselor preferences, and assessment issues. *The Counseling Psychologist, 29,* 18–54.

Quintana, S. M., and Bernal, M. E. (1995). Ethnic minority training in counseling psychology: Comparisons with clinical psychology and proposed standards. *The Counseling Psychologist, 23,* 102–121.

Ramos-Sánchez, L. (2009). Counselor bilingual ability, counselor ethnicity, acculturation and Mexican-Americans' perceived counselor credibility. *Journal of Counseling and Development, 87,* 311–318.

Ramos-Sánchez, L., and Atkinson, D. R. (2009). The relationship between Mexican American acculturation, cultural values, gender, and help-seeking intentions. *Journal of Counseling and Development, 87,* 62–71.

Ramos-Sánchez, L., and Shapiro, J. (2009). Cultural and linguistic training for practitioners working with Latinos: Development of a Latino training model. Manuscript submitted for publication.

Ramos-Sánchez, L., Atkinson, D. R., and Fraga, E. (1999). Mexican Americans' bilingual ability, counselor bilingualism cues, counselor ethnicity, and perceived counselor credibility. *Journal of Counseling Psychology, 46,* 125–131.

Reeves, K. (1986). Hispanic utilization of an ethnic mental health clinic. *Journal of Psychosocial Nursing, 24,* 23–26.

Robertson, D. T., and Morris, J. R. (2000). Multicultural counseling: Historical context and current training considerations. *The Western Journal of Black Studies, 24,* 239–253.

Rogler, L. H., Malgady, R. G., and Rodriguez, O. (1989). *Hispanics and mental health: A framework for research.* Malabara, FL: Krieger Publishing Co.

Romero, A. J., Edwards, L. M., and Corkery, S. (2013). Assessing and treating Latinos: Overview of mental health research. In F. A. Paniagua, and A. M. Yamada (Eds.), *Handbook of multicultural mental health: Assessment and treatment of diverse populations.* (2nd Edition). San Diego, CA: Elsevier.

Ruelas, S. R., Atkinson, D. R., and Ramos-Sánchez, L. (1998). Counselor helping model, participant ethnicity and acculturation level, and perceived counselor credibility. *Journal of Counseling Psychology, 45,* 98–103.

Ruiz, P. (2002). Commentary: Hispanic access to health/mental health services. *Psychiatric Quarterly, 73,* 85–91.

Ruiz, R. A., and Padilla, A. M. (1977). Counseling Latinos. *Personnel and Guidance Journal, 55,* 401–408.

Sanchez, A. R., and Atkinson, D. R. (1983). Mexican-American cultural commitment, preference for counselor ethnicity, and willingness to use counseling. *Journal of Counseling Psychology, 30,* 215–220.

Sandoval, M. C., and De La Roza, M. C. (1986). A cultural perspective for serving the Hispanic client. In H. Lefley (Ed.), *Cross-cultural training for mental health professionals* (pp. 151–181). Illinois: Charles C. Thomas.

Santiago-Rivera, A. L., and Altarriba, J. (2002). The role of language in therapy with the Spanish-English bilingual client. *Professional Psychology: Research and Practice, 33,* 30–38.

Santiago-Rivera, A. L., Arredondo, P., and Gallardo-Cooper, M. (2002). *Counseling Latinos and la familia.* Thousand Oaks, CA: Sage.

Shapiro, J., and Simonsen, D. (1994). Education/support group for Latino families of children with Down's syndrome. *Mental Retardation, 32*, 403–415.

Shim, R. S., Compton, M. T., Rust, G., and Kaslow, N. J. (2009). Race-ethnicity as a predictor of attitudes toward mental health treatment seeking. *Hospital and Community Psychiatry, 60*, 1336–1341.

Slattery, J. M., and Knapp, S. (2003). In-home family therapy and wraparound services for working with seriously at-risk children and adolescents. In L. VandeCreek, and T. L. Jackson (Eds.), *Innovations in clinical practice: Focus on children and adolescents* (pp. 135–149). Saratoga, FL: Professional Resource Press/ Professional Resource Exchange.

Suárez-Orozco, C., Todorova, I. L. G., and Louie, J. (2002). Making up for lost time: The experience of separation and reunification among immigrant families. *Family Process. 41*, 625–643.

Sue, D. W., and Sue, D. (2008). *Counseling the culturally different: Theory and practice*. (5th Edition). Toronto, Canada: John Wiley and Sons, Inc.

Sue, D. W., and Sue, D. (2013). *Counseling the culturally different: Theory and practice*. (6th Edition). Toronto, Canada: John Wiley and Sons, Inc.

Sullivan, K. T., Ramos-Sánchez, L., and McIver, S. D. (2007). Predicting the use of campus counseling services for Asian/Pacific Islander, Latino/Hispanic, and White students: Problem severity, gender, and generational status. *Journal of College Counseling, 10*, 103–116.

Tran, A. G. T. T., Lee, R. M., and Burgess, D. J. (2010). Perceived discrimination and substance use of Hispanic/Latino, African-born Black, and Southeast Asian immigrants. *Cultural Diversity and Ethnic Minority Psychology, 16*, 226–236.

Vazquez-Nuttal, E., Avila-Vivas, Z., and Morales-Barreto, G. (1984). Working with Latin American families. *The Family Therapy Collections, 5*, 74–90.

Vega, W. A., and Gil, A. (1998). *Drug and ethnicity in early adolescence*. New York, NY: Plenum Press.

Vega, W. A., and Sribney, W. M. (2011). Understanding the Hispanic health paradox through a multi-generational lens: A focus on behavior disorders. In C. Gustavo, L. J. Crockett, and M. A. Miguel (Eds.), *Health disparities in youth and families: Research and applications* (pp. 151–168). New York, NY: Springer Science.

Vega, W. A., Sribney, W. M., and Achara-Abrahams, I. (2003). Co-occurring alcohol, drug and other psychiatric disorders among Mexican-origin people of the United States. *American Journal of Public Health, 93*, 1057–1064.

Vega, W. A., Kolody, B., Aguilar-Gaxiola, S., and Catalano, R. (1999). Gaps in services utilization by Mexican Americans with mental health problems. *American Journal of Psychiatry, 156*, 928–934.

Vega, W. A., Kolody, B., Valle, R., and Weir, J. (1991). Social networks, social support, and their relationship to depression among immigrant Mexican women. *Human Organization, 50I*, 154–162.

Vega, W. A., Sribney, W. M., Aguilar-Gaxiola, S., and Kolody, B. (2004). 12-month prevalence of DSM-III-R psychiatric disorders among Mexican Americans: Nativity, social assimilation, and age determinants. *Journal of Nervous and Mental Disease, 192*, 532–541.

Wells, K. B., Hough, R. L., Golding, J. M., Burnam, M. A., and Karno, M. (1987). Which Mexican-Americans underutilize health services? *American Journal of Psychiatry, 7*, 918–922.

Zea, M. C., Quezada, T., and Belgrave, F. Z. (1994). Latino cultural values: Their role in adjustment to disability. *Journal of Social Behavior and Personality, 9*, 185–200.

Zinn, M. B. (1982). Familism among Chicanos: A theoretical review. *Journal of Social Relations, 10*, 224–238.

12

PARENTING AND CHILDREN'S MENTAL HEALTH IN MEXICAN AMERICAN FAMILIES

Chelsea Klinkebiel, Nicole L. Harris, and Joaquin P. Borrego, Jr.

Introduction

The topic of mental health in Mexican American youth is an important one, as past research suggests that Latino children and adolescents may be more at risk for certain difficulties. For example, previous research has shown that Latino children and teenagers report higher levels of depressive symptoms than Caucasian or African American youth (Twenge and Nolen-Hoeksema, 2000). Studies examining depression specifically in Mexican American youth have also shown higher levels of self-reported depressive symptoms in these children and adolescents in comparison to youth in other ethnic groups (Hill *et al.*, 2003; Joiner *et al.*, 2001; Roberts *et al.*, 1997). Less has been shown in terms of externalizing behavior-problems between ethnic groups, with past studies showing no differences in parent- and child-reported conduct problems between Mexican American youth and other ethnic groups (Hill *et al.*, 2003). The purpose of this chapter is to explicate the various risk factors, protective factors, and unique social and cultural factors that may not only contribute to the mental health of Mexican American children and adolescents but also may interplay in the relationship between parenting and the mental health of these youth.

Parent behavior has been implicated as an important contributing factor to children's internalizing and externalizing symptoms in various parenting models (Baumrind, 1966; Goodman and Gotlib, 1999; McLeod *et al.*, 2007; Patterson, 1982). Most models of the relationships between parenting and children's mental health have been primarily based on European American families, and less research has focused on the application of these models with Latino populations. It is possible that distinct cultural and social factors may interact in the relationship between parenting and child outcomes. Therefore, before examining the relationships between parenting and children's mental health in Mexican American families, it is important to discuss the factors that encompass the broader social context in which parenting occurs, and which may play a role in the relationship between parenting and child functioning.

Social and Cultural Factors

Socio economic Status

The most recent census report indicates that approximately 26 percent of citizens of Mexican descent live at or below the poverty line (U.S. Census Bureau, 2010), and Latino families have been shown to be two to three times more likely to live in poverty than Caucasian, non-Hispanic families (Proctor and Dalaker, 2002). Given this overrepresentation, it appears that these families are more likely to encounter factors that may place the family- and child development at risk. Financial difficulties can be stressful not only for the adults but children as well. For example, Wadsworth *et al.* (2008) found that poverty-related stressors (e.g. economic strain) have far reaching effects in Hispanic and Caucasian households when compared to African Americans. Namely, Latino children reported lesser physical as well as psychological well-being and were more likely to experience anxiety and depression. In addition to higher levels of stress related to poverty, low-income status may also include less access to needed health and mental health services, less satisfactory education, and housing that is lower in quality as well as neighborhoods that are less safe.

Neighborhood Context

Most recent estimates indicate that approximately 63 percent of all Latino children are living in low-income families with the majority also living in economically disadvantaged neighborhoods (Gonzales *et al.*, 2011; National Center for Children in Poverty, 2010). Mexican Americans are at a greater risk for negative outcomes related to their neighborhood context (White *et al.*, 2012). Elementary school children living in economically disadvantaged neighborhoods, for instance, reported more stressful life events which were then predictive of aggression a year later (Attar *et al.*, 1994). Along these lines, Roosa *et al.* (2005) found that the association between children's' negatively perceived neighborhood conditions (i.e. neighborhood quality and crime) and their externalizing behavior was partially mediated by the amount of stressful life events reported, conflict with parents, and association with deviant peers. Unfortunately, Mexican American families are less likely to go from a high- to low-poverty neighborhood than to relocate from a low- to a high-poverty area (South *et al.*, 2005). Therefore, children and families may experience stress associated with both financial constraints and underprivileged neighborhoods.

Conversely, researchers have also examined the ways in which Mexican Americans' neighborhood context can also serve as a protective factor even when economically disadvantaged (e.g. Lee and Ferraro, 2007). Roosa *et al.*, (2003) have suggested that this apparent inconsistency in findings may be the result of research using the term *neighborhoods* and *communities* interchangeably. The authors conceptualize neighborhoods as a particular residential geographic location whereas communities are comprised mostly of individuals with a shared identity or bond and include numerous institutions (e.g. churches, schools, youth centers, etc.). Neighborhoods that serve as ethnic enclaves, or communities, for example, have been found to buffer against psychological distress in older Mexican Americans (Gerst *et al.*, 2011). Additionally, research has shown that when low-income immigrant families were in neighborhoods that were comprised predominately of Mexican immigrants, they reported fewer problems with adapting to American culture (Roosa *et al.*, 2009). Finally, studies have shown that when parents perceived their neighborhoods as being higher quality and more socially organized, they were more likely to rely on community members for support monitoring their children's behavior, and experienced greater parental efficacy (Byrnes *et al.*, 2011; Ceballo and Hurd, 2008).

Education

Highly related to socioeconomic status and community resources, education is another area in which Latino youth face many risk factors. Previous research shows that Latino students are more likely to drop out of school than Caucasian youth, with this risk increasing for Mexican American students who live in urban environments with schools that are poorer in quality (Kao and Thompson, 2003). Additionally, previous research has shown that Mexican American students often show, on average, lower levels of academic achievement than students in other ethnic groups, with family socioeconomic status and resources (i.e. income and parent's education level) accounting for a significant amount of variance in these differences (Altschul, 2012; Leventhal *et al.*, 2006). Financial restraints can also significantly impact perceived access to educational resources later in life. More specifically, parental economic hardships can also have detrimental effects on the educational aspirations of adolescents. Previous research by Ojeda and Flores (2008) showed that perceived educational barriers had a significant negative impact on the highest level of education that high school students hoped to attain.

Cultural Values

Much research has been devoted to the examination of the socialization of children with cultural values. Some predominant values in Mexican American culture that may play a major role in the socialization of children include *respeto* and *familismo*. In previous research, Mexican American mothers have indicated that children are expected to respect and obey their parents and have rated *respeto* as one of the most important cultural values to transmit to children (Calzada *et al.*, 2010). This cultural value emphasizes the importance of obedience and showing respectful behavior to parents, elders, and individuals of authority. Another key cultural value in Mexican American families is *familismo*, which emphasizes the importance of interdependence among family members as well as family connectedness and respect for family members (Sotomayor-Peterson *et al.*, 2012). These cultural values are seen as potentially beneficial for Mexican American youth, given that relationships in families who emphasize these values may be stronger and provide more social support (Harwood *et al.*, 2002). Additionally, previous research has suggested that these family values, important in Mexican American culture, may buffer against life stressors and risk factors for mental health problems (Berkel *et al.*, 2010).

Literature Review

Parenting in Mexican American Families

Due to the influence of cultural values such as *respeto*, it has often been proposed that Mexican American parents may be more likely to place more emphasis on teaching children to be obedient and utilize control in their interactions with children than parents from other ethnic groups. Indeed, previous research has often focused on the dimension of control in Latino families, and results have shown that Mexican American parents are more likely to use authoritarian parenting practices than Caucasian parents (Chilman, 1993; Martinez, 1988; Varela *et al.*, 2004), although some research has shown no differences in parenting style between Mexican American parents and parents from other ethnic groups (e.g. Caucasian and African American; Medora *et al.*, 2001), other studies *have* shown differences in specific parenting behaviors between Caucasian and Mexican American parents. In a 1994 study, Knight *et al.* found that, based on both mother and child reports of parenting behaviors, Mexican American mothers utilized more rejection, more control, and less-consistent discipline. Differences in hostile control and consistency of discipline have also been shown in more recent studies (Hill *et al.*, 2003), with both mother and child reports showing higher levels of this type of control as well as inconsistent discipline in Mexican American mothers than in Caucasian mothers. Some studies, however, have found contrary results, with behavioral observations showing Mexican American mothers to be less likely to use controlling behaviors with their children (Moreno, 1997).

Given that cultural factors may play an important role in parenting, studies that simply compare ethnic groups (e.g. Mexican American vs. Caucasian) may fail to illustrate within-group differences that may lead to mixed results in findings of differences in parenting styles and parent behaviors. It has been widely recognized that environmental factors such as socio-economic status may play a large part in findings from studies examining family relations, and the many components of socioeconomic status must be acknowledged when discussing families that may differ in the ways that they function and interact. These multiple adverse experiences can place families at risk for high levels of stress, and this may be one pathway through which differences in parenting behaviors occur in Mexican American families. Recent studies drawing on family models of stress (Conger *et al.*, 2000; cited in Parke *et al.*, 2004) have shown that more economic hardship is associated with higher levels of distress in parents, which is predictive of negative parenting practices. For example, in a study of low-income Latina mothers (predominantly Mexican American and Puerto Rican), Prelow *et al.* (2010) found that various environmental risk factors (financial strain, neighborhood crime, and low-quality housing) predicted maternal psychological distress, which predicted lower levels of positive parenting behavior (e.g. monitoring and involvement). This relationship among economic hardship, parent distress, and parent behaviors was also found by White *et al.* (2009) in a sample of Mexican American mothers and fathers, with higher levels of economic difficulties predicting higher levels of parental depressive symptoms, and higher levels of depressive symptoms predicting less warmth and less consistent discipline by parents. Therefore, it appears that environmental risk factors and the associated high levels of distress, may place these families at risk for impaired parenting. In addition to these more global parenting behaviors, research has also shown relationships between higher levels of parent stress and specific behaviors such as physically aggressive discipline by Mexican American parents (Altschul and Lee, 2011), with more highly distressed parents more likely to use coercive discipline methods such as spanking, hitting, and slapping.

It should be noted that although Mexican American families may be at higher risk to experience economic hardship and, therefore, higher levels of stress, previous studies have also identified protective factors that may buffer against adverse outcomes. For example, Behnke *et al.* (2008) examined the role of family cohesiveness in the relationship between economic stress and negative parenting behaviors in Mexican American families. Results from this study showed that family cohesiveness mediated this relationship, suggesting that families with higher levels of cohesiveness may not experience interactions that are as negative. Other studies have also suggested that social support from others may buffer the negative impact of economic stress in Mexican American families, with results showing that higher levels of support buffer the relationship between environmental stressors and depressive symptoms (Cardoso *et al.*, 2010; Prelow *et al.*, 2010). Given that Latino families may include high levels of support, this is likely an important protective factor for Mexican American families experiencing, for example, financial strain.

In addition to broad social factors, more specific cultural factors specific to Mexican American families have also been examined in their relation to parenting styles and behaviors. One such factor is immigration status. In a 1993 study, Buriel found that parents of first- and second-generation children reported a parenting style emphasizing child responsibility (e.g. earlier child autonomy and strict parenting), while parents of third-generation children reported a parenting style emphasizing concern (e.g. more support and control). This study also showed that parental and child characteristics related to parenting styles, with mothers' education level, and language spoken between parents and children relating to the degree to which parents emphasized responsibility or concern. Specifically, mothers with higher education levels were more likely to emphasize concern, as were mothers and fathers who spoke Spanish with their children less. Buriel (1993) posited that these two factors were likely highly related to acculturation, with families focusing more on values and parenting practices related to concern as they become more acculturated. Acculturation is a very important cultural factor to take into account when examining parenting differences within the Mexican American culture, as families may differ greatly in the amount that they endorse certain cultural values and parenting practices.

Acculturation and Parenting

Acculturation typically refers to cultural changes that may occur as a result of exposure to the predominant culture (in this case, European American; Berry, 1997). Acculturation has been linked to both parenting beliefs and parenting behaviors. In an examination of the incidence of unfavorable parenting beliefs, psychological distress, and health risk behaviors in Mexican American women (as compared to European Americans), Acevedo (2000) utilized language preference (English versus Spanish) as a proxy for acculturation. Within the Mexican American sample, unmarried Spanish dominant speakers were more likely to endorse parenting beliefs associated with punitive parenting (e.g. use of corporal punishment).

Level of acculturation can also influence the way in which parents conceptualize their children's course of development. As noted by Gutierrez and Sameroff (1990), perceptions of how children develop can serve as the basis from which parents judge appropriate behavior. The authors proposed that the more acculturated parents are, the more likely they are to endorse more flexible, perspectivistic beliefs about their children's development as opposed to rigid, categorical beliefs. In this study, *perspectivistic* beliefs were classified as perceptions that outcomes are determined in many ways, and *categorical* beliefs were deemed as those that assign one cause to a single outcome. It was found that the more acculturated mothers were (utilizing the Acculturation Rating Scale for Mexican Americans (ARSMA), Cuellar *et al.*, 1980), the more likely they were to endorse perspectivistic beliefs and assess child outcomes as being the result of an interplay between constitutional and environmental factors (when compared to European Americans). Overall, Mexican American mothers who were highly acculturated but also maintained a bicultural perspective were the *most* likely to endorse perspectivistic beliefs.

The acculturative process may also greatly influence parenting behavior and the overall quality of the parent–child relationship. Studies finding differences in parenting behavior between Mexican American and Caucasian parents have also found within-group differences based on acculturation level, or variables related to high or low acculturation. For example, Hill *et al.* (2003) found that primarily Spanish-speaking versus English-speaking Mexican American parents used more hostile control and inconsistent discipline. These results have also been shown by Dumka *et al.* (1997) who found that less acculturated mothers used more inconsistent discipline, and by Parke *et al.* (2004) who found that more highly acculturated parents used lower levels of hostile parenting. However, results suggesting the opposite relationship have also been shown. For example, Altschul and Lee (2011) found that among Latina mothers (primarily of Mexican descent), some indicators of acculturation (religious involvement, and endorsement of traditional gender beliefs) were not associated with corporal punishment. However, Latina mothers born outside of the United States used corporal punishment with children significantly less than Latina mothers born in the US.

Within families, the acculturative process can occur at different rates, with parents typically taking longer than their children to adopt the host culture (Phinney *et al.*, 2000). In a longitudinal study, Schofield *et al.* (2008) examined the impact of these acculturation gaps on later child outcomes. Additionally, the authors assessed the quality of the parent–child relationship as a potential moderator. Results indicated that perceived gaps in acculturation were related to greater father–child conflict as a function of low relationship quality. Father–child acculturation gaps were also related to child externalizing and internalizing behaviors. Interestingly, these same gaps were not related to mother–child conflict. As noted by the authors, this difference may be due to role of the father as the enforcer of family norms and customs. Notwithstanding, the validity of the acculturation gap hypothesis has been met with mixed results. Lau *et al.* (2005), for instance, found that acculturation gaps between parents and their adolescent children were not associated with increased conflict or negative conduct. Future research is needed to explicate the role of acculturation in the quality of the parent–child relationship.

Parenting, Child Outcomes, and the Role of Acculturation

Previous research on parenting styles and behavior and child outcomes has primarily focused on European American populations. These studies have shown that children of parents who utilize high levels of control and harsh or coercive behaviors but low levels of nurturing and warm parenting behaviors (Authoritarian) show more adjustment problems, such as higher levels of internalizing symptoms and conduct problems than children whose parents utilize moderate amounts of both control and warmth with their children (Authoritative; Lamborn *et al.*, 1991).

Although there is less research on these relationships in Mexican American families, some results show the same outcomes in Mexican American children exposed to parenting characterized as harsh and coercive and warm and nurturing. These studies have primarily used self-report measures of parent behaviors and/or parenting styles as well as self-report measures of children's problematic symptoms or behaviors. One commonly used measure of parenting behaviors in these studies is the Child's Report of Parent Behavior Inventory (*CRPBI*, Schaefer, 1965). This self-report measure includes both parent and child report versions and consists of eighteen possible parenting factors made up of specific parent behaviors. Commonly examined parenting factors from this measure include those seen as positive, such as *Acceptance*, as well as those characterized as negative, such as *Inconsistent Discipline* and *Hostile Control*. Child symptoms and behavior problems are also commonly measured with self-report measures, with many studies utilizing the broad-band scales such as the Child Behavior Checklist (*CBCL*; Achenbach, 1991) to measure internalizing and externalizing behavior problems, or using other measures for more specific symptoms.

Both internalizing and externalizing symptoms and their relationship to parenting behaviors were examined in a study by Dumka *et al.* (1997). This study utilized a sample of Mexican immigrant and Mexican American families with fourth-grade children. Parent behaviors measured in this study included mother-reported supportive parenting (Acceptance scale of the CRPBI) and *Inconsistent Discipline*. As predicted, mothers' supportive parenting was related to lower levels of child conduct problems and child depressive symptoms, while mother's inconsistent discipline was related to higher levels of both child depressive symptoms and conduct problems. A similar relationship between parenting factors and child internalizing symptoms in Mexican American families was shown in a study by Barrera *et al.* (2002) in which parents' supportive parenting was examined in its relation to child outcomes with families of children between the ages of 11 and 15. In this study, the *Acceptance* subscale of the CRPBI as well as other measures of parental involvement in children's everyday lives and monitoring made up the construct of supportive parenting. Results showed that supportive parenting was associated with lower levels of youth-reported depressive and anxiety symptoms.

Additional parenting factors that have been examined in Mexican American families include harsh or hostile behaviors that may put children at risk for emotional and behavioral problems. For example, Mexican American parents' self-reported behaviors on the *Hostile Control* subscale have been shown to predict adolescent externalizing symptoms (Gonzales *et al.*, 2011). Higher levels of authoritarian parenting have been shown to be related to higher levels of internalizing and externalizing problems in young Mexican American children (Calzada *et al.*, 2012). However, past research has also failed to find an association between hostile parent behavior (as measured by the *Hostile Control* subscale of the CRPBI) and Mexican American children's externalizing symptoms (Parke *et al.*, 2004).

An explanation for these mixed findings may be elucidated by the examination of cultural factors and the ways that they may play into relationships between parenting behaviors and child outcomes. For example, it has been suggested that the use of higher levels of control by Latina mothers may not be associated with negative outcomes such as those seen in Caucasian children whose parents utilize high control (Grau *et al.*, 2009). Previous research has shown that parental behaviors deemed controlling such as intrusiveness and hostile control are associated with less negative outcomes in children of less acculturated Mexican American mothers (Gonzales, 2000 and Ispa *et al.*, 2004, both cited in Grau *et al.*, 2009). This may suggest that higher control is seen as a positive parenting factor and may not lead to as many negative outcomes in children of less acculturated parents (Grau *et al.*, 2009). If less acculturated parents highly endorse the Mexican American values of *respeto* and *familismo*, it is possible that these parenting behaviors are part of the strong, positive bond between parents and children and may be associated with protective factors related to these values. Indeed, in the previously described study by Hill *et al.* (2003), differences among the amount of control and positive parenting practices were found between predominantly Spanish- versus English-speaking Mexican American parents (with language as a proxy for acculturation). Specifically, among Spanish-speaking Mexican American parents, hostile control and acceptance were positively correlated, but for English-speaking Mexican American parents, these parenting factors were unrelated. Hill *et al.* (2003) posit that in families where individuals may be less acculturated and facing more acculturative stress, parenting that is high in warmth but also in control may lead to more positive outcomes in children. Therefore, depending on how much they endorse cultural values such as *respeto* or *familismo*, parents may utilize certain amounts of control with children, and these parenting behaviors may not be considered to put children at risk if they occur in the context of these values (Halgunseth *et al.*, 2006).

Parenting Interventions with Mexican American Families

Like families from other ethnic and racial minority groups, Mexican American families also experience environmental and family stressors that may warrant professional mental and behavioral health services. In this context, there is a growing awareness that services should be culturally relevant for Mexican American and other ethnic and racial minority families (Cardemil, 2010; Lau, 2006) and that culture-related factors (e.g. *familismo*) should be assessed and addressed in the context of provision of mental health services (Barker *et al.*, 2010).

Fortunately, there are also a growing number of interventions that have been shown to be effective with Mexican-origin and other Latino families (please see Zayas *et al.*, 2009, for a more extensive review of the parenting intervention literature). Results from recent literature reviews (e.g. Ho *et al.*, 2010; Huey and Polo, 2008) and outcome studies (e.g. Martinez and Eddy, 2005; McCabe and Yeh, 2009) suggest that interventions have been shown to be effective with Mexican American, Latino, and other ethnic and racial minority groups.

Summary

As in other cultural groups, parenting plays an important role in the development and psychological well-being of children in Mexican American families. In addition to the quality of parent–child relationships, there are also other psychosocial processes (e.g. acculturation) that may impact parenting practices and the psychological well-being of Mexican American children.

Within-group differences may be equally as important as between-group differences when examining the relationship between parenting and child outcomes. Although identifying risk factors is useful in the development of programs and interventions, identifying existing protective factors is crucial to developing culturally appropriate models of family outcomes. Much more research on parenting practices and child functioning that addresses these areas is needed in order to provide services that are most appropriate for these families.

Future Directions and Challenges

As discussed previously, researchers are increasingly examining the role of various cultural and social factors in the relationship between parenting and children's functioning. One variable, acculturation, appears to be very important, as it may influence parenting beliefs and practices. One limitation of previous research examining acculturation is that many studies utilize language preference of parents as an indicator of acculturation. Given that acculturation encompasses many other domains than just language (e.g. beliefs, customs, values; Broesch and Hadley, 2012), it is important for researchers to utilize methods to measure for acculturation that include multiple constructs. Additionally, instruments that can measure both acculturation and enculturation may more effectively capture unique bicultural processes that influence individual and family functioning (Gonzales *et al.*, 2009). Lastly, examining the acculturation levels of various family members is important, as this may play a role in each individual's attitudes and acceptance of parenting practices and parenting interventions.

Another limitation of past research on parenting in Mexican American families includes the way in which parenting variables are measured. Many studies have utilized self-report measures of parenting behaviors that include broad constructs such as support and control (which are made up of various discrete behaviors). The use of these broad constructs to describe parent behavior may mean that more specific parenting differences related to cultural variables may be missed in the reporting of research findings. Additionally, given the heterogeneity of Latino families, it is possible that various parenting constructs may be understood and accepted differently by parents with diverse backgrounds and varying acculturation levels. The use of self-report measures also means that specific behaviors and interaction patterns between parents and children that may play a role in the development and maintenance of externalizing and/or internalizing behavior problems may be overlooked. Therefore, behavioral observations should be used when possible to identify specific behaviors and unique interaction patterns that family members may engage in. Recent data with Mexican American families suggests that readily-available coding systems (e.g. *Dyadic Parent–Child Interaction Coding System*, Eyberg *et al.*, 2004) appear to be appropriate as they can assist in detecting families with clinically elevated child behavior problems (McCabe *et al.*, 2010).

Lastly, many studies of the relationship between parenting and child functioning in Mexican American families have focused on older children and adolescents, with fewer studies examining child outcomes in young children. Therefore, it is not clear whether the relationships between parenting and child outcomes generalize to those in early childhood. Given that influence and control by parents is often the greatest during early childhood years, examining parent–child relationships and interactions during this time may identify early pathways of risk and resilience. Additionally, future research should examine parenting factors and child functioning across a variety of developmental periods in order to discover how children of different ages may experience unique risk- or protective factors.

Policy Implications

As others have detailed (e.g. Carlo *et al.*, 2009), much of the previous research on development and psychological functioning with Latino populations has taken a problem-focused approach, with less emphasis on normative developmental trajectories and protective factors. This is especially evident in research literature on parenting, and in order to understand the relationship between parenting and risk for psychopathology in specific ethnic minority populations, it is important to know what typical, optimal development entails. It is also important to understand the protective factors unique to Mexican American families that may be different from those seen in traditional models of developmental psychopathology. Existing literature has identified two factors—risk factors (e.g. acculturative stress, discrimination, and poverty) and protective factors (e.g. positive peer- and family relationships, good coping skills)—for Latino youth (Kuperminc *et al.*, 2009). Incorporating these factors into models of pathways from parenting to child functioning will help to guide services and interventions that are culturally appropriate.

Also important to consider is the significant amount of heterogeneity among those who identify as Mexican-origin. In addition to demographic factors such as language use, generation status, educational attainment, and socioeconomic status, there are also within-group differences, for example, acculturation level, ethnic identity, and varying degrees of adherence to culture-related practices such as *familismo, respeto*, and certain parenting behaviors (e.g. use of corporal punishment). It would be erroneous for professionals to assume that all Mexican Americans adhere to the same cultural practices and to the same degree. Assessing for differences along certain dimensions (e.g. acculturation) may provide more useful information that guides the services that are provided for these families. Therefore, assessment methods (e.g. self-report measures and/or behavioral observations) that are reliable and valid for Mexican American families should be identified and utilized. As stated previously, it is important to know how family members understand and endorse certain parenting practices as well as what they see as typical and normal child functioning.

Lastly, to assure cultural and ecological validity, professionals should regularly assess for acceptability of treatment goals, acceptability of treatment procedures, and satisfaction with both the process and outcome of the intervention (Foster and Mash, 1999). As noted above, there is growing literature to suggest that evidence-based interventions are being found to be effective with ethnic minority families, including Mexican American families. In spite of this encouraging information, it would be erroneous to assume that all interventions would be effective with all Mexican American families. Professionals should assess the degree to which treatment goals and procedures are found to be acceptable by Mexican American families. As an example, a study by Borrego, Jr. *et al.* (2007) found that Mexican American families find interventions such as response cost and time-out (e.g. taking away privileges after misbehaving, isolating child for period of time after misbehaviour) as more acceptable than treatment procedures such as differential attention (i.e. ignore when misbehaving and pay attention when behaving appropriately). In this way, researching components of interventions that may be more acceptable to families, and finding ways to culturally adapt interventions will help to educate practitioners about services that are more culturally appropriate. As stated above, however, policies that allow for individualized assessment of treatment needs will be more culturally responsive, and can prevent the widespread use of treatments deemed appropriate for Mexican Americans, but that are provided for families *solely* based on their ethnicity (Lopez *et al.*, 2012).

References

Acevedo, M. C. (2000). The role of acculturation in explaining ethnic differences in the prenatal health-risk behaviors, mental health, and parenting beliefs of Mexican American and European American at-risk women. *Child Abuse and Neglect, 24*, 111–127. doi:10.1016/S0145-2134(99)00121-0

Achenbach, T. M. (1991). *Manual for Child Behavior Checklist/4-18 and 1991 Profile*. Burlington, VT: University of Vermont, Department of Psychiatry.

Altschul, I. (2012). Linking socioeconomic status to the academic achievement of Mexican American youth through parent involvement in education. *Journal of the Society for Social Work and Research, 3*, 13–30. doi:10.5243/jsswr.2012.2

Altschul, I., and Lee, S. J. (2011). Direct and mediated effects of nativity and other indicators of acculturation on Hispanic mothers' use of physical aggression. *Child Maltreatment, 16*, 262–274. doi: 10.1177/1077559511421523

Attar, B. K., Guerra, N. G., and Tolan, P. H. (1994). Neighborhood disadvantage, stressful life events, and adjustment in urban elementary-school children. *Journal of Clinical Child Psychology, 23*, 391–400. doi: 10.1207/s15374424jccp2304_5

Barker, C.H., Cook, K., and Borrego, Jr., J. (2010). Addressing cultural variables in parent training programs with Latino families. *Cognitive and Behavioral Practice, 17*, 157–166. doi: 10.1016/j.cbpra.2010.01.002

Barrera, M., Prelow, H. M., Dumka, L. E., Gonzales, N. A., Knight, G. P., Michaels, M. L., Roosa, M. W., and Tein, J. Y. (2002). Pathways from family economic conditions to adolescents' distress: Supportive parenting, stressors outside the family, and deviant peers. *Journal of Community Psychology, 30*, 135–152. doi: 10.1002/jcop.10000

Baumrind, D. (1966). Effects of authoritative parental control on child behavior. *Child Development, 37*, 887–907. doi: 10.2307/1126611

Behnke, A. O., Macdermid, S. M., Coltrane, S. L., Parke, R. D., Duffy, S., and Widaman, K. F. (2008). Family cohesion in the lives of Mexican American and European American parents. *Journal of Marriage and Family, 70*, 1045–1059. doi: 10.1111/j.1741-3737.2008.00545.x

Berkel, C., Knight, G. P., Zeiders, K. H., Tein, J., Roosa, M. W., Gonzales, N. A., and Saenz, D. (2010). Discrimination and adjustment for Mexican American adolescents: A prospective examination of the benefits of culturally related values. *Journal of Research on Adolescence, 20*, 893–915. doi: 10.1111/j.1532-7795.2010.00668.x

Berry, J. W. (1997). Immigration, acculturation, and adaptation. *Applied Psychology: An International Review, 46*, 5–34. doi: 10.1080/026999497378467

Borrego, Jr., J., Ibanez, E. S., Spendlove, S. J., and Pemberton, J. R. (2007). Treatment acceptability among Mexican American parents. *Behavior Therapy, 38*, 218–227. doi: 10.1016/j.beth.2006.08.007

Broesch, J., and Hadley, C. (2012). Putting culture back into acculturation: Identifying and overcoming gaps in the definition and measurement of acculturation. *The Social Science Journal, 49*, 375–385. doi: 10.1016/j.soscij.2012.02.004

Buriel, R. (1993). Childrearing orientations in Mexican American families: The influence of generation and sociocultural factors. *Journal of Marriage and the Family, 55*, 987–1000. doi: 10.2307/352778

Byrnes, H. F., Miller, B. A., Chen, M., and Grube, J. W. (2011). The role of mothers' neighborhood perceptions and specific monitoring strategies in youths' problem behavior. *Journal of Youth and Adolescence, 40*, 347–360. doi: 10.1007/s10964-010-95381

Calzada, E. J., Fernandez, Y., and Cortes, D. E. (2010). Incorporating the cultural value of *respeto* into a framework of Latino parenting. *Cultural Diversity and Ethnic Minority Psychology, 16*, 77–86. doi: 10.1037/a0016071

Calzada, E. J., Huang, K. Y., Anicama, C., Fernandez, Y., and Brotman, L. M. (2012). Test of a cultural framework of parenting with Latino families of young children. *Cultural Diversity and Ethnic Minority Psychology, 18*, doi: 10.1037/a0028694

Cardemil, E. V. (2010). Cultural adaptations to empirically supported treatments: A research agenda. *The Scientific Review of Mental Health Practice*, 7, 8–21.

Cardoso, J. B., Padilla, Y. C., Sampson, M. (2010). Racial and ethnic variation in the predictors of maternal parenting stress. *Journal of Social Services Research*, 36, 429–444. doi: 10.1080/01488376. 2010.510948

Carlo, G., Villarruel, F. A., Azmitia, M., and Cabrera, N. J. (2009). Perspectives and recommendations for future directions in U.S. Latino psychology. In F. A. Villarruel, G. Carlo, J. M. Grau, M. Azmitia, N. J. Cabrera, and J. T. Chahin (Eds.), *Handbook of Latino psychology: Developmental and community-based perspectives* (pp. 415–418). Thousand Oaks, CA: Sage Publications, Inc.

Ceballo, R., and Hurd, N. (2008). Neighborhood context, SES, and parenting: Including a focus on acculturation among Latina mothers. *Applied Developmental Science*, 12, 176–180. doi: 10.1080/ 10888690802387997

Chilman, C. S. (1993). Mexican and Spanish-origin American families. In H. P. McAdoo (Ed.), *Family ethnicity: Strength in diversity* (pp. 141–163). Thousand Oaks, CA: Sage.

Cuellar, I., Harris, L. C., and Jasso, R. (1980). An acculturation scale for Mexican American normal and clinical populations. *Hispanic Journal of Behavioral Sciences*, 2, 199–217.

Dumka, L. E., Roosa, M. W., and Jackson, K. M. (1997). Risk, conflict, mothers' parenting, and children's adjustment in low-income, Mexican immigrant, and Mexican American families. *Journal of Marriage and the Family*, 59, 309–323. doi: 10.2307/353472

Eyberg, S. M., Nelson, M. M., Duke, M., and Boggs, S. R. (2004). *Manual for the dyadic parent–child interaction coding system (3rd edition)*. Unpublished manuscript.

Foster, S. L., and Mash, E. J. (1999). Assessing social validity in clinical treatment research: Issues and procedures. *Journal of Consulting and Clinical Psychology*, 67, 308–319.

Gerst, K., Miranda, P. Y., Eschbach, K., Sheffield, K. M., Peek, M. K., and Markides, K. S. (2011). Protective neighborhoods: Neighborhood proportion of Mexican Americans and depressive symptoms in very old Mexican Americans. *Journal of American Geriatric Association*, 59, 353–358. doi: 20.1111/j.1532-5415.2010.03244.x

Gonzales, N. A., Fabrett, F. C., and Knight, G. P. (2009). Acculturation, enculturation, and the psychosocial adaptation of Latino youth. In F. A. Villarruel, G. Carlo, J. M. Grau, M. Azmitia, N. J. Cabrera, and J. T. Chahin (Eds.), *Handbook of U.S. Latino psychology: Developmental and community-based perspectives.* (pp.115–134). Thousand Oaks, CA: Sage Publications, Inc.

Gonzales, N. A., Coxe, S., Roosa, M. W., White, R. M. B., Knight, G. P., Zeiders, K. H., and Saenz, D. (2011). Economic hardship, neighborhoods context, and parenting: Prospective effects on Mexican-American adolescents' mental health. *American Journal of Community Psychology*, 47, 98–113. doi: 10.1007/s10464-010-9366-1

Goodman, S. H., and Gotlib, I. H. (1999). Risk for psychopathology in the children of depressed mothers: A developmental model for understanding mechanisms of transmission. *Psychological Review*, 106, 458–490. doi: 10.1037/0033-295X.106.3.458

Grau, J. M., Azmitia, M., and Quattlebaum, J. (2009). Latino families: Parenting, relational, and developmental processes. In F. A. Villarruel, G. Carlo, J. M. Grau, M. Azmitia, N. J. Cabrera, and J. T. Chahin (Eds.), *Handbook of U.S. Latino psychology: Developmental and community-based perspectives.* (pp.153–169). Thousand Oaks, CA: Sage Publications, Inc.

Gutierrez, J., and Sameroff, A. (1990). Determinants of complexity in Mexican-American and Anglo-American mothers' conceptions of child development. *Child Development*, 61, 384–394. doi: 10.2307/1131099

Halgunseth, L. C., Ispa, J. M., and Rudy, D. (2006). Parental control in Latino families: An integrated review of the literature. *Child Development*, 77, 1282–1297. doi:10.1111/j.1467-8624. 2006.00934.x

Harwood, R., Leyendecker, B., Carlson, V., Asencio, M., and Miller, A. (2002). Parenting among Latino families in the U.S. In M. H. Bornstein (Ed.), *Handbook of parenting: Vol 4: Social conditions and applied parenting* (2nd edn., pp. 21–46). Mahwah, NJ: Lawrence Erlbaum Associates.

Hill, N. E., Bush, K. R., and Roosa, M. W. (2003). Parenting and family socialization strategies and children's mental health: Low-income Mexican-American and Euro-American mothers and children. *Child Development*, 74, 189–204. doi: 10.1111/1467-8624.t01-1-00530

Ho, J. K., McCabe, K. M., Yeh, M., and Lau, A. S. (2010). Evidence-based treatments for conduct problems among ethnic minorities. In R. C. Murrihy, A. D. Kidman, and T. H. Olendick (Eds.), *Clinical handbook of assessing and treating conduct problems in youth* (pp. 455–488). New York, NY: Springer.

Huey, S. J., Jr., and Polo, A. J. (2008). Evidence-based psychosocial treatments for ethnic minority youth. *Journal of Clinical Child and Adolescent Psychology, 37,* 262–301.

Joiner, T. E., Perez, M., Wagner, K. D., Berenson, A., and Marquina, G. S. (2001). On fatalism, pessimism, and depressive symptoms among Mexican-American and other adolescents attending an obstetrics-gynecology clinic. *Behaviour Research and Therapy, 39,* 887–896. doi: 10.1016/S0005-7967(00)00062-0

Kao, G., and Thompson, J. S. (2003). Racial and ethnic stratification in educational achievement and attainment. *Annual Review of Sociology, 29,* 417–442. doi:10.1146/annurev.soc.29.010202.100019

Knight, G. P., Virdin, L. M., and Roosa, M. (1994). Socialization and family correlates of mental health outcomes among Hispanic and Anglo American children: Considerations of cross-ethnic scalar equivalence. *Child Development, 65,* 212–224. doi: 10.2307/1131376

Kuperminc, G. P., Wilkins, N. J., Roche, C., and Alvarez-Jimenez, A. (2009). Risk, resilience, and positive development in Latino youth. In F. Villarruel, G. Carlo, J. M. Grau, M. Azmitia, N. Cabrera, and J. Chahin (Eds.), *Handbook of U.S. Latino psychology: Developmental and community-based perspectives* (pp. 213–233). Thousand Oaks, CA: Sage Publications.

Lamborn, S. D., Mounts, N. S., Steinberg, L., and Dornbusch, S. M. (1991). Patterns of competence and adjustment among adolescents from authoritative, authoritarian, indulgent, and neglectful families. *Child Development, 62,* 1049–1065. doi: 10.2307/1131151

Lau, A. S. (2006). Making the case for selective and directed cultural adaptations of evidence-based treatments: Examples from parent training. *Clinical Psychology: Science and Practice, 13,* 295–310. doi: 10.1111/j.1468-2850.2006.00042.x

Lau, A. S., McCabe, K. M., Yeh, M., Garland, A. F., Wood, P. A., and Hough, R. L. (2005). The acculturation gap-distress hypothesis among high-risk Mexican American families. *Journal of Family Psychology, 19,* 367–375. doi:10.1037/0893-3200.13.3.367

Lee, M., and Ferraro, K. F. (2007). Neighborhood residential segregation and physical health among Hispanic Americans: Good, bad, or benign? *Journal of Health and Social Behavior, 48,* 131–148. doi: 10.1177/002214650704800203

Leventhal, T., Xue, Y., and Brooks-Gunn, J. (2006). Immigrant differences in school-age children's verbal trajectories: A look at four racial/ethnic groups. *Child Development, 77,* 1359–1374. doi:10.1111/j.1467-8624.2006.00940.x

Lopez, S., Barrio, C., Kopelowicz, A., and Vega, W. A. (2012). From documenting to eliminating disparities in mental health care for Latinos. *American Psychologist, 67,* 511–523. doi: 10.1037/a0029737

Martinez, C. R., and Eddy, J. M. (2005). Effects of culturally adapted parent management training on youth behavioral health outcomes. *Journal of Consulting and Clinical Psychology, 73,* 841–851. doi:10.1037/0022-006X.73.5.841

Martinez, E. A. (1988). Child behavior in Mexican American/Chicano families: Maternal teaching and child-rearing practices. *Family Relations, 37,* 275–280.

McCabe, K. M., and Yeh, M. (2009). Parent–child interaction therapy for Mexican Americans: A randomized clinical trial. *Journal of Clinical Child and Adolescent Psychology 38,* 753–759. doi: 10.1080/15374410903103544

McCabe, K. M., Yeh, M., Lau, A., Argote, C. B., and Liang, J. (2010). Parent–child interactions among low-income Mexican American parents and preschoolers: Do clinic-referred families differ from nonreferred families? *Behavior Therapy, 41,* 82–92. doi:10.1016/j.beth.2009.01.003

McLeod, B. D., Wood, J. J., Weisz, J. R. (2007). Examining the association between parenting and childhood anxiety: A meta-analysis. *Clinical Psychology Review, 27,* 155–172. doi: 10.1016/j.cpr.2006.09.002

Medora, N. P., Wilson, S., and Larson, J. H. (2001). Attitudes toward parenting strategies, potential for child abuse, and parental satisfaction of ethnically diverse low-income U.S. mothers. *The Journal of Social Psychology, 141,* 335–348. doi: 10.1080/00224540109600555

Moreno, R. P. (1997). Everyday instruction: A comparison of Mexican American and Anglo mothers and their preschool children. *Hispanic Journal of Behavioral Sciences, 19,* 527–539. doi: 10.1177/07399863970194010

National Center for Children in Poverty. (2010). *Basic facts about low-income children, 2010. Children under age 18.* New York: Mailman School of Public Health, Columbia University.

Ojeda, L., and Flores, L. Y. (2008). The influence of gender, generation level, parents' education level, and perceived barriers on the educational aspirations of Mexican American high school students. *The Career Development Quarterly, 57,* 84–94.

Parke, R. D., Coltrane, S., Duffy, S., Buriel, R., Dennis, J., Powers, J., French, S., and Widaman, K. F. (2004). Economic stress, parenting, and child adjustment in Mexican American and European families. *Child Development, 75,* 1632–1656. doi: 10.1111/j.1467-8624.2004.00807.x

Patterson, G. R. (1982). *Coercive family process.* Eugene, OR: Castalia Publishing Company.

Phinney, J. S., Ong, A., and Madden, T. (2000). Cultural values and intergenerational value discrepancies in immigrant and non-immigrant families. *Child Development, 71,* 528–539. doi: 10.1111/1467-8624.00162

Prelow, H. M., Weaver, S. R., Bowman, M. A., and Swenson, R. R. (2010). Predictors of parenting among economically disadvantaged Latina mothers: Mediating and moderating factors. *Journal of Community Psychology, 38,* 858–873. doi: 10.1002/jcop.20400

Proctor, B. D., and Dalaker, J. (2002). U.S. Census Bureau, Current Population Reports, P60-219. *Poverty in the United States: 2001.* Washington, DC: U.S. Government Printing Office.

Roberts, R. E., Roberts, C. R., and Chen, Y. R. (1997). Ethnocultural differences in prevalence of adolescent depression. *American Journal of Community Psychology, 25,* 95–110. doi: 10.1023/A:1024649925737

Roosa, M. W., Jones, S., Tein, J. Y., and Cree, W. (2003). Prevention science and neighborhood influences on low-income children's development: Theoretical and methodological issues. *Journal of Community Psychology, 44,* 15–27. doi: 10.1023/A:1023070519597

Roosa, M. W., Weaver, S. R., White, R. M. B., Tein, J., Knight, G. P., Gonzales, N., and Saenz, D. (2009). Family and neighborhood fit or misfit and the adaptation of Mexican Americans. *American Journal of Community Psychology, 44,* 15–27. doi:10.1007/s10464-009-9246-8

Roosa, M. W., Deng, S., Ryu, E., Burrell, G. L., Tein, J., Jones, S., Lopez, V., and Crowder, S. (2005). Family and child characteristics linking neighborhood context and child externalizing behavior. *Journal of Marriage and Family, 67,* 515–529. doi: 10.1007/s10464-009-9246-8

Schaefer, E. S. (1965). Children's reports of parental behavior: An inventory. *Child Development, 36,* 417–424.

Schofield, T. J., Parke, R. D., Kim, Y., and Coltrane, S. (2008). Bridging the acculturation gap: Parent–child relationship quality as a moderator in Mexican American families. *Developmental Psychology, 44,* 1190–1994. doi: 10.1037/a0012529

Sotomayor-Peterson, M., Figueredo, A. J., Christensen, D. H., and Taylor, A. R. (2012). Couples' cultural values, shared parenting, and family emotional climate within Mexican American families. *Family Process, 51,* 218–233. doi:10.1111/j.1545-5300.2012.01396.x

South, S. J., Crowder, K., and Chavez, E. (2005). Exiting and entering high-poverty neighborhoods: Latinos, blacks and Anglos compared. *Social Forces, 84,* 873–900. doi: 10.1353/sof.2006.0037

Twenge, J. M., and Nolen-Hoeksema, S. (2000). Age, gender, race, socioeconomic status, and birth cohort differences on the children's depression inventory: A meta-analysis. *Journal of Abnormal Psychology, 111,* 578–588. doi: 10.1037//0021-843X.111.4.578

U.S. Census Bureau. (2010). Income, poverty, and health insurance coverage in the United States: 2009. Retrieved from http://www.census.gov/prod/2010pubs/p60-238.pdf

Varela, R. E., Vernberg, E. M., Sanchez-Sosa, J. J., Riveros, A., Mitchell, M., and Mashunkashey, J. (2004). Parenting style of Mexican, Mexican American, and Caucasian-Non-Hispanic families: Social context and cultural influences. *Journal of Family Psychology, 18,* 651–657. doi:10.1037/0893-3200.18.4.651

Wadsworth, M. E., Raviv, T., Reinhard, C., Wolff, B., DeCarlo Santiago, C., and Einhorn, L. (2008). An indirect effects model of the association between poverty and child functioning: The role of children's poverty-related stress. *Journal of Loss and Trauma, 13,* 156–185. doi: 10.1080/15325020701742185

White, R. M. B., Roosa, M. W., and Zeiders, K. H. (2012). Neighborhood and family intersections: Prospective implications for Mexican American adolescents' mental health. *Journal of Family Psychology.* Advance online publication. doi:10.1037/a0029426

White, R. M. B., Roosa, M. W., Weaver, S. R., and Nair, R. L. (2009). Cultural and contextual influences on parenting in Mexican American families. *Journal of Marriage and Family*, *71*, 61–79. doi: 10.1111/j.1741-3737.2008.00580.x

Zayas, L. H., Borrego, Jr., J., and Domenech-Rodríguez, M. (2009). Parenting interventions and Latino families: Research findings, cultural adaptations, and future directions. In F. Villarruel, G. Carlo, J. M. Grau, M. Azmitia, N. Cabrera, and J. Chahin (Eds.), *Handbook of U.S. Latino psychology: Developmental and community-based perspectives* (pp. 291–308). Thousand Oaks, CA: Sage Publications.

13

THE CULTURAL ADAPTATION AND MENTAL HEALTH OF MEXICAN AMERICAN ADOLESCENTS

Nancy A. Gonzales, Michaeline Jensen, Zorash Montano, and Henry Wynne

Introduction

In response to dramatic population shifts of the past two decades, there has been a proliferation of research on cultural factors related to the mental health and adaptation of Mexican heritage children and adolescents living in the United States (hereafter termed "Mexican American" youth). A central focus of this research is to understand how processes of cultural adaptation impact mental health problems and other health disparities experienced by this large and growing population. The current chapter reviews this literature, focusing primarily on the past decade of research, which best captures the diverse cultural contexts and experiences to which Mexican American youth are currently exposed.

We use the term *cultural adaptation* to refer collectively to the dual processes of acculturation and enculturation (Berry, 2003; Knight *et al.*, 2009). Acculturation is the term originally used to describe the cultural changes that result at both the group level and the individual psychological level from sustained contact between two or more distinct cultures (Berry *et al.*, 1986). At the individual level, this process may result in the gradual incorporation of cultural beliefs, values, behaviors, and language of the host culture, as well as changes in one's identification with, and sense of belonging to the host culture. Simultaneously, individuals also adapt to the cultural beliefs, values, behaviors, and language of their heritage culture and develop an understanding and sense of belonging to their ethnic group (i.e. enculturation). Acculturation and enculturation processes are ongoing across generations, including for recent immigrants, youth born in the US to immigrant parents, as well as for later generations (see also Caldera, Velez-Gomez, and Lindsey, Chapter 1). Understanding processes of cultural adaptation within and across these groups has been a primary focus of research with Mexican Americans. Rather than providing an exhaustive review, this chapter summarizes major findings on the relation between cultural adaptation and mental health, in which there has been some consensus across studies to suggest intervention and policy recommendations.

Mexican American Youth at Risk

This chapter will focus primarily on research, targeting adolescents between the ages of 10–18. Research shows that Latino youth, especially those of Mexican origin, are at elevated risk for a host of negative outcomes compared to their non-Latino peers, and many of these disparities appear for the first time during adolescence. Latino adolescents have a higher likelihood of suffering from a mood disorder (including anxiety, major depression, dysthymia, bipolar, and comorbid disorders) than non-Latino White teens and other ethnic groups (Anderson and Mayes, 2010). Evidence also supports disparities in mood and anxiety symptoms for Mexican Americans specifically when compared to non-Latino Whites (Glover et al., 1999; Siegel et al., 1998). Latino adolescents report elevated rates of alcohol and illicit drug use (Johnston et al., 2004; Swendsen et al., 2012), with Mexican American teens being more likely than teens from other Latino subgroups (e.g. Cubans and Puerto Ricans) to drink frequently and heavily (Nielsen and Ford, 2001). Among Latino subgroups, Mexican American (along with Puerto Rican) teens are at greatest risk for marijuana use (Delva et al., 2005). Latino adolescents are also the least likely racial/ethnic group to report condom use, the most likely to report using no method of contraception, and have the highest teen pregnancy rates among any racial or ethnic group (Center for Disease Control and Prevention, 2012; Hamilton and Ventura, 2012).

However, studies that find that Latino adolescents are at increased risk must be contrasted with research showing that Latino immigrants (both adults and children) have better mental health than their US-born counterparts and non-Latino Whites, despite being more economically and socially disadvantaged ("the immigrant paradox"; Alegría et al., 2008). It has also been shown that the mental health of immigrants declines over time in the host country (Alegría et al., 2008). When examined with adolescent samples, the immigrant paradox is most consistently supported by outcomes of adolescent risk-taking and problem behavior; for instance, prevalence of sexual risk-taking and conduct disorder increase significantly across generations, with those whose families have been in the US for a longer time experiencing higher rates (Breslau et al., 2011; Guarini et al., 2011). First generation Mexican immigrant adolescents are significantly less likely than second and third generation teens to use alcohol and marijuana, binge drink, or be convicted of a DUI (Cavanagh, 2007; Eitle et al., 2009; Maldonado-Molina et al., 2011). Data on suicide rates also support the immigrant paradox, with lower suicide intentions and attempt rates reported among first generation Latino youth (Peña et al., 2008).

Despite ample evidence showing that increased acculturation and US exposure are related to poor mental health and risky behaviors, there are many examples in which expected patterns are *not* supported (Guilamo-Ramos et al., 2004; Tschann et al., 2002). Altogether, the growing body of research aimed at testing and explaining these inconsistencies reveals a complex set of risk and protective processes that are not just a function of birthplace or simple linear progressions across generations. Rather, mental health may be increased or decreased by social processes and experiences associated with cultural adaptation that vary depending on factors such as place of birth, English proficiency, the broader community context, and affiliation with one's ethnic culture (see also Klinkebiel et al., Chapter 12). Additionally, these factors often have additive, subtractive, or multiplicative properties. The following discussion of processes that can help explain these nuances is organized around three points of convergence: (1) processes of cultural adaptation, particularly *acculturation*, increase exposure and vulnerability to culture-related stressors; (2) processes of *enculturation* offer protective benefits for youth that remain connected to their ethnic culture and its values; and (3) bicultural youth, high on dimensions of acculturation *and* enculturation, may be the most resilient.

Cultural Adaptation and Acculturative Stress

The dual processes of acculturation and enculturation present challenges to the daily lives of Mexican American youth, both within and outside of the family, such as language barriers, real and perceived discrimination, and culture-related conflicts with peers and family members. These acculturative stressors escalate during adolescence because youth have increased exposure to peer and community contexts, and normative developmental processes such as increased peer affiliation and risk-taking, identity development and autonomy-striving, all combine to heighten culturally-linked tensions. Literature examining acculturative stress has found it to be linked with internalizing and externalizing problems in youth, and may help to explain why cultural adaptation can lead to such psychological problems as depression for some youth but not for others (Gil et al., 1994; Hovey and King, 1996; Romero and Roberts, 2003). Below we summarize findings on the two most frequently studied dimensions of acculturative stress: perceived discrimination and family-related stressors.

Perceived Discrimination and Mexican American Adolescents

High levels of perceived discrimination are consistently related to negative mental health outcomes for Mexican American adolescents (Berkel et al., 2010; Delgado et al., 2011). Mexican American youth describe discrimination, based on English fluency, immigration concerns, negative stereotypes, poverty, and skin color (Edwards and Romero, 2008). Stereotypes often include expectations of academic incompetence and for Latino boys, assumptions about the propensity for violence and delinquency (Gibbs, 1998) that lead to more explicit forms of discrimination (e.g. being questioned by police officers). In addition, minority status frequently includes real or perceived structural barriers to success in mainstream society, including reduced access to social, economic, and educational resources (Baca Zinn and Wells, 2000; García Coll and Magnuson, 2000). Perceived discrimination has been associated with lower self-esteem, and higher depressive symptoms for Mexican American adolescents (Romero and Roberts, 2003; Umaña-Taylor and Updegraff, 2007). Furthermore, in one of the few longitudinal studies to examine the effects of discrimination, Berkel et al. (2010) found that perceived discrimination predicted increases in internalizing symptoms for Mexican American early adolescents over a two-year period. In another study, higher perceived discrimination was related to PTSD symptoms, higher alcohol and drug use, involvement in fights, and more sexual partners (Flores et al., 2010).

However, there is variability across and within groups, as well as individual variability in adolescents' exposure and vulnerability to discrimination. For example, studies indicate that US-born and more acculturated Latino adolescents are more sensitized and vulnerable to the effects of discrimination against their group (Umaña-Taylor and Updegraff, 2007). Specifically, among a largely Mexican American sample, Umaña-Taylor (op.cit.) found that Latino youth were more vulnerable to low self-esteem and depressive symptoms as a result of discrimination if they had a strong orientation to the mainstream culture, but not if they had a low mainstream orientation. It is possible that US-born and highly acculturated Latinos are more susceptible to negative ethnic prejudices and stereotypes when they become more invested in the majority culture, and spend significant amounts of time in mainstream social contexts. There also is evidence that the deleterious effects of discrimination may be more salient and impactful for Mexican-origin male adolescents than for females (Brittain et al., 2013; Umaña-Taylor et al., 2012).

Acculturation and Family Stress

Several studies have shown increased acculturation is associated with the erosion of family bonding and diminished family functioning. For example, the relationship between youth acculturation and problem behavior is mediated by increased family conflict (Gonzales *et al.*, 2006; Smokowski and Bacallao, 2006), parents' decreased monitoring of adolescents (Fridrich and Flannery, 1995), disruptions in parent–child bonds (McQueen *et al.*, 2003) and decreased parental involvement (Dinh *et al.*, 2002). These acculturation-related family processes have also been associated with depression in some cases (Gonzales *et al.*, 2006; Bacallao and Smokowski, 2007).

The link between acculturation and adolescent problem behavior has been attributed most frequently to intergenerational conflict that results when family members adjust their values and norms to better align with US society (e.g. Szapocznik *et al.*, 1990). Intergenerational acculturation discrepancies are purported to produce a clash of values and expectations between parents and teens, leading to increased family conflict, parent–child alienation, and youth maladjustment (Smokowski *et al.*, 2008). For example, Martinez (2006) operationalized differential acculturation as greater youth "Americanism" relative to parents and found a relation with youth substance use in a sample of Mexican American early adolescents. That relationship was fully mediated by the effects of differential acculturation on family cultural stress and effective parenting practices. However, several studies failed to support the acculturation discrepancy hypothesis (Pasch *et al.*, 2006; Smokowski *et al.*, 2008). For example, Pasch (op.cit.) did not support the discrepancy theory, but found that parent and child acculturation were both predictive of increased rates of adolescent sexual experiences and increased family conflict. Several other studies also report that parents' increased acculturation is associated with increased family conflict, including parent–child conflict and interparental conflict (Flores *et al.*, 2004; Gonzales *et al.*, 2006). Perhaps as Latino parents' experience shifts in cultural values regarding family hierarchies, and child respect and obedience, they adopt less controlling parenting strategies and greater tolerance for expressions of conflict and autonomy. Although these shifts have also been associated with some improvements in family functioning (Cabrera *et al.*, 2006; Hill *et al.*, 2003), they may increase vulnerability for problematic conflict processes if families in cultural transition are not equipped to manage the unfamiliar tensions and dynamics of parent–child disagreements that emerge in adolescence.

The Protective Benefits of Traditional Cultural Orientation

A major advance in research with Mexican American populations in the past decade is the recognition that an individual's orientation toward his or her traditional ethnic culture is equally important for understanding adaptation within the US, and that aspects of traditional culture may provide important resources to promote positive adjustment. Although widely acknowledged for some time in the theoretical literature (e.g. Phinney, 1990), the protective benefits of traditional culture have only recently been examined in empirical studies (e.g. Gonzales *et al.*, 2008). In this section we focus on cultural values and ethnic identity, the two most frequently studied cultural resources.

Traditional Cultural Values

An alternative to the acculturative stress explanation of the immigrant paradox, and the increasing risk that comes with acculturation and more time spent in the US, is the hypothesis that changes in adherence to traditional Mexican cultural values—such as respect, religiosity, traditional gender roles, and familism—may account for differences in mental health outcomes based on immigrant status (Gonzales *et al.*, 2008). In fact, endorsement of traditional cultural values has been found to mediate the relation between immigrant status, Anglo orientation, Mexican orientation, and internalizing, externalizing, and academic outcomes (Berkel *et al.*, 2010; Gonzales *et al.*, 2008).

The association between increased problem behavior among more acculturated youth has been explained as a decrease in the importance of the value of respect (*respeto*), which is undermined when youth are exposed to the individualistic US value system (Pantin *et al.*, 2003). Traditional Mexican culture also emphasizes emotional restraint—which is linked to a collectivistic ideal—and the construct of *simpatía* that refers to a sense of empathizing with others, respecting them, and remaining agreeable, even if this requires personal sacrifice (Varela *et al.*, 2007). Similarly, shifts in traditional gender roles can increase the risk of substance use and early sexual activity, particularly for females, though research is currently parsing out exactly what elements of traditional gender roles (e.g. assertive vs. aggressive masculinity) are protective and which are harmful (Kulis *et al.*, 2003; Kulis *et al.*, 2010). Traditional religious values can also protect against antisocial behaviors and substance use, perhaps by discouraging or prohibiting certain behaviors, by promoting ties with prosocial people, and through affiliation with religious institutions that serve as a source of support (Hodge *et al.*, 2011; Marsiglia *et al.*, 2005).

The construct of *familism* refers to an individual's strong identification with and attachment to nuclear and extended family and includes feelings of loyalty, reciprocation, and solidarity among family members (e.g. Sabogal *et al.*, 1987). Familism values are considered the most important defining characteristic of Mexican Americans and other Latino subgroups in the US (Keefe and Padilla, 1987), and growing evidence suggests they play an important role in mental health outcomes for Mexican American youth. Higher levels of familism among adolescents relate directly to positive outcomes such as decreased aggressive behaviors, fewer conduct problems and risk taking, and less rule-breaking (Germán *et al.*, 2009; Marsiglia *et al.*, 2009; Smokowski and Bacallao, 2006). Youth familism values are also related to fewer depressive symptoms, internalizing problems, and social problems (Smokowski *et al.*, 2007). Higher affiliative obedience, a related construct referring to the extent to which children honor the hierarchical structure of the traditional family, has been related to lower depressive symptomatology (Polo and Lopez, 2009).

Theory suggests that familism values may not only be directly related to positive outcomes, but also serve as a buffer against the ill effects of stressors frequently experienced by Latino youth, with evidence suggesting that strong familism values and family pride protect against deviant peer affiliations, perceived discrimination, and cultural conflicts (Germán *et al.*, 2009; Gil *et al.*, 1994). The protective nature of familism values can perhaps be attributed to the increased social support available within families high in familism values (DeGarmo and Martinez, 2006; Gonzalez *et al.*, 2012), and which can be drawn upon when facing stressors. It is also possible that commitment to honoring family obligations may include a commitment to school success and achievement for which parents made sacrifices (Fuligni *et al.*, 1999), motivation to avoid behaviors (e.g. deviant acts, promiscuity) that might bring shame (*verguenza*) to the family, or a sense of purpose and meaning that helps to promote positive engagement and greater resilience (Telzer *et al.*, 2013). As suggested by social identification theory, teens high in familism who are more connected to their native culture may also be more capable of viewing the positive aspects of that culture when faced with negative messages and discrimination (Tajfel and Forgas, 2000). Among Latino adolescents, family pride has been shown to protect against stressors like discrimination, acculturation and language conflicts, and perceptions of a closed society (Gil *et al.*, 1994).

Research suggests that some of the effects of familism values may lie in their influence on family processes and interactions. Studies show that familism values promote healthy family interactions (Hovey and King, 1996; Smokowski *et al.*, 2008), reduced family conflict (Smokowski and Bacallao, 2006), and also predict greater willingness to engage in services to promote family well-being and youth development (Dillman Carpentier *et al.*, 2007). Evidence also has shown that familism values at the neighborhood level influence youth directly by decreasing problem behaviors and indirectly by strengthening the affective quality of family relationships (Gonzales *et al.*, 2011). However, recent findings also suggest that different facets of familism may function in qualitatively different ways. Telzer, Gonzales, and Fuligni (2013) showed that among Mexican origin adolescents family obligation values were related to lower adolescent substance use, and that this effect seemed to be mediated by decreased associations with deviant peers and increased disclosure to parents. However, in the same study and in contrast to findings focused on youth values, actual family assistance behaviors were associated with greater cigarette, alcohol, marijuana, and illicit drug use for youth in high conflict homes. These findings underscore the importance of considering how traditional cultural values can serve both risk and protective roles depending on the broader context and the demands to which youth are exposed.

Ethnic Identity

Ethnic identity describes the psychological process by which individuals explore their ethnic background, determine the meaning of their ethnicity, and come to feel positively about their ethnic background (Umaña-Taylor *et al.*, 2004). As its definition suggests, ethnic identity is a key component of an individual's enculturation (Knight *et al.*, 1993), and plays an important role in the way immigrants confront the challenges in their new countries (Phinney, 1990). Studies repeatedly find a moderately strong positive relation between ethnic identity and self-esteem (Phinney *et al.*, 1997; Umaña-Taylor *et al.*, 2004). Moreover, studies of Mexican origin adolescents have found that higher ethnic identity is related to less externalizing symptoms and less alcohol use, and these relations are mediated through self-esteem (Schwartz *et al.*, 2007; Zamboanga *et al.*, 2009). It is believed that this relation is due to ethnic identity providing positive feelings about one's identity, which helps confront ethnically based stereotypes and attributions (Tajfel and Turner, 1986). Accordingly, strong ethnic identity has been found to be a protective factor against perceived discrimination (Romero and Roberts, 2003; Umaña-Taylor *et al.*, 2011; Umaña-Taylor *et al.*, 2012).

Recently, there has been a proliferation of research on the protective role of ethnic identity against substance use in Mexican American youth. For example, a recent study found that those students endorsing higher ethnic identity were less likely to report mixed use of alcohol and drugs, heavy drinking, regular cigarette smoking, and regular marijuana use (Love *et al.*, 2006). Ethnic identity may also influence substance use by playing a role in substance use decisions and norms. A study found that those adolescents reporting higher ethnic identity perceived more parental antidrug norms, approved less of peer drug use, had higher antidrug norms, and higher refusal efficacy (Ndiaye *et al.*, 2009). Further, youth endorsing higher ethnic identity had less positive expectations of substance use and had fewer substance use intentions. Country of origin further moderated effects on antidrug norms. Mexico-born preadolescents who reported higher ethnic identity perceived more peer antidrug norms, and American-born youth who endorsed higher ethnic identity perceived fewer peer antidrug norms.

Although ethnic identity has emerged as a protective factor in an overwhelming number of studies, some studies have had mixed findings (Marsiglia *et al.*, 2004; Zamboanga *et al.*, 2009).

Marsiglia and colleagues (2004) examined the varying relation of ethnic identity and drug use in different ethnic groups, including Mexican Americans, African Americans, and non-Hispanic Whites. Stronger ethnic identity predicted lower drug use for non-Hispanic Whites, but for Mexican Americans and individuals of mixed heritage, strong ethnic identity was related to higher current rates of alcohol and cigarette use. On the other hand, ethnic identity was related to more antidrug use norms but this relation was weaker for the Mexican American group. In a study of Mexican American, male juvenile offenders, those in the high ethnic identity group had higher initial frequency of binge drinking, suggesting they were at increased risk, though they also showed a greater decline of binge drinking with age (Losoya *et al.*, 2008). Conversely, those in the moderate and low ethnic identity groups endorsed heavier initial frequencies of marijuana use, indicating that ethnic identity was protective against early age marijuana use, though the moderate ethnic identity group had the steepest decline in marijuana use with age. These findings do not support blanket conclusions about the role of ethnic identity and substance use, but rather highlight its dynamic nature, both interacting with other variables and changing over time.

Research also indicates that the role of ethnic identity may vary by gender, with males seemingly enjoying more protective benefits than females (Kulis *et al.*, 2010; Nagoshi *et al.*, 2011; Umaña-Taylor *et al.*, 2012). For example, Kulis and colleagues (2010) found that for males living longer in the US, stronger ethnic identity was associated with decreased substance use, decreased use intentions, and fewer pro drug norms. On the other hand, females living longer in the US and reporting stronger ethnic identity had more alcohol use, pro drug norms, and friends who endorsed substance use. Umaña-Taylor *et al.*, (2012) also found that ethnic identity affirmation provided protective benefits for Mexican American males, but not females, attenuating the negative impact of discrimination on their academic adjustment, including teacher reports of externalizing behavior in school. The authors of these two studies suggest that ethnic identity may emerge as a stronger protective factor for males because they are more at risk for substance use (e.g. less parental monitoring, more substance-using opportunities), and for adjustment difficulties because they are more influenced by extra-familial contexts and thus, ethnic identity plays a more protective role.

Bicultural Adaptation: The Best of Both Worlds

Although having strong identification with Mexican culture may be a positive resource for youth, it is also important for Mexican origin youth to be able to function successfully in US society. Several scholars have argued that the most resilient youth, irrespective of where they were born, may be those who have developed strong ties with and the ability to interact effectively within, both ethnic and mainstream contexts (e.g. Félix-Ortiz and Newcomb, 1995; LaFromboise *et al.*, 1993). Bicultural individuals are theoretically able to interact with, and take advantages of social connections and opportunities within the mainstream culture, while retaining the protective resources of their traditional culture that enable them to cope with culturally related stressors in their communities and families. Bicultural individuals also appear to benefit from the ability to shift their sociocognitive perceptual schemas in order to fit situational demands (Haritatos and Benet-Martínez, 2002). Schwartz *et al.* (2007) suggest that biculturalism is potentially "greater than the sum of its parts," a condition separate from endorsement of either of the component cultures.

Although the number of studies that have tested this proposition are still few in number, beneficial effects of bicultural adaptation have been found in studies with diverse groups of

Latino youth, and with divergent methodologies (Coatsworth *et al.*, 2005; Parke and Buriel, 2007). In studies with Mexican American youth specifically, Losoya and colleagues (2008) found that those adolescents who were moderate in Mexican affiliation and moderate in Anglo affiliation had lower initial levels of heavy drinking and marijuana use and remained stable over time. Biculturalism has also been found to predict a lower risk for aggressive behaviors, conduct problems, and substance use as well as lower levels of depressive and internalizing symptoms (Bauman and Summers, 2009; Marsiglia *et al.*, 2009). A study of bilingualism—one aspect of biculturalism—found Mexican youth who only spoke English were significantly more likely to drop out of school than bilingual youth who were proficient in English and Spanish (Feliciano, 2001). Finally, there is evidence that the whole family unit, including both parents and children, benefits from biculturality. Smokowski *et al.* (2008) found that strong involvement in both one's culture of origin and US culture were associated with higher family cohesion, high familism, and low levels of parent–adolescent conflict. Miranda *et al.* (2000) found that bicultural families displayed lower levels of conflict and demonstrated more commitment and support among family members when compared to low- and high-acculturated families.

Future Directions and Challenges

Despite compelling evidence that Mexican origin adolescents experience a decline in mental health and an increase in risk-taking behavior with greater exposure to US culture, the past decade of research aimed at unpacking this phenomenon does not support such broad generalizations. What has been revealed, instead, is a far more nuanced set of dynamics at play. Although the process of adapting to US culture is associated with increased exposure to challenges within and outside the family, it also presents opportunities, such as greater integration with peer groups and access to resources like education, health care, and community services. Adolescents who are positioned to take advantage of these opportunities, by virtue of their ability to interact and engage with the mainstream US culture, will be better prepared to make positive contributions to their communities as young adults, but only if they do not succumb to the increased risks that come with such engagement. Greater understanding of these risks, and the individual and environmental conditions that promote positive adaptation in the context of these risks, has been a significant contribution of research on Mexican American youth in recent years. Notwithstanding the progress that has been made, research on cultural adaptation and mental health of Mexican American youth is still in its infancy and there are notable gaps. With so much focus on risky adolescent behaviors, such as substance use, research on other mental health outcomes such as depression and anxiety, and serious mental disorder, lags considerably behind. The focus on adolescent risky behavior has likely perpetuated the immigrant paradox which is less often supported when other outcomes are considered. There also is a need for more research on the development of youth competencies (e.g. Armenta *et al.*, 2011) and research with younger children.

Our current understanding of the interplay between culture and other contextual factors also is limited. Evidence reviewed in this chapter highlights the conditional nature of cultural adaptation and its effects on mental health outcomes, with variability due to many interacting factors. In particular, there is evidence that gender and nativity can be associated with very different experiences and vulnerabilities for Mexican American youth. There also is evidence that the broader community context, shapes and constrains youth and family vulnerabilities. For example, White *et al.* (2012) showed that the contextual amplification of early puberty previously reported to increase the risk for mental health problems in economically disadvantaged communities (e.g. Ge *et al.*, 2002), was not supported for Mexican American adolescents. Lower income communities characterized by a larger proportion of Mexican American families (ethnic enclaves) did not amplify risk as previously shown, but instead offered protective benefits for Latina teens at risk due to early puberty. A few other studies suggest there may be important cultural dimensions of Mexican American neighborhoods that outweigh putative negative community characteristics like disadvantage (Denner *et al.*, 2001; Gonzales *et al.*, 2011). Cultural adaptation also is likely to vary between established ethnic enclaves and newer receiving communities (e.g. North Carolina, South Carolina, Kentucky, Tennessee—where the Hispanic population has more than doubled since 2000; Ennis *et al.*, 2011). Although current research better reflects these communities, there has been little attention to contextual conditions that may account for differential effects across communities.

Ample evidence supports traditional Mexican cultural values and the protective benefits of ethnic identity, but there is evidence that these empowering aspects of traditional culture also can have a downside. For example, Varela *et al.* (2007) highlight the fact that Latino youth are often taught to place their needs secondary to the needs of the collective group and family, and to exercise greater self-regulation and control of emotions. Although this may help to account for lower rates of risk-taking and problem behavior among less acculturated youth, it is possible that an emphasis on self-regulation and control of emotions may stifle understanding and managing of internal states, increasing risk for internalizing problems. Zayas *et al.* (2010) found that strong adherence to traditional values may increase risk for suicide attempts among Latina teens when they fail to comply with family expectations, particularly related to traditional gender roles and female sexuality. Likewise, Fuligni and colleagues (2005) emphasize the multiple benefits of a strong sense of family obligation in Mexican immigrant families, but have found these obligations can undermine educational success and the pursuit of higher education. One important lesson that this chapter highlights for future research is the need to consider multiple domains of functioning and test alternative models to avoid overly simplistic accounts of culture and its effects on youth development and mental health.

A final point that should not be underestimated is that cultural adaptation unfolds in the context of other normative social, biological, and developmental processes that are relevant across culture groups. Mexican heritage, place of birth, and ethnic identity are not inherently risk nor protective factors for emotional or behavioral problems, but it is the ways in which these aspects of culture intersect with key developmental and social processes, as well as with aspects of individual variability (e.g. genetic vulnerability), that explain which youth are most at risk for maladjustment. For example, the adverse effects of poverty and social inequality contribute the lion's share of variance, explaining rates of symptoms and disorders for Mexican American youth—as it does for all other cultural groups in the US and across the globe (Wilkinson and Marmot, 2003). Cultural influences can amplify risk processes and developmental trajectories, but must be understood in combination with these broader social determinants, and with the developmental tasks and challenges that youth encounter at specific stages of development (García Coll *et al.*, 1996).

Implications for Policy and Practice

Research on Mexican American youth has generated several important findings that can inform theory and guide services and policy. Although Mexican Americans face substantial challenges as cultural minorities in the US, and they experience disparities in income, education, as well as their mental health and psychological functioning, they also have many strengths as a group that comprise an important key to fostering resilient outcomes. Institutions, service agencies, and intervention programs that work with Mexican American youth could potentially do more to reduce the public health burden of health disparities for this population if they adopt a strengths-based approach that supports Mexican American youth in retaining and being proud of their traditional culture, while simultaneously helping them fully engage within the mainstream culture. Such an approach is a far cry from some of the anti-immigrant policies currently advocated, but the alternative is most likely to produce generations of disenfranchised youth and costly public health consequences for these youth and society at large. Research also indicates a strengths-based, bicultural agenda should be applied when working with the parents and families of these youth. Cultural adaptation presents multiple challenges for all family members, that requires each of them to respond as individuals. For example, parents' experience of acculturation stressors impacts their own psychological functioning and parenting which, in turn, impacts youth adjustment (White *et al.*, 2009). Language barriers and feelings of marginalization are typically more pronounced for immigrant parents than for their children, particularly those who have limited opportunities to interact in mainstream settings (Garrison *et al.*, 1999). These parents will experience the greatest difficulty linking to their children's schools or accessing other needed services for family members. Efforts to engage families in their schools and communities are more likely to succeed if offered with respect for cultural differences and traditions, not as a choice between cultures.

References

Alegría, M., Canino, G., Shrout, P. E., Woo, M., Duan, N., Vila, D., Torres, M., Chin, C., and Meng, X.-L. (2008). Prevalence of mental illness in immigrant and non-immigrant U.S. Latino groups. *The American Journal of Psychiatry*, 165(3), 359–369. doi: 10.1176/appi.ajp.2007.07040704

Anderson, E. R., and Mayes, L. C. (2010). Race/ethnicity and internalizing disorders in youth: A review. *Clinical Psychology Review*, 30(3), 338–348. doi: 10.1016/j.cpr.2009.12.008

Armenta, B. E., Knight, G. P., Carlo, G., and Jacobson, R. P. (2011). The relation between ethnic group attachment and prosocial tendencies: The mediating role of cultural values. *European Journal of Social Psychology*, 41(1), 107–115. doi: 10.1002/ejsp.742

Bacallao, M. L., and Smokowski, P. R. (2007). The costs of getting ahead: Mexican family system changes after immigration. *Family Relations*, 56, 52–66.

Baca Zinn, M., and Wells, B. (2000). Diversity within Latino families: New lessons for family social science. In D. H. Demo, K. R. Allen, and M. A. Fine (Eds.), *Handbook of family diversity* (pp. 252–273). New York, NY: Oxford University Press.

Bauman, S., and Summers, J. J. (2009). Peer victimization and depressive symptoms in Mexican American middle school students: Including acculturation as a variable of interest. *Hispanic Journal of Behavioral Sciences*, 31(4), 515–535. doi: 10.1177/0739986309346694

Berkel, C., Knight, G. P., Zeiders, K. H., Tein, J. Y., Roosa, M. W., Gonzales, N. A., and Saenz, D. (2010). Discrimination and adjustment for Mexican American adolescents: A prospective examination of the benefits of culturally related values. *Journal of Research on Adolescence*, 20(4), 893–915. doi: 10.1111/j.1532-7795.2010.00668.x

Berry, J. W. (2003). Origin of cross-cultural similarities and differences in human behavior: An eco-cultural perspective. *Cultural guidance in the development of the human mind*, 97–109.

Berry, J. W., Trimble, J. E., and Olmedo, E. L. (1986). Assessment of acculturation. In W. J. L. J. W. Berry (Ed.), *Field methods in cross-cultural research* (pp. 291–324). Thousand Oaks, CA: Sage Publications, Inc.

Breslau, J., Borges, G., Saito, N., Tancredi, D. J., Benjet, C., Hinton, L., and Medina-Mora, M. E. (2011). Migration from Mexico to the United States and conduct disorder: A cross-national study. *Archives of General Psychiatry*, 68(12), 1284–1293. doi: 10.1001/archgenpsychiatry.2011.140

Brittain, A. S., Toomey, R. B., Gonzales, N. A., and Dumka, L. E. (in press). Perceive discrimination and Mexican American adolescents' internalizing and externalizing behaviors: Examining the moderating role of coping strategies, gender, and acculturation. *Applied Developmental Science*.

Cabrera, N. J., Shannon, J. D., West, J., and Brooks-Gunn, J. (2006). Parental interactions with Latino infants: Variation by country of origin and English proficiency. *Child Development*, 77(5), 1190–1207. doi: 10.1111/j.1467-8624.2006.00928.x

Cavanagh, S. E. (2007). Peers, drinking, and the assimilation of Mexican American youth. *Sociological Perspectives*, *50*(3), 393–416. doi: 10.1525/sop.2007.50.3.393

Center for Disease Control and Prevention. (2012). Youth risk behavior surveillance—United States, 2011. *Morbidity and Mortality Weekly Report*, *61*(4).

Coatsworth, J. D., Maldonado-Molina, M., Pantin, H., and Szapocznik, J. (2005). A person-centered and ecological investigation of acculturation strategies in Hispanic immigrant youth. *Journal of Community Psychology*, *33*(2), 157–174. doi: 10.1002/jcop.20046

DeGarmo, D. S., and Martinez, C. R. (2006). A culturally informed model of academic well-being for Latino youth: The importance of discriminatory experiences and social support. *Family Relations*, *55*(3), 267–278. doi: 10.1111/j.1741-3729.2006.00401.x

Delgado, M. Y., Updegraff, K. A., Roosa, M. W., and Umaña-Taylor, A. J. (2011). Discrimination and Mexican-origin adolescents' adjustment: The moderating roles of adolescents', mothers', and fathers' cultural orientations and values. *Journal of Youth and Adolescence*, *40*(2), 125–139. doi: 10.1007/s10964-009-9467-z

Delva, J., Wallace, J. M., Jr., O'Malley, P. M., Bachman, J. G., Johnston, L. D., and Schulenberg, J. E. (2005). The epidemiology of alcohol, marijuana, and cocaine use among Mexican American, Puerto Rican, Cuban American, and other Latin American eighth-grade students in the United States: 1991–2002. *American Journal of Public Health*, *95*(4), 696–702. doi: 10.2105/AJPH.2003.037051

Denner, J., Kirby, D., Coyle, K., and Brindis, C. (2001). The protective role of social capital and cultural norms in Latino communities: A study of adolescent births. *Hispanic Journal of Behavioral Sciences*, *23*(1), 3–21. doi: 10.1177/0739986301231001

Dillman Carpentier, F., Mauricio, A., Gonzales, N., Millsap, R., Meza, C., Dumka, L., German, M., and Genalo, M. (2007). Engaging Mexican origin families in a school-based preventive intervention. *The Journal of Primary Prevention*, *28*(6), 521–546. doi: 10.1007/s10935-007-0110-z

Dinh, K. T., Roosa, M. W., Tein, J.-Y., and Lopez, V. A. (2002). The relationship between acculturation and problem behavior proneness in a Hispanic youth sample: A longitudinal mediation model. *Journal of Abnormal Child Psychology*, *30*(3), 295–309. doi: 10.1023/A:1015111014775

Edwards, L. M., and Romero, A. J. (2008). Coping with discrimination among Mexican descent adolescents. *Hispanic Journal of Behavioral Sciences*, *30*(1), 24–39. doi: 10.1177/0739986307311431

Eitle, T. M., Wahl, A.-M. G., and Aranda, E. (2009). Immigrant generation, selective acculturation, and alcohol use among latina/o adolescents. *Social Science Research*, *38*(3), 732–742. doi: 10.1016/j.ssresearch.2009.01.006

Ennis, S. R., Rios-Vargas, M., and Albert, N. G. (2011). The Hispanic population: 2010. *2010 Census Briefs*. http://www.census.gov/prod/cen2010/briefs/c2010br-04.pdf

Feliciano, C. (2001). The benefits of biculturalism: Exposure to immigrant culture and dropping out of school among Asian and Latino youths. *Social Science Quarterly*, *82*(4), 865–879. doi: 10.1111/0038-4941.00064

Félix-Ortiz, M., and Newcomb, M. D. (1995). Cultural identity and drug use among Latino adolescents. In G. Botvin, S. Schinke, and M. Orlandi (Eds.), *Drug abuse prevention with multiethnic youth* (pp. 147–165). Newbury Park, CA: Sage.

Flores, E., Tschann, J. M., Vanoss Marin, B., and Pantoja, P. (2004). Marital conflict and acculturation among Mexican American husbands and wives. *Cultural Diversity and Ethnic Minority Psychology*, *10*(1), 39–52. doi: 10.1037/1099-9809.10.1.39

Flores, E., Tschann, J. M., Dimas, J. M., Pasch, L. A., and De Groat, C. L. (2010). Perceived racial/ethnic discrimination, posttraumatic stress symptoms, and health risk behaviors among Mexican American adolescents. *Journal of Counseling Psychology*, *57*(3), 264–273. doi: 10.1037/a0020026

Fridrich, A. H., and Flannery, D. J. (1995). The effects of ethnicity and acculturation on early adolescent delinquency. *Journal of Child and Family Studies*, *4*(1), 69–87. doi: 10.1007/BF02233955

Fuligni, A. J., Tseng, V., and Lam, M. (1999). Attitudes toward family obligations among American adolescents with Asian, Latin American, and European backgrounds. *Child Development*, *70*(4), 1030–1044. doi: 10.1111/1467-8624.00075

Fuligni, A. J., Witkow, M., and Garcia, C. (2005). Ethnic identity and the academic adjustment of adolescents from Mexican, Chinese, and European backgrounds. *Developmental Psychology*, *41*(5), 799–811. doi: 10.1037/0012-1649.41.5.799

García Coll, C., and Magnuson, K. (2000). Cultural differences as sources of developmental vulnerabilities and resources: A view from developmental research. In S. J. Meisels and J. P. Shonkoff (Eds.), *Handbook of early childhood intervention* (pp. 94–111). Cambridge, UK: Cambridge University Press.

García Coll, C., Crnic, K., Lamberty, G., Wasik, B. H., Jenkins, R., García, H. V., and Mcadoo, H. P. (1996). An integrative model for the study of developmental competencies in minority children. *Child Development*, 67(5), 1891–1914. doi: 10.1111/j.1467-8624.1996.tb01834.x

Garrison, E. G., Roy, I. S., and Azar, V. (1999). Responding to the mental health needs of Latino children and families through school-based services. *Clinical Psychology Review*, 19(2), 199. doi: 10.1016/S0272-7358(98)00070-1

Ge, X., Brody, G. H., Conger, R. D., Simons, R. L., and Murry, V. M. (2002). Contextual amplification of pubertal transition effects on deviant peer affiliation and externalizing behavior among African American children. *Developmental Psychology*, 38(1), 42–54. doi: 10.1037/0012-1649.38.1.42

Germán, M., Gonzales, N. A., and Dumka, L. (2009). Familism values as a protective factor for Mexican-origin adolescents exposed to deviant peers. *The Journal of Early Adolescence*, 29(1), 16–42. doi: 10.1177/0272431608324475

Gibbs, J. T. (1998). African American adolescents. In J. T. G. L. N. Huang (Ed.), *Children of color: Psychological interventions with culturally diverse youth* (updated edn.) (pp. 171–214). San Francisco, CA: Jossey-Bass.

Gil, A. G., Vega, W. A., and Dimas, J. M. (1994). Acculturative stress and personal adjustment among Hispanic adolescent boys. *Journal of Community Psychology*, 22(1), 43–54. doi: 10.1002/1520-6629(199401)22:1<43::AID-JCOP2290220106>3.0.CO;2-T

Glover, S. H., Pumariega, A. J., Holzer III, C. E., Wise, B. K., and Rodriguez, M. (1999). Anxiety symptomatology in Mexican American adolescents. *Journal of Child and Family Studies*, 8(1), 47–57. doi: 10.1023/A:1022994510944

Gonzales, N. A., Deardorff, J., Formoso, D., Barr, A., and Barrera Jr., M. (2006). Family mediators of the relation between acculturation and adolescent mental health. *Family Relations: An Interdisciplinary Journal of Applied Family Studies*, 55(3), 318–330. doi: 10.1111/j.1741-3729.2006.00405.x

Gonzales, N. A., Coxe, S., Roosa, M. W., White, R. M., Knight, G. P., Zeiders, K. H., and Saenz, D. (2011). Economic hardship, neighborhood context, and parenting: Prospective effects on Mexican American adolescents' mental health. *American Journal of Community Psychology*, 47(1–2), 98–113. doi: 10.1007/s10464-010-9366-1

Gonzales, N. A., German, M., Kim, S. Y., George, P., Fabrett, F. C., Millsap, R., and Dumka, L. E. (2008). Mexican American adolescents' cultural orientation, externalizing behavior and academic engagement: The role of traditional cultural values. *American Journal of Community Psychology*, 41(1–2), 151–164. doi: 10.1007/s10464-007-9152-x

Gonzalez, L. M., Stein, G. L., Shannonhouse, L. R., and Prinstein, M. J. (2012). Latina/o adolescents in an emerging immigrant community: A qualitative exploration of their future goals. *Journal for Social Action in Counseling and Psychology*, 4(1), 83–102.

Guarini, T. E., Marks, A. K., Patton, F., and Coll, C. G. (2011). The immigrant paradox in sexual risk behavior among Latino adolescents: Impact of immigrant generation and gender. *Applied Developmental Science*, 15(4), 201–209. doi: 10.1080/10888691.2011.618100

Guilamo-Ramos, V., Jaccard, J., Johansson, M., and Tunisi, R. (2004). Binge drinking among Latino youth: Role of acculturation-related variables. *Psychology of Addictive Behaviors*, 18(2), 135–142. doi: 10.1037/0893-164x.18.2.135

Hamilton, B. E., and Ventura, S. J. (2012). Birth rates for U.S. teenagers reach historic lows for all age and ethnic groups. *NCHS data brief, no 89*. Hyattsville, MD: National Center for Health Statistics.

Haritatos, J., and Benet-Martínez, V. (2002). Bicultural identities: The interface of cultural, personality, and socio-cognitive processes. *Journal of Research in Personality*, 36(6), 598–606. doi: 10.1016/S0092-6566(02)00510-X

Hill, N. E., Bush, K. R., and Roosa, M. W. (2003). Parenting and family socialization strategies and children's mental health: Low-income Mexican-American and Euro–American mothers and children. *Child Development*, 74(1), 189–204. doi: 10.1111/1467-8624.t01-1-00530

Hodge, D. R., Marsiglia, F. F., and Nieri, T. (2011). Religion and substance use among youths of Mexican heritage: A social capital perspective. *Social Work Research*, 35(3), 137–146. doi: 10.1093/swr/35.3.137

Hovey, J. D., and King, C. A. (1996). Acculturative stress, depression, and suicidal ideation among immigrant and second-generation Latino adolescents. *Journal of the American Academy of Child and Adolescent Psychiatry, 35*(9), 1183–1192. doi: 10.1097/00004583-199609000-00016

Johnston, L. D., O'Malley, P. M., Bachman, J. G., and Schulenberg, J. E. (2004). Demographic subgroup trends for various licit and illicit drugs, 1975–2006 *(Monitoring the Future Occasional Paper No. 60)*. Ann Arbor, MI: Institute for Social Research.

Keefe, S. E., and Padilla, A. M. (1987). *Chicano ethnicity*. University of New Mexico Press.

Knight, G. P., Bernal, M. E., Garza, C. A., Cota, M. K., and Ocampo, K. A. (1993). Family socialization and the ethnic identity of Mexican American children. *Journal of Cross-Cultural Psychology, 24*(1), 99–114. doi: 10.1177/0022022193241007

Knight, G. P., Gonzales, N. A., Saenz, D. S., Bonds, D. D., Germán, M., Deardorff, J., . . . and Updegraff, K. A. (2009). The Mexican American cultural values scale for adolescents and adults. *The Journal of Early Adolescence, 30*(3), 444–481.

Kulis, S., Marsiglia, F. F., and Hurdle, D. (2003). Gender identity, ethnicity, acculturation, and drug use: Exploring differences among adolescents in the southwest. *Journal of Community Psychology, 31*(2), 167–188. doi: 10.1002/jcop.10041

Kulis, S., Marsiglia, F. F., and Nagoshi, J. L. (2010). Gender roles, externalizing behaviors, and substance use among Mexican American adolescents. *Journal of Social Work Practice in the Addictions, 10*(3), 283–307. doi: 10.1080/1533256X.2010.497033

LaFromboise, T., Coleman, H. L., and Gerton, J. (1993). Psychological impact of biculturalism: Evidence and theory. *Psychological Bulletin, 114*(3), 395–412. doi: 10.1037/0033-2909.114.3.395

Losoya, S., Knight, G., Chassin, L., Little, M., Vargas-Chanes, D., Mauricio, A., and Piquero, A. (2008). Trajectories of acculturation and enculturation in relation to heavy episodic drinking and marijuana use in a sample of Mexican American serious juvenile offenders. *Journal of Drug Issues, 38*(1), 171. doi: 10.1177/002204260803800108

Love, A. S., Yin, Z., Codina, E., and Zapata, J. T. (2006). Ethnic identity and risky health behaviors in school-age Mexican American children. *Psychological Reports, 98*(3), 735–744. doi: 10.2466/PR0.98.3.735-744

Maldonado-Molina, M. M., Reingle, J. M., Jennings, W. G., and Prado, G. (2011). Drinking and driving among immigrant and US-born Hispanic young adults: Results from a longitudinal and nationally representative study. *Addictive Behaviors, 36*(4), 381–388. doi: http://dx.doi.org/10.1016/j.addbeh.2010.12.017

Marsiglia, F. F., Parsai, M., and Kulis, S. (2009). Effects of familism and family cohesion on problem behaviors among adolescents in Mexican immigrant families in the southwest United States. *Journal of Ethnic and Cultural Diversity in Social Work: Innovation in Theory, Research and Practice, 18*(3), 203–220. doi: 10.1080/15313200903070965

Marsiglia, F. F., Kulis, S., Hecht, M. L., and Sills, S. (2004). Ethnicity and ethnic identity as predictors of drug norms and drug use among preadolescents in the US southwest. *Substance Use and Misuse, 39*(7), 1061–1094. doi: 10.1081/JA-120038030

Marsiglia, F. F., Kulis, S., Nieri, T., and Parsai, M. (2005). God forbid! Substance use among religious and non-religious youth. *American Journal of Orthopsychiatry, 75*(4), 585–598. doi: 10.1037/0002-9432.75.4.585

Martinez, C. R. (2006). Effects of differential family acculturation on Latino adolescent substance use. *Family Relations, 55*(3), 306–317. doi: 10.1111/j.1741-3729.2006.00404.x

McQueen, A., Greg Getz, J., and Bray, J. H. (2003). Acculturation, substance use, and deviant behavior: Examining separation and family conflict as mediators. *Child Development, 74*(6), 1737–1750. doi: 10.1046/j.1467-8624.2003.00635.x

Miranda, A. O., Estrada, D., and Firpo-Jimenez, M. (2000). Differences in family cohesion, adaptability, and environment among Latino families in dissimilar stages of acculturation. *The Family Journal, 8*(4), 341–350. doi: 10.1177/1066480700084003

Nagoshi, J. L., Marsiglia, F. F., Parsai, M., and Castro, F. G. (2011). The moderating effects of ethnic identification on the relationship between parental monitoring and substance use in Mexican heritage adolescents in the southwest United States. *Journal of Community Psychology, 39*(5), 520–533. doi: 10.1002/jcop.20449

Ndiaye, K., Hecht, M. L., Wagstaff, D. A., and Elek, E. (2009). Mexican-heritage preadolescents' ethnic identification and perceptions of substance use. *Substance Use and Misuse, 44*(8), 1160–1182. doi: 10.1080/10826080802544133

Nielsen, A. L., and Ford, J. A. (2001). Drinking patterns among Hispanic adolescents: Results from a national household survey. *Journal of Studies on Alcohol, 62*(4), 448–456.

Pantin, H., Schwartz, S. J., Sullivan, S., Coatsworth, J. D., and Szapocznik, J. (2003). Preventing substance abuse in Hispanic immigrant adolescents: An ecodevelopmental, parent-centered approach. *Hispanic Journal of Behavioral Sciences, 25*(4), 469–500. doi: 10.1177/0739986303259355

Parke, R. D., and Buriel, R. (1997). Socialization in the family: Ethnic and ecological perspectives. In N. Eisenberg (Ed.) and W. Damon (Series Ed.), *Handbook of child psychology: Vol. 3. Social, emotional, and personality development* (5th edn., pp. 463–552). New York: Walley.

Pasch, L. A., Deardorff, J., Tschann, J. M., Flores, E., Penilla, C., and Pantoja, P. (2006). Acculturation, parent-adolescent conflict, and adolescent adjustment in Mexican American families. *Family Process, 45*(1), 75–86. doi: 10.1111/j.1545-5300.2006.00081.x

Peña, J. B., Wyman, P. A., Brown, C. H., Matthieu, M. M., Olivares, T. E., Hartel, D., and Zayas, L. H. (2008). Immigration generation status and its association with suicide attempts, substance use, and depressive symptoms among Latino adolescents in the USA. *Prevention Science, 9*(4), 299–310. doi: 10.1007/s11121-008-0105-x

Phinney, J. S. (1990). Ethnic identity in adolescents and adults: Review of research. *Psychological Bulletin, 108*(3), 499–514. doi: 10.1037/0033-2909.108.3.499

Phinney, J. S., Cantu, C. L., and Kurtz, D. A. (1997). Ethnic and American identity as predictors of self-esteem among African American, Latino, and White adolescents. *Journal of Youth and Adolescence, 26*(2), 165–185. doi: 10.1023/A:1024500514834

Polo, A. J., and Lopez, S. R. (2009). Culture, context, and the internalizing distress of Mexican American youth. *Journal of Clinical Child and Adolescent Psychology, 38*(2), 273–285.

Romero, A. J., and Roberts, R. E. (2003). Stress within a bicultural context for adolescents of Mexican descent. *Cultural Diversity and Ethnic Minority Psychology, 9*(2), 171–184. doi: 10.1037/1099-9809.9.2.171

Sabogal, F., Marín, G., Otero-Sabogal, R., Marín, B. V., and Perez-Stable, E. J. (1987). Hispanic familism and acculturation: What changes and what doesn't? *Hispanic Journal of Behavioral Sciences, 9*(4), 397–412. doi: 10.1177/07399863870094003

Schwartz, S. J., Zamboanga, B. L., and Jarvis, L. H. (2007). Ethnic identity and acculturation in Hispanic early adolescents: Mediated relationships to academic grades, prosocial behaviors, and externalizing symptoms. *Cultural Diversity and Ethnic Minority Psychology, 13*(4), 364–373. doi: 10.1037/1099-9809.13.4.364

Siegel, J. M., Aneshensel, C. S., Taub, B., Cantwell, D. P., and Driscoll, A. K. (1998). Adolescent depressed mood in a multiethnic sample. *Journal of Youth and Adolescence, 27*(4), 413–427. doi: 10.1023/A:1022873601030

Smokowski, P. R., and Bacallao, M. L. (2006). Acculturation and aggression in Latino adolescents: A structural model focusing on cultural risk factors and assets. *Journal of Abnormal Child Psychology, 34*(5), 659–673. doi: 10.1007/s10802-006-9049-4

Smokowski, P. R., Chapman, M. V., and Bacallao, M. L. (2007). Acculturation risk and protective factors and mental health symptoms in immigrant Latino adolescents. *Journal of Human Behavior in the Social Environment, 16*(3), 33–55. doi: 10.1300/10911350802107710

Smokowski, P. R., Rose, R., and Bacallao, M. L. (2008). Acculturation and Latino family processes: How cultural involvement, biculturalism, and acculturation gaps influence family dynamics. *Family Relations: An Interdisciplinary Journal of Applied Family Studies, 57*(3), 295–308. doi: 10.1111/j.1741-3729.2008.00501.x

Swendsen, J., Burstein, M., Case, B., Conway, K., Dierker, L., He, J., and Merikangas, K. (2012). Use and abuse of alcohol and illicit drugs in US adolescents: Results of the national comorbidity survey—adolescent supplement. *Archives of General Psychiatry, 69*(4), 390. doi:10.1001/archgenpsychiatry.2011.1503

Szapocznik, J., Kurtines, W., Santisteban, D. A., and Rio, A. T. (1990). Interplay of advances between theory, research, and application in treatment interventions aimed at behavior problem children and adolescents. *Journal of Consulting and Clinical Psychology, 58*(6), 696–703. doi: 10.1037/0022-006X.58.6.696

Tajfel, H., and Forgas, J. P. (2000). Social categorization: Cognitions, values and groups. In *Stereotypes and prejudice: Essential readings* (pp. 49–63). New York, NY: Psychology Press.

Tajfel, H., and Turner, J. C. (1986). The social identity theory of intergroup behaviour. In S. Worchel and W. G. Austin (Eds.), *Psychology of intergroup relations* (2nd edn.). Chicago: Nelson Hall.

Telzer, E. H., Gonzales, N., and Fuligni, A. J. (2013). Family obligation values and family assistance behaviors: Protective and risk factors for Mexican American adolescents' substance use. *Journal of Youth and Adolescence.* doi: 10.1007/s10964-013-9941-5

Tschann, J. M., Flores, E., Marin, B. V., Pasch, L. A., Baisch, E. M., and Wibbelsman, C. J. (2002). Interparental conflict and risk behaviors among Mexican American adolescents: A cognitive-emotional model. *Journal of Abnormal Child Psychology, 30*(4), 373–385. doi: 10.1023/A:1015718008205

Umaña-Taylor, A. J., and Updegraff, K. A. (2007). Latino adolescents' mental health: Exploring the interrelations among discrimination, ethnic identity, cultural orientation, self-esteem, and depressive symptoms. *Journal of Adolescence, 30*(4), 549–567. doi: 10.1016/j.adolescence.2006.08.002

Umaña-Taylor, A. J., Updegraff, K. A., and Gonzales-Backen, M. A. (2011). Mexican-origin adolescent mothers' stressors and psychosocial functioning: Examining ethnic identity affirmation and familism as moderators. *Journal of Youth and Adolescence, 40*(2), 140–157. doi: 10.1007/s10964-010-9511-z

Umaña-Taylor, A. J., Yazedjian, A., and Bámaca-Gómez, M. (2004). Developing the ethnic identity scale using Eriksonian and social identity perspectives. *Identity: An International Journal of Theory and Research, 4*(1), 9–38. doi: 10.1207/S1532706XID0401_2

Umaña-Taylor, A. J., Wong, J. J., Gonzales, N. A., and Dumka, L. E. (2012). Ethnic identity and gender as moderators of the association between discrimination and academic adjustment among Mexican-origin adolescents. *Journal of Adolescence, 35*(4), 773–786. doi: http://dx.doi.org/10.1016/j.adolescence.2011.11.003

Varela, R. E., Steele, R. G., and Benson, E. R. (2007). The contribution of ethnic minority status to adaptive style: A comparison of Mexican, Mexican American, and European American children. *Journal of Cross-Cultural Psychology, 38*(1), 26–33. doi: 10.1177/0022022106295439

White, R., Deardorff, J., and Gonzales, N. A. (2012). Contextual amplification or attenuation of pubertal timing effects on depressive symptoms among Mexican American girls. *Journal of Adolescent Health.* doi: 10.1016/j.jadohealth.2011.10.006

White, R., Roosa, M. W., Weaver, S. R., and Nair, R. L. (2009). Cultural and contextual influences on parenting in Mexican American families. *Journal of Marriage and Family, 71*(1), 61–79. doi: 10.1111/j.1741-3737.2008.00580.x

Wilkinson, R. G., and Marmot, M. (2003). *Social determinants of health: The solid facts.* World Health Organization.

Zamboanga, B. L., Schwartz, S. J., Jarvis, L. H., and Van Tyne, K. (2009). Acculturation and substance use among Hispanic early adolescents: Investigating the mediating roles of acculturative stress and self-esteem. *The Journal of Primary Prevention, 30*(3–4), 315–333. doi: 10.1007/s10935-009-0182-z

Zayas, L., Gulbas, L. E., Fedoravicius, N., and Cabassa, L. J. (2010). Patterns of distress, precipitating events, and reflections on suicide attempts by young Latinas. *Social Science and Medicine, 70*(11), 1773–1779. doi: http://dx.doi.org/10.1016/j.socscimed.2010.02.013

PART V

Perspectives on Physical Health

14

NUTRITIONAL RESILIENCE IN MEXICAN IMMIGRANT/MEXICAN AMERICANS

How might Food Intake Contribute to the Hispanic Paradox?

Guadalupe X. Ayala and Elva M. Arredondo

Introduction

The study of what and how we eat is important, given the link between diet and the prevention and control of obesity and other chronic diseases (Block *et al.*, 1992; Boeing *et al.*, 2012; Gotay, 2005; Key *et al.*, 2004). Research on Mexican immigrant/Mexican American families is particularly worthwhile given the growth of this population in the US (US Census Bureau, 2010). Most nutrition research involving Mexican immigrant/Mexican American families, including our own, has focused on dietary behavioral risk factors and how these are related to greater risk for health problems than in the general population. For example, research indicates that US Hispanics[1] are more likely to drink a sugary beverage at least once a day compared with non-Hispanic Whites (Han and Powell, 2013). Similar findings have been observed for fast food consumption (Sorkin and Billimek, 2012). These two behaviors, in turn, are associated with risk for obesity, including in a Mexican-origin sample (Ayala *et al.*, 2008b).

In this chapter, we take a different approach. First, we examine protective versus risk factors on diet, and we examine these factors at multiple levels of influence as defined in the Social Ecological Framework (Elder *et al.*, 2007). Regarding the former, examining protective factors helps us to identify where to begin building an assets-based intervention. Regarding the latter, this helps us to identify potentially modifiable factors at the individual, interpersonal, organizational, and community levels of influence. Emphasis is placed at the interpersonal level given the importance of family and social ties in the Mexican culture (Marín and Triandis, 1985). In this process, we also acknowledge the moderating role of acculturation at each level of the Social Ecological Framework. This perspective is described in detail below and depicted in Figure 14.1. We then describe how we targeted increases in these protective factors by describing the American Cancer Society-funded family-based intervention known as *Entre Familia: Reflejos de Salud* (Within the family: Reflections of Health). We conclude this chapter with reflections on the field of Mexican-origin family health in the US.

Theoretical Framework: Food from a Multi-Level Perspective

The Socio-Ecological Model for Latino Health Promotion, (see Figure 14.1; Elder *et al.*, 2009) depicts four levels of influence on health behaviors, and the people within these spheres of

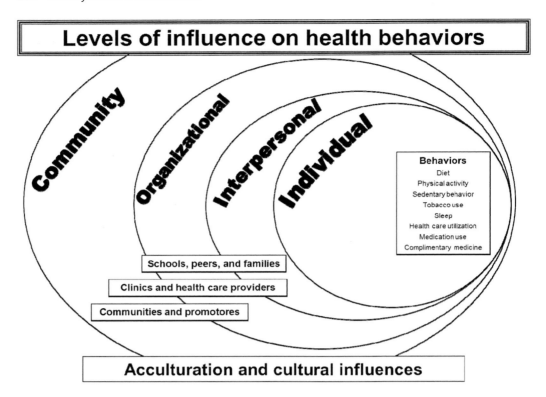

FIGURE 14.1 Socio-Ecological Model for Latino Health Promotion.

influence that have an impact on our health behaviors (e.g. health care providers within clinics). The model was developed in collaboration with fellow investigators at the Institute for Behavioral and Community Health, a research institute affiliated with San Diego State University (www.ibachsd.org). It is based on Bronfenbrenner's (Bronfenbrenner, 1979) Social Ecological Framework and similar work by Stokols (Stokols, 1996) and Green and Kreuter (Green and Kreuter, 2005), as well as our individual and collective experiences implementing a variety of health behavior change interventions in the community, initially addressing tobacco and alcohol use among adolescent Mexican-origin immigrants to preventing and controlling childhood obesity by working with families and recreation centers (Elder *et al.*, 2013), among others (Elder *et al.*, in press). The model illustrates the importance of recognizing the concurrent levels of influence on behavior (individual, interpersonal, organizational, community), and the importance of both social (i.e. people) and physical (i.e. places) environmental factors.

In this chapter, we present evidence of dietary protective factors at three levels of influence. At the individual level, we examine racial/ethnic differences in the consumption of fruit and vegetables (FVs), given its association with health outcomes (Key *et al.*, 2004). At the interpersonal level, we focus specifically on family influences given that Mexican-origin people have a strong sense of identification with and attachment to both nuclear and extended family members (Andaya *et al.*, 2011; Marín and Triandis, 1985). This collective identity and importance of family have clear implications for designing interventions that target the social environment, including those that promote loyalty, unity, reciprocity, and solidarity within families and communities (Smith and Ryan, 2006). At this level, we also present familial influences given their strong association with healthy eating (Pearson *et al.*, 2009). Finally, community influences have clear implications for health, including features of the physical (Sallis and Glanz, 2009) and social environments (Wansink, 2004). For example, the availability of fresh FVs in small stores frequented by Mexican immigrants/Mexican Americans facilitates their purchase and consumption (Emond *et al.*, 2012).

Finally, we consider the moderating role of acculturation given its association with a plethora of individual, interpersonal, and community-level influences on Latinos' health behaviors and health outcomes. Acculturation is a bidimensional process in which individuals, through continuous, first-hand contact with a cultural group dominant to one's own, learn and/or adopt certain aspects of the dominant culture while retaining most or some aspects of their culture of origin (Berry, 2003; Cuellar and Arnold, 1995; Marín and Gamba, 1996). There is ample evidence that this process of change in language use, behaviors, values, etc., is associated with dietary changes, most notably in the unhealthy direction (Ayala *et al.*, 2008a). Evidence also suggests that the acculturation process is associated with changes in parenting practices (Ward, 2008), and recent research suggests that dimensions consistent with the concept of acculturation at the neighborhood level (e.g. neighborhood ethnic density) are associated with healthier neighborhoods as defined by access to FVs (Dubowitz *et al.*, 2008b). Thus, our analysis will extend the protective analysis further by examining the moderating role of acculturation.

Literature Review

Individual-Level Protective Factors

Among the most consistent protective factor exhibited by Mexican-origin individuals is greater consumption of fiber compared with the non-Hispanic white population (King *et al.*, 2012). These consumption patterns reflect greater consumption of fresh FVs compared with other racial/ethnic groups (Blanck *et al.*, 2008). There is also evidence that gender may moderate this relationship. For example, Carvajal and colleagues (Carvajal *et al.*, 2002) found a greater percentage of Latino boys consuming five or more FVs compared with non-Latino boys; no differences were observed among girls.

Two important dietary behaviors include food shopping behaviors and food preparation techniques. Public health research on the food shopping behavior of US Latinos is limited. However, the food industry has produced several reports. In the second of two seminal reports, food industry researchers found that Latinos spend over one third more money per week on groceries compared with non-Latinos, irrespective of income and acculturation levels (FMI, 2005). The higher expenditure on groceries among Latinos was attributed to younger age, larger household sizes, a desire for freshness, and more frequent trips to the grocery store. Importantly, a larger percentage of their grocery store purchases occurred in locations other than their primary grocery store, most notably in smaller Latino-targeted food stores such as the *tiendas*, an environment that may support healthy eating as described below.

Moderating Role of Acculturation

One of the social mechanisms that appear to influence the relationship between diet and health outcomes is the acculturation process. In a systematic review published in the Journal of the American Dietetic Association, we reported that "irrespective of the samples included and the operationalization of acculturation used, being less acculturated was associated with healthier levels of nutrient consumption" (Ayala *et al.*, 2008a, p. 1339). The most pronounced and consistent relationship observed was between acculturation and FV consumption. Irrespective of how acculturation was operationalized, greater acculturation to the US culture was associated with less FV consumption. In other words, retaining traditional values and behaviors (or simply being born outside the US) is associated with better dietary behaviors, including greater consumption of FVs.

Supportive Interpersonal Factors

A systematic review of the relationship between family variables and healthy eating identified a number of family-related correlates and determinants of children's FV intake (Pearson *et al.*, 2009). The review found that having these foods available in the home, having parents that set limits on what is consumed, parental encouragement, and parental modeling of healthy eating were associated with children's FV intake (Pearson *et al.*, 2009). There is also evidence that Hispanic parent–child dyads have a stronger resemblance on dietary intake compared with non-Hispanic parent–child dyads (Beydoun and Wang, 2009). This greater correspondence between what children consume and what their parents consume supports a focus at the interpersonal level. In this section we focus on several types of familial/parental factors including family meal decision-making and family meal sharing.

Family Meal Decision-making

Hispanic families are typically characterized as operating within a patriarchal structure which influences decision making (Cromwell and Ruiz, 1979). The majority of studies involving non-Hispanic families suggest that households that embraced traditional gender roles were more likely to make meal choices that reflected the husband's preference, which often involved less healthful choices. Research from our group sheds a slightly different picture. A study involving Mexican-origin families examined the dietary intake of women living in households where they engaged in solitary meal decision-making (i.e. a traditional gender role) compared to women living in households where these decisions were shared with partners and/or children (Arredondo *et al.*, 2006). Adjusting for socio-demographic factors (income, education, and employment) and acculturation levels, women in traditional decision-making households consumed significantly less saturated fat per day than women in shared decision-making households. These findings suggest that when Latin*as* are in control of meal decisions, the family is more likely to eat healthy. This is further supported by research on the role that children play in meal decision-making. In a qualitative study involving Mexican-origin mothers living in Texas, providing food for one's child was "an essential source of satisfaction and happiness and connected to their identities as mothers" (pp. 1–15; Johnson *et al.*, 2011). Unfortunately this attachment can often translate into engaging in permissive or indulgent meal decision-making behavior, a behavior associated with less consumption of healthy foods among Hispanics (Chaidez and Kaiser, 2011; Hoerr *et al.*, 2009) and greater risk for obesity among Hispanic boys (Hughes *et al.*, 2011) and Mexican-origin children in general (Olvera and Power, 2010).

Family Meal Sharing

Families who consume meals together have children who eat more FVs and drink fewer soft drinks compared to families who do not (Gillman *et al.*, 2000). Baseline data from *Aventuras para niños*, a childhood obesity intervention for Mexican-origin families, suggested that consumption of breakfast as a family at least four times per week was positively related to children's consumption of FVs (Andaya *et al.*, 2011). In a diverse sample that included Hispanic immigrants, eating five or more dinners per week with family was associated with less risk for childhood obesity (Tovar *et al.*, 2013). These findings may be explained by additional evidence that among multi-ethnic families, eating meals together is associated with greater parental encouragement for healthy eating (Poulos *et al.*, 2013). Among Mexican-origin parents, eating meals together is perceived as more pleasurable and an effective weight control method (Flores *et al.*, 2012). Notwithstanding the protective effects of family meals, a national study determined that among low-income Hispanic boys, more frequent family meals were associated with a marginally significant increased risk for obesity (Rollins *et al.*, 2010). More research is needed to clarify these associations, including examining the moderating role of parenting practices.

Parental Factors, Including Parenting Practices

A number of studies show a link between children's contexts such as the home environment and children's risk for becoming overweight (Davison and Birch, 2001). More specifically, parenting practices have been linked to children's health. For example, there is evidence that positive maternal involvement in feeding (e.g. monitor and set limits) among Mexican-origin families is associated with a lower BMI among children (Tschann *et al.*, 2013). Similarly, Matheson and colleagues (Matheson *et al.*, 2006) determined that parental modeling of healthy food consumption among Mexican-origin mothers was associated with fewer calories consumed among children. In short, there is consistent evidence that planning and encouraging of healthy eating by parents is related to healthier food consumption among children (Cullen *et al.*, 2003).

In a study involving 810 predominantly Mexican-origin parents regarding their children's physical activity and eating practices, results suggested that parents who monitored their children's diet and physical activity had children who ate more healthy—defined as (i) eating FVs (e.g. 100 percent orange juice, green salad, fruit, vegetables—not potatoes), (ii) low-fat dairy foods (e.g. cheese, milk, yogurt), (iii) low-sugar cereals (e.g. oatmeal, Kix®, Cheerios®), (iv) wheat bread and (v) crackers—and were more physically active. Similarly, there was a positive association between parents' reinforcement of healthy behaviors and children's health practices (Arredondo *et al.*, 2006). In this study, parents who disciplined their children when eating unhealthy foods or drinking unhealthy beverages (e.g. sodas) had boys who were less likely to engage in these behaviors. This pattern was not evident among girls. These findings suggest that certain parenting behaviors may protect Mexican-origin children from engaging in unhealthy eating and their impact on children's health practices may vary by the child's gender.

Home Availability and Accessibility of FVs

A strong correlate of FV intake among children is their availability and accessibility in the home (Blanchette and Brug, 2005). Given these findings, researchers have recently examined factors associated with greater availability and accessibility of FVs. In a study involving Hispanic families, Dave and colleagues (Dave *et al.*, 2010) found that parental practices to promote FV intake ($p<0.001$), like parent role modeling ($p<0.001$), were positively associated with greater availability and accessibility of FVs in the home. In addition, parents who stated that fast food was inexpensive and convenient were less likely to have FVs available and accessible in the home. Similarly, Matheson and colleagues found that in food-secure (i.e., confident of having regular and consistent access to nutritional food) versus food-insecure households, Mexican-origin mothers who displayed a positive attitude toward making healthful foods more available in the home had children who consumed more fruits and fewer calories from fat (Matheson *et al.*, 2006).

Moderating Role of Acculturation

Few studies have examined the moderating role of acculturation on the relationship between interpersonal factors and diet, and findings are mixed depending on the interpersonal factor in question and how acculturation is operationalized. Being less acculturated appears to be associated with eating breakfast together and more generally, eating more family meals together (Vera-Becerra *et al.*, 2013). Similarly, Dave and colleagues (Dave *et al.*, 2010) found that Spanish-speaking Hispanic families had greater availability and accessibility of fresh FVs in their homes compared with English-speaking families (p<0.001). On the other hand, there is also evidence for the negative influence of acculturation. For example, in terms of parenting practices, Kaiser and colleagues (Kaiser *et al.*, 2001) determined that less- versus more-acculturated mothers were more likely to offer alternatives when their child refused to eat; yet more acculturated mothers viewed bribes, threats, and punishment as ineffective child feeding strategies compared with less acculturated mothers.

Protective Communities

Cross-sectional studies have shown positive associations between proximity of small food stores offering a variety of FVs and greater FV intake (Bodor *et al.*, 2008). Availability of supermarkets is related to overall diet quality (Laraia *et al.*, 2004). Most studies also demonstrate differential access to supermarkets and other food stores by neighborhood deprivation (e.g. poorer neighborhoods have less access) (Cubbin *et al.*, 2001), ethnic composition (Dubowitz *et al.*, 2008a; Moore and Diez Roux, 2006), and area-level wealth (Reidpath *et al.*, 2002)—all factors relevant to the study of Latino health. There is also evidence that small grocery stores in racial/ethnic minority neighborhoods are less likely to carry healthy food selections than those in predominantly white neighborhoods (18- versus 58 percent) (Horowitz *et al.*, 2004). Thus, evidence supports the importance of the community level of influence, and the larger body of research suggests that, for the most part, poorer and ethnically diverse neighborhoods do not support healthy eating.

However, despite the wealth of data on racial/ethnic disparities in access to healthy foods, several recent studies suggest that not all racially-/ethnically-diverse neighborhoods are the same. For example, in a review by Larson and colleagues (2009), one study determined that Hispanic neighborhoods are more likely to have a supermarket (Moore and Diez Roux, 2006). Our own research comparing the availability of fresh FVs in small Mexican immigrant/Mexican American grocery stores (*tiendas*) to supermarkets suggests no disparities in access to fresh produce (Emond *et al.*, 2012). In fact, the cost to purchase sufficient fresh FVs to meet dietary guidelines was $3.00 cheaper in *tiendas* versus supermarkets, with no difference in quality of the produce. *Tiendas* have been identified as important sources of food for other Latino immigrant populations in the US (Fish *et al.*, 2013). Similarly, Gloria and colleagues (Gloria and Steinhardt, 2010) found no differences in availability of healthy foods in small stores by neighborhood income-level. These findings may be explained by the fact that the research was conducted in Texas with a large Mexican immigrant/Mexican American population, a context that is likely to include many *tiendas*. These findings are important, because availability of FVs is associated with healthier eating practices among Latinos. Zenk *et al.* (Zenk *et al.*, 2009) found a positive relationship between neighborhood availability of FVs and Latinos intake of FVs compared with African Americans. For each additional food store in the neighborhood with fresh produce, Latinos consumed a third of a serving more of FVs compared with others.

Application of Theory to Intervention Research: The Entre Familia *Study*

Given evidence on the various levels of influence, our research also takes a social ecological perspective (Ayala *et al.*, in press; Elder *et al.*, 2006, 2009). At the individual level, we have intervened with women using health communication strategies that emphasize factors influential in dietary decision-making and behavior, including, but not limited to time, culture, and material resources (Elder *et al.*, 2005, 2006, 2009). At the interpersonal level, we have intervened with families to promote parenting skills related to dietary and physical activity behaviors (Ayala *et al.*, 2010). And at the community level, we have intervened with Latino grocery stores (*tiendas*) to try and improve access to healthy foods (Ayala *et al.*, 2011). To illustrate the application of theory to our intervention, here we describe a study targeting the individual- and interpersonal levels.

Recently completed research funded by the American Cancer Society, is the *Entre Familia: Reflejos de Salud* (Within the family: Reflections of Health) study. This study was a 10-session family-based intervention designed to promote healthy eating among Mexican immigrants/Mexican American residents of the Imperial County, CA, a county on the Southern tip of the state of California, on the US–Mexico border. Similar to other border communities, Imperial County has the highest rates of obesity and diabetes in the state (e.g. 39 percent childhood obesity compared with 28 percent in the state). *Entre Familia* is a partnership between faculty in the Graduate School of Public Health at San Diego State University and practitioners with *Clínicas de Salud del Pueblo, Inc.*, a federally-qualified health center with ten sites in Imperial and Riverside counties. Using focus groups and other formative research data, a *promotora* (Community Health Worker) training manual, a 9-part DVD series and an accompanying family manual were created to promote healthy eating. The *promotoras* were identified from among individuals in the community who had the leadership skills and motivation to work with families to promote healthy eating. Over the course of four months, the *promotoras* met with the families once a week for the first two months and then biweekly thereafter to watch the DVD and complete components of the family manual. Consistent with the influences described above, the *promotora* worked with the family to set goals such as increasing the number of meals that the family eats together as one strategy to promote healthy eating (referred to as a *Promesa*—Promise—see Figure 14.2). After the family set their weekly goal, the *promotora* engaged them in a behavior change exercise that complimented the goal and reinforced family involvement. This family intervention was effective at improving the mothers' (Ayala *et al.*, 2011) and the children's dietary intake (Horton *et al.*, in press) and the mothers' food shopping and preparation strategies as defined by Kristal and colleagues (Kristal *et al.*, 1999). Future analyses will examine whether the intervention was effective at improving parenting practices to promote healthy eating (Larios *et al.*, 2009) and family meals.

Summary

This chapter is part of a larger effort to understand the many positive aspects of Mexican immigrant families' lives that may explain their more positive health outcomes, despite worse socioeconomic status as measured by income, employment, and education, compared with the general population. This phenomenon is referred to as the Hispanic or Immigrant Health Paradox (Franzini *et al.*, 2001). Despite this initial advantage, however, successive generations of Mexican immigrant fare worse on a number of health indicators (Pew Hispanic Center, 2010). Thus, it is imperative that researchers and practitioners identify potential assets among immigrants upon which to build more effective interventions. Importantly, although we identified a number of differences between Mexican-origin families compared with others, the assets identified may not

FIGURE 14.2 The *Entre Familia* Study "Promise"

be unique to Mexican-origin families. Thus, the potential to generalize some of the lessons learned, to interventions with other immigrant groups represents an important line of inquiry for future research.

Future Directions and Challenges

Despite the many positive factors identified, Mexican-origin communities in the US, and others that are similar, are plagued by a variety of negative factors. They consume too much fast food (Elder *et al.*, 2009); high-fat, high sugar foods are common at social events (Ayala *et al.*, 2005); schools and worksites have easier access to unhealthy foods than to healthy foods (Emmons *et al.*, 1999); and at the community level, there is a greater density of fast food restaurants compared with others (Lee *et al.*, 2010). Thus, although a focus on protective factors can help to identify assets upon which to build an intervention, efforts are still needed to create a socially and physically supportive environment.

Policy Implications

Statistics show that 50 percent of Latino children who are currently 2–5 years of age will have diabetes by the time they are adults (Pew Hispanic Center, 2010). These statistics will not only impact health care costs, but the future prosperity of these individuals. Practitioners and policymakers alike are trying to identify strategies to prevent this. For example, federal programs such as the American Reinvestment and Recovery Act of 2009, the Patient Protection and Affordable Care Act, and the Healthy Food Financing Initiative have bolstered healthy corner store efforts by providing $650 million, $100 million, and $50 million in funding, respectively, to support efforts to increase access to healthy, affordable food. Similarly, the newest initiative of the Special Supplemental Nutrition Program for Women, Infants, and Children (WIC) has encouraged small stores to provide healthy food options in ethnically diverse neighborhoods (Ayala *et al.*, 2012). By making healthy food options more available, underserved communities may be more inclined to buy FVs and make healthy home meals. In addition to making healthy foods more accessible, policy makers can take steps to reduce the marketing of unhealthy foods to Latino families. Children are exposed to considerable marketing of unhealthy foods and beverages, and research shows that exposure to unhealthy food marketing increases children's risk for unhealthy eating and obesity (IOM, 2006). Policies that limit exposure to unhealthy food marketing would support parents' efforts to purchase healthy foods.

Notes

1   The terms Hispanic and Latino are used interchangeably throughout to be consistent with the manner in which they were reported on the original source. Where possible, country of origin is used to further specify the population.

References

Andaya, A., Arredondo, E. M., Alcaraz, J. E., Lindsay, S. P., and Elder, J. P. (2011). The association between family meals, TV viewing during meals, and fruit, vegetables, soda, and chips intake among Latino children. *Journal of Nutrition Education and Behavior, 43*(5), 308–315. doi: 10.1016/j.jneb.2009.11.005

Arredondo, E., Elder, J. P., Ayala, G. X., Campbell, N. R., Baquero, B., and Duerkson, S. (2006). Is parenting style related to children eating and physical activity in Latino children. *Health Education Research, 21*(6), 862–871.

Ayala, G. X., Baquero, B., and Klinger, S. (2008a). A systematic review of the relationship between acculturation and diet among Latinos in the United States: Implications for future research. *Journal of The American Dietetic Association, 108*(8), 1330–1344.

Ayala, G. X., Maty, S., Cravey, A., and Webb, L. (2005). Mapping social and environmental influences on health: A community perspective. In B. Israel and E. Eng (Eds.), *Multiple Methods for Conducting Community-based Participatory Research for Health* (pp. 188–209). San Francisco, CA: Jossey-Bass.

Ayala, G. X., Carnethon, M., Arredondo, E., Delamater, A., Perreira, K., Van Horn, L., . . . Isasi, C. R. (in press). Theoretical foundations of the Study of Latino (SOL) Youth: Implications for obesity and cardiometabolic risk. *Annals of Epidemiology*.

Ayala, G. X., Elder, J. P., Campbell, N. R., Arredondo, E. M., Baquero, B., Crespo, N. C., and Slymen, D. J. (2010). Longitudinal intervention effects on parenting of the Aventuras para Niños study. *American Journal of Preventive Medicine, 38*(2), 154–162.

Ayala, G. X., Ibarra, L., Arredondo, E., Horton, L., Hernandez, E., Parada, H., . . . Elder, J. P. (2011). Promoting healthy eating by strengthening family relations: Design and implementation of the Entre Familia: Reflejos de Salud intervention. In R. E. H. Landrine (Ed.), *Cancer Disparities: Causes and Evidence-Based Solutions*. New York, NY: Springer.

Ayala, G. X., Rogers, M., Arredondo, E. M., Campbell, N. R., Baquero, B., Duerksen, S. C., and Elder, J. P. (2008b). Away-from-home food intake and risk for obesity: Examining the influence of context. *Obesity, 16*(5), 1002–1008. doi: 10.1038/oby.2008.34

Ayala, G.X., Laska, M.N., Zenk, S.N., Tester, J., Rose, D., Odoms-Young, A., McCoy, T., Gittelsohn, J., Foster, G.D., and Andreyeva, T. (2012). Stocking characteristics and perceived increases in sales associated with the introduction of new food products approved by the Special Supplemental Nutrition Program for Women, Infants, and Children. *Public Health Nutrition*, *15*(9), 1771–9.

Berry, J. W. (2003). Conceptual approaches to acculturation. In K. M. Chun, P. Balls Organista, and G. Marín (Eds.), *Acculturation: Advances in Theory, Measurement, and Applied Research* (pp. 17–37). Washington, DC: American Psychological Association.

Beydoun, M. A., and Wang, Y. (2009). Parent–child dietary intake resemblance in the United States: Evidence from a large representative survey. *Social Science and Medicine*, *68*(12), 2137–2144. doi: 10.1016/j.socscimed.2009.03.029

Blanchette, L., and Brug, J. (2005). Determinants of fruit and vegetable consumption among 6–12-year-old children and effective interventions to increase consumption. *Journal of Human Nutrition and Dietetics*, *18*(6), 431–443.

Blanck, H. M., Gillespie, C., Kimmons, J. E., Seymour, J. D., and Serdula, M. K. (2008). Trends in fruit and vegetable consumption among US men and women, 1994–2005. *Preventing Chronic Disease*, *5*(2), 1–10.

Block, G., Patterson, B., and Subar, A. (1992). Fruit, vegetables, and cancer prevention: A review of the epidemiological evidence. *Nutrition and Cancer*, *18*(1), 1–29.

Bodor, J. N., Rose, D., Farley, T. A., Swalm, C., and Scott, S. K. (2008). Neighbourhood fruit and vegetable availability and consumption: The role of small food stores in an urban environment. *Public Health Nutrition*, *11*(4), 413–420.

Boeing, H., Bechthold, A., Bub, A., Ellinger, S., Haller, D., Kroke, A., . . . Watzl, B. (2012). Critical review: Vegetables and fruit in the prevention of chronic diseases. *European Journal of Nutrition*, *51*(6), 637–663. doi: 10.1007/s00394-012-0380-y

Bronfenbrenner, U. (1979). *The Ecology of Human Development: Experiments by Nature and Design*. Cambridge, MA: Harvard Univ. Press.

Carvajal, S. C., Hanson, C. E., Romero, A. J., and Coyle, K. K. (2002). Behavioural risk factors and protective factors in adolescents: A comparison of Latinos and non-Latino whites. *Ethnicity and Health*, *7*(3), 181–193.

Chaidez, V., and Kaiser, L. L. (2011). Validation of an instrument to assess toddler feeding practices of Latino mothers. *Appetite*, *57*(1), 229–236. doi: 10.1016/j.appet.2011.05.106

Cromwell, R. E., and Ruiz, R. A. (1979). The myth of macho dominance in decision making within Mexican and Chicano Families. *Hispanic Journal of Behavioral Sciences*, *1*(4), 355–73.

Cubbin, C., Hadden, W. C., and Winkleby, M. A. (2001). Neighborhood context and cardiovascular disease risk factors: The contribution of material deprivation. *Ethnicity and Disease*, *11*(4), 687–700.

Cuellar, I., and Arnold, B. (1995). Acculturation Rating Scale for Mexican Americans-II: A revision of the original ARSMA scale. *Hispanic Journal of Behavioral Sciences*, *17*(3), 275.

Cullen, K. W., Baranowski, T., Owens, E., Marsh, T., Rittenberry, L., and de Moor, C. (2003). Availability, accessibility, and preferences for fruit, 100% fruit juice, and vegetables influence children's dietary behavior. *Health Education and Behavior*, *30*(5), 615–626.

Dave, J. M., Evans, A. E., Pfeiffer, K. A., Watkins, K. W., and Saunders, R. P. (2010). Correlates of availability and accessibility of fruits and vegetables in homes of low-income Hispanic families. *Health Education Research*, *25*(1), 97–108.

Davison, K., and Birch, L. (2001). Childhood overweight: A contextual model and recommendations for future research. *Obesity Reviews*, *2*, 159–171.

Dubowitz, T., Subramanian, S. V., Acevedo-Garcia, D., Osypuk, T. L., and Peterson, K. E. (2008b). Individual and neighborhood differences in diet among low-income foreign and U.S.-born women. *Women's Health Issues: Official Publication of The Jacobs Institute of Women's Health*, *18*(3), 181–190. doi: 10.1016/j.whi.2007.11.001

Dubowitz, T., Heron, M., Bird, C. E., Lurie, N., Finch, B. K., Basurto-Dávila, R., . . . Escarce, J. J. (2008a). Neighborhood socioeconomic status and fruit and vegetable intake among Whites, Blacks, and Mexican Americans in the United States. *The American Journal of Clinical Nutrition*, *87*(6), 1883–1891.

Elder, J., Ayala, G., McKenzie, T., Litrownik, A., Gallo, L., Arredondo, E., . . . Kaplan, R. (in press). A three decade evolution to transdisciplinary research: Community health research in California-Mexico border communities. *Progress in Community Health Partnerships: Research, Education, and Action*.

Elder, J. P., Ayala, G. X., Parra-Medina, D., and Talavera, G. A. (2009). Health communication in the Latino community: Issues and approaches. *Annual Review of Public Health, 30*, 227–251.

Elder, J. P., Ayala, G. X., Campbell, N. R., Arredondo, E. M., Slymen, D. J., Baquero, B., Engelberg, M. (2006). Long-term effects of a communication intervention for Spanish-dominant Latinas. *American Journal of Preventive Medicine, 31*(2), 159–166.

Elder, J. P., Ayala, G. X., Campbell, N. R., Slymen, D., Lopez-Madurga, E. T., Engelberg, M., and Baquero, B. (2005). Interpersonal and print nutrition communication for a Spanish-Dominant Latino population: Secretos de la Buena Vida. *Health Psychology, 24*(1), 49–57. doi: 10.1037/0278-6133.24.1.49

Elder, J. P., Crespo, N. C., Corder, K., Ayala, G. X., Slymen, D. J., Lopez, N. V., . . . McKenzie, T. L. (2013). Childhood obesity prevention and control in city recreation centres and family homes: The MOVE/me Muevo Project. *Pediatric Obesity.*

Elder, J. P., Lytle, L., Sallis, J. F., Young, D. R., Steckler, A., Simons-Morton, D., . . . Ribisl, K. (2007). A description of the social-ecological framework used in the trial of activity for adolescent girls (TAAG). *Health Education Research, 22*(2), 155–165.

Emmons, K. M., Linnan, L. A., Shadel, W. G., Marcus, B., and Abrams, D. B. (1999). The working healthy project: A worksite health-promotion trial targeting physical activity, diet, and smoking. *Journal of Occupational and Environmental Medicine, 41*(7), 545–555.

Emond, J.A., Madanat, H.N., and Ayala, G.X. (2012). Do Latino and non-Latino grocery stores differ in availability and affordability of healthy food items in a low income, metropolitan region? *Public Health Nutrition, 15*, 360–9.

Fish, C. A., Brown, J. R., and Quandt, S. A. (2013). African American and Latino low income families' food shopping behaviors: Promoting fruit and vegetable consumption and use of alternative healthy food options. *Journal of Immigrant and Minority Health / Center For Minority Public Health.*

Flores, G., Maldonado, J., and Durán, P. (2012). Making tortillas without lard: Latino parents' perspectives on healthy eating, physical activity, and weight-management strategies for overweight Latino children. *Journal of the Academy of Nutrition and Dietetics, 112*(1), 81–89. doi: 10.1016/j.jada.2011.08.041

FMI. (2005). El Mercado: A perspective on U.S. Hispanic shopping behavior.

Franzini, L., Ribble, J. C., and Keddie, A. M. (2001). Understanding the Hispanic paradox. *Ethnicity and Disease, 11*(3), 496–518.

Gillman, M. W., Rifas-Shiman, S. L., Frazier, A. L., Rockett, H. R., Camargo, C. A., Jr., Field, A. E., . . . Colditz, G. A. (2000). Family dinner and diet quality among older children and adolescents. *Archives of Family Medicine, 9*(3), 235–240.

Gloria, C. T., and Steinhardt, M. A. (2010). Texas nutrition environment assessment of retail food stores (TxNEA-S): Development and evaluation. *Public Health Nutrition, 13*(11), 1764–1772.

Gotay, C. C. (2005). Behavior and cancer prevention. *Journal of Clinical Oncology, 23*(2), 301–310.

Green, L. W., and Kreuter, M. W. (2005). *Health Program Planning: An Educational and Ecological Approach.* New York, NY: McGraw-Hill Higher Education.

Han, E., and Powell, L. M. (2013). Consumption patterns of sugar-sweetened beverages in the United States. *Journal of the Academy of Nutrition and Dietetics, 113*(1), 43–53. doi: 10.1016/j.jand.2012.09.016

Hoerr, S. L., Hughes, S. O., Fisher, J. O., Nicklas, T. A., Liu, Y., and Shewchuk, R. M. (2009). Associations among parental feeding styles and children's food intake in families with limited incomes. *The International Journal of Behavioral Nutrition and Physical Activity, 6*, 55–55. doi: 10.1186/1479-5868-6-55

Horowitz, C. R., Colson, K. A., Hebert, P. L., and Lancaster, K. (2004). Barriers to buying healthy foods for people with diabetes: Evidence of environmental disparities. *American Journal of Public Health, 94*(9), 1549–1554.

Horton, L. A., Parada, H. P., Slymen, D., Arredondo, E., Ibarra, I., and Ayala, G. X. (in press). Improving children's diets in a family intervention: Entre Familia: Reflejos de Salud. *Salud Publica de Mexico.*

Hughes S.O., Power, T.G., Papaioannou, M.A., Cross, M.B., Nicklas, T.A., Hall, S.K., and Shewchuk, R.M. (2011). Emotional climate, feeding practices, and feeding styles: An observational analysis of the dinner meal in Head Start families. *The International Journal of Behavioral Nutrition and Physical Activity, 10*(8), 60.

Institute of Medicine, Committee on Food Marketing and the Diets of Children and Youth. (2006). *Food Marketing to Children and Youth: Threat or Opportunity?* Washington, DC: National Academies Press. Available from: http://www.iom.edu/Reports/2005/Food-Marketing-to-Children-and-Youth-Threat-or-Opportunity.aspx

Johnson, C. M., Sharkey, J. R., and Dean, W. R. (2011). It's all about the children: A participant-driven photo-elicitation study of Mexican-origin mothers' food choices. *BMC Women's Health*, *11*, 41–41. doi: 10.1186/1472-6874-11-41

Kaiser, L. L., Melgar-Quiñonez, H. R., Lamp, C. L., Johns, M. C., and Harwood, J. O. (2001). Acculturation of Mexican-American mothers influences child feeding strategies. *Journal of the American Dietetic Association*, *101*(5), 542–547.

Key, T. J., Schatzkin, A., Willett, W. C., Allen, N. E., Spencer, E. A., and Travis, R. C. (2004). Diet, nutrition and the prevention of cancer . . . Diet, Nutrition and the Prevention of Chronic Diseases: scientific background papers of the Joint WHO/FAO Expert Consultation (Geneva, 28 January-1 February 2002). *Public Health Nutrition*, 7(1A), 187–200.

King, D. E., Mainous, A. G., III, and Lambourne, C. A. (2012). Trends in dietary fiber intake in the United States, 1999–2008. *Journal of the Academy of Nutrition and Dietetics*, *112*(5), 642–648. doi: 10.1016/j.jand.2012.01.019

Kristal, A. R., Shattuck, A. L., and Patterson, R. E. (1999). Differences in fat-related dietary patterns between Black, Hispanic and White women: Results from the Women's Health Trial Feasibility Study in Minority Populations. *Public Health Nutrition*, *2*(3), 253–262.

Laraia, B. A., Siega-Riz, A. M., Kaufman, J. S., and Jones, S. J. (2004). Proximity of supermarkets is positively associated with diet quality index for pregnancy. *Preventive Medicine*, *39*(5), 869–875.

Larios, S. E., Ayala, G. X., Arredondo, E. M., Baquero, B., and Elder, J. P. (2009). Development and validation of a scale to measure Latino parenting strategies related to children's obesigenic behaviors. The parenting strategies for eating and activity scale (PEAS). *Appetite*, *52*(1), 166–172.

Larson, N. I., Story, M. T., and Nelson, M. C. (2009). Neighborhood environments: Disparities in access to healthy foods in the U.S. *American Journal of Preventive Medicine*, *36*(1), 74–81.

Lee, R. E., Heinrich, K. M., Medina, A. V., Regan, G. R., Reese-Smith, J. Y., Jokura, Y., and Maddox, J. E. (2010). A picture of the healthful food environment in two diverse urban cities. *Environmental Health Insights*, *4*, 49–60.

Marín, G., and Gamba, R. J. (1996). A new measurement of acculturation for Hispanics: The bidimensional acculturation scale for. *Hispanic Journal of Behavioral Sciences*, *18*(3), 297.

Marín, G., and Triandis, H. (1985). Allocentrism as an important characteristic of the behavior of L.A. and Latinos. In R. Diaz-Guerrero (Ed.), *Cross-Cultural and National Studies of Social Psychology* (pp. 85–104). Amsterdam: North Hall.

Matheson, D. M., Robinson, T. N., Varady, A., and Killen, J. D. (2006). Do Mexican-American mothers' food-related parenting practices influence their children's weight and dietary intake? *Journal of the American Dietetic Association*, *106*(11), 1861–1865.

Moore, L. V., and Diez Roux, A. V. (2006). Associations of neighborhood characteristics with the location and type of food stores. *American Journal of Public Health*, *96*(2), 325–331. doi: 10.2105/ajph.2004.058040

Olvera, N., and Power, T. G. (2010). Brief report: Parenting styles and obesity in Mexican American children: A longitudinal study. *Journal of Pediatric Psychology*, *35*(3), 243–249. doi: 10.1093/jpepsy/jsp071

Pearson, N., Biddle, S. J. H., and Gorely, T. (2009). Family correlates of fruit and vegetable consumption in children and adolescents: A systematic review. *Public Health Nutrition*, *12*(2), 267–283.

Pew Hispanic Center. (2010). *Demographic profile of Hispanics in California, 2008*. Washington, DC: Pew Research Center.

Poulos, N. S., Pasch, K. E., Springer, A. E., Hoelscher, D. M., and Kelder, S. H. (2013). Is frequency of family meals associated with parental encouragement of healthy eating among ethnically diverse eighth graders? *Public Health Nutrition*, 1–6.

Reidpath, D. D., Burns, C., Garrard, J., Mahoney, M., and Townsend, M. (2002). An ecological study of the relationship between social and environmental determinants of obesity. *Health and Place*, *8*(2), 141–145.

Rollins, B. Y., Belue, R. Z., and Francis, L. A. (2010). The beneficial effect of family meals on obesity differs by race, sex, and household education: The national survey of children's health, 2003–2004. *Journal of the American Dietetic Association*, *110*(9), 1335–1339. doi: 10.1016/j.jada.2010.06.004

Sallis, J. F., and Glanz, K. (2009). Physical activity and food environments: Solutions to the obesity epidemic. *The Milbank Quarterly*, *87*(1), 123–154.

Smith, C., and Ryan, A. (2006). Change for Life/Cambia tu vida: A health promotion program based on the stages of change model for African descendent and Latino adults in New Hampshire. *Preventing Chronic Disease, 3*(3), 1–11.

Sorkin, D. H., and Billimek, J. (2012). Dietary behaviors of a racially and ethnically diverse sample of overweight and obese Californians. *Health Education and Behavior: The Official Publication Of The Society For Public Health Education, 39*(6), 737–744. doi: 10.1177/1090198111430709

Stokols, D. (1996). Translating social ecological theory into guidelines for community health promotion. *American Journal of Health Promotion, 10*(4), 282–298.

Tovar, A., Hennessy, E., Must, A., Hughes, S. O., Gute, D. M., Sliwa, S., . . . Economos, C. D. (2013). Feeding styles and evening family meals among recent immigrants. *The International Journal of Behavioral Nutrition and Physical Activity, 10*(1), 84–84.

Tschann, J. M., Gregorich, S. E., Penilla, C., Pasch, L. A., de Groat, C. L., Flores, E., . . . Butte, N. F. (2013). Parental feeding practices in Mexican American families: Initial test of an expanded measure. *The International Journal of Behavioral Nutrition and Physical Activity, 10*, 6–6. doi: 10.1186/1479-5868-10-6

US Census Bureau, C. (2010). 2006–2008 American Community Survey 3-Year Estimates.

Vera-Becerra, L. E., Lopez, M. L., and Kaiser, L. L. (2013). Child feeding practices and overweight status among Mexican immigrant families. *Journal of Immigrant and Minority Health / Center For Minority Public Health.*

Wansink, B. (2004). Environmental factors that increase the food intake and consumption volume of unknowing consumers. [Article]. *Annual Review of Nutrition, 24*(1), 455–479. doi: 10.1146/annurev.nutr.24.012003.132140

Ward, C. L. (2008). Parental perceptions of childhood overweight in the Mexican American population: An integrative review. *The Journal of School Nursing, 24*(6), 407–416. doi: 10.1177/1059840508324555

Zenk, S. N., Lachance, L. L., Schulz, A. J., Mentz, G., Kannan, S., and Ridella, W. (2009). Neighborhood retail food environment and fruit and vegetable intake in a multiethnic urban population. *American Journal of Health Promotion: AJHP, 23*(4), 255–264.

15

INDIGENOUS HEALTH AND COPING RESOURCES IN MEXICAN AMERICAN COMMUNITIES

Rebecca A. Lopez

Introduction

Many immigrant communities encounter unique problems in coping with and finding resources for basic needs. As addressed in earlier chapters, extended family members, parentified children and *compadrazco* family systems can provide important information and supports for Mexican American families in many areas of need. But in the area of health care, resources may be inaccessible due to low income, legal status, language or cultural incompatibilities. With increasing attacks on public safety nets and with the increased scrutiny of undocumented populations there exists an ongoing burden of finding even minimal health care options in many of our Mexican American enclaves. As the nation's economic and political vagaries continue to disproportionately impact the poor and undocumented, it is important to assess the availability of any alternative health care resources for the poorest consumers.

Although acculturation has diminished the knowledge and practice of many oral traditions and folk practices, the unique history of Mexican Americans as both the oldest immigrants to this country, as well as the most numerous, recent émigrés suggest opportunities for a rekindling of many time-honored beliefs and practices. When no other formal health care options are available, the Mexican culture may provide informal, "complementary" health care systems retained of traditional Mexican Indian folk paradigms. These remnants of "parallel" belief systems and indigenous practices may constitute the only resources for some ethnic enclaves that cannot access formal, mainstream systems due to finances or due to cultural inaccessibility. For some Mexican Americans, the need to fulfill health care needs can mean calling upon traditional, informal, indigenous health care systems.

Literature Review

Cultural Beliefs About Health and Illness

Culture influences symptom presentation, beliefs about causes of disease and discomfort, as well as attitudes toward, and choices about treatment. Latinos, as well as other members of minority cultures in the United States, enjoy a tradition of folk medicine based on beliefs of indigenous rural populations with limited access to established Western medical practices (Suarez, 2000). When Latinos migrate to the United States, these beliefs are combined synergistically with

Western medical beliefs and Anglo cultural beliefs about health in a melange of perceptions about health and disease that inform the attitudes of Latinos in this country. Kleinman (1980) noted a medical pluralism available to the immigrant, ranging from the professional medical sector, to the natural and spiritual folk sector, to a popular sector of home remedies. While acculturated Latinos tend to prefer a family physician to folk medicine practice, the continual interaction among immigrants from Mexico reinforces the traditional beliefs about health (Suarez, 2000). Alternative cultural explanations of disease are part of the process of "everyday reasoning" that people draw on to explain illness (Hunt and Mattingly, 1998, p. 267). A folk belief about the causes of illness can be seen as complementing, rather than challenging, the dominant model of Western medicine. Western medicine draws on *beliefs* as does folk medicine; the difference is that the beliefs of the dominant culture are legitimized by science and professionalization. As persons with health problems attempt to contextualize their experiences of disease, they will draw on many forms of reasoning, including biographical, to enable them to manage their experiences.

Patient experience and patient belief is a newly legitimized field of inquiry in medicine and allied fields, due to the recognition that wellness and recovery depend on an understanding of the systems of meaning that patients bring to their experience of illness (Bade, 1999; Belliard and Ramirez-Johnson, 2005; Oomen *et al.*, 1999). Patients and medical providers may have entirely different narratives about what causes disease and the actual impact of culture on physiological response to social interaction (Butler *et al.*, 2009)—a persistent negotiation referred to as a sociocultural "tug of war" by Bateson (1994).

From this broader perspective of health dynamics, modern medicine omits potential social contributors to illness as they seek to diagnose the causes of illness in some Mexican American patients through strict scientific, intellectual investigation (Castillo, 1997). Folk medicine provides a broader perspective which takes into account the cultural significance and the personal and social meanings of illness (Mezzich *et al.*, 1996). Well-known folk illnesses, such as *susto* (fear or shock), *coraje* (extreme, often suppressed anger), *mal ojo* (evil eye), have made their way into the common nomenclature to describe health beliefs for growing Latino populations. Debate continues as to the pervasiveness of these traditional explanations for illness, and for their treatment through the use of home remedies and informal folk doctors. While many suggest it is a resource utilized only by the poorest recent immigrants (Krajewski-Jaime, 1991), folk medical systems may constitute a viable "conceptual bridge" that can help interpret the full impact of disease (Hunt, 1998; p. 305).

The Dual Health Perspective and Indigenous Health Practices

It is important to acknowledge the dual health perspective held by many Mexicans, as it is a perspective that differs in important ways from the formal beliefs and practices of mainstream US health institutions. Centuries of contrasting philosophical, religious and geo-political factors have evolved two systems of thought to explain sickness and health in indigenous Mexican populations in contrast with Western European systems. Western European medicine has historically been formed on the basis of theoretical foundations and techniques emanating from a dependence on "scientific investigation." (Telles and Karno, 1994, p. 234). It is a perspective that is "neutral and impersonal and . . . grounded in scientific objectivism" (Mezzich *et al.*, 1996, p. 6). Centuries of blending of Spanish and indigenous scientific and religious beliefs created an amalgam of the scientific rationality perspective with the supernatural elements indigenous peoples of Mexico had employed for centuries which served to explain cause and effect in health and illness. Applewhite (1995) is among many who suggest the persistence of beliefs in a metaphysical and spiritual world that not only explained illness, but also provided indigenous resources for cures of such psychosocial illnesses. In sum, it has evolved within the Mestizo (Spanish–Indian) culture as a perspective that recognizes that illness is more than scientific, and is equally impacted by psychological and social contexts. Niska and Snyder's (1999) work revealed young, Mexican American parents who described the concept of health as ". . .more than freedom from illness" (p. 229). The parents in their studies held a perception of true health that was defined as inclusive of the "physical, emotional, social interactional and spiritual integration of their . . . family" (p. 229). Utilizing a strict Western European practice of diagnosis and intellectual investigation would omit critical social and familial factors, viewed in the Mexican culture to contribute to illness (Mezzich *et al.*, 1996; Castillo, 1997). Indigenous folk medicine provides a broader perspective which takes into account the cultural significance, and places the illness within a context of personal and social dynamics that can be every bit as virulent as bacteriological causes recognized by mainstream Western European medicine (Mezzich *et al.*, 1996).

Krajewski-Jaime (1991) contributed further to our understanding of the dual perspective by suggesting three central aspects of folk medicine among Latinos: first, the social contributions of family and kin in diagnosing and treating illness; second, the melding of religion and illness which then sanctions the use of spiritual healing practices; and third, the universality of many of these remnants of health beliefs, symptoms, and practices among Latino communities (p. 161). Building on the distinctions of the dual perspective is the perspective that health can only be preserved with the maintaining of homeostasis among all systems of the individual—psychological, social, and interpersonal:

> . . . a healthy body is maintained through the balancing of biological needs and social-interpersonal expectations, physical and spiritual harmony, and individual and cultural–familial attachments.
>
> *(Vargas and Koss-Chioino, 1992, p. 115)*

A particular Mexican value of *personalismo* is often used to describe Mexican American social interactions and helps to explain the primacy of positive social relationships as an important aspiration in daily life (Applewhite, 1995; Appleby *et al.*, 2001; Green, 1995). Cox and Ephross (1998) suggested the "marginal-to-poor level of existence" make informal, traditional, and personal social networks particularly important for "the information, practical assistance, contacts. . .(and) major sources of support and integration into the new society" (p. 87). Within today's ethnic Mexican American communities, Mexican traditions and belief systems can persist in a collective isolation, particularly when surrounded by mainstream resources which are hostile or inaccessible, or are perceived as such. Rivera and Erlich (1984) refer to the concept of "neo-gemeinschaft" which is thought to typify ethnic minority communities. These are relatively homogenous and closed communities where English is not often spoken; where there is a shared experience of racism and oppression among many extended family networks. Individuals are expected to nourish relationships among groups, rather than engage in strengthening individual abilities (Green, 1995). The value of *personalismo* prevails to value respect for authority, loyalty, and family attachments, more so than mainstream culture. These collective goals supersede the need for strict role assignment among family members in favor of more functional and fluid roles and tasks that may even overlook generational expectations.

The interplay of multiple dynamics in Latino health and illness was also investigated by Falicov (1998), who typified Latino health belief systems as possessing three distinct qualities: ". . . belief in traditional folk illness; belief in hot/cold theories of illness; and belief in the supernatural, magic and bewitchment . . ." (p. 132). For centuries, indigenous Mexican belief systems were believed to be governed by a holistic perspective that an imbalance in any of the bio-psycho-social components of an individual could cause illness. Disease and illness were recognized as emanating from powerful supernatural forces inflicted either by God or by persons with special powers (Davidow, 1999). The supernatural had the power both to inflict illness and ruin, as well as heal and nurture the individual (Kiev, 1968). Mexican folk medicine today reflects remnants of these belief systems originated by native American Indian naturalist religions and the Western European, Roman Catholic spiritual notion of health or illness as "God's will" that can be attributable to an established, religious deity (Davidow, 1999; p. 49). This dual health perspective is a prime example of the hybrid *Mestizo* culture (Spanish and Indian) which has formed the basis for many health, spiritual, and family practices today:

> *Mestizo* refers to a dynamic, synergistic process developed from the amalgamation of peoples, philosophies, and cultures bridging the European continent and the Americas; the intermingling of physical, psychological, cultural and spiritual ties between the Spaniard and the Indian.
>
> *(Vargas and Koss-Chioino, 1992, p. 105)*

Traditional Folk Illnesses

The umbrella term of *curanderismo* is commonly used to refer to indigenous Mexican folk healing, inclusive of a variety of centuries-old practices, treatments, and perceived afflictions. *Curanderismo* for some Mexican American families includes a perception of illness both as a biological event (as in the Western European perspective) and as a "social-interpersonal matrix" of causes and cures (Vargas and Koss-Chioino, 1992, p. 114). Folk illnesses are differentiated from other microbial illnesses in that they are viewed for their potential for personal transmission, and/or due to their supernatural origin (Trotter, 2001). With the powerful inculcation and subjugation of indigenous Mexicans by the Spaniards, an additional health and illness paradigm entered the mainstream of Mexican belief systems and practices. The Western European Hippocratic theories of humoral pathology incorporated the perspective that physical health was to be viewed as dependent on a constant balance of the body's four humors: the hot fluids of blood and yellow bile, and the cold fluids of phlegm and black bile (Davidow, 1999; Levine, 1993). The symmetry of a distressed individual could be restored through ingesting foods and herbs with contrasting qualities and powers, often under the guidance of an expert in knowledge of the special properties of various foods and herbs (Levine, 1993). These attempts to seek balance very often provided a ready personal and spiritual explanation for the unexplained illness (Castillo, 1997).

Along with the illness or imbalance created with conflicting foods or herbs, equally powerful in causing imbalance were considered to be the *mal aires* or *mal de aire* (or bad airs) (Alegria *et al.*, 1977). These were felt to cause a range of illnesses from mild pains or cramps to extreme conditions of paralysis in individuals. Malevolent, cold drafts can serve to explain the cause of everything from headaches, to tuberculosis and must be restored to harmony with "hot" foods (Levine, 1993; p. 155). Likewise, the "hot" illnesses, which can include digestive maladies, kidney ailments, rashes, and sore throat, must be remedied with foods of opposing forces (Ripley, 1986). Pregnancy, in particular, is also thought to be a "hot" imbalance, requiring "cold" foods to restore balance (Levine, 1993; p. 140). While there may be wide ambiguity and variation in the consistent categorizing of individual foods, there is some agreement that foods such as pork, eggs, and dairy products are so strong in their properties as to very often be the source of such imbalance (Krajewski-Jaime, 1991; Gonzalez-Lee and Simon, 1990).

A particular folk illness that has moved from the supernatural in nature to the physiological is the condition of *empacho*. At its extreme, more than indigestion, *empacho* is believed to be caused by food or concentrations of saliva that cannot be dislodged from the sides of the stomach, leading to stomach pain, constipation, bloating or other digestive disorders, often with a nervous or psychological basis (Green, 1995; Abril, 1977).

A unique body of disorders involving spiritual and socio-personal imbalances forms the bulk of the more serious folk illnesses—the most feared perhaps being those which could be construed by Western European practitioners as potential mental disorders, although modern diagnostic clinicians are diversifying their categorizations of culture-bound and culturally influenced behaviors. This group of illnesses is composed of the personally transmitted, supernatural illnesses of *mal ojo* (or evil eye), and *embrujo* (or supernatural hex) (Green, 1995; Levine, 1993). *Mal ojo* (also expressed as *mal de ojo* or simply *ojo*) can cause headaches, fever, or even death in the person who has been the subject of intense and covetous glances as Green (1995) depicts:

> The eyes of another person can be the virulent agent for initiating this condition . . . Children are particularly susceptible to the admiring looks of adults, and women may be exposed to danger from the glances of men (p. 65).

The social taboo of *envidia,* or intense jealousy, may precede *mal ojo* when a known or unknown person desires what another person possesses. Such an imbalance in this relationship can be remedied if the injured party is physically touched by the perpetrator to break the spell. *Envidia* is felt to be the cause of several negative physical manifestations such as insomnia, fever, vomiting or restlessness (Alegria *et al.*, 1977). Equally powerful is the condition of *embrujo* (also known as *embrujada* or *mal puesto*). *Un embrujo* is thought to be an intentionally directed, personally transmitted hex which signifies an imbalance between positive energies and evil spirits (Vargas and Koss-Chioino, 1992).

Another group of folk maladies which can be the result of human or supernatural instigation is comprised of *susto* and *espanto* (Levine, 1993). *Susto*—and most often *espanto*—have been described as "soul loss" by Levine (1993) or "spirit attack" by Castillo (1997), first indicated by physical weakness, but then escalating to depression, introversion, and apathy among other symptoms. *Susto* is typified by serious fright as a result of a traumatic incident, which may or may not involve human interaction. *Susto* is thought to particularly occur in the childhood years. Left untreated, death can be the ultimate outcome (Mezzich *et al.*, 1996; Castillo, 1997). Perhaps more serious is a variant of *susto* termed *espanto*, which is said to be caused by extreme fright due to supernatural causes that have caused the soul to separate from one's body (Krajewski-Jaime, 1991). Symptoms of *espanto*, initially, are comparable to those of *susto,* but may escalate to include anorexia, insomnia, and hallucination (Abril, 1977; Chesney *et al.*, 1980).

Traditional Folk Practitioners and Treatments

The "folk systems" used by some Mexican Americans today incorporate folk and religious treatments to provide culturally accessible health care resources. It is a system composed of practitioners who have been informally trained or who are recognized as having inherited the "*don*," or gift of healing (Trotter, 2001).

General Healers

The *curandero* (male) or *curandera* (female) is recognized as a folk healer with the ability to both diagnose illness and provide therapeutic, psychosocial interventions in the natural physical and psychological realm, as well as the supernatural realm. (Chesney *et al.*, 1980; Trotter and Chavira, 1997). They are empowered with the ability to counteract the power of an evil spell (*un embrujo* or *mal puesto*) which has been cast on the patient. *Curanderos* are able to serve as a link with spirits who can direct positive or negative forces in assisting the patient (Trotter and Chavira, 1997). Healers utilize what Castillo (1997) refers to as "transformational healing symbols" which may include herbs, medications, massage, prayer, holy objects, incantations, penance for sin, proverbs, scripture or sacred words (pp. 82–83). The healer is often said to perform "*una limpia*" (Levine, 1993) or "*una barrida*" (Applewhite, 1995) or "*un baño*" (Appleby *et al.*, 2001), all of which figuratively translate to "a spiritual cleansing", although the *curandero* may also engage in physically bathing or wiping down the patient with a variety of substances. As in the case of *mal de ojo*, the touch of the person who cast the ill will is sought out to break the negative bond. If that does not occur, the victim may choose to seek out a *curandero* who has particular expertise in the use of spiritual, religious, and rudimentary medical implements. Treatments have traditionally included the use of eggs, herbs, oils, candle lighting, laying on of hands, and prayer (Abril, 1977; Applewhite, 1995). *Curanderos* may treat a full range of physical, mental, and spiritual afflictions, even to the point of performing exorcisms (Applewhite, 1995).

Spiritualists

For those community members who believe that spiritual assistance is solely needed, treatment by *espiritualistas* may be sought out (Trotter and Chavira, 2001). These faith healers, likewise, have no particular, formal medical expertise, are predominantly women and are most revered. They may be referred to as *señoras* or *espiritistas* or *espiritualistas* as above, and are sought out to heal the soul only. Their expertise lies in reading spiritual cards or performing a seance to discern problem relationship areas and outcomes for the spiritually anguished client (Gonzalez-Lee and Simon, 1990; Trotter and Chavira, 1997).

Herbalists

Another tier of folk health practitioners involves the *yerberos* or *hierbistas* (herbalists), (Applewhite, 1995; Levine, 1993). *Yerberos* may maintain a public "*botánica*" or small shop where natural herbs, homeopathic medicines, and religious amulets are made available for purchase, along with medical consultation and direction (Gomez-Beloz and Chavez, 2001). They may dispense *estafiate* as a purgative tea for *empacho* (Krajewski-Jaime, 1991); *yerbabuena* (peppermint) teas for stomach pain and for discomfort attending pregnancy (Sherraden and Barrera, 1997); *manzanilla* (chamomile) for a wide range of physical and emotional ailments, including labor pains (Giachello, 1994); *flor de tila* (linden blossom) for insomnia; or *borraja* (borage) to cut a fever (Trotter and Chavira, 1997). Torres (1983) undertook extensive, early research in documenting hundreds of herbs used as analgesics, antidotes, anti-emetics, antiseptics, disinfectants, expectorants, purgatives, sedatives, and stimulants. One particular herb is noted for its "magical" properties, *pirul* (pepper tree), and is thought to be used by *curanderos* to cure *susto* or *mal de aire*. Trotter and Chavira (1997) note the use of such medicinal herbs by *curanderos* who may prescribe teas, herbal baths or poultices as a form of "primitive chemotherapy" (p. 74).

Physical Healers

A final category of practitioners includes those who deal exclusively with physical imbalances. These are the *sobadores* (or *sobaderos*) (traditional masseuses) and *parteras* (lay midwives) (Giachello,

1994; Sherraden and Barrera, 1997). *Sobadores* may perform simple massages (*masajes*) to alleviate pain and tension; or they may also be instrumental in treating *empacho* or in manipulating sprains (Gonzalez-Lee and Simon, 1990). More experienced *sobadores* may be called upon to function as *hueseros*, or bone-setters (Trotter and Chavira, 1997).

Family Variations of Folk Practices

Many Mexican American families practice their own traditions of folk medicine within their home and extended family networks. Candle-lit religious altars may be established in the home for commemorative, religious, and healing purposes. The use of home-made poultices, herbal treatments, and religious amulets are those practices transferred from generation to generation and which form a group of remedios caseros (home remedies) (Applewhite, 1995; Gomez-Beloz and Chavez, 2001; Sherraden and Barrera, 1997). Supportive professionals such as the yerbero (herbalist) dispense the needed medicinal herbs as illness warrants, not unlike several other American ethnic minority communities. Most typical of the herbs found in a majority of Mexican American homes where folk healing is practiced are thought to include manzanilla and yerba buena (Sherraden and Barrera, 1997).

Curanderismo may persist for practical reasons, which confront many needy Mexican Americans for whom formal health care systems are not available. Lack of medical insurance, language barriers, lack of knowledge of and accessibility to mainstream medical services have also served to sustain an informal system of health care providers and home remedies (Guendelman, 1991; Davidow, 1999; Mueller *et al.*, 1998; Zambrana, 1995). Equally important may be the lack of culturally sensitive providers available to this isolated population (Price and Elliot, 1993), as well as possible interpretive biases inherent in cross-cultural interactions between providers and consumers (Varela *et al.*, 2004). One of the primary reasons that Mexican folk traditions may persist is that some of the folk illnesses defy ontological explanations or descriptions that can be readily understood by mainstream doctors (Mezzich *et al.*, 1996). The mother who seeks medical care for her child who is believed to be suffering from *caida de mollera* (fallen fontanel) may often be confronted by a medical staff who view the child's dehydration and fever to be the result of "parental ignorance, superstition, or simply as abuse and/or neglect" (Krajewski-Jaime, 1991, p. 157). In contrast, a *curandero* may offer understanding and relief for the parent in a culturally sensitive and relevant context, perhaps to the point of treating the child for *mal ojo* when all other explanations have failed.

Some research suggests the use of folk medicine is but a small percentage of actual Mexican American health care practices (Chesney *et al.*, 1980; Higginbotham *et al.*, 1990). In Baer and Bustillo's (1993) study, 53 percent of Mexican American farmworkers in one sample self-medicated using available, traditional resources. Yet, others suggest that reliance on folk healers and treatments may not necessarily be determined by social status or by level of acculturation:

> . . . it is critical to understand which behaviors result from oppression, discrimination and poverty and which are reflections of ethnic values and norms.
>
> *(Cox and Ephross, 1998, p. 13)*

Coping with Stress through the Conceptualization of Coraje

Coping with stress may be a health imperative encountered by many in the Mexican American community due to the socioeconomic realities of Latino subjugation as a minority group in the

US. Several Mexican American cultural traits bear relevance for the manner in which our communities are able to survive and cope through the travails of minority status.

Latinos are thought by some to be a personable and perhaps more "acquiescent" minority population (Marín *et al.*, 1992). *Simpatía*, or the desire to maintain harmony and remain agreeable with others, has been noted as a Latino cultural tendency in early studies by Marín and Marín (1991), and contemporary study by Varela *et al.* (2007). As mentioned earlier, the *personalismo* which is often used to describe Mexican American social interactions speaks to the primacy of positive social relationships as a goal in everyday life, often requiring the sublimation of individual needs (Appleby *et al.*, 2001; Applewhite, 1995).

A third Latino cultural trait is *respeto*, which refers to the personal behavior whereby respect is shown to others on the basis of age, gender, and authority (Antshel, 2002). In turn, those who treat others with respect are due respect. This is a cultural expectation that recognizes not only social class, but the inherent worth of even the most marginalized groups.

The conflict between maintaining *simpatía* and attaining due *respeto* when confronted with a discriminatory environment may pose a psychic predicament for Mexican Americans seeking compliance with cultural demands. Minorities, more so than the white population, may be exposed to higher levels of stress due to their social conditions of oppression; and they may have fewer tangible resources to cope with the stresses of racial discrimination and blocked opportunity (Williams and Williams-Morris, 2000). Latinos and African Americans in particular have higher levels of stress—as measured by global stress measures—than Whites (Magai *et al.*, 2003; Rodriguez-Calcagno and Brewer, 2005). High levels of stress in these groups are associated with poor mental and physical health status (Finch *et al.*, 2001; Harrell *et al.*, 2003).

Researchers as early as Freud (1961) explored the implications of emotional inhibition for psychological illness. More recent research foci explore emotion regulation for its physiological impact—particularly the psychic stress that can compromise vascular health (Butler *et al.*, 2009; Ostir *et al.*, 2006) and the immune system (Pert *et al.*, 1998). Pert (op. cit.) argued that "emotional expression generates balance in the neuropeptide-receptor network" that is key to the immunological system (p. 30). While the relationship of emotional experience to causes and treatment of illness has not been adequately researched in mainstream medicine, research from allied fields suggests the strength of this relationship in the form of a "psychosomatic network comprising biochemical substrates of emotion" (Pert, op. cit., p. 31). The authors suggest that medical interventions should encourage self-assertion and self-expression in persons suffering from disease, as a way to promote healing. Self-assertion and self-expression should be viewed for their potential conflict with traditional Latino concepts such as collective perspectives and *personalismo*.

The connection between stress, anger, and disease among Mexican Americans has undergone limited scrutiny and empirical study, except to suggest that there is greater somatization of stress among some Latino groups (Varela *et al.*, 2007). Research has shown that acculturation and more interaction with American culture can predict significant medical and mental health consequences (Padilla and Borrero, 2006). Harrell *et al.* (2003) cite the "physiological arousal and negative health sequelae" (p. 243) that is produced with racism in the US. Perceived discrimination is cited by Finch *et al.* (2001), Kessler *et al.* (1999), and by Schultz *et al.* (2000) as affecting morbidity and mortality in Mexican Americans. Perceived powerlessness in some minority populations is also linked to specific negative health outcomes in work by Bade (1999).

Social Situations

The ability to maintain cooperative and harmonious relationships in social exchanges in light of oppressive and exploitative circumstances encountered by Latinos in the US can be facilitated by having a "place" to hold the anger and frustration. *Coraje* is an affective state characterized varyingly as feelings of frustration and powerlessness (Bade, 1999); as an extreme emotional state (Caban and Walker, 2006); as anger resulting from betrayal (Loewe and Freeman, 2000); and as intense anger (Coronado *et al.*, 2004). *Coraje* may then be thought of as a culturally relevant "relief valve" which allows the person to feel anger, yet not express the anger openly. It has been loosely translated in a number of Spanish and Latin American Indian dialects as excessive anger (*enojo*), ire (*colerina* and *ira*) and as emotion so intense as to cause the "blood to boil" ("*me hierve la sangre*") (Villasenor-Bayardo, 2003–04, p. 8). In common parlance in some parts of Mexico, a person who has a reputation for being angry very often is referred to as "*el corajud*," or the angry one.

Such strong emotional states are believed to lead to "susceptibility to illness or to actual physiological dysfunction" (Suarez, 2000, p. 201). The emotional imbalance is viewed by some as a cause of excessive production of *bilis* (or bile) in the body which causes imbalances in physiological systems (Villasenor-Bayardo, 2003–2004). *Coraje* has been specifically named by subjects in numerous studies as a perceived contributor to miscarriage (Castaneda *et al.*, 2003); digestive ailments (Villasenor-Bayardo, 2003–2004); and diabetes (Coronado *et al.*, 2004; Loewe and Freeman, 2000; Lopez-Amador and Ocampo-Barrio, 2007; Mullenax, 2004; Weller *et al.*, 1999).

Diabetes

The prevalence of diabetes among Mexican Americans constitutes a compelling illustration of one health condition where the Mexican dual health perspective can be seen. We are compelled to explore this, given the current alarming rates of diabetes, and the possibility that, for some, *coraje* may be looked to as one cause of the illness. Latinos are at a disproportionately high risk for type 2 diabetes, also known as non-insulin dependent diabetes mellitus, compared with non-Hispanic Whites (Caruli *et al.*, 2005; Coronado *et al.*, 2004). Estimates are that Latinos over 50 years of age in the United States have twice the rate of diabetes diagnoses as Whites (National Diabetes Information Clearinghouse, 2005). Perhaps more significantly, Latinos are twice as likely to suffer serious complications from diabetes, such as diabetic retinopathy, than are non-Hispanic Whites (Factline, 2006; Haan *et al.*, 2003); and they are more likely to be hospitalized for uncontrolled diabetes and its complications (Laditka and Laditka, 2006).

The main causes of diabetes cited in the medical literature are a genetic predisposition to the disease, which Latinos may inherit from their native Indian ancestry, and a diet high in sugar and fat resulting in high glucose and insulin concentrations (Stern and Haffner, 1992). The dual health perspective employed by many Latinos in America suggest there may be divergent perspectives of the causes of diabetes between Latinos and formal Western medical experts. One study of Latino patients with Type 2 diabetes (Loewe and Freeman, 2000) attributed the onset of diabetes to a sudden crisis or trigger, including emotional trauma caused by various crises and "anger (*coraje*) resulting from an episode of betrayal and domestic violence" (p. 387). In studies by both Cherrington *et al.* (2006) and Coronado *et al.* (2004), a stressful emotional state was believed by subjects to cause extreme changes in the blood sugar levels resulting in the onset of diabetes. Weller *et al.* (1999) explored 4 Latino groups in 3 countries (2 sites in US Latino communities, and 1 group each in Mexico and Guatemala) but found consistent belief in emotional causes of diabetes in only the Mexican sample.

Emerging Interpretation of Coraje

In one recent study, 71 Mexican American, bilingual, professional women were asked to translate *coraje* into their own words (Lopez, 2012; unpublished raw data). The responses were many variations of the words "anger" (n = 29), "rage" (n = 23) and "frustration" (n = 15). Elaborations on "anger" and "rage" included upset, stifling anger, mad, serious anger, fury, and pissed off. After "anger" and "rage", the third most noted translation of *"coraje"* included the term "frustration." Others added additional words to define the concept including: stress, disappointment, resentment, annoyed, insult, injustice, and unexpressed anger. Social situations identified by the sample (injustice, disrespect, discrimination) were foremost for at least 50 percent of the subjects. Though given the opportunity to do so, none of the subjects noted non-personal objects or situations (such as a flat tire or a bounced check) as situations creating *coraje*. Instead, perceived imbalances in human interactions and presumed violations of the Latino cultural traits of *respeto* and *simpatía* were most mentioned as causing feelings of *coraje*. Responses to the statements about the relationship between *coraje* and health provided an interesting indication of knowledge and misperceptions about the role of strong emotions as a contributing factor to physical illness. While there was general agreement that *coraje* could manifest in health consequences (e.g. high blood pressure, headaches, and general illness), notably, a significant percentage of the respondents (who were all college-educated women) stated they were "not sure" that *coraje* could contribute to the onset of diabetes. This bears implications for the help-seeking behaviors of Mexican Americans who may attribute actual physical illness to social and interpersonal conflict as defined by the Latino value system.

Summary

The formal and indigenous resources available to contemporary Mexican American communities may be diverse—or may be limited. Language barriers, generational distinctions, socio-environmental stressors, isolation from country of origin, and elapsed time since emigration to the US will all contribute to the use of available institutional services versus reliance on home remedies and complementary community resources. These factors also contribute to the very nature of the individual's spiritual and personal belief systems that form the basis for their perceptions of what constitutes illness and wellness. This very broad range of health and illness contexts suggests numerous needs and outcomes as the Mexican American community seeks relief in culturally sanctioned sources and in acculturally learned sources.

Future Directions and Challenges

The use of traditional belief systems and the expression of Latino-centric values and concepts as coping mechanisms may be only one resource among Latino Americans who may incorporate traditional indigenous beliefs into their help-seeking behavior. Practitioners, researchers, and policymakers, however, are challenged to make no assumptions about these practices. Rather, it should be only one factor to be considered when approaching the needs of Latino communities. Successfully engaging the Latino consumer with knowledge of, and sensitivity to traditional practices may serve as a starting point toward a productive relationship with those seeking help. The holistic approach must be employed when addressing community needs, as well as the needs within our multi-generational family systems who may share only remnants of traditional belief systems—or who may have no affinity for traditional practices. So too should practitioners, researchers, and policymakers accept the potential paradigm shift that moves us away from "blaming the victims" in our communities for their health care practices. The looming challenge is to hold accountable those social systems that increasing studies show to exacerbate illness in our communities that confront discrimination and inequity. Advocating for recognition of these societal dynamics is, indeed, a challenge for all who work with Latino communities.

Policy Implications

The implications for cross-cultural health care, education, and pluralistic inclusion of alternative belief systems such as folk medicine and diverse Latino health perspectives are many. Recognition of the socioeconomic conditions faced by Latinos in the US can set the foundation for recognizing potential levels of stress and need for services in culturally diverse communities. While some suggest that the use of folk nomenclature and belief systems is exaggerated for ethnic communities and has been diluted over generations, there appears to be a continuing awareness that these additional health and illness nosologies persist even in Mexican American multi-generational, professional, and educated communities. Practitioners are encouraged to eschew narrow health care paradigms that are not inclusive of diverse patient and provider explanatory models of illness. Given the increasing diversity and health care needs of our ethnic enclaves, we can stress the inadequacy of narrow constructs that exclude indigenous and culturally specific health belief systems that may persist among immigrant populations. From policy and research perspectives, there is an exigency to further explore the impact of social class and conditions on health and illness outcomes. Given immigration, repatriation, and underlying economic dynamics that particularly affect Latino communities, it is insufficient to rely on static policies that have not kept pace with the changing face of Latinos in the US. Research that explores the acculturative loss of traditional resources is an imperative if we are to truly gauge the full extent of resources available to our communities. Other quality of life indicators, such as strong family supports and religious supports may also contribute to ameliorating the negative aspects of life in impoverished communities. The broader perspective of linking social class, economic status, perceived power, and health outcomes among our society's sub groups may yield important conclusions for circumspect health policies that can impact both the physical and social conditions that foster disease, and may help us to better understand the persistence of indigenous health care systems in our communities today. Increased research in the area of health promotion, through the recognition of the roles of poverty and discrimination, such as posed by Ryan *et al.* (2006) and by De Vogli *et al.* (2007), would begin to broaden our discussion about why immigrant groups (including Latinos) tend to incur more illness the longer they reside in the US.

References

Abril, I.F. (1977). Mexican-American folk beliefs. *American Journal of Maternal and Child Nursing*, May–June, 168–173.

Alegria, D., Guerra, E., Martinez, C. and Meyer, G. (1977). *El hospital invisible*: A study of *curanderismo*. *Archives of General Psychiatry*, *34*(11), 1354–1357.

Antshel, K.M. (2002). Integrating culture as a means of improving treatment adherence in the Latino population. *Psychology, Health and Medicine*, 7, 435–449.

Appleby, G.A., Colon, E. and Hamilton, J. (2001). *Diversity, Oppression and Social Functioning*. Needham Heights, MA: Allyn and Bacon.

Applewhite, S.L. (1995, Nov.). *Curanderismo*: Demystifying the health beliefs and practices of elderly Mexican Americans. *Health and Social Work*, *20*(4), 247–253.

Bade, B.L. (1999). *Is there a Doctor in the Field? Underlying Conditions Affecting Access to Health Care for California Farmworkers and their Families*. University of California, Riverside: California Policy Research Center.

Baer, R.D. and Bustillo, M. (1993). *Susto* and *mal de ojo* among Florida farmworkers: Emic and etic perspectives. *Medical Anthropology Quarterly*, 7, 90–100.

Bateson, M. (1994). *Peripheral Visions: Learning Along the Way*. New York: Harper.

Belliard, J.C. and Ramirez-Johnson, J. (2005). Medical pluralism in the life of a Mexican immigrant woman. *Hispanic Journal of Behavioral Sciences*, *27*(3), 267–285.

Butler, E.A., Lee, T.L. and Gross, J.J. (2009). Does expressing your emotions raise or lower your blood pressure? The answer depends on cultural context. *Journal of Cross-Cultural Psychology*, 40(3), 510–517.

Caban, A. and Walker, E.A. (2006). Systematic review of research on culturally relevant issues for Hispanics with diabetes. *The Diabetes Educator*, 32(4), 584–595.

Caruli, L., Rondinella, S., Lombardini, S., Canedi, I., Loria, P. and Caruli, N. (2005). Review article: Diabetes, genetics and ethnicity. *Alimentary Pharmacology and Therapeutics*, 22, 16–19.

Castaneda, X., Billings, D.L. and Blanco, J. (2003). Abortion beliefs and practices among midwives (*parteras*) in a rural Mexican town. *Women and Health*, 37(2), 73–87.

Castillo, R.J. (1997). *Culture and Mental Illness. A Client-Centered Approach.* Pacific Grove, CA: Brooks/ Cole Pub.

Cherrington, A., Ayala, G.K., Sleath, B. and Corbie-Smith, G. (2006). Examining knowledge, attitudes and beliefs about depression among Latino adults with type-2 diabetes. *The Diabetes Educator*, 32(4), 603–613.

Chesney, A.P., Thompson, B.L., Guevara, A., Vela, A. and Schottstaedt, M.F. (1980). Mexican American folk medicine: Implications for the family physician. *Journal of Family Practice*, 11(4), 567–574.

Coronado, G., Thompson, B., Tejeda, S. and Godina, R. (2004). Attitudes and beliefs among Mexican Americans about type 2 diabetes. *Journal of Health Care for the Poor and Underserved*, 15, 576–588.

Cox, C.B. and Ephross, P.H. (1998). *Ethnicity and Social Work Practice.* New York: Oxford University Press.

Davidow, J. (1999). *Infusions of Healing.* New York: Fireside Press.

De Vogli, R., Ferrie, J.E., Chandola, T., Kivimski, M. and Marmot, G. (2007). Unfairness and health: Evidence from the Whitehall II study. *Journal of Epidemiology and Community Health*, 61, 513–518.

Factline (2006). Tracking Health in Underserved Communities. National Library of Medicine. Retrieved from: http://www.meharry.org/F1/

Falicov, C.J. (1998). *Latino Families in Therapy: A Guide to Multicultural Practice.* New York: Guilford Press.

Finch, B.K., Hummer, R.A., Kol, B. and Vega, W.A. (2001). The role of discrimination and acculturative stress in the physical health of Mexican-origin adults. *Hispanic Journal of Behavioral Science*, 23, 399–429.

Freud, S. (1961). *Civilization and its Discontents* (J. Strachey, trans.) New York: W.W. Norton.

Garza, M. (1998, June). Healing spirits. *Hispanic*, June, 7–11.

Giachello, A.L. (1994). Maternal/perinatal health. In C. Molina and M. Aguirra-Molina (Eds.) *Latino Health in the U.S.* Washington, DC: American Public Health Association, 135–187.

Gomez-Beloz, A. and Chavez, N. (2001). The *botanica* as a culturally appropriate health care option for Latinos. *Journal of Alternative and Complementary Medicine*, 7(5), 537–545.

Gonzalez-Lee, T. and Simon, H.J. (1990). *Interviewing the Latino patient: A Cross Cultural Perspective.* New Jersey: Prentice Hall.

Green, J.W. (1995). *Cultural Awareness in the Human Services.* Needham Heights, MA: Allyn and Bacon.

Guendelman, S. (1991). Health care users residing on the Mexican border: What factors determine choice of the U.S. or Mexican health system? *Medical Care*, 29(5), 419–427.

Haan, M., Mungas, M., Gonzalez, H., Ortiz, T., Acharya, A. and Jagust, W. (2003). Prevalence of dementia in older Latinos: The influence of Type 2 diabetes mellitus, stroke and genetic factors. *Journal of the American Geriatric Society*, 51, 169–177.

Harrell, J.P., Hall, S. and Taliaferro, J. (2003). Physiological responses to racism and discrimination: An assessment of the evidence. *American Journal of Public Health*, 93(2), 243–248.

Higginbotham, L., Trevino, F.M. and Ray, L.A. (1990). Utilization of *curanderos* by Mexican Americans: Prevalence and predictors. *American Journal of Public Health*, 80, 32–35.

Hunt, L.M. (1998). Moral reasoning and the meaning of cancer: Causal explanations of oncologists and patients in Southern Mexico. *Medical Anthropology Quarterly, New Series, Vol. 12*(3), 298–318.

Hunt, L.M. and Mattingly, C. (1998). Diverse rationalities and multiple realities in illness and healing. *Medical Anthropology Quarterly*, 12, 267–272.

Kessler, R.C., Mickelson, K.D. and Williams, D.R. (1999). The prevalence, distribution and mental health correlates of perceived discrimination in the United States. *Journal of Health and Social Behavior*, 40(3), 208–230.

Kiev, A. (1968). *Curanderismo: Mexican American Folk Psychiatry.* New York: The Free Press.

Kleinman, A. (1980). *Patients and Healers in the Context of Culture.* Berkeley: University of California Press.

Krajewski-Jaime, E.R. (1991, March–April). Folk healing among Mexican American families as a consideration in the delivery of child welfare and child health care services. *Child Welfare, 52*(2), 157–167.

Laditka, J. and Laditka, S. (2006). Race, ethnicity and hospitalization for six chronic ambulatory care sensitive conditions in the USA. *Ethnicity and Health, 11*, 247–263.

Levine, S. (1993). *Dolor y Alegria: Women and Social Change in Urban Mexico.* Madison, WI: University of Wisconsin Press.

Loewe, R. and Freeman, J. (2000). Interpreting diabetes mellitus: Differences between patient and provider models of disease and their implications for clinical practice. *Culture, Medicine and Psychiatry, 24*, 379–401.

Lopez, R.A. (2012). [The conceptualization of anger as *coraje*]. Unpublished raw data.

Lopez-Amador, K.H and Ocampo-Barrio, P. (2007). Creencias sobre su enfermedad, habitos de alimentaction, actividad fisica y tratamiento en un grupo de diabeticos Mexicanos. [Patient beliefs on their disease, eating habits, physical activity, and treatment in a group of Mexican subjects with diabetes] *Archivos en Medicina Familiar, 9*(2), 80–86.

Magai, C., Kerns, M.D., Gillespie, M. and Huang, B. (2003). Anger experience and anger inhibition in sub-populations of African-American and European American older adults and relationship to circulatory disease. *Journal of Health Psychology, 8*(4), 413–432.

Marín, G. and Marín, B.V. (1991). *Research with Hispanic Populations.* Newbury Park, CA: Sage.

Marín, G., Gamba, R.J. and Marín, B.V. (1992). Extreme response style and acquiescence among Hispanics: The role of acculturation and education. *Journal of Cross Cultural Psychology, 23*(4), 498–509.

Mezzich, J.E., Kleinman, A., Fabrega, H. and Parron, D.L. (Eds.) (1996). *Culture and Psychiatric Diagnosis.* Washington, DC: American Psychiatric Press.

Mueller, K.J., Patil, K. and Boilesen, E. (1998). The role of uninsurance and race in healthcare utilization by rural minorities. *Health Services Research, 33*, 597–601.

Mullenax, N.A. (2004). The "Latino disease:" A case study of diabetes in East Los Angeles. In Samuels and Associates. *The Social and Environmental Experiences of Diabetes: Implications for Diabetes Prevention, Management and Treatment Programs. A Series of Case Studies.* Woodland Hills: The California Endowment.

National Diabetes Information Clearinghouse. (2005). The diabetes epidemic among Hispanic and Latino Americans. Adapted from National Institute of Diabetes and Digestive and Kidney Diseases. National Diabetes Statistics fact sheet. Bethesda, MD: U.S. Department of Health and Human Services, National Institute of Health.

Niska, K. and Snyder, M. (1999). The meaning of family health among Mexican American first-time mothers and fathers. *Journal of Family Nursing, 5*, 218–233.

Oomen, J.S., Owen, L.J. and Suggs, L.S. (1999). Culture counts: Why current treatment models fail Hispanic women with type 2 diabetes. *The Diabetes Educator, 25*(2), 220–225.

Ostir, G.V., Markides, K.S. and Ottenbacher, K.I. (2006). Hypertension in older adults and the role of positive emotions. *Psychosomatic Medicine, 68*, 727–733

Padilla, A. and Borrero, N. (2006). The effects of acculturative stress on the Hispanic family. In P. Wong and L. Wong (Eds.) *Handbook of Multicultural Perspectives on Stress and Coping.* New York: Springer, 299–319.

Pert, C., Dreher, H. and Ruff, M. (1998). The psychosomatic network: Foundations of mind-body medicine. *Alternative Therapies, 4*, 30–41.

Price, S. and Elliot, B. (1993). Health experience by minority families. *Family Health Care, 1*, 6–8.

Ripley, G.D. (1986). Mexican-American folk remedies: Their place in health care. *Texas Medicine/Folk Medicine, 82*, 41–44.

Rivera, R. and Erlich, J. (1984). An assessment framework for organizing in emerging minority communities. In F. Cox, J. Erlich, J. Rothman and J. Tropman (Eds.) *Tactics and Techniques of Community Practice* (2nd Ed.). Itasca, IL: F.E. Peacock, 98–108.

Rodriguez-Calcagno, M. and Brewer, E.W. (2005). Job stress among Hispanic professionals. *Hispanic Journal of Behavioral Sciences, 27*(4), 504–516.

Ryan, A.M., Gee, G.C. and Laflamme, D.F. (2006). The association between self-reported discrimination, physical health and blood pressure. *Journal of Health Care for the Poor and Underserved, 17*, 115–132.

Schultz, A., Williams, D., Israel, B., Becker, A., Parker, E., James, S.A. and Jackson, J. (2000), Unfair treatment, neighborhood effects, and mental health in the Detroit metropolitan area. *Journal of Health and Social Behavior, 41*(3), 314–332.

Sherraden, M.S. and Barrera, M.E (1997). Culturally protective health practices: Everyday pregnancy care among Mexican immigrants. *Journal of Multicultural Social Work, 6*(1–2), 93–115.

Stern, M. and Haffner, S. (1992). Type II Diabetes among Mexican Americans: A public health challenge. In A. Furino (Ed.) *Health policy and the Hispanic.* Boulder, Colo: Westview Press, 57–76.

Suarez, Z. (2000). Hispanics and health care. In P. Cafferty and D. Engstrom (Eds.) *Hispanics in the United States: An Agenda for the Twenty First Century.* New Brunswick: Transaction Publishers, 195–237.

Telles, C. and Karno, M. (1994). *Latino Mental Health: Current Research and Policy Perspectives.* UCLA Neuropsychiatric Institute: Author.

Torres, E. (1983). *Traditional Mexican American Herbal Remedies.* Texas: Nieves Press.

Trotter, R.T. (2001). *Curanderismo*: A picture of Mexican American folk healing. *Journal of Alternative and Complementary Medicine, 7*(2), 129–131.

Trotter, R.T. and Chavira, J.A. (1997). *Curanderismo: Mexican American Folk Healing.* Georgia: University of Georgia Press.

Varela, R.E., Steele, R.C. and Benson, E.R. (2007). The contribution of ethnic minority status to adaptive style: A comparison of Mexican, Mexican American, and European American children. *Journal of Cross-cultural Psychology, 38*(1), 26–33.

Varela, R.E., Vernberg, E.M., Sanchez-Sosa, J.J., Riveros, A., Mitchell, M. and Mashunkashey, J. (2004). Anxiety reporting and culturally associated interpretation biases and cognitive schemas: A comparison of Mexican, Mexican American, and European American families. *Journal of Clinical Child and Adolescent Psychology, 33,* 237–247.

Vargas, L.A. and Koss-Chioino, J.D. (Eds.) (1992). *Working with Culture: Psychotherapeutic Interventions with Ethnic Minority Children and Adolescents.* San Francisco: Jossey-Bass.

Villasenor-Bayardo, S.J. (2003–2004). *Los sindromos culturales en America Latina. Revista Universidad de Guadalajara, Coleccion de Babel,* 30/invierno, pp. 1–25.

Weller, S.C., Baer, R.D., Pachter, L.M., Trotter, R.T., Glazer, M., Garcia de Alba Garcia, J.E. and Klein, R.E. (1999). Latino beliefs about diabetes. *Diabetes Care, 22* (5 May), 722–728.

Williams, D.R. and Williams-Morris, R. (2000). Racism and mental health: The African American experience. *Ethnicity and Health, 5*(3–4), 243–268.

Zambrana, R. (1995). *Understanding Latino Families: Scholarship, Policy and Practice.* Thousand Oaks, CA: Sage.

16

THE PSYCHOLOGY OF HEALTH

Physical Health and the Role of Culture and Behavior in Mexican Americans

John M. Ruiz, Heidi A. Hamann, James García, and Simon J. Craddock Lee

Introduction

Racial/ethnic minorities in the United States generally experience disproportionate burdens of illness and disease. Like non-Hispanic (NH) Blacks, Hispanics/Latinos experience a range of psychosocial and physical health disparities, including lower income and education, high rates of obesity and high rates of chronic diseases. Yet surprisingly, Latinos (including Mexican Americans) experience lower incidence of several leading causes of death, as well as lower all-cause mortality relative to NH Whites; this phenomenon is commonly referred to as the Hispanic/Latino mortality paradox. This chapter will review the available evidence concerning disease rates and health outcomes, while also presenting a discussion of cultural pathways which may moderate and mediate the observed findings.

Although the expressed focus of this book is to characterize the Mexican American experience, the associated physical health data for this population is in many instances, lacking. Hence, we will describe data on Latinos in general and specify Mexican Americans when data are available. Given striking demographic and health differences between US and foreign-born Latinos, including those of Mexican descent, we will refer to nativity status where possible.

Literature Review

Socio-Demographic Profile

Socio-demographic factors, including socioeconomic status (SES), are amongst the most robust psychosocial predictors of mental and physical health (Ruiz *et al.*, 2012). Latinos (including Mexican Americans) experience significant socioeconomic disparities relative to NH Whites, including substantial disparities in education, employment, wages, and individual-, childhood-, and household poverty (U.S. Department of Education, 2009; U.S. Department of Labor Statistics, 2013). The Latino SES profile appears similar to, and in many cases worse, than that of NH Blacks. Together these data suggest that Latino and Mexican American income is significantly skewed to the lower end of the economic spectrum and should constitute a significant risk factor for health.

Health Care

Health Insurance

Robust evidence supports the connection between health insurance coverage and objective health benefits, including lower disease incidence, early diagnosis, better disease management, lower morbidity, along with lower disease-specific and all-cause mortality (Ayanian *et al.*, 2000; Ng *et al.*, 2012). A recent longitudinal analysis of the Third National Health and Nutrition Examination Survey (NHANES III) data demonstrated that the uninsured were at 80 percent greater risk of mortality after adjusting for age and gender, and at 40 percent greater risk when accounting for 9 additional risk factors, including income, education, smoking, and race/ethnicity (Wilper *et al.*, 2009).

Consistent with their broader comparative SES profile, the percentage of uninsured Latinos in general (29.1%), and people of Mexican descent specifically (33%), is significantly greater than the general population (15.4%) and non-Hispanics (NH Whites: 11.1%; NH Blacks: 19.0%; Gonzalez-Barrera and Lopez, 2013). There is also a significant insurance coverage gap between native and foreign-born persons of Mexican descent living in the US (20% uninsured among persons of Mexican descent born in the US vs. 57 percent of those born outside the US; Gonzalez-Barrera and Lopez, 2013). Hence, there is considerable heterogeneity amongst Latinos in terms of insurance coverage, with the best case scenario suggesting a disparity similar in degree to NH Black–White differences.

Usual Source of Care and Access

Having a physician or usual source of health care is a critical gateway to maintaining health and managing disease (DeVoe *et al.*, 2003). Evidence also suggests that managed, continuous care lowers need for hospitalization and overall health care costs (Weiss and Blustein, 1996). Latinos in general (and particularly those of Mexican descent) are less likely to have a usual source of care compared to non-Hispanics. In 2006–7 approximately 34.3% of Latinos and 39% of persons of Mexican descent did not have a usual source of care, a rate approximately twice that of NH Blacks (18.9%) and NH Whites (15.2%). Although SES is a factor in health care access, it does not account for the entirety of these observed differences. Notably, these disparities extend to children (Flores and Tomany-Korman, 2008), adolescents (Lau *et al.*, 2012), and the elderly (Chen *et al.*, 2005). Among adults these disparities are associated with lower rates of preventive care services such as blood pressure checks, mammograms, colo-rectal screenings, and smoking cessation (Rodriguez *et al.*, 2009).

Latinos with a usual source of care generally report lower satisfaction with the quality of their physician interactions and lower overall health care satisfaction relative to non-Hispanics (Rodriguez *et al.*, 2009; Saha *et al.*, 2003). Lower overall satisfaction is further linked to reluctance to engage with the health care setting and lower adherence (Yang *et al.*, 2009). To address these discrepancies in patient–health care alliances, there is growing use of community health care workers (*promotores de salud*). *Promotores* are community members who function as liaisons between the community and the health care providers (American Public Health Association, 2013) and have been used successfully in community outreach, patient education, and health program enhancement, particularly among Latinos (Ramirez *et al.*, 2013; Raphael *et al.*, 2013). Moreover, the success of the promotores model has led to its endorsement by a range of health care suppliers, as well as the US Department of Health and Human Services (2011).

Finally, Latinos will often turn to spiritual health as both a complement and/or alternative to US system-based medical care (Ruiz and Steffen, 2011). For example, a national telephone survey of 3,728 Latinos found that 69% considered spiritual healing as very important to physical health, with 60% engaging in prayer, 49% having asked others to pray for them, and 6% having consulted a *curandero* or spiritual healer (Reyes-Ortiz *et al.*, 2009). Together, the data suggest that although Latinos are generally not as engaged with traditional care as non-Hispanic patients, they value and pursue opportunities to receive care including through culturally specific channels.

Health Behaviors

Smoking

Smoking is the most modifiable risk factor for disease, and accounts for approximately 440,000 deaths (one of every five deaths) in the United States annually (CDC, 2013). Hispanic middle-school-age students are nearly twice as likely to smoke compared to NH Blacks and Whites (CDC, 2012a), but high school Latino adolescents are less likely than NH Whites. In addition to traditional predictors of youth smoking, acculturation and proximity to tobacco retailers are associated with increased risk (West *et al.*, 2010). Although peer pressure appears to be a universal predictor, positive social expectations of smoking from peers appear to be especially salient for Latino-, including Mexican American youth (Wilkinson *et al.*, 2008).

The smoking prevalence rate amongst Latino adults is 12.9 percent, a rate that is declining and is far below the national average of 19 percent and rates of other minority groups (Blacks: 19.4%; NH American Indian/Alaska Natives: 31.5%; Go *et al.*, 2013). Amongst Latinos, individuals of Puerto Rican descent have the highest smoking rates, followed by Cubans, Mexicans, and persons from Central or South America (Daviglus *et al.*, 2012). Nationally, the prevalence of smoking is higher amongst men compared to women, 21.6% vs. 16.5% respectively. These gender differences are more pronounced amongst Latinos (men: 17.0% vs. women: 8.6%).

Amongst those classified as smokers, Latinos tend to consume fewer cigarettes per day relative to non-Hispanics (Substance Abuse and Mental Health Services Administration [SAMHSA], 2011). Relative to non-Hispanics, Latinos also smoke fewer days per month and consume fewer cigarettes per day. Moreover, Latinos as a group may absorb less nicotine from a given cigarette compared to non-Hispanics. A study of 2,136 smokers published in the *Journal of the American Medical Association*, documented that when number of cigarettes is held constant, levels of continine (a nicotine biomarker reflecting consumption rate) are lower for Latinos relative to non-Hispanics (Caraballo *et al.*, 1998). This difference may reflect variations in a variety of factors, including differences in consumption rate or metabolism of nicotine.

Overall, Latinos are less likely to smoke than other racial/ethnic groups, and among smokers they smoke fewer cigarettes and absorb lower levels of nicotine. There is also considerable within-group variation by descent and gender. The lower smoking rates amongst Latinos may have important health benefits which we will revisit later in this chapter.

Obesity

US incidence of obesity has reached epidemic proportions, with staggering financial and human health implications. Such findings have led the National Heart, Lung, and Blood Institute (NHLBI) to designate obesity prevention research as a "top-tier" (i.e. highest level) priority (NHLBI, 2001). More than two thirds of US adults are considered overweight, with one third or 72 million adults classified as obese (body mass index > 30.0; Flegal *et* al., 2012). Both women and men of Mexican descent have rates of obesity (women: 45.8%; men: 36.5%) that are lower than NH Blacks (women: 54.4%; men; 38.7%) but higher than NH Whites (women: 32.9%; men: 34.7%).

Like adult obesity, rates among children are steadily increasing to a current prevalence rate of over 11% (National Center for Health Statistics, 2013). Latino boys of Mexican descent have higher rates of obesity (19.1%) compared to both NH White (8.8%) and NH Black (15.7%) boys. In contrast, Latina girls of Mexican descent have obesity rates (9.9%) comparable to NH White girls (9.2%) but lower than NH Black girls (14.2%).

A nuanced picture is emerging with respect to acculturation and obesity amongst Latinos (including Mexican Americans; Caprio *et al.*, 2008). First, since lower parental acculturation is associated with valuing heavier infants, child feeding practices may mediate obesity outcomes (Contento *et al.*, 2003). Second, as children get older, their own level of acculturation strongly influences their weight through diet and behavior change (Allen *et al.*, 2007). More acculturated Latino and Mexican American children and adolescents exercise less and consume fewer fruits and vegetables, more soda, and more between-meal snacks throughout the day. Third, higher levels of acculturation continue to influence greater obesity risk in adulthood (Kaplan *et al.*, 2004).

Physical Fitness

Physical activity is an important moderator of obesity, cardiovascular disease, diabetes and metabolic conditions, some forms of cancer, mobility and healthy aging, health-related quality of life, and all-cause mortality (U.S. Department of Health and Human Services, 2013). Despite their relatively higher rates of obesity, Mexican American youth tend to be more physically active and are more likely to achieve weekly physical activity recommendation goals than NH White youths (Nyberg *et al.*, 2011). Like all youth, Latino physical activity levels decrease with age, with acculturation as a key moderator of decreased physical activity among Latino youth. In particular, higher acculturation is associated with an increase in sedentary activities such as watching TV, working on computers, etc. The Robert Wood Johnson Foundation (Nyberg *et al.*, 2011) notes that aspects of the built environment, such as availability and quality of parks and recreational spaces are a further barrier, particularly among lower SES Latinos.

Amongst adults, NH Blacks and Latinos generally engage in less leisure-time physical activity such as running, walking, attending a gym, etc. relative to NH Whites (Marshall *et al.*, 2007). However, when physical activity is conceptualized more broadly as a function of daily activity and assessed objectively with activity monitors such as accelerometers, Latinos are observed to be more active than other groups (Ham and Ainsworth, 2010). Such findings may help to explain a recent observation in the National Health and Nutrition Examination Survey (NHANES) that Latinos (including those of Mexican descent) have higher VO_2 max levels (i.e. gold-standard measure of cardiovascular and aerobic fitness) relative to non–Hispanics (Ceaser *et al.*, 2013).

Alcohol Use

Excessive alcohol use is associated with a broad range of physical, mental, and social health challenges. The Center for Disease Control and Prevention (2012a) estimates that by age 13, over 25 percent of Latino youth have tried alcohol compared to the national average of 20.5 percent. Amongst 9th to 12th grade students (14–18 years) Latinos' alcohol use is similar to NH Whites and significantly greater than NH Blacks. Among Latinos, Spanish and Cuban youth are most likely to use alcohol, with Mexican adolescents amongst the lowest at 15.7 percent (SAMHSA, 2011). Higher acculturation, particularly the loss of *familismo*, is predictive of increased risk for alcohol use (Blanco *et al.*, 2013; Gil *et al.*, 2000).

A mixed picture of alcohol use patterns emerge for Latino adults. Compared to NH Whites, Latinos have lower prevalence of use and lower rates of dependence, yet higher binge drinking rates (National Institute on Alcohol Abuse and Alcoholism, 2010). Like adolescents, higher acculturation is associated with greater risk of dependence (Ramisetty-Mikler *et al.*, 2010). However the country of origin differences observed among adolescents reverse in adults, such that persons of Cuban descent have the lowest rates, whereas those of Mexican and Puerto Rican descent have the highest (Ramisetty-Mikler, op. cit.). Such differences are critical to identifying intervention points for adolescents and adults.

Summary

In summary, Latinos including those of Mexican descent are the largest racial/ethnic minority group in the US, making them substantial consumers of health care. Latinos as a group are characterized by a range of socio-demographic disparities which generally predict health and disease risk. Despite relatively better rankings on a few key health behaviors such as smoking and alcohol use, the overall profile is one of greater health risk relative to NH Whites.

Physical Health Status

Self-reported Health

Self-reported health is an established predictor of mortality in healthy and chronic illness populations (Nielsen *et al.*, 2008; Phillips *et al.*, 2010). In light of their socioeconomic disparities, including poor access to quality- and continuous health care, Latinos as a group report lower self-reported health relative to NH Whites—a disparity that remains after accounting for SES—and is consistent across immigration status (Hayes *et al.*, 2011; Luckett *et al.*, 2011).

Comparative Mortality

Despite a risk profile similar to NH Blacks, Latinos live longer than NH Whites, an epidemiological phenomenon commonly referred to as the Hispanic or Latino mortality paradox (Ruiz and Steffen, 2011). The paradoxical nature of this relationship evoked healthy skepticism amongst researchers with a host of explanatory hypotheses. An overarching concern was the accuracy of data—which relied heavily on census counts and accurate reporting of ethnicity on death certificates to estimate death rates (cf., Smith and Bradshaw, 2006). However, several studies have now documented that the effects of ethnic misclassification on death certificates are negligible and do not alter the observed effect (Arias *et al.*, 2010). Additional explanatory hypotheses including, (1) the possibility that Latinos participated in the census but returned to their country of origin before death leading to statistical immortality (i.e. the Salmon bias hypothesis) and, (2) the possibility that only the healthiest Latinos emigrated to the US (e.g. the healthy migrant hypothesis) have been debunked by analysis of nationally representative data (Abraido-Lanza *et al.*, 1999). Finally, a meta-analysis of the 58 prospective studies involving more than 4.6 million participants found an overall 17.5 percent Latino mortality advantage relative to non-Hispanics (Ruiz *et al.*, 2013), an effect similar to the 20 percent Latino advantage determined using the estimation methodology (Arias *et al.*, 2010). Together, these findings leave little doubt regarding the validity of the effect.

Of particular interest within the Latino paradox is that Latino infant mortality rates (5.27 deaths per 1,000 live births) are lower than the national average (6.05), with estimates suggesting a rate similar to or less than that of NHs Whites (5.05) and far lower than NH Blacks (11.42; Hoyert and Xu, 2012). These differences in survival are most pronounced during the neo-natal period (28 days to 1 year) and are not explained by weight or gestational age.

Notably, there are significant variations in longevity and the strength of the Latino Paradox amongst Latinos. In general, persons of Mexican and Central or South American descent live significantly longer than other Latinos (Hoyert and Xu, 2012). In contrast, those of Puerto Rican descent have the highest early all-cause and disease-specific mortality rates (Hajat *et al.*, 2000; Hoyert and Xu, 2012). The reasons for such variance are unclear but may reflect important cultural and/or behavioral factors. For example, data from the Hispanic Community Health Study/Study of Latinos (HCHS/SOL; Daviglus *et al.*, 2012) show that smoking rates amongst Latinos are highest for those of Puerto Rican descent. Robust data also demonstrates that foreign-born Latinos live longer than US born Latinos, both within and outside the US (Abraido-Lanza *et al.*, 1999; Borrell and Lancet, 2012).

In summary, these findings, derived from a variety of methodologies, demonstrate significant all-cause, disease-specific, and infant survival advantages among Latinos relative to non-Hispanics and further, that foreign-born Latinos have a greater advantage than US born Latinos. The range of ages and conditions across which these observations are made suggest that associated mechanisms are likely basic and not disease- or condition-specific.

Specific Diseases and Conditions

The mortality findings have given way to discussions of a broader health paradox for Latinos (Gallo *et al.*, 2009). Here we review current evidence for the major causes of death and health disability, with an emphasis on comparative statistics to discern advantages and disparities.

Cardiovascular Diseases

Cardiovascular diseases (CVD) are a constellation of conditions which occur primarily in adulthood and generally reflect compromised blood flow. An estimated 83.6 million American adults have one or more types of CVD including 77.9 million cases of hypertension (i.e. high blood pressure) and 15.4 million cases of coronary heart disease (CHD; Go *et al.*, 2013). A robust list of risk factors which predict CVDs, particularly CHD, are: (1) non-modifiable factors (e.g. age, sex, and family history), (2) socio-demographic factors, (3) behavioral factors (smoking, diet, and physical activity), and (4) medical factors/comorbidities, including cholesterol, hypertension, and diabetes.

The Hispanic Community Health Study/Study of Latinos (HCHS/SOL; Sorlie *et al.*, 2010), a multisite, prospective population-based study of 16,000 Latinos, is unique in that it aims to stratify risk by Hispanic/Latino backgrounds. Cross-sectional data from HCHS/SOL has demonstrated high rates of medical CVD risk factors among Latinos; 80 percent of men and 71 percent of women had at least one major risk, and Puerto Ricans had the highest levels of risk (Daviglus *et al.*, 2012). Additional population-level evidence demonstrates that although Latinos tend to have acceptable levels of low density lipoproteins (i.e. LDL, "bad cholesterol") they have substantially lower levels of high density lipoproteins (i.e. HDL, "good cholesterol").

Despite their CVD risk factor profile, Latinos have lower rates of most CVDs (Go *et al.*, 2013). For example, the American Heart Association reports the prevalence of CVDs for men in the US in 2010 was 44.4% for NH Blacks, 36.6% for NH Whites, and 33.4% for Mexican Americans (Go *et al.*, 2013). Similar differences were observed for women, with the CVD rates highest for NH Black women (48.9%) and lowest for Mexican American women (30.7%). Latinos are also less likely to receive secondary prevention treatments such as statins (Kim *et al.*, 2012) and are less likely to undergo tertiary interventions such as coronary artery bypass grafting (CABG) surgery (Parikh *et al.*, 2009).

Mexican Americans experience higher rates of undiagnosed CVD, and amongst those diagnosed, they are significantly less likely to be receiving adequate treatment relative to non-Hispanics (Go *et al.*, 2013). Despite these disparities, the incidence of cardiovascular events such as myocardial infarction (MI, i.e. heart attack) is either similar to or lower, relative to NH Whites. Moreover, a meta-analysis of 11 prospective studies of persons diagnosed with CHD published between 1990 and 2010 determined the Latino mortality odds ratio to be 0.75, or a 25 percent lower compared to non-Hispanics (Ruiz *et al.*, 2013).

The discrepancy between CVD risk and outcomes is perplexing and in need of further research. One possibility is that the traditional risk factors for CVD are not valid for predicting disease in Latinos. For example, although HDL and diabetes are well-validated risk markers, neither is very predictive of CVD outcomes in Latinos (Willey *et al.*, 2011). It is also possible that cultural factors may provide resilience to offset risks and buffer against disease progression; such cultural moderators of disease and mortality risk are further described later in this chapter.

Cancer

Despite steady declines in mortality over the past decade, cancer remains the second leading cause of death nationally, accounting for over 580,000 deaths annually (American Cancer Society, 2013). Non-Hispanic Blacks have the highest likelihood of developing and dying from cancer compared to all other racial/ethnic groups. In contrast, Latinos have lower cancer incidence and mortality compared to NH Whites, although there are significant disparities for some types of cancer. For example, Latinas are 30 percent less likely to develop breast cancer, but 60 percent more likely to develop cervical cancer, and more than twice as likely to develop stomach cancer compared to NH White women (CDC, 2013). Latino men are 20 percent less likely to be diagnosed with prostate cancer but 70 percent more likely to have stomach cancer. Additionally, Latino men and women are at twice the risk of developing cancer of the liver compared to NH Whites.

The American Cancer Society (2013) attributes much of the racial/ethnic cancer disparities to health care access issues. For example, stomach, cervical, and liver cancers are all linked to infections or viral pathogens, which may suggest a common immune-mediated pathway contributing to these disparities. Although vaccines are available for cervical cancer, Latino utilization rates are markedly low (Jemal *et al.*, 2013). In addition, Latinos are often diagnosed at more advanced disease stages (Ramirez *et al.*, 2013), are more likely to experience treatment initiation delays following an abnormal screening (Smith *et al.*, 2013), and are less likely to received adjuvant treatments (e.g. radiation) following surgical intervention relative to NH Whites (Bickell *et al.*, 2006).

Nativity is emerging as an important moderator of cancer risk and outcomes. Several studies have now found that foreign-born Latinos experience lower incidence of cancers, particularly in women at younger ages (Horn-Ross *et al.*, 2012). Amongst those with cancer, foreign-born Latinos tend to get diagnosed at later stages (Montealegre *et al.*, 2013). However, in the context of late stage cancers, foreign-born Latinos have a survival advantage relative to US born Latinos and NH Whites (Montealegre *et al.*, 2013; Patel *et al.*, 2013). There is some evidence that acculturation increases screening uptake, which may increase incidence figures. However, the reasons for the advantage remain speculative (Ruiz and Steffen, 2011).

Unfortunately, data on Latinos and cancer risk remain limited in many respects. First, The National Cancer Institute's Surveillance, Epidemiology, and End Results (SEER) database, from which population-level cancer epidemiology statistics are derived, has only reported Latino rates since 1992 and constricts understanding of historical trends (American Cancer Society, 2013). In addition, certain states were not added to the registries until 1997, which further impacts trend analysis. Second, people in the SEER database are coded as Latino, based on medical record data and Spanish surnames, both of which have significant flaws, contributing to under-representation. Third, available data is largely aggregated at the umbrella-term level which potentially masks important distinctions in this heterogeneous population.

Diabetes

Diabetes is a chronic illness characterized by excessive blood glucose (sugar; hyperglycemia) due to chronic insulin deficiency. Failure to control diabetes can lead to significant health risks including loss of vision, compromised blood flow, neuropathy, end stage renal disease, heart disease, stroke, and death (CDC, 2011). The most common types of diabetes are Type 1 (insulin-dependent) or "juvenile onset"—reflecting its common diagnosis in childhood, although it can be diagnosed at any age—and Type 2 (non insulin-dependent) which accounts for 95 percent of all diabetes cases and is strongly tied to family history and lifestyle factors.

Amongst Latinos, the risk of Type 1 and 2 diabetes varies as a function of age. For example, data from the SEARCH for Diabetes in Youth Study documented that below the age of 10 years, the vast majority of Latino cases were of Type 1 diabetes. However, Type 2 diabetes was more common among youth ages 15–19 years, an effect driven by females (Lawrence *et al.*, 2009). Latino and Mexican American children and adolescents from lower SES families are at particularly high risk, with evidence implicating reduced physical activity due to environmental barriers coupled with higher consumption of sodas and saturated fats (Bortsov *et al.*, 2011). In addition to behavioral mediators, emerging hypotheses are exploring biological/ genetic vulnerabilities among Latinos, including among Mexican American children and adolescents (cf. Fowler *et al.*, 2013).

Amongst adults, prevalence rates of diabetes rise sharply with age and vary significantly by race and ethnicity. For example, the CDC reports the prevalence of diabetes in 2011 was 2.6% for the 20–44 years age group, 11.7% for those 45–64 years, and 18.9% for those above 65 years (CDC, 2012b). With respect to groups, NH Whites had the lowest prevalence rates at 7.1%, followed by Asian Americans at 8.4%, Latinos at 11.8%, NH Blacks at 12.6%, and American Indian and Alaska Natives at 16.1%. These disparities reflect long-standing historical trends (Schiller *et al.*, 2012). Persons of Mexican and Puerto Rican descent experience diabetes prevalence rates that are 1.9 to 3 times that of NH Whites and Cubans (Harris *et al.*, 1998) with greater downstream risk of diabetes-related mortality (Kochanek *et al.*, 2012).

Emerging data suggest several important caveats to the Latino-diabetes picture. First, Type 1 diabetes accounts for the majority of cases under age 10; Type 2 the majority after age 10. Second, Type 2 diabetes appears to strike Latinos at younger ages than non-Hispanics (CDC, 2012b). Third, Latinos are more likely to be diagnosed compared to NH Whites but less likely to receive medical screenings such as foot or eye examinations (Hertz *et al.*, 2006). Fourth, Latinos as a group are more likely to experience clinical consequences of diabetes and are 1.5 times as likely to die of the disease compared to NH Whites (Kochanek *et al.*, 2012). Differences in care may contribute to these observed disparities.

Communicable Diseases

Latinos suffer disproportionate rates of communicable diseases relative to non-Hispanics. For example, Latinos account for approximately 75 percent of newly diagnosed tuberculosis cases (Winston *et al.*, 2010) and are at twice the risk of Hepatitis A, gonorrhea, and syphilis infection compared to NH Whites (CDC, 2013; Hoyert and Xu, 2012). With respect to HIV/AIDS, Latinos accounted for approximately 20 percent of new infections despite accounting for less than 16 percent of the US population in 2009 (CDC, 2012c). Comparatively, Latinos are 3 times as likely to be diagnosed with HIV/AIDS relative to NH Whites. Although Latino men are significantly more likely to be diagnosed with HIV than women, Latina women are 5 times more likely to be diagnosed with HIV compared to NH White women. The AIDS-related mortality rates for Latino/Latina men and women are approximately 2.5 and 3.6 times the rate respectively, of NH White men and women.

Despite Latinos' lower SES profile, their infant/childhood immunization rates are comparable to those of NH Whites (CDC, 2012c). Amongst older adults, Latinos are 20 percent less likely to get the annual influenza (flu) vaccination and 40 percent less likely to be immunized for pneumonia (National Center for Health Statistics, 2013).

Future Directions and Challenges

Several risk and resilience factors may influence the observed differences in disease incidence and outcomes, including potential biological (e.g. genetics, immune functioning), behavioral (e.g. diet, smoking), psychological (e.g. stress, positivity), social (e.g. cultural, discrimination), and socio-demographic (e.g. SES, health care access) differences. For example, emerging evidence demonstrates significant heterogeneity in smoking-related lung cancer risk, with Latinos experiencing the lowest rates of risk among persons who smoke less than 30 cigarettes per day (Haiman *et al.*, 2006). This effect may be due to several factors: behavioral differences in the amount of cigarettes smoked, the depth of inhalation, or biological differences in immune response or cellular resistance to the damaging properties of smoking exposure.

Cultural factors are often posited as important resilience mechanisms explaining paradoxical health findings among Latinos (Gallo *et al.*, 2009). Collectivistic coping as well as specific values such as *familismo* (importance of maintaining close family [broadly defined] relationships), *personalismo* (valuing and building warm, affiliative social ties), and *simpatía* (valuing the expression of kindness and maintaining interpersonal harmony) may engender social capital and social support, which are robust moderators of health outcomes (Holt-Lunstad *et al.*, 2010). Indirect evidence generally supports this hypothesis. Latinos (particularly foreign-born) living in lower SES, low-acculturated ethnic enclaves or "barrios" experience a multitude of health benefits, including greater infant survival (Shaw and Pickett, 2013), lower incidence of breast and other cancers (Eschbach *et al.*, 2005), greater likelihood of surviving an illness (Patel *et al.*, 2013), and lower all-cause mortality (Eschbach *et al.*, 2004). Several of these studies demonstrate the moderating effect of ethnic density by contrasting with a low SES, low Latino density neighborhood. In addition, much of this evidence is derived from Mexican American populations (Eschbach *et al.*, 2004), with some demonstrating a transitive advantage to non-Hispanics (cf., Shaw and Pickett, 2013).

Conceptually, the observed health outcome may reflect advantages at different time points in the disease course. For example, Latinos may be more resistant to illness, may experience slower disease progression, and/or may experience a survival and recovery advantage. Importantly, moderating and mediating mechanisms may differ at each time point. For example, immunological factors may be important moderators of smoking-related lung cancer risk whereas social support may be a more critical moderator of recovery following lung cancer treatment. Further study is needed to explicate these relationships to improve targeting of interventions.

Policy Implications

Given the size and growth of the Latino population in the US, understanding their health is a national priority. Not surprisingly, Latinos and Mexican Americans have considerable sociodemographic risks including low incomes, education, access to healthcare, and high rates of obesity and undiagnosed diseases. Yet surprisingly, Latinos experience lower infant mortality, adult all-cause mortality, and lower incidence of heart disease and many cancers compared to their NH White counterparts. These positive outcomes should not belie risks and vulnerabilities within this population, and efforts should continue to be made to achieve optimal health. However, these paradoxical findings may serve as a unique opportunity to identify sources of resilience leading to the development of interventions for all.

References

Abraido-Lanza, A. F., Dohrenwend, B. P., Ng-Mak, D. S., and Turner, J. B. (1999). The Latino mortality paradox: A test of the "salmon bias" and healthy migrant hypotheses. *American Journal of Public Health*, *89*, 1543–1548.

Allen, M. L., Elliott, M. N., Morales, L. S., Diamant, A. L., Hambarsoomian, K., and Schuster, M. A. (2007). Adolescent participation in preventive health behaviors, physical activity, and nutrition: Differences across immigrant generations for Asians and Latinos compared with Whites. *American Journal of Public Health*, *97*, 337–343.

American Cancer Society (2013). *Cancer Facts and Figures, 2013*. Atlanta: American Cancer Society. Retrieved from http://www.cancer.org/acs/groups/content/@ epidemiologysurveilance/documents/document/acspc-036845.pdf [Accessed November 19, 2013].

American Public Health Association (2013). Community health workers section, Retrieved from http://www.apha.org/membergroups/sections/aphasections/chw [Accessed November 16, 2013].

Arias, E., Eschbach, K., Schauman, W. S., Backlund, E. L., and Sorlie, P. D. (2010). The Hispanic morality advantage and ethnic misclassification on US death certificates. *American Journal of Public Health*, *100*, S171–S177.

Ayanian, J. Z., Weissman, J. S., Schneider, E. C., Ginsburg, J. A., and Zaslavsky, A. M. (2000). Unmet health needs of uninsured adults in the United States. *Journal of the American Medical Association*, *284*, 2061–2069.

Bickell, N. A., Wang, J. J., Oluwole, S., Schrag, D., Godfrey, H., Hiotis, K., Mendez, J., and Guth A. A. (2006). Missed opportunities: Racial disparities in adjuvant breast cancer treatment. *Journal of Clinical Oncology*, *24*, 1357–1362.

Blanco, C., Morcillo, C., Alegria, M., Dedios, M. C., Fernandez-Navarro, P., Regincos, R., and Wang, S. (2013). Acculturation and drug use disorders among Hispanics in the U.S. *Journal of Psychiatric Research*, *47*, 226–232.

Borrell, L. N., and Lancet, E. A. (2012). Race/ethnicity and all-cause mortality in US adults: Revisiting the Hispanic paradox. *American Journal of Public Health*, *102*, 836–843.

Bortsov, A. V., Liese, A. D., Bell, R. A., Dabelea, D. D'Agostino, R. B., Jr., Hamman, R. F., Klingensmith, G. J., Lawrence, J. M., Maahs, D. M., McKeown, R., Marcovina, S. M., Thomas, J., Williams, D. E., and Mayer-Davis, E. J. (2011). Sugar-sweetened and diet beverage consumption is associated with cardio-vascular risk factor profile in youth with Type 1 diabetes. *Acta Diabetologica*, *48*, 275–282.

Caprio, S., Daniels, S. R., Drewnowski, A., Kaufman, F. R., Palinkas, L. A., Rosenbloom, A. L., and Schwimmer, J. B. (2008). Influence of race, ethnicity, and culture on childhood obesity: Implications for prevention and treatment. A consensus statement of shaping American's health and obesity society. *Diabetes Care, 31*, 2211–2221.

Caraballo, R. S., Giovino, G. A., Pechacek, T. F., Mowery, P. D., Richter, P. A., Strauss, W. J., . . . Maurer, K. R. (1998). Racial and ethnic differences in serum cotinine levels of cigarette smokers. *JAMA: The Journal of the American Medical Association, 280*(2), 135–139.

Ceaser, T. G., Fitzhugh, E. C., Thompson, D. L., and Bassett, D. R. Jr. (2013). Association of physical activity, fitness, and race: NHANES 1999–2004. *Medicine and Science in Sports and Exercise, 45*, 286–293.

Center for Disease Control and Prevention (2011). National diabetes fact sheet, 2011. Retrieved from http://www.cdc.gov/diabetes/pubs/pdf/ndfs_2011.pdf [Accessed November 13, 2013].

Center for Disease Control and Prevention (2012a). Youth risk behavior surveillance—United States, 2011. Surveillance Summaries, 61, 1–162. Retrieved from http://www.cdc.gov/mmwr/pdf/ss/ss6104. pdf [Accessed November 26, 2013].

Center for Disease Control and Prevention (2012b). *Diabetes Report Card, 2012*. Center for Disease Control and Prevention. Atlanta, GA: U.S. Department of Health and Human Services. Retrieved from http://www.cdc.gov/diabetes/pubs/pdf/diabetesreportcard.pdf [Accessed November 19, 2013].

Center for Disease Control and Prevention (2012c). Sexually transmitted disease surveillance 2011. Atlanta, GA: U.S. Department of Health and Human Services. Retrieved from http://www.cdc.gov/ std/stats11/Surv2011.pdf [Accessed November 24, 2013].

Center for Disease Control and Prevention (2013). QuickStats: Number of deaths from 10 leading causes—National Vital Statistics System, United States, 2010. *Morbidity and Mortality Weekly Report, 62*, 155. Retrieved from http://www.cdc.gov/mmwr/preview/mmwrhtml/mm6208a8.htm [Accessed November 4, 2013].

Chen, J. Y., Diamant, A., Pourat, N., and Kagawa-Singer, M. (2005). Racial/ethnic disparities in the use of preventive services among the elderly. *American Journal of Preventive Medicine, 29*, 388–395.

Contento, I. R., Basch, C., Zybert, P. (2003). Body image, weight, and food choices of Latina women and their young children. *Journal of Nutrition Education and Behavior, 35*, 236–248.

Daviglus, M. L., Talavera, G. A., Avilés-Santa, M. L., Allison, M., Cai, J., Criqui, M. H., and Stamler, J. (2012). Prevalence of major cardiovascular risk factors and cardiovascular diseases among Hispanic/ Latino individuals of diverse backgrounds in the United States. *Journal of the American Medical Association, 308*, 1775–1784.

DeVoe, J. E., Fryer, G. E., Phillips, R., and Green, L. A. (2003). Receipt of preventive care among adults: Insurance and usual source of care. *American Journal of Public Health, 93*, 786–791.

Eschbach, K., Mahnken, J. D., and Goodwin, J. S. (2005). Neighborhood composition and incidence of cancer among Hispanics in the United States. *Cancer, 103*, 1036–1044.

Eschbach, K., Ostir, G. V., Patel, K. V., Markides, K. S., and Goodwin, J. S. (2004). Neighborhood context and mortality among older Mexican Americans: is there a barrio advantage? *American Journal of Public Health, 94*, 1807–1812.

Flegal, K. M., Carroll, M. D., Kit, B. K., and Ogden, C. L. (2012). Prevalence of obesity and trends in distribution of body mass index among US adults, 1999–2010. *Journal of the American Medical Association, 307*, 491–497.

Flores, G., and Tomany-Korman, S. C. (2008). Racial and ethnic disparities in medical and dental health, access to care and use of services in U.S. children. *Pediatrics, 121*, 286–298.

Fowler, S. P., Puppala, S., Arya, R., Chittoor, G., Farook, V.S.S., Schneider, J., . . . Duggirala, R. (2013). Genetic epidemiology of cardiometabolic risk factors and their clustering patterns in Mexican American children and adolescents: The SAFARI study. *Human Genetics, 132*, 1059–1071.

Gallo, L. C., Penedo, F. J., Espinosa de los Monteros, K., and Arquelles, W. (2009). Resiliency in the face of disadvantage: Do Hispanic cultural characteristics protect health outcomes? *Journal of Personality, 77*, 1707–1746.

Gil, A. G., Wagner, E. F., and Vega, W. A. (2000). Acculturation, familismo and alcohol use among Latino adolescent males: Longitudinal relations. *Journal of Community Psychology, 28*, 443–458.

Go, A. S., Mozaffarian, D., Roger, V. L., Benjamin, E. J., Berry, J. D., Borden, W. B., . . . Turner, M. B. (2013). Heart disease and stroke statistics—2013 update: A report from the American Heart Association. *Circulation, 127*(1), 6–245.

Gonzalez-Barrera, A., and Lopez, M. H. (2013). A demographic portrait of Mexican-origin Hispanics in the United States. Washington, DC: Pew Hispanic Center. Retrieved from http://www.pewhispanic.org/files/2013/05/2013-04_Demographic-Portrait-of-Mexicans-in-the-US.pdf [Accessed November 5, 2013].

Haiman, C. A. Stram, D. O., Wilkens, L. R., Pike, M. C., Kolonel, L. N., Henderson, B. E., and Le Marchand, L. (2006). Racial/ethnic differences in smoking-related risk of lung cancer. *New England Journal of Medicine*, *354*, 333–342.

Hajat, A., Lucas, J. B., and Kington, R. (2000). Health outcomes among Hispanic subgroups: Data from the National Health Interview Survey, 1992–1995. *Advance Data*, *25*, 1–14.

Ham, S. A., and Ainsworth, B. E. (2010). Disparities in data on *Healthy People 2010* Physical activity objectives collected by accelerometry and self-report. *American Journal of Public Health*, *100*, S263–S268.

Harris, M. I., Flegal, K. M., Cowie, C. C., Eberhardt, M. S., Goldstein, D. E., Little, R. R., . . . Byrd-Holt, D. D. (1998). Prevalence of diabetes, impaired fasting glucose, and impaired glucose tolerance in US adults: The Third National Health and Nutrition Examination Survey, 1988–1994. *Diabetes Care*, *21*(4), 518–524.

Hayes, D. K., Greenlund, K. J., Denny, C. H., Neyer, J. R., Croft, J. B., and Keenan, N. L. (2011). Racial/ethnic and socioeconomic disparities in health-related quality of life among people with coronary heart disease, 2007. *Preventing Chronic Disease*, *8*, A78.

Hertz, R. P., Unger, A. N., and Ferrario, C. M. (2006). Diabetes, hypertension, and dyslipidemia in Mexican Americans and non-Hispanic whites. *American Journal of Preventive Medicine*, *30*(2), 103–110.

Holt-Lunstad, J., Smith, T. B., and Layton, J. B. (2010). Social relationships and mortality risk: A meta-analytic review. *PLoS Medicine*, *7*.

Horn-Ross, P. L., Chang, E. T., Clarke, C. A., Keegan, T. H., Rull, R. P., Quach, T., and Gomez, S. L. (2012). Nativity and papillary thyroid cancer incidence rates among Hispanic women in California. *Cancer*, *118*, 216–222.

Hoyert, D. L., and Xu, J. (2012). Deaths: preliminary data for 2011. *National vital statistics report*, *61*. Hyattsville, MD: National Center for Health Statistics. Retrieved from http://www.cdc.gov/nchs/data/nvsr61/nvsr61_06.pdf [Accessed November 19, 2013].

Jemal, A., Simard, E. P., Dorell, C., *et al.*, (2013). Annual report to the nation on the status of cancer, 1975–2009, featuring the burden and trends in human papillomavirus (HPV)—associated cancers and HPV vaccination coverage levels. *Journal of the National Cancer Institute*, *105*, 175–201.

Kaplan, M. S., Huguet, N., Newsom, J. T., and McFarland, B. H. (2004). The association between length of residence and obesity among Hispanic immigrants. *American Journal of Preventive Medicine*, *27*(4), 323–326.

Kim, G., Ford, K. L., Chiriboga, D. A., and Sorkin, D. H. (2012). Racial and ethnic disparities in health-care use, delayed care, and management of diabetes mellitus in older adults in California. *Journal of the American Geriatric Society*, *60*, 2319–2325.

Kochanek, K. D., Xu, J., Murphy, S. L., Minino, A. M., and Kung, H. C., Division of Vital Statistics (2012). Deaths: final data for 2009. *National vital statistics reports*, *60*(3). National Center for Health Statistics. Hyattsville, MD. Retrieved from http://www.cdc.gov/nchs/data/nvsr60/nvsr60_03.pdf [Accessed November 18, 2013].

Lau, M., Lin, H., and Flores, G. (2012). Racial/ethnic disparities in health and health care among U.S. adolescents. *Health Services Research*, *47*, 2031–2059.

Lawrence, J. M., Mayer-Davis, E. J., Reynolds, K., Beyer, J., Pettitt, D. J., D'Agostino, R. B., Jr., Marcovina, S. M., Imperatore, G., Hamman, R. F., and the SEARCH for Diabetes in Youth Study Group (2009). Diabetes in Hispanic American Youth: Prevalence, incidence, demographics, and clinical characteristics: The SEARCH for Diabetes in Youth Study. *Diabetes Care*, *32*, S123–S132.

Luckett, T., Goldstein, D., Butow, P. N., Gebski, V., Aldridge, L. J., McGrane, J., Ng, W., and King, M. T. (2011). Psychological morbidity and quality of life of ethnic minority patients with cancer: A systematic review and meta-analysis. *Lancet Oncology*, *12*, 1240–1248.

Marshall, S. J., Jones, D. A., Ainsworth, D. A., Reis, J. P., Levy, S. S., and Macera, C. A. (2007). Race/ethnicity, social class, and leisure-time physical inactivity. *Medicine and Science in Sports and Exercise*, *39*, 44–51.

Montealegre, J. R., Zhou, R., Amirian, E. S., Follen, M., and Scheurer, M. E. (2013). Nativity disparities in late-stage diagnosis and cause-specific survival among Hispanic women with invasive cervical cancer: An analysis of surveillance, epidemiology, and end results data. *Cancer Causes and Control, 24*, 1985–1994.

National Center for Health Statistics (US) (1994). *Plan and operation of the third National Health and Nutrition Examination Survey, 1988–94* (No. 32). National Center for Health Statistics.

National Center for Health Statistics (2013). Health, United States, 2012: With special feature on emergency care. Hyattsville, MD. Retrieved from http://www.cdc.gov/ nchs/data/hus/hus12.pdf [Accessed November 17, 2013].

National Heart, Lung, and Blood Institute (2001). Prevention of cardiovascular disease: National Heart, Lung, and Blood Institute task force report on research in prevention of cardiovascular disease. Retrieved from http://www.nhlbi.nih.gov/resources/docs/cvdrpt.htm [Accessed November 16, 2013].

National Institute on Alcohol Abuse and Alcoholism (2010). Alcohol use and alcohol use disorder in the United States, a 3-year follow-up: Main findings from the 2004–2005 wave 2 national Epidemiological Survey on Alcohol and Related Conditions (NESARC). Retrieved from http://pubs.niaaa.nih.gov/publications/NESARC_DRM2/ NESARC2DRM.pdf [Accessed November 27, 2013].

Ng, D. K., Brootman, D. J., Lau, B., and Young, J. H. (2012). Insurance status, not race, is associated with mortality after an acute cardiovascular event in Maryland. *Journal of General Internal Medicine, 27*, 1368–1376.

NHANES Laboratory Procedure Manuals and Mobile Exam Center Components Descriptions (1988). Available at: http://www.cdc.gov/nchs/data/nhanes/nhanes_05_06/lab_d.pdf

Nielsen, A. B., Siersma, V., Hiort, L. C., Drivsholm, T., Kreiner, S., and Hollnagel, H. (2008). Self-rated general health among 40-year-old Danes and its association with all-cause mortality at 10-, 20-, and 29 years' follow-up. *Scandinavian Journal of Public Health, 36*, 3–11.

Nyberg, K., Ramirez, A., and Gallion, K. (2011). Physical activity, overweight and obesity among Latino youth. Salud American. Princeton, NJ: Robert Wood Johnson Foundation. Retrieved from http://www.rwjf.org/content/dam/web-assets/2011/12/physical-activity-overweight-and-obesity-among-latino-youth [Accessed on November 26, 2013].

Parikh, S. V., Enrquez, J. R., Selzer, F., Slater, J. N., Laskey, W. K., Wilensky, R. L., . . . Holper, E. M. (2009). Association of a unique cardiovascular risk profile with outcomes in Hispanic patients referred for percutaneous coronary intervention (from the National Heart, Lung, and Blood Institute Dynamic Registry). *American Journal of Cardiology, 104*, 775–779.

Patel, M. I., Schupp, C. W., Gomez, S. L., Chang, E. T., and Wakelee, H. A. (2013). How do social factors explain outcomes in non-small-cell lung cancer among Hispanics in California? Explaining the Hispanic paradox. *Journal of Clinical Oncology, 31*, 3572–3578.

Phillips, A. C., Der, G., and Carroll, D. (2010). Self-reported health, self-reported fitness, and all-cause mortality: Prospective cohort study. *British Journal of Health Psychology, 15*, 337–346.

Ramirez, A. G., Perez-Stable, E. J., Penedo, F. J., Talavera, G. A., Carrillo, J. E., Fernandez, M. E., Holden, A. E., Munoz, E., San Miguel, S., and Gallion, K. (2013). Navigating Latinas with breast screen abnormalities to diagnosis: The Six Cities Study. *Cancer, 119*, 1298–1305.

Ramisetty-Mikler, S., Caetano, R., and Rodriguez, L. A. (2010). The Hispanic Americans Baseline Alcohol Survey (HABLAS): Alcohol consumption and sociodemographic predictors across Hispanic national groups. *Journal of Substance Use, 15*, 402–416.

Raphael, J. L., Rueda, A., Lion, K. C., and Giordano, T. P. (2013). The role of lay health care workers in pediatric chronic disease: A systematic review. *Academic Pediatrics, 13*, 408–420.

Reyes-Ortiz, C. A., Rodriguez, M., and Markides, K. S. (2009). The role of spirituality healing with perceptions of the medical encounter among Latinos. *Journal of General Internal Medicine, 24*, 542–547.

Rodriguez, M. A., Bustamante, A. V., and Ang, A. (2009). Perceived quality of care, receipt of preventive care, and usual source of health care among undocumented and other Latinos. *Journal of General Internal Medicine, 24*, 508–513.

Ruiz, J. M., and Steffen, P. (2011). Latino Health. In H. S. Friedman (Ed.), *The Oxford Handbook of Health Psychology*. Oxford University Press: New York.

Ruiz, J. M., Steffen, P., and Prather, C. C. (2012). Socioeconomic status and health. In A. Baum, T. A. Revenson, and J. E. Singer (Eds.), *Handbook of Health Psychology*. Mahwah, NJ: Lawrence Erlbaum Associates.

Ruiz, J. M., Steffen, P., and Smith, T. B. (2013). The Hispanic mortality paradox: A systematic review and meta-analysis of the longitudinal literature. *American Journal of Public Health, 103,* e1–e9.

Saha, S., Arbelaez, J. J., and Cooper, L. A. (2003). Patient-physician relationships and racial disparities in the quality of health care. *American Journal of Public Health, 93,* 1713–1719.

Schiller, J. S., Lucas, J. W., Ward, B. W., and Peregoy, J. A. (2012). Summary health statistics for U.S. adults: National Health Interview Survey, 2010. National Center for Health Statistics. *Vital Health Statistics, 10.* Washington, DC. Retrieved from http://www.cdc.gov/nchs/data/series/sr_10/sr10_252.pdf [Accessed November 18, 2013].

Shaw, R. J., and Pickett, K. E. (2013). The health benefits of Hispanic communities for non-Hispanic mothers and infants: Another Hispanic paradox. *American Journal of Public Health, 103,* 1052–1057.

Smith, D. P., and Bradshaw, B. S. (2006). Rethinking the Hispanic paradox: Death rates and life expectancy for U.S. non-Hispanic white and Hispanic populations. *American Journal of Public Health, 96,* 1686–1692.

Smith, E. C., Ziogas, A., and Anton-Culver, H. (2013). Delay in surgical treatment and survival after breast cancer diagnosis in young women by race/ethnicity. *JAMA Surgery, 148,* 516–523.

Sorlie, P. D., Aviles-Santa, L. M., Wassertheil-Smoller, S., Kaplan, R. C., Daviglus, M. L., Giachello, A. L., . . . Heiss, G. (2010). Design and implementation of the Hispanic Community Health Study/Study of Latinos. *Annals of Epidemiology, 20,* 629–641.

Substance Abuse and Mental Health Services Administration (2011). Past month cigarette use among racial and ethnic groups. *The NDSHU report: substance use among Hispanic adolescents.* Rockville, MD: Center for Behavioral Health Statistics and Quality. Retrieved from http://www.samhsa.gov/data/2k11/WEB_SR_007/WEB_SR_007.htm [Accessed November 13, 2013].

U.S. Department of Education, National Center for Education Statistics (2009). *Condition of Education 2009* (NCES 2009-081), indicators 2, 3, 12, 13, and 20. Washington, DC: U.S. Government Printing Office.

U.S. Department of Health and Human Services (2011). HHS action plan to reduce racial and ethnic disparities: A nation free of disparities in health and health care. Washington, DC: U.S. Department of Health and Human Services. Retrieved from http://minorityhealth.hhs.gov/npa/files/Plans/HHS/HHS_Plan_complete.pdf [Accessed November 16, 2013].

U.S. Department of Health and Human Services (2013). Healthy People 2020. Office of Disease Prevention and Health Promotion. Washington, DC. Retrieved from http://www.healthypeople.gov/2020/default.aspx [Accessed November 17, 2013].

U.S. Department of Labor Statistics (2013). Labor force characteristics by race and ethnicity, 2012. *BLS Reports, Report 1044,* October. Retrieved from http://www.bls.gov/cps/cpsrace2012.pdf [Accessed November 4, 2013].

Weiss, L. J., and Blustein, J. (1996). Faithful patients: The effect of long-term physician-patient relationships on the cost and use of health care by older Americans. *American Journal of Public Health, 86,* 1742–1747.

West, J. H, Blumberg, E. J., Kelley, N. H. J., Hill, L., Sipan, C. L., Schmitz, K. E., and Hovell, M. F. (2010). Does proximity to retailers influence alcohol and tobacco use among Latino adolescents? *Journal of Immigrant and Minority Health, 12,* 626–633.

Wilkinson, A. V., Waters, A. J., Vasudevan, V., Bondy, M. L., Prokhorov, A. V., and Spitz, M. R. (2008). Correlates of susceptibility to smoking among Mexican origin youth residing in Houston, Texas: A cross-sectional analysis. *BMC Public Health, 8,* 337.

Willey, J. Z., Rodriguez, C. J., Carlino, R. G., Moon, Y. P., Paik, M. C., Boden-Albala, B., and Elkind, M. S. (2011). Race-ethnic differences in the association between lipid profile components and risk of myocardial infarction: The Northern Manhattan Study. *American Heart Journal, 161,* 886–892.

Wilper, A. P., Woolhandler, S., Lasser, K. E., McCormick, D., Bor, D. H., and Himmelstein, D. U. (2009). Health insurance and mortality in US adults. *American Journal of Public Health, 99,* 2289–2295.

Winston, C., Pratt, R., Armstrong, L., and Navin, T. (2010). Decrease in reported tuberculosis cases—United States, 2009. *Morbidity and Mortality Weekly Report (MMWR), 59,* 289–294.

Yang, Y., Thumula, V., Pace, P. F., Banahan III, B. F., Wilkin, N. E., and Lobb, W. B. (2009). Predictors of medication nonadherence among patients with diabetes in Medicare Part D programs: A retrospective cohort study. *Clinical Therapeutics, 31*(10), 2178–2188.

17

PROMOTING THE HEALTH OF MEXICAN AMERICAN INFANTS AND YOUNG CHILDREN

Margaret O'Brien Caughy and Luisa Franzini

Introduction

Children of Latino heritage represent the fastest growing group among children in the United States. According to the US Bureau of the Census (2009) the proportion of the child population under age 18 in the US of Hispanic origin has more than doubled in the last three decades, from 9 percent in 1980 to 22 percent in 2009. This trend is anticipated to continue, with the proportion of children of Hispanic origin projected to comprise 27 percent of the entire US population of children in 2021 (U.S. Bureau of the Census, 2009). Country of origin data from the 2004 American Community Survey indicated that those of Mexican origin comprise the largest proportion of Hispanics, accounting for almost two-thirds of Hispanic individuals in the United States (U.S. Bureau of the Census, 2007).

Literature Review

Health Status of Mexican American Infants and Young Children

With regards to health status, Mexican American infants and young children display more optimal health outcomes in some domains while appearing vulnerable to greater risks for poor health in other domains. Infants who are born low birth weight (less than 2500 grams or 5.5 pounds) or very low birth weight (less than 1500 grams or 3.3 pounds) are at greater risk of morbidity and mortality than infants born with a birth weight in the normal range. Rates of low birth weight and infant mortality vary significantly with socioeconomic status. For instance, for births in the United States between 2003 and 2005, infant mortality rates were highest among mothers with 9–11 years of education (9.30 deaths per 1000 live births) and lowest among mothers with 16 years of education or more (4.15 deaths per 1000 live births) (United States Department of Health and Human Services [US DHHS], 2010).

Public health epidemiologists have coined the term "Hispanic Paradox" to refer to the fact that Hispanics[1] display more optimal pregnancy outcomes despite exposure to greater socioeconomic risk factors. Rates of high school graduation are lower among Hispanics (69.6%) compared with non-Hispanic Whites (88.6%) (U.S. Bureau of the Census, 2007). Poverty rates are higher among Hispanics overall (22%) compared with non-Hispanic Whites (8.8%), and

TABLE 17.1 Low birth weight, very low birth weight, and infant mortality rates by race/ethnicity, United States 2003–2006

Race/ethnic category	Low Birth Weight	Very Low Birth Weight	Infant Mortality
	(%)	(%)	(per 1000)
White, non–Hispanic	7.21	1.10	5.71
Black, non–Hispanic	13.53	2.73	13.61
Hispanic:			
Mexican	6.46	1.01	5.50
Puerto Rican	9.94	1.72	8.11
Cuban	6.99	1.13	4.53
Central/South American	6.71	1.03	4.78
Other Hispanic	8.41	1.24	6.59
Other non–Hispanic	7.93	1.04	5.27
All births	7.70	1.30	5.85

Source: United States Department of Health and Human Services (US DHHS) (2010). Linked Birth/Infant Death Records 2003–2005, CDC WONDER On-line Database. Retrieved Feb 16, 2010 11:18:27 AM, from http://wonder.cdc.gov/lbd-current.html; and United States Department of Health and Human Services (US DHHS) (2010). Natality Public-Use Data 2003–2006, CDC WONDER Online Database Retrieved April 7, 2010, from http://wonder.cdc.gov/natality-current.html.

slightly higher among Hispanics of Mexican origin (23.6%) (U.S. Bureau of the Census, 2007). Despite lower socioeconomic status, however, Hispanics have lower rates of low birth weight births and infant mortality.

Franzini *et al.* (2001) provide a comprehensive review of the epidemiological literature on the Hispanic Paradox. Lower rates of low birth weight births, preterm births, and infant mortality among Hispanics appear to be a "real" health advantage and not merely an artifact resulting from data reliability or selection bias. In 2006, the low birth weight rate among Hispanics was 7.0%, and the very low birth weight rate was 1.2%. The rate of very low birth weight births among Hispanics was the same as the rate for the non-Hispanic Whites, and the rate of low birth weight was lower than that of non-Hispanic Whites (7.3%) (Martin *et al.*, 2009).

The health advantage of improved pregnancy outcomes in the face of socioeconomic disadvantage is not observed equally across all Hispanic subgroups. Generally, the best pregnancy outcomes among Hispanics are observed among those of Mexican, Cuban, and Central/South American origin, whereas Puerto Ricans display rates of poor pregnancy outcome which are intermediate to those of non-Hispanic Whites and African Americans (Buekens *et al.*, 2000; de la Rosa, 2002; Franzini *et al.*, 2001; Fuentes-Afflick *et al.*, 1999; Mendoza *et al.*, 1991). As shown in Table 17.1, rates of adverse pregnancy outcome for Hispanics, especially Mexican Americans, were lower than for non-Hispanic Whites. Therefore, Mexican American infants are more likely to enter the world as healthy newborns despite the fact their mothers faced greater risks during pregnancy related to exposure to poverty.

Threats to the Health of Mexican American Infants and Young Children

Despite the advantages Mexican American infants enjoy with regards to more optimal pregnancy outcomes, Mexican American children are more likely to experience poor health in other domains. For example, Flores *et al.* (2005) used data from the National Survey of Early

Childhood Health (NSECH) to examine how health status and access to health care varied by race/ethnicity. The NSECH was a telephone survey of families with children between 4 and 35 months of age conducted in 2000 with 2,068 respondents, oversampled for Black and Latino children. The parents of Latino children in this sample were significantly less likely to rate their child's health as "excellent" or "very good" compared to non-Hispanic White and non-Hispanic Black children (72%, 90%, and 79%, respectively). Latino children were also significantly more likely to be uninsured than other children. Among Latino parents, 31% reported their child had been uninsured at least once in the last 12 months compared to 9% for non-Hispanic White children and 18% for non-Hispanic Black children. This rate of uninsured status is higher than reported by Current Population Survey (CPS) conducted by the US Census in 2008, which reported that 17.2% of Latino children were uninsured compared to 6.7% of non-Hispanic Whites and 10.7% of non-Hispanic Blacks (DeNavas-Walt et al., 2009). This discrepancy may result from the fact that the NSECH data reported by Flores et al. (2005) focused on children under the age of 3 years, while the CPS estimates included all children under the age of 18 years.

Flores et al. (2002) present a summary of the data regarding health disparities evident among Latino children and youth. For example, Latino children are disproportionately affected by poor oral health. Specifically, Mexican American preschoolers have higher rates of dental caries, and Mexican American adolescents have higher rates of untreated dental caries compared with non-Hispanic White and non-Hispanic Black children and youth. Latino children and youth are also more likely to be overweight or obese compared to other race/ethnic groups. In a study involving 173 Mexican American nine-year-old children in San Antonio, Treviño et al. (1999) reported a very high prevalence of risk factors for Type 2 diabetes including low intake of fruits and vegetables, higher than recommended intake of saturated fats, low levels of physical fitness, high proportions of body fat, and high prevalence of first- or second-degree relatives with diabetes.

Health disparities among Hispanic youth have also been reported for adolescents. Although Hispanic adolescents report later initiation of sexual activity, they are less likely to report use of contraception. Consequently, estimated pregnancy rates among Hispanic adolescent females are higher than non-Hispanic Black or non-Hispanic White adolescents (132.8, 128.0, and 45.2 per thousand, respectively, in 2004–2006) (Gavin et al., 2009). Hispanic adolescents are also more likely to report higher rates of persistent feelings of sadness, with 36.3% of Hispanic youth participating in the Youth Risk Behavior Survey (YRBS; Kolbe et al., 1993) in 2007 reporting symptoms of persistent sadness during the prior 12 months compared with 26.2% of non-Hispanic White youth and 29.2% of non-Hispanic Blacks (Centers for Disease Control and Prevention [CDC], 2010). In addition, 10.2% of Hispanic youth reported attempting suicide in the prior 12 months compared with 5.6% for non-Hispanic whites and 7.7% of non-Hispanic blacks. These patterns are most striking for Hispanic female adolescents, 42.3% of whom reported feeling persistently hopeless and 14% of whom reported having attempted suicide in the last year. There is a growing empirical literature of the unique stressors related to immigrant status and acculturation and their relation to the psychosocial well-being of Hispanic youth (Romero and Roberts, 2003; Smokowski and Bacallao, 2007; Smokowski et al., 2010).

Despite higher rates of identified mental health needs, Hispanic youth also report lower rates of utilization of behavioral health services (Alegria, et al., 2004; Castaneda, 1994; Coker et al., 2009; Zimmerman, 2005). The evidence regarding whether these disparities are explained by socioeconomic factors is conflicting, with some researchers reporting that disparities in mental health care utilization for Hispanic youth disappear when socioeconomic factors are controlled (Coker et al., 2009), and others reporting they do not (Zimmerman, 2005). Regardless, we still have insufficient information regarding the barriers to mental health services among Hispanic youth in general as well as Mexican American youth specifically (Alegria *et al.*, 2004; Castaneda, 1994; Flores *et al.*, 2002).

Ensuring the Health of Mexican American Infants and Young Children: A Life Course Perspective

In recent years, the field of public health, and the field of maternal and child health in particular, has embraced a life-course perspective for explaining and addressing race/ethnic disparities in pregnancy outcomes, child health, and adult health (Braveman and Barclay, 2009; Kotelchuck, 2003; Lu and Halfon, 2003). Although similar in some regards to the lifespan perspective espoused by developmental sociologists and psychologists (e.g. Baltes, 1980; Elder and Rockwell, 1979), the life-course perspective in public health is more narrow. The life-course perspective in public health was instigated primarily by evidence of a relation between pregnancy outcomes and physical health status later in life (e.g. the "Barker Hypothesis"; Barker, 1990), whereas a developmental lifespan approach examines how contextual, chronological, and historical processes across the lifespan affect well-being in a wide range of outcomes. Although the Barker Hypothesis is controversial, the application of a life-course perspective to understanding disparities in pregnancy outcome has contributed to a greater appreciation among public health professionals for the importance of a woman's health outside of pregnancy and how experiences early in life contribute to a woman's health status once she becomes of childbearing age (Lu and Halfon, 2003).

The very existence of the paradox of better pregnancy outcomes among Mexican American infants in the face of economic risk confounds many of the basic tenets of the public health life course approach. Our ability to effectively address disparities in the health status of Mexican American infants and young children would be enhanced if the public health life-course perspective were to incorporate elements of developmental lifespan (Baltes, 1980; Elder and Rockwell, 1979) and ecological approaches (Bronfenbrenner and Ceci, 1994; Bronfenbrenner, 1984; Garcia Coll *et al.*, 1996). What all these perspectives have in common is the belief that the determinants of development must be understood within the context of developmental stage, historical time, family, and community. An appreciation of these contextual elements is critical for the identification of sources of risk and resilience for the health of Mexican American children and youth.

Mexican American Communities and Families: Assets and Vulnerabilities

Guided by a lifespan and ecological perspective, we know that risk and protective factors for the health of infants and young children accrue at both the family and community levels. At the family-level, compromised parental health, both physical and psychological, can compromise infant and child health and development. Some of the pathways from parental health to child health are indirect. For example, poor parental physical health is associated with an increased risk of poverty for some children (Wagmiller *et al.*, 2008), which in turn is associated with increased risk for poor health. Likewise, poor psychological status of the mother during the post-partum period is associated with decreased utilization of well-baby care, recommendations for putting babies on their back to sleep, and childhood immunizations (Zajicek-Farber, 2009). Empirical data regarding rates of post-partum and maternal depression among Mexican-origin women are scant. Heilemann *et al.* (2004) reported that more than half of their sample of pregnant and post-partum Mexican-origin women reported depressive symptoms higher than the cut point for concern on the Centers for Epidemiologic Studies—Depression (CES-D) screening tool, and more than a quarter of their sample scored over 24 on the CES-D, putting them in the category of being high risk for depression.

At the community level, a diverse set of factors have been identified as affecting child health over and above family and child factors. Community-level factors such as neighborhood economic impoverishment, neighborhood social climate, the built environment, and the presence of neighborhood resources have been linked with a range of measures of child well-being including infant mortality/low birth weight, childhood injury, asthma, childhood overweight/ obesity, and child behavior problems (Burdette and Whitaker, 2005; Caughy et al., 2008; Franzini et al., 2007; Gordon-Larsen et al., 2006; Kohen et al., 2002; Molnar et al., 2004; Papas et al., 2007; Rauh et al., 2008; Sellstrom and Bremberg, 2006). Studies of community-level effects on child health and development specifically focused on Hispanic youth are limited, and most that exist focus on adolescents. Living in a high density Hispanic neighborhood appears to be protective for both Hispanic adolescents and adults. Several researchers have reported that Hispanic adolescents living in higher density Hispanic neighborhoods are less likely to engage in risky behavior (Molnar et al., 2003; Upchurch et al., 2001). These findings are echoed in research on neighborhood effects for depression among Mexican American older adults. Ostir et al. (2003) reported that risk of depression decreased with increasing proportion of Mexican American residents in the neighborhood. With regards to children, Molnar et al. (2003) found that risk of parent-to-child physical aggression declined with increasing numbers of friends and relatives in the neighborhood. Therefore, understanding the determinants of health status among Mexican American infants and young children requires the consideration of both the family and community context in which they live.

Community Characteristics of Mexican American Families

Conclusions can be drawn from the broader research on community influences on child health to identify a number of characteristics of Mexican American communities which may provide sources of resilience or risk for the health of Mexican American infants and young children, and we will use data from our own studies to examine the prevalence of these factors among Mexican American families in Texas.

In 2002, we completed a survey of a diverse sample of 3,203 adults living in 13 different communities in Houston and in the Lower Rio Grande Valley. The 11 communities located in Houston were all low/medium income communities selected to represent both older, established residential neighborhoods as well as more recently developed neighborhoods. One of the communities selected in the Lower Rio Grande Valley was an urban neighborhood, while the other was a "colonia" (e.g. an incorporated area with limited access to public services). Respondents were chosen using a multi-stage probability sampling process by which city blocks were sampled first, followed by dwelling units, followed by respondents. Survey questions covered a wide range of topics including perceived characteristics of the respondent's neighborhood, health status, community involvement, and, for those with children, discipline practices and involvement in their child's education.

Of the 3,203 survey respondents, 1,376 were of Mexican-origin, and of those, 917 (66.6%) had a child or youth under the age of 18 living in their home. We will use these data to illustrate the characteristics of communities and families in which Mexican American children are being raised, and to identify potential sources of risk and resilience for child health. To capture the heterogeneity of Mexican American families who participated in the survey, we stratified the data by nativity (US-born versus foreign-born) and residence location (Houston or the Lower Rio Grande Valley).

Characteristics of the communities in which these families lived are displayed in Table 17.2. The indicators in the top half of the table are structural indicators drawn from the US Census in 2000. Poverty rates were significantly higher for Mexican American survey participants as compared with both the Texas poverty rate in 2000 (14.7%), as well as the US poverty rate in 2000 (11.3%). Poverty rates were highest for foreign-born residents of the Lower Rio Grande Valley, and lowest for US-born Mexican Americans in Houston. Similar patterns were seen in the other economic indicators including child poverty, economic impoverishment, and unemployment. Economic impoverishment is an index created from 2000 census variables as recommended by Sampson and his colleagues (Morenoff and Sampson, 1997; Sampson *et al.*, 1997, 1999). This scale was comprised of percent of individuals below the poverty line, percent receiving public assistance, percent unemployed, and percent of households that are female-headed with children, each of which was standardized against the State of Texas as a whole and averaged to yield an index of concentrated economic impoverishment. As this is a z-score, it can be seen that while all Mexican American respondents lived in neighborhoods with levels of concentrated economic impoverishment greater than the average for the state, those in the Lower Rio Grande Valley lived in communities more than three standard deviations above the mean level of economic impoverishment for the state.

Survey participants lived in neighborhoods which were home to a high proportion of Hispanic residents, with the proportion of Hispanic residents ranging from 63% for US-born Mexicans living in Houston to more than 85% for foreign-born Mexicans living in the lower Rio Grande Valley. Mexican American respondents in the lower Rio Grande Valley lived in neighborhoods with a higher proportion of individuals who were not English-speaking, but interestingly, foreign-born Mexican American respondents in Houston lived in neighborhoods with a higher proportion of foreign-born residents than did foreign-born Mexican Americans in the Valley.

Neighborhood residential stability is also an important indicator of community context because the average length of tenure in the neighborhood influences the development of social cohesion and other forms of neighborhood social support. While Mexican Americans living in the Valley experienced a lower proportion of residents moving in and out within one year, they also had fewer residents in their neighborhood that had been there for an extended period of time, or for more than three decades.

Not all features of neighborhoods that have important implications for child health can be ascertained from data sources such as the census. Therefore, we also asked survey participants about the physical and social environment of their neighborhood, and their responses to these items are displayed at the bottom of Table 17.2. All scales were converted to t-scores to facilitate comparison across scales. *Physical/social disorder* tapped the perception that graffiti, trash, and people loitering in the neighborhood were problems. High levels of physical and social disorder in the neighborhood can influence child health by increasing risk for injury and/or decreasing opportunities for safe outdoor play (Berg and Medrich, 1980; Burdette and Whitaker, 2005; Molnar *et al.*, 2004; O'Campo *et al.*, 2000; Reading *et al.*, 1999). As a whole, Mexican Americans in the sample lived in neighborhoods with a significantly higher level of physical and social disorder than non-Hispanic Whites, 3.57 versus 1.69, $t = 11.01$, $p < .001$. The average level of disorder for neighborhoods of non-Hispanic Black participants, 3.84, was higher than the average level for Mexicans, but not significantly higher. As can be seen in Table 17.2, the average level of neighborhood disorder was highest among foreign-born Mexican American respondents living in the lower Rio Grande Valley.

Exchange with neighbors taps the degree to which neighbors help one another out such as by watching another neighbor's property when they are out of town or borrowing things from one

TABLE 17.2 Neighborhood Characteristics of Mexican-origin Respondents with Children by Nativity and Residence Location

	Houston				Lower Rio Grande				
	US-Born (N = 200)		Foreign-born (N = 448)		US-Born (N = 79)		Foreign-Born (N = 190)		F
	Mean	SD	Mean	SD	Mean	SD	Mean	SD	
Neighborhood structural characteristics									
Poverty rate	$24.84_{a,b,c}$	14.00	$30.01_{c,d,e}$	12.46	$35.03_{a,d}$	16.72	$40.11_{b,e}$	19.90	36.98***
Child poverty rate	17.55_a	10.81	21.96_a	10.45	27.36_a	18.38	32.74_a	21.95	40.96***
Economic impoverishment	$0.81_{a,b,c}$	2.28	$1.60_{a,d,e}$	1.98	$3.01_{b,d}$	0.75	$3.26_{c,e}$	0.82	53.24***
Unemployment rate	$10.30_{a,b,c}$	7.00	$12.10_{c,d,e}$	7.21	$14.76_{a,d}$	6.16	$14.51_{b,e}$	5.58	16.04***
% Hispanic	$62.83_{a,b,c}$	30.14	$73.91_{c,d,e}$	26.31	$84.13_{a,d}$	13.86	$85.45_{b,e}$	14.33	32.14***
% foreign born	31.17_a	15.63	$36.30_{a,b,c}$	14.58	30.40_b	9.17	32.29_c	9.77	10.00**
% non-English speaking	7.64_a	5.63	9.43_a	5.17	13.06_a	6.71	15.16_a	7.44	64.12***
% in neighborhood ≤1 year	$21.54_{a,b}$	9.58	$21.55_{c,d}$	9.73	$12.19_{a,c}$	5.90	$11.27_{b,d}$	4.80	85.84***
% in neighborhood 30+ years	$9.25_{a,b}$	7.02	$9.04_{c,d}$	5.61	$2.81_{a,c}$	3.68	$2.65_{b,d}$	3.66	86.57***
Perceptions of neighborhood physical and social characteristics									
Physical/social disorder	3.23_a	2.91	3.34_b	3.04	4.10	3.33	$4.56_{a,b}$	3.75	8.23**
Exchange with neighbors	$4.78_{a,b}$	2.36	$4.19_{a,c,d}$	2.47	5.36	2.19	$5.64_{a,b,d}$	2.30	18.69***
Collective efficacy	6.24_a	1.48	$5.88_{a,b}$	1.37	6.34	1.44	6.54_b	1.32	11.34**
Supportive environment for children	6.31	2.08	6.25_a	2.26	7.05_a	2.07	6.76	2.46	4.46*
Fear of retaliation	4.43	2.39	4.64	2.61	4.66	2.61	4.81	2.80	0.68
Fear of victimization	$5.28_{a,b}$	2.92	6.54_a	2.94	5.80	2.93	6.25_b	3.00	8.84**

Note: a) Means with the same subscript letter are significantly different; b) $p < .05$; ** $p < .01$; *** $p < .001$

another. Mexican Americans overall reported lower rates of neighborly exchange compared with non-Hispanic Whites and non-Hispanic Blacks, 4.56 vs. 5.20 vs. 5.22, respectively, $F = 19.47$, $p > .001$. However, this masks the variability within the Mexican American group, which can be seen in Table 17.3. Both US-born and foreign-born Mexican Americans living in the lower Rio Grande Valley reported higher levels of neighborhood exchange than either non-Hispanic Whites or non-Hispanic blacks, and lower levels were seen among Mexicans living in the urban center of Houston.

Collective efficacy was a term coined by Sampson (Sampson *et al.*, 1997, 1999) which measures the degree of social cohesion in the neighborhood as well as the degree to which the neighborhood comes together to address common problems. As with neighborhood exchange, average levels of collective efficacy for Mexican Americans as a whole was lower than for non-Hispanic Whites and non-Hispanic Blacks, 6.15 vs. 6.80 vs. 6.34, respectively, $F = 24.69$, $p < .001$. However, like neighborhood exchange, levels of neighborhood collective efficacy were significantly higher among those living in the Lower Rio Grande Valley, especially those who were foreign-born.

The scale *Supportive environment for children* assessed the degree to which neighbors watch out for children, as well as the degree to which the neighborhood provided a safe environment for play, and *Fear of victimization* tapped the degree to which respondents were concerned about being the victim of a crime in their neighborhood (Coulton *et al.*, 1996). Foreign-born Mexican Americans in Houston reported the highest levels of fear of victimization, and US-born Mexican Americans in the Valley reported the most supportive neighborhoods for children.

The data from our surveys with Mexican-origin parents in Houston and the Lower Rio Grande Valley illustrates that Mexican American children and youth are exposed to communities characterized by both risk and protective factors. Mexican American parents in our sample lived in neighborhoods characterized by high levels of economic impoverishment, physical incivilities, and fear of crime. However, these neighborhoods also had high levels of neighborhood social cohesion and neighborhood involvement. Improving the health of Mexican American infants and young children will depend on our ability to reduce neighborhood risk factors while preserving and enhancing strengths of Mexican American communities.

Family Environments for Mexican American Children

Our survey also included a number of items tapping characteristics of the family such as social support, community involvement, health status, employment benefits, and, for families with children, involvement with their child's education. Social support measures included counts of numbers of friends and relatives, as well as a measure of the respondent's perception of support, for childrearing in particular. As can be seen in Table 17.3, across all social support measures, it was evident that foreign-born Mexican Americans living in Houston were more isolated from sources of social support compared with their US-born counterparts living there, as well as Mexican Americans living in the Lower Rio Grande Valley. Compared to non-Hispanic Whites and non-Hispanic Blacks, Mexican Americans engaged in more activities in the neighborhood, such as visiting friends and family, attending church, engaging in volunteer activities, and shopping, 5.35 vs. 3.47 vs. 5.35, respectively, $F = 89.48$, $p < .001$. As shown in Table 17.3, although level of involvement in neighborhood activities was high among all subgroups of Mexican Americans, it was significantly higher among foreign-born Mexican Americans living in the Rio Grande Valley.

Religiosity is another source of support for families. In a previous report, we detailed the race/ethnic differences in both organizational and non-organizational religious participation in this

TABLE 17.3 Family Characteristics of Mexican-origin Respondents with Children, by Nativity and Residence Location

	Houston				Rio Grande Valley				
	US-Born		Foreign-born		US-Born		Foreign-born		
	Mean	SD	Mean	SD	Mean	SD	Mean	SD	F
Social support									
Close friends	3.89_a	3.03	$2.96_{a,b,c}$	2.67	3.96_b	3.38	4.14_c	3.54	9.35***
Close relatives	4.42_a	3.42	3.29_a	2.96	3.90	3.17	3.90	3.41	6.11***
Friends/relatives seen 1+x/mo.	4.87_a	3.61	3.66_a	3.00	4.06	3.55	4.27	3.61	6.23***
Friends/relatives in neighborhood	3.02	3.00	2.35_a	2.62	2.30	3.09	3.20_a	3.55	4.99**
Support for raising children	3.63_a	2.06	2.57_a	1.99	3.88_b	1.87	3.63_c	2.20	16.98***
Religion									
Religiosity (organizational)	6.07_a	2.63	6.10_b	2.53	5.84_c	2.74	$6.85_{a,b,c}$	2.50	4.82**
Religiosity (non–organizational)	11.58	2.38	11.43_a	2.14	11.00_b	2.58	$12.01_{a,b}$	1.64	4.98**
Community involvement									
Activities in neighborhood	5.24_a	2.23	5.43_b	1.99	5.71	1.81	$6.15_{a,b}$	1.66	8.31***
Membership in organizations	0.68_a	1.08	$0.36_{a,b}$	0.79	0.61	1.10	0.68_b	1.05	7.99***
Health status									
Physical health status	51.14_a	8.61	51.82_b	7.21	50.18	7.99	$47.79_{a,b}$	9.50	11.26***
Mental health status	51.65_a	9.34	51.17_b	8.80	50.82_c	9.19	$46.57_{a,b,c}$	9.41	13.56***
Has health benefits through job (%)	60.4		46.0		75.0		44.6		$\chi^2 = 13.86$**
Involvement in school	%		%		%		%		χ^2
Discusses school w/child 1+x/wk (%)	94.6		92.3		89.8		93.7		1.77
Participates in school activities 1+x/mo (%)	59.5		57.7		50.9		52.7		2.21
In touch w/ teachers 1+x/mo	76.2		77.2		76.3		72.3		1.41
Volunteer at school 1+x/mo	47.2		42.4		26.4		24.1		21.42***

Note: a) Means with the same subscript letter are significantly different; b) $p < .05$; * $p < .05$; ** $p < .01$; *** $p < .001$

sample and its relation to physical and mental health status (Franzini *et al.*, 2005). Overall, non–Hispanic Blacks in the sample reported the highest level of religiosity, followed by Hispanics. Among Mexican Americans, those who were foreign-born and living in the Lower Rio Grande Valley reported significantly higher levels of religiosity compared with other Mexican Americans.

As detailed previously, compromised parental health status is associated with an increased risk for poor child health. In this survey, physical and mental health were measured using the Physical Component Summary (PCS) and the Mental Component Summary (MCS) of the SF-12 with ranges between 0 and 100, and higher scores indicating better health (Ware *et al.*, 2003). Overall, better physical and mental health was seen among those Mexican American parents living in Houston, and the lowest levels of health were seen among foreign-born Mexican Americans living in the lower Rio Grande Valley (Table 17.3).

Approximately 70 percent of the families interviewed had at least one person in the household who was currently employed, and 40 percent of the respondents themselves were employed at least part-time. For respondents who were employed, we asked whether they received health benefits through their employer, and only 52.7 percent did. Even among those employed full-time, only 62.3 percent received health benefits. Rates of health benefits differed significantly by subgroup, with US-born Mexican Americans living in the lower Rio Grande Valley being most likely to have health benefits.

Finally, for respondents with school-age children, we asked about their level of involvement in their child's education. All of the parents reported high levels involvement, with more than 90 percent reporting they discussed school work with their child at least once per week, and three quarters reporting they were in touch with their child's teacher at least once per month. The only difference which emerged between groups was that Mexican Americans living in the Lower Rio Grande Valley were less likely to volunteer in their child's school than those living in Houston. We also compared school involvement between English-speaking and Spanish-speaking parents. Although there were no differences in level of involvement in terms of discussing school work, participating in school activities, and staying in touch with the teacher, Spanish-speaking parents were less likely to volunteer at their child's school.

Summary

Supporting the Healthy Development of Mexican American Infants and Young Children

The lifespan and ecological perspectives in the field of human development emphasize the need to consider the contextual forces both within and outside the family when identifying sources of risk and resilience. The field of public health has recently begun to recognize the importance of health status during infancy and early childhood as a potential determinant of health in adulthood (Barker, 1990; Hall, 2007; Klebanoff *et al.*, 1999; Lu and Halfon, 2003; Wise, 2009). This "lifespan" perspective, however, would be enhanced by incorporating a greater appreciation for contextual influences of family and community as well as the interactions between these domains. Mexican Americans are among one of the fastest growing demographic groups in this country. Ensuring the health of Mexican American infants and young children presents challenges to the field of public health that could be more readily addressed if we had a better understanding of not only the risk factors for poor health, but also the assets present in Mexican American families and communities that can be capitalized upon to improve health outcomes.

Future Directions and Challenges

Mexican American families are one of the fastest growing demographics in the United States. Mexican American infants are less likely to be born low birth weight than other infants, but older Mexican American children are more likely to experience poor health in a variety of domains. The high levels of social capital, collective efficacy, and social support seen in a number of Mexican American communities and families are sources of resilience which should be supported and enhanced in order to ensure the healthy development of Mexican American infants and young children. The work summarized here has a number of implications for research, policy, and practice with Mexican American families and young children.

First, it is clear that the empirical data available are insufficient when it comes to the determinants of health in Mexican American children. More research is needed that recognizes the heterogeneity within Latino families of different countries of origin, and more research is needed on Mexican American families specifically because of their large numbers relative to other Latino groups in the US. Furthermore, research on the health of Latino children should report the country of origin of participants to facilitate the compilation of empirical knowledge specific to different groups of Latinos.

Along these lines, more research is needed which recognizes the importance of the communities in which Mexican American children live, for their healthy growth and development. Future research studies should investigate the characteristics unique to Mexican American communities and identify the factors important for supporting healthy pregnancy outcomes which might enhance continued healthy development across the lifespan. Intervention initiatives which inadvertently undermine the strengths related to community cohesion and involvement in Mexican American communities must be avoided.

Policy makers and public health professionals must recognize the heterogeneity within and among Mexican American communities and families as they seek to develop culturally competent approaches to the development and implementation of preventive interventions to improve health. Failure to recognize this heterogeneity and rather to implement a "one size fits all" to policy development and implementation, will not only result in ineffective prevention initiatives but may also result in unintended consequences such as undermining the inherent strengths of Mexican American families and communities. Policies and programs which recognize and build upon these strengths will hold the greatest promise for promoting the healthy development of Mexican American infants and young children.

Policy Implications

Supporting Communities to Support Healthy Development

The existence of the "Hispanic Paradox", wherein Hispanic infants, and Mexican American infants in particular, experience positive pregnancy outcomes despite facing significant socioeconomic disadvantages, has been supported by numerous empirical investigations (Buekens et al., 2000; de la Rosa, 2002; Franzini et al., 2001). Although researchers have repeatedly documented the Hispanic Paradox, we still have very little understanding of what protective factors are operating within Hispanic families and communities to support healthy pregnancies. As we demonstrated with our data from Mexican American families living in Texas, there is considerable variability in the family and community contexts in which Mexican American infants and young children grow and develop. More research is needed to determine if variability in those family and community contexts may explain variations in health outcomes for Mexican

Americans. For example, there was evidence from our data that Mexican American families in Texas differed significantly in terms of the levels of social support they received, the amount of involvement in their neighborhood in which they engaged, and the degree of neighborhood social cohesion which they experienced. Although research on neighborhood context and health status has documented the positive association between neighborhood social cohesion— or "social capital"—and better health outcomes for both children and adults (Dorsey and Forehand, 2003; Mulvaney and Kendrick, 2005; Szreter and Woolcock, 2004), very little of this research has focused on Mexican American families and their communities.

However, Mexican Americans are also living in communities that can impart significant risk for the development of infants and young children. As we demonstrated with our data from Texas, Mexican American families are living in neighborhoods experiencing significantly higher levels of economic impoverishment and physical and social disorder, with poverty rates two to three times as high as the national average. The links between neighborhood economic conditions and physical structure and the healthy development of children has been demonstrated in a large empirical literature (Aneshensel and Sucoff, 1996; Gordon-Larsen et al., 2006; Leventhal and Brooks-Gunn, 2000; Papas et al., 2007; Sampson et al., 2002; Sellstrom and Bremberg, 2006). The forces shaping the economic status of a neighborhood operate at a macro level through the institution of economic policies which determine the distribution of resources and the location of businesses and industry (Jargowsky, 1997; Wilson, 1987). Policy makers need to be aware of how economic policies affect the well-being of communities, and take steps to ensure that adequate resources in the form of retail services, medical care, schools, and recreational facilities are available to all communities. With regards to Mexican American communities in particular, it is important that any policies to improve economic and physical conditions also support and enhance the strong sense of community engagement already present in these neighborhoods. Policies that undermine the strong sense of community in Mexican American neighborhoods will be counter-productive in terms of improving the health of residents. Rather, effective efforts to improve Mexican American neighborhoods should rely on a process of community engagement wherein the voice of the community and community priorities are incorporated as a central focus in neighborhood revitalization efforts.

Improving Access to Health Care

A common theme in the literature on the health of Latino children is the accessibility of affordable and culturally competent medical care. Flores et al. (2002) reported that lack of insurance was a major barrier to health care access for Latino children, citing failed outreach efforts to enroll Latino children in public health insurance programs, such as Medicaid and SCHIP, and lack of materials in Spanish for Spanish-speaking parents. A few advances have been made since this report. Mendoza (2009) cited changes in the reauthorization of SCHIP which will no longer require documented immigrant children to be in this country for 5 years before accessing public health insurance as a factor which should improve the access of immigrant children to health care. However, policy changes may be insufficient for addressing the disparities in health insurance coverage. In the 2007 Kaiser Survey of Children's Health Coverage (Kaiser Commission on Medicaid and the Uninsured, 2009b), it was found that low-income citizen children in mixed-status families (e.g. families in which the child is a citizen but the parent is a non-citizen) were twice as likely to be uninsured as children in families in which the parent was a citizen. This disparity was due primarily to the lower availability of employer-provided health insurance in mixed-status families, as well as lower rates of participation in public health insurance programs such as Medicaid and SCHIP. Hispanic parents were much less likely to be aware of Medicaid and SCHIP. In addition, Hispanic parents were more likely to report misperceptions of eligibility requirements for Medicaid/SCHIP, as well as lack of knowledge regarding how and where to apply for the programs.

Health Care Reform and Mexican American Child Health

Since President Barack Obama took office in January 2009, two major pieces of health care legislation were signed into law including the reauthorization of the Children's Health Insurance Program (CHIPRA) and the Patient Protection and Affordable Care Act (e.g. health care reform) in March 2010. Improving the health of Mexican American infants and young children requires an understanding of the implications of this legislation for the health care access for this population. As part of the Personal Responsibility and Work Opportunity Reconciliation Act—often referred to as welfare reform—passed in 1996, states were prohibited from using federal funds to provide health insurance coverage to legally resident immigrants who had been in the United States for less than 5 years (Kaiser Commission on Medicaid and the Uninsured, 2009a). Obviously, a five-year waiting period for accessing health care would have significant negative effects on the health of pregnant women, infants, and young children. However, seventeen states (including California and Texas) elected to use state funds to provide health care coverage to legally resident immigrant pregnant women and children who had been in the country less than five years.

CHIPRA lifted the ban and allowed states to use federal funds to cover recent, legally resident immigrant children and pregnant women effective April 1, 2009. In addition, CHIPRA expanded resources available for dental care and mental care and included provisions to streamline the enrollment process. These provisions of CHIPRA were not altered by the health care reform act passed in March 2010. The extension of health care access to legally resident immigrant children and pregnant women who have been in the US less than 5 years has obvious implications for the health of Mexican infants and young children. However, a failure to address the health care access issues for undocumented immigrants means that many Mexican American infants and children will be at risk for poor health outcomes, especially those living in mixed status families.

Improving Access to Culturally Appropriate Health Care

Although improving access to health care is a necessary component, it is not sufficient for ensuring access to the quality health care for Mexican American children and youth. Flores et al. (2002) summarized the evidence that deficiencies in health care quality as indicated by lower referral rates for diagnostic tests and lower rates of prescriptions for appropriate therapies disproportionately affect Latino children. In addition, Flores et al. (2005) reported that Hispanic parents were most likely to report that their provider never or only sometimes understood their child-rearing preferences and their child's needs. Improving the health care quality available to Mexican American children necessitates we increase the accessibility to not only affordable but also family-centered, culturally competent medical care. On the health care delivery side, efforts are needed to increase the number of bilingual providers who are sensitive to the needs to Mexican American families.

Note

1 For the purposes of this paper, we use the term "Hispanics" to refer to all Hispanic subgroups when data specific to Mexican Americans are not available. When data are subgroup specific, we use the term "Mexican American".

References

Alegria, M., Canino, G., Lai, S., Ramirez, R. R., Chavez, L., Rusch, D., and Shrout, P. E. (2004). Understanding caregivers' help-seeking for Latino children's mental health care use. *Medical Care, 42*, 447–455.

Aneshensel, C. S., and Sucoff, C. A. (1996). The neighborhood context of adolescent mental health. *Journal of Health and Social Behavior, 37*(4), 293–310.

Baltes, P. B. (1980). Life-span developmental psychology. *Annual Review of Psychology, 31*, 65–110.

Barker, D. J. P. (1990). Fetal and infant origins of adult disease: The womb may be more important than the home. *British Medical Journal, 301*(6761), 1111.

Berg, M., and Medrich, E. A. (1980). Children in four neighborhoods: The physical environment and its effect on play and play patterns. *Environment and Behavior, 12*(3), 320–348.

Braveman, P., and Barclay, C. (2009). Health disparities beginning in childhood: A life-course perspective. *Pediatrics, 124*, S163–S175.

Bronfenbrenner, J., and Ceci, S. J. (1994). Nature-nurture reconceptualized in developmental perspective: A bioecological model. *Psychological Review, 101*(4), 568–586.

Bronfenbrenner, U. (1984). Ecology of the family as a context for human development. *Developmental Psychology, 22*(6), 723–742.

Buekens, P., Notzon, F., Kotelchuck, M., and Wilcox, A. (2000). Why do Mexican Americans give birth to few low-birth-weight infants? *American Journal of Epidemiology, 152*(4), 347–351.

Burdette, H. L., and Whitaker, R. C. (2005). A national study of neighborhood safety, outdoor play, television viewing and obesity in preschool children. *Pediatrics, 116*, 657–662.

Castaneda, D. M. (1994). A research agenda for Mexican-American adolescent mental health. *Adolescence, 29*(113), 225–239.

Caughy, M. O., O'Campo, P. J., and Nettles, S. M. (2008). The effect of residential neighborhood on child behavior problems in first grade. *American Journal of Community Psychology, 42*(1–2), 39–50.

Centers for Disease Control and Prevention (CDC) (2010). 1991–2009 High School Youth Risk Behavior Survey Data. Retrieved March 18, 2010 http://apps.nccd.cdc.gov/youthonline

Coker, T. R., Elliott, M. N., Kataoka, S., Schwebel, D. C., Mrug, S., Grunbaum, J. A., . . . Schuster, M. A. (2009). Racial/ethnic disparities in the mental health care utilization of fifth grade children. *Academic Pediatrics, 9*, 89–96.

Coulton, C. J., Korbin, J. E., and Su, M. (1996). Measuring neighborhood context for young children in an urban area. *American Journal of Community Psychology, 24*(1), 5–33.

de la Rosa, I. (2002). Perinatal outcomes among Mexican Americans: A review of an epidemiological paradox. *Ethnicity and Disease, 12*, 480–487.

DeNavas-Walt, C., Proctor, B. D., and Smith, J. C. (2009). Income, poverty and health insurance coverage in the United States: 2008. In *Current Population Reports: Consumer Income*. Washington, D.C.: U.S. Government Printing Office.

Dorsey, S., and Forehand, R. (2003). The relation of social capital to child psychosocial adjustment difficulties: The role of positive parenting and neighborhood dangerousness. *Journal of Psychopathology and Behavioral Assessment, 25*(1), 11–23.

Elder, G. H., Jr., and Rockwell, R. C. (1979). The life-course and human development: An ecological perspective. *International Journal of Behavioral Development, 2*(1), 1–21.

Flores, G., Fuentes-Afflick, E., and Barbot, O. (2002). The health of Latino children: Urgent priorities, unanswered questions, and a research agenda. *JAMA, 288*(1), 82–90.

Flores, G., Olson, L., and Tomany-Korman, S. C. (2005). Racial and ethnic disparities in early childhood health and health care. *Pediatrics, 115*, e183–e193.

Franzini, L., Ribble, J. C., and Keddie, A. M. (2001). Understanding the Hispanic Paradox. *Ethnicity and Disease, 11*(3), 496–518.

Franzini, L., Ribble, J. C., and Wingfield, K. A. (2005). Religion, sociodemographic and personal characteristics, and self-reported health in whites, blacks, and Hispanics living in low-socioeconomic status neighborhoods. *Ethnicity and Disease, 15*(3), 469–484.

Franzini, L., Elliott, M. N., Cuccaro, P., Schuster, M., Gilliland, J., Grunbaum, J. A., . . . Tortolero, S. R. (2007). Influences of physical and social neighborhood environments on children's physical activity and obesity. *American Journal of Public Health, 99*, 271–278.

Fuentes-Afflick, E., Hessol, N. A., and Perez-Stable, E. J. (1999). Testing the epidemiologic paradox of low birth weight in Latinos. *Archives of Pediatric and Adolescent Medicine, 153*(2), 147–153.

Garcia Coll, C., Lamberty, G., Jenkins, R., McAdoo, H. P., Crnic, K., Wasik, B. H., and Garcia, H. V. (1996). An integrative model for the study of developmental competencies in minority children. *Child Development, 67*(5), 1891–1914.

Gavin, L., MacKay, A. P., Brown, K., Harrier, S., Ventura, S., Kann, L., . . . Ryan, G. (2009). Sexual and reproductive health of persons aged 10–24 years: United States, 2002–2007. *Morbidity and Mortality Weekly Report, 58*(SS-6), 1–60.

Gordon-Larsen, P., Nelson, M. C., Page, P., and Popkin, B. M. (2006). Inequality in the built environment underlies key health disparities in physical activity and obesity. *Pediatrics, 117*, 417–424.

Hall, S. S. (2007). Small and thin: The controversy over the fetal origins of adult health. *The New Yorker, 83*(36), 52.

Heilemann, M. V., Frutos, L., Lee, K. A., and Kury, F. S. (2004). Protective strength factors, resources and risks in relation to depressive symptoms among childbearing women of Mexican descent. *Health Care for Women International, 25*, 88–106.

Jargowsky, P. A. (1997). *Poverty and place: Ghettos, barrios and the American city.* New York: Russell Sage Foundation.

Kaiser Commission on Medicaid and the Uninsured. (2009a). CHIP Tips: New federal funding available to cover immigrant children and pregnant women. Washington, DC: Kaiser Family Foundation.

Kaiser Commission on Medicaid and the Uninsured. (2009b). Covering uninsured children: Reaching and enrolling citizen children with non-citizen parents. Washington, DC: Kaiser Family Foundation.

Klebanoff, M. A., Secher, N. J., Mednick, B. R., and Schulsinger, C. (1999). Maternal size at birth and the development of hypertension during pregnancy. *Archives of Internal Medicine, 159*, 1607–1612.

Kohen, D. E., Brooks-Gunn, J., Leventhal, T., and Hertzmann, C. (2002). Neighborhood income and physical and social disorder in Canada: Associations with young children's competencies. *Child Development, 73*, 1844–1860.

Kolbe, L. J., Kann, L., and Collins, J. L. (1993). Overview of the youth risk behavior surveillance system. *Public Health Reports, 108*(Suppl 1), 2.

Kotelchuck, M. (2003). Building on a life-course perspective in maternal and child health. *Maternal and Child Health Journal, 7*(1), 5–11.

Leventhal, T., and Brooks-Gunn, J. (2000). The neighborhoods they live in: The effects of neighborhood residence on child and adolescent outcomes. *Psychological Bulletin, 126*(2), 309–337.

Lu, M. C., and Halfon, N. (2003). Racial and ethnic disparities in birth outcomes: A life-course perspective. *Maternal and Child Health Journal, 7*(1), 13–30.

Martin, J. A., Hamilton, B. E., Sutton, P. D., Ventura, S. J., Menacker, F., Kirmeyer, S., and Mathews, T. J. (2009). Births: Final data for 2006. *National Vital Statistics Reports Vol. 57.* Hyattsville, MD: National Center for Health Statistics.

Mendoza, F. S. (2009). Health disparities and children in immigrant families: A research agenda. *Pediatrics, 124*, S187–S195.

Mendoza, F. S., Ventura, S. J., Valdez, B., Castillo, R., Saldivar, L. E., Baisden, K., and Martorelli, R. (1991). Selected measures of health status for Mexican-American, mainland Puerto Rican, and Cuban-American children. *JAMA, 265*, 227–232.

Molnar, B. E., Gortmaker, S. L., Bull, F. C., and Buka, S. L. (2004). Unsafe to play? Neighborhood disorder and lack of safety predict reduced physical activity among urban children and adolescents. *American Journal of Health Promotion, 18*(5), 378–386.

Molnar, B. E., Buka, S. L., Brennan, R. T., Holton, J. K., and Earls, F. (2003). A multilevel study of neighborhoods and parent-to-child physical aggression: Results from the Project on Human Development in Chicago neighborhoods. *Child Maltreatment: Journal of the American Professional Society on the Abuse of Children, 8*(2), 84–97.

Morenoff, J. D., and Sampson, R. J. (1997). Violent crime and the spatial dynamics of neighborhood transition: Chicago, 1970–1990. *Social Forces, 76*, 31–64.

Mulvaney, C., and Kendrick, D. (2005). Depressive symptoms in mothers of pre-school children: Effects of deprivation, social support, stress and neighbourhood social capital. *Social Psychiatry and Psychiatric Epidemiology, 40*, 202–208.

O'Campo, P., Rao, R. P., Gielen, A. C., Royalty, W., and Wilson, M. (2000). Injury-producing events among children in low-income communities: The role of community characteristics. *Journal of Urban Health*, 77(1), 34–49.

Ostir, G. V., Eschbach, K., Markides, K. S., and Goodwin, J. S. (2003). Neighborhood composition and depressive symptoms among older Mexican Americans. *Journal of Epidemiology and Community Health*, 57(12), 987–992.

Papas, M. A., Alberg, A. J., Ewing, R., Helzlsouer, K. J., Gary, T. L., and Klassen, A. C. (2007). The built environment and obesity. *Epidemiologic Reviews*, 29, 129–143.

Rauh, V. A., Landrigan, P. J., and Claudio, L. (2008). Housing and health: Intersection of poverty and environmental exposures. *Annals of the New York Academy of Science*, 1136, 276–288.

Reading, R., Langford, I. H., Haynes, R., and Lovett, A. (1999). Accidents to preschool children: Comparing family and neighborhood risk factors. *Social Science and Medicine*, 48, 321–330.

Romero, A., and Roberts, R. E. (2003). Stress within a bicultural context for adolescents of Mexican descent. *Cultural Diversity and Ethnic Minority Psychology*, 9(2), 171–184.

Sampson, R. J., Morenoff, J. D., and Earls, F. (1999). Beyond social capital: Spatial dynamics of collective efficacy for children. *American Sociological Review*, 64(5), 633–660.

Sampson, R. J., Morenoff, J. D., and Gannon-Rowley, T. (2002). Assessing "neighborhood effects": Social processes and new directions in research. *Annual Review of Sociology*, 28, 443–478.

Sampson, R. J., Raudenbush, S. W., and Earls, F. (1997). Neighborhoods and violent crime: A multilevel study of collective efficacy. *Science*, 277, 918–924.

Sellstrom, E., and Bremberg, S. (2006). The significance of neighbourhood context to child and adolescent health and well-being: A systematic review of multilevel studies. *Scandinavian Journal of Public Health*, 34, 544–554.

Smokowski, P. R., and Bacallao, M. L. (2007). Acculturation, internalizing mental health symptoms, and self-esteem: Cultural experiences of Latino adolescents in North Carolina. *Child Psychiatry and Human Development*, 37, 273–292.

Smokowski, P. R., Rose, R., and Bacallao, M. L. (2010). Influence of risk factors and cultural assets on Latino adolescents' trajectories of self-esteem and internalizing symptoms. *Child Psychiatry and Human Development*, 41, 133–155.

Szreter, S., and Woolcock, M. (2004). Health by association? Social capital, social theory, and the political economy of public health. *International Journal of Epidemiology*, 33(4), 650–667.

Treviño, R. P., Marshall, R. M., Hale, D. E., Rodriguez, R., Baker, G., and Gomez, J. (1999). Diabetes risk factors in low-income Mexican-American children. *Diabetes Care*, 22(2), 202–207. doi: 10.2337/diacare.22.2.202

U.S. Bureau of the Census. (2007). The American Community—Hispanics: 2004. *American Community Survey Reports*. Washington, DC.

U.S. Bureau of the Census. (2009). POP3: Racial and ethnic composition: Percentage of U.S. children ages 0–17 by race and Hispanic origin, 1980–2008 and projected 2009–2021. Retrieved April 9, 2010, from http://www.childstats.gov/AMERICASCHILDREN/demo.asp

United States Department of Health and Human Services (US DHHS) (2010). Linked Birth/Infant Death Records 2003–2005, CDC WONDER On-line Database. Retrieved Feb 16, 2010 11:18:27 AM, from http://wonder.cdc.gov/lbd-current.html

Upchurch, D. M., Aneshensel, C. S., and Mudgal, J. (2001). Sociocultural contexts of time to first sex among Hispanic adolescents. *Journal of Marriage and the Family*, 63, 1158–1169.

Wagmiller, R. L., Lennon, M. C., and Kuang, L. (2008). Parental health and children's economic well-being. *Journal of Health and Social Behavior*, 49(1), 37–55.

Ware, J. E. J., Turner-Bowker, D. M., Kosinski, M., and Gandek, B. (2003). *SF-12V2y: How to score version 2 of the SF-12t Health Survey*. Lincoln, RI: QualityMetric, Inc.

Wilson, W. J. (1987). *The truly disadvantaged: The inner city, the underclass, and public policy*. Chicago: University of Chicago Press.

Wise, P. H. (2009). Confronting social disparities in child health: A critical appraisal of life-course science and research. *Pediatrics*, 124, S203–S211.

Zajicek-Farber, M. L. (2009). Postnatal depression and infant health practices among high-risk women. *Journal of Child and Family Studies, 18*, 236–245.

Zimmerman, F. J. (2005). Social and economic determinants of disparties in professional help-seeking for child mental health problems: Evidence from a national sample. *Health Services Research, 5 (Part 1)*, 1514–1533.

PART VI

Conclusions

18

PERSPECTIVES AND RECOMMENDATIONS FOR FUTURE DIRECTIONS

Eric W. Lindsey and Yvonne M. Caldera

This book brings together writings on Mexican American children and family life that highlight existing knowledge, recent advances, and emerging themes. Compilation of the scholarship in this volume was guided by three major goals: (1) to focus specifically on information pertaining to Mexican American children and families, (2) to include a multidisciplinary perspective in the information presented, and (3) to adopt a strength-based perspective in reviewing information about Mexican American children and families. In so doing, the information collected offers a glimpse into the diversity and complexity of issues examined by researchers, and outlines recommendations for policy makers and practitioners working with Mexican American children and families.

Focusing on Mexican American Children and Families

Based on a growing chorus of theorists and researchers calling attention to the between-group diversity among Latino populations, the past decade has seen a surge in research focusing specifically on Mexican Americans. The guiding principle of this body of work has been that empirical findings based on data from other Latino populations should not be generalized to Mexican American children and families. Additionally, efforts have been made to move away from comparative research in studying Latino populations to focus instead on examining within-group variations.

The chapters in this volume reveal that, although limited, the empirical focus on Mexican American children and families is justified, and progress in understanding the unique experience of Mexican Americans is being made. It is clear that tremendous heterogeneity exists within the Mexican American population. The history and cultural context of contemporary Mexican American families present particular opportunities and challenges for socialization strategies and family dynamics. Likewise, variations in goals and values from one family to another, as well as across individuals, have been linked to differences among Mexican American children and parents. These points are clearly made in Chapter 1 by Caldera, Velez-Gomez, and Lindsey, who review information concerning the secular trends seen in the composition of the Mexican American population over the last 50 years, and identify some of the dominant cultural values found to be associated with characteristics of Mexican American family life. In addition, in Chapter 2, Quintana, Chavez, and Ramírez Stege review the most recent literature concerning ethnic identity formation among Mexican American youth, making the point that past and current perceptions of what it means to be of Mexican origin have unique implications for the adjustment of Mexican American children and adolescents. In a related vein, Klinkebiel, Harris, and Borrego, Jr. in Chapter 12 summarize research documenting how particular parenting practices found among Mexican American families are related to children's mental health outcomes in ways that differ from other ethnic groups, as well as variations across Mexican American parents' use of particular socialization strategies.

Several authors included in this volume describe differences in sociocultural experiences across Mexican American families, and examine processes that lead to within-group heterogeneity in Mexican American family dynamics. Multiple chapters also reveal that this body of research has begun to disentangle the influence of ethnicity from other social context variables (e.g. socioeconomic status and community or neighborhood factors). For example, in Chapter 4, Aldoney, Karberg, Malin, and Cabrera outline an ecological-systems model for understanding Mexican American children's school readiness, and review empirical data that supports the idea that multiple levels of the environment in which Mexican American families live interact to account for variations in children's school readiness. In addition, Ayala and Arredondo, in Chapter 14, point to evidence that attitudes held toward food and nutrition, as well as environmental factors that play a role in access to food, account for unique patterns of health among Mexican Americans relative to other ethnic groups. Similarly, in Chapter 15, Lopez describes how cultural beliefs in natural medicine and use of indigenous remedies for physical ailments may be linked to patterns of health outcomes found among Mexican American families.

Future research must continue to explore similarities and differences in developmental and family processes among Mexican Americans and other Latino subgroups. Both variations among Mexican Americans and differences between Mexican Americans and other Hispanic White Americans are important to consider. There is also a tremendous need for empirical research that examines public policies and interventions aimed at Mexican American families, the majority of which have been based on science conducted with other Latino groups, with little attention given to their applicability to Mexican American populations. For example, in Chapter 10, Suizzo identifies how intervention programs designed specifically to incorporate strategies that target unique cultural values and characteristics of Mexican American families have produced measureable improvements in children's adjustment to school. Additional program evaluation research that examines processes and outcomes of interventions specifically targeting Mexican American children and families will aid in improved efficacy of such programs.

Focus on Multidisciplinary Research

A thorough understanding of the cultural, intrapersonal, and interpersonal forces that influence Mexican American children and families necessitates the adoption of a multidisciplinary perspective. The chapters in this volume reveal that theory and research designed to understand Mexican American families is increasingly based in multiple disciplines. Each discipline brings to bear unique approaches to understanding the strengths of Mexican Americans, as well as the challenges they confront. A comparison of the different chapters contained in the handbook reveals that in some cases authors from separate disciplines apply their unique expertise to explore the same issue, and reveal distinctive information that can be applied to developing solutions. For instance, in Chapter 14, Ayala and Arredondo, point to evidence from the field of nutrition that attitudes held toward food, as well as environmental factors that influence access to food, account for unique patterns of health among Mexican Americans relative to other ethnic groups. In turn, in Chapter 16, Ruiz, Hamann, García, and Craddock Lee use a bio-psychosocial model of health to outline how cultural beliefs and unique behavioral patterns influence health outcomes among Mexican Americans. The chapters overlap in examining the psychological phenomena surrounding health behavior among Mexican Americans, but each offers a discrete perspective on the factors that contribute to health outcomes.

In other instances, authors incorporate elements from multiple conceptual frameworks in their specific chapter. For example, in Chapter 17, O'Brien Caughy and Franzini outline how a combination of the public health life-course approach, the developmental lifespan perspective, and ecological systems theory offer researchers and practitioners greater insight into the patterns of health outcomes observed among Mexican American infants and young children. Together, these and other chapters in the handbook illustrate how different disciplines can come together to offer new perspectives in understanding existing empirical data.

The strength of a multidisciplinary perspective is that it offers the opportunity to open new areas of research through the transmission of knowledge, tools, methodology, and solutions generated in one discipline, to other disciplines. In this way, advances in theory and model testing are more likely to be achieved through multidisciplinary discussions and collaborations. Chapter 3 by White, Knight, and Roosa illustrates how this might be accomplished by outlining steps for researchers to use culturally informed theory in studying Mexican American children and families. In addition, Arzubiaga, Brinkerhoff, and Granville Seeley, in Chapter 7, highlight how the concept of space can be incorporated into the methodology of research from other disciplines to expand conceptualizations of the lives of Mexican Americans. These chapters, and others in the handbook, indicate that future research should embrace a multidisciplinary perspective that brings together different fields of knowledge to generate new expertise, and to use that expertise to create new instruments, models, and approaches that couldn't occur if they were separately handled.

The underlying message of the handbook as a whole is that a multidisciplinary perspective can bring together what appears to be disparate pieces of information in a way that serves to advance existing theory, research, and policy related to Mexican American children and families. The work collected in this volume reveals that there continues to be a critical need for researchers to develop conceptual frameworks that foster research and that tests specific hypotheses about expected differences among Mexican Americans and other ethnic groups, and why such differences exist. This work would help to identify concepts and mechanisms specific to Mexican Americans, as well as those that cut across other ethnic groups. This work would also facilitate the development of policies and interventions that benefit Mexican Americans and allow for the integration of findings from different domains and periods of the lifespan.

Finally, this research would assist the construction of transnational models that serve to contextualize the unique experiences of Mexican Americans. To date, the literature is piecemeal, and collaboration among scholars working in different fields and different periods of development has been limited. Some conceptual models and theories are available, but research that tests aspects of those theories is lagging. Based on these observations, we recommend developing new theories and conceptual models, and enriching existing ones, by promoting and supporting multidisciplinary research efforts.

Focus on Normative Development and Strengths of Mexican Americans

The information reviewed in this volume encourages an understanding of the unique normative developmental trajectories of Mexican American children and families. For example, in Chapter 9, Zepeda and Rodriguez provide a thorough summary of the current state of empirical literature on the distinct pattern of development among dual language learners, and in so doing outline the trajectory of bilingual development among Mexican American children. In Chapter 5, Lindsey and Caldera review existing research on the manifestation of coparenting among Mexican American families, highlighting the role that qualitative research has played in understanding unique patterns of coparenting in Mexican American families. The focus on normative developmental processes indicates that it is important for researchers to continue to examine the psychometric properties of measures used with Mexican Americans, and to test equivalence of models across different ethnic groups. Such research is valuable to ensure that measures are psychometrically adequate and to examine the universality or cultural specificity of psycho-logical and behavioral models. To apply these more refined techniques it will be necessary to design more sophisticated investigations with large sample sizes. However, it is important not to undervalue qualitative and more basic descriptive research, which furthers the accumulation of a rich foundation of knowledge and information regarding Mexican Americans. Thus, we recommend that qualitative as well as quantitative, and descriptive as well as explanatory research efforts are needed to adequately address the gaps in the literature. These more complex quantitative, qualitative, and mixed-methods approaches will require that we review existing methodologies to ensure that scholars have the tools to take on this challenge.

Contrary to the cultural-deficit ideological perspective that permeates much of the research on minority populations, the scholarship represented in this book highlights the personal and social strengths and assets found among Mexican American children and families. For example, Chapter 6 by Lopez, Ruvalcaba and Rogoff, identifies the practice of attentive helpfulness as a unique cultural characteristic of Mexican American families. In addition, Gonzales, Jensen, Montano, and Wynne, in Chapter 13, synthesize existing literature on how processes of acculturation and encculturation interact to build resilience among Mexican American adolescents. Furthermore, rather than focus on problems and pathology, the contributors to this volume also highlight factors that protect and strengthen Mexican American children and families. For instance, Midobuche, Benavides, and Koca in Chapter 8, identify the characteristics that empirical literature suggests are associated with academic resilience among Mexican American students. In addition, Ramos-Sánchez in Chapter 11, reviews information pertaining to the intentions behind Mexican Americans' use of counseling services. We believe that the emphasis on strength-based research in the Handbook contributed to the variation in study topics found in the volume, and produced a collection of scholarship with a more holistic and balanced perspective on understanding Mexican Americans. Furthermore, it is hoped that the information contained in this volume will contribute to the development of more valid intervention and policy programs for use with Mexican American populations.

Based on the information obtained from the focus on normative research, it is recommended that researchers continue to conduct research with normative populations that highlight strengths, resilience, and well-being. When this research is integrated with problem-focused approaches, it will provide a more comprehensive view of Mexican Americans which will contribute to the development of theories and polices. However, for the determination of developmental trajectories, multicohort longitudinal studies are necessary because they enable the researcher to disentangle age, cohort, and period effects by showing whether the same changes with age are observed in different cohorts studied in different time periods.

Another important goal to be derived from the information in this volume is identifying cultural factors that are important resources and strengths to shield Mexican American individuals and families from some of the negative consequences of exposure to stressors, and that help account for paradoxes such as lower rates of psychiatric disorder among Mexican Americans as compared with non-Hispanic whites. At the same time, the information suggests that we need to develop and refine intervention strategies that enhance parents' abilities to promote success for their children. Such strategies need to be developed in partnership with communities and schools. The high levels of social capital, collective efficacy, and social support seen in a number of Mexican American communities and families are sources of resilience which should be supported and enhanced in order to ensure the healthy development of Mexican American infants and young children. Attention to human capabilities and adaptive systems that promote healthy development and functioning have the potential to inform policy and programs that foster competence and human capital and aim to improve the health of communities and nations while also preventing problems.

Summary

Mexican American families are a rapidly growing segment of the US population. The work summarized in this handbook suggests that in order to develop policy and programs that are relevant to these families and their children we must build a foundation of research that focuses specifically the experiences of Mexican Americans. As a step in this direction, the chapters included in this handbook provide an overview of existing information on Mexican American families from a multidisciplinary perspective. The information presented in these chapters highlights the diversity within Mexican American families and documents how variability in cultural and social experiences is related to the well-being and adjustment of Mexican Americans. In addition, the work in this handbook underscores the value of taking a strength-based perspective in studying the lives of Mexican American children and families. It is clear from the information presented in the chapters that an important goal for future inquiry should be to identify protective factors that reduce the negative effect of risk factors and result in positive outcomes for Mexican American families and children.

AUTHOR INDEX

SUBJECT INDEX